Biodiversity Laws, Policies and Science in Europe, the United States and China

Giovanni Antonelli • Tianbao Qin •
Maria Vittoria Ferroni • Alex Erwin
Editors

Biodiversity Laws, Policies and Science in Europe, the United States and China

Springer

Editors
Giovanni Antonelli
Ministry of Culture
Rome, Italy

Tianbao Qin
School of Law
Wuhan University
Wuhan, China

Maria Vittoria Ferroni
Department of Political Sciences
Sapienza University of Rome
Rome, Italy

Alex Erwin
Florida International University
Miami, FL, USA

ISBN 978-3-031-56217-4 ISBN 978-3-031-56218-1 (eBook)
https://doi.org/10.1007/978-3-031-56218-1

This Springer imprint is published by the registered company Springer Nature Switzerland AG
The registered company address is: Gewerbestrasse 11, 6330 Cham, Switzerland

Thanks to Dr. Emanuele Merlino, Cons. Francesco Gilioli, Cons. Donato Luciano and Cons. Giorgio Carlo Brugnoni for their trust and mentorship.

Thanks to Pres. Chiara Colosimo and Undersecretary Giovanbattista Fazzolari for their leadership and service.

Thanks to Deputy Minister Vannia Gava, Hon. Silvia Fregolent and Dr. Francesco Giubilei for their contribution.

Thanks to my parents for their unconditional love.

Giovanni Antonelli

Foreword

Biodiversity: Laws, Policy, and Science in Europe, the United States, and China

The term *biodiversity* was introduced by entomologist E.O. Wilson in 1986 to refer to what is known as *biological diversity*, which is what—in the 1992 Convention on Biological Diversity (CBD)—was defined as *the variety and variability of living organisms from all sources, including inter alia terrestrial, marine and other aquatic ecosystems, and the ecological complexes of which they are part.*

Over the years, the protection of biodiversity has been achieved mainly through the creation of protected areas, the development of strategies and national and supranational plans and programs to ensure their implementation, and the raising of awareness among all stakeholders within sectoral policies. To date, about 75% of land and 66% of marine ecosystems have already been significantly modified. Out of the eight million known animal and plant species, one million are reported to be endangered—a risk that anthropogenic action is accelerating at a thousand times the natural rate. Human activity represents the dominant force in this process; moreover, the mass of man-made products generated by humans (buildings, roads, concrete...) has surpassed the natural one that encompasses the totality of all life on the planet.

The results achieved in the European context to halt biodiversity loss have shown that much remains to be done despite the efforts deployed and the many successes achieved; in particular, the analysis of the work carried out in recent years has shown that the main challenge remains that of effectively integrating the conservation and sustainable use of biodiversity into sector policies, a process closely linked to the harmonization of national legislation in a biodiversity manner. It should be recalled that the first forms of protection were developed at the level of international law, with the World Charter for Nature, adopted by the United Nations General Assembly (1982), and then especially with the "Our Common Future" Report, with which the work of the Brundtland Commission was concluded in 1987, highlighting the importance of biodiversity for sustainable development. But the real turning point came with the adoption at the United Nations Conference in Rio de Janeiro in 1992 of the *Convention on Biological Diversity* (CBD). In Italy, the recent constitutional reform, which took place in February 2022, was a further important piece in this framework, which is likely to push in the direction of an implementation of the legal protection of biodiversity and the acquisition by it of increasing relevance in the legal system. With this reform, in fact, the text of Article 9 of the Italian Constitution was not only amended with the inclusion of an express reference to the Republic's duty to protect the environment, but reference was also made to biodiversity and ecosystems; thus, according to the new paragraph 3 of Article 9, the Republic *protects the environment, biodiversity and ecosystems.* This clearly marked the overcoming of a conception of environmental protection strictly, or perhaps exclusively, related to the protection of natural beauty.

Efforts to date, however, have not been sufficient to halt, or even significantly curb, the severe biodiversity loss that is taking place. It is therefore necessary to adopt new biodiversity policies and strategies. In this regard, the CBD COP15 set four goals for 2050 and 23 "targets" for 2030 that will be preparatory to the adoption of a "Vision for biodiversity" that will have to ensure "humanity in harmony with nature by mid-century," i.e., without generating further negative impacts on natural environments.

In this light, the intention to phase out, or at least reform, subsidies that threaten the world's biodiversity to the tune of $500 billion a year is certainly positive. According to the United Nations Environment Programme (UNEP), governments spend $500 billion to $1 trillion a year on subsidies that are harmful to the environment and biodiversity. It is also desirable that resources of at least $200 billion a year be mobilized in this decade to finance restoration actions, money to be raised in the *Global Environmental Fund.*

Another issue that is high on the international agenda today is the dissemination of knowledge about the heritage of biological diversity present in the territory. This objective should be pursued through the dissemination of research, monitoring, and projects; the dissemination of effective education on the concept of biodiversity even at the school level; and the promotion of environmental tourism aimed at enhancing biodiversity heritage.

In recent European Union policies, the concept of "No Net Loss," i.e., no net loss of biodiversity for all new infrastructure from 2030, has appeared, initiating its adoption on selected projects in areas of high biodiversity importance, starting in 2025. This concept is based on the idea that all possible and unavoidable residual impacts generated by human activities on biodiversity and ecosystems should include dedicated and targeted actions to compensate for the net loss associated with the impact itself.

The United States is home to more than 1300 endangered plant and animal species, and about 40% of land and marine areas are made up of protected areas. In a January 27 executive order, the government initiated the *30 by 30* program, a concrete commitment to protect 30% of US marine and inland areas by 2030. To fulfill the commitment, an area of nearly two million square kilometers will need to be dedicated to protection over the next 10 years. Although the steps forward are concrete and promising, there is still a lot of work to be done in such a vast and diverse territory. It should be noted that the United States of America, due to *bipartisan* divisions and opposition from various interest groups, has never ratified the CBD, yet it has always maintained a very active and dynamic role in its work. Indeed, their *status* has granted them ample opportunities for input and, most importantly, the ability to influence the international debate, engaging key players in decision-making and creating new incentives for conservation efforts worldwide.

China is home to nearly 38,000 species of higher plants, essentially trees, shrubs, and ferns; more than 8100 species of vertebrate animals; more than 1400 species of birds; and 20% of the world's fish species. Many of China's wild species are endemic, which means they are found nowhere else in the world. It also contains parts of four global hot spots of the world's biodiversity, places that have large numbers of endemic species and are also seriously endangered. The Indo-Burmans, the mountains of southwestern China, the eastern Himalayas, and the mountains of Central Asia are home to species such as the giant panda, the Asiatic black bear, the endangered Sichuan partridge, the Xizang alpine toad, the Sichuan spear, and the golden pheasant. China is also adopting a vision to protect biodiversity, so much so that their Constitution speaks of "ecological civilization," in which sense they seem to be making strides in reconciling environmental impacts with achieving economic goals.

Pope Francis recently issued an alarm and a call for co-responsibility in the face of the climate change emergency before it is too late and without always relying on the *technocratic paradigm*. The Holy Father's words cannot remain ignored; rather, they must represent an even greater responsibility on issues that are becoming increasingly urgent and impactful.

For all this, we welcome additional tools for technical and cultural insights.

Ministry for Environment and Energy Security, Rome, Italy
6 October 2023

Vannia Gava

Foreword

Environmental Protection and Biodiversity: Legislative Policies and the Work of Public Decision-Makers at the National and Supranational Levels

The regulatory process aimed at decarbonization and climate neutrality has its roots in an age-old debate, which, however, has seen its first appreciable and global results since December 12, 2015, when the 21st Conference of the Parties to the United Nations Framework Convention on Climate Change (*COP21 of the UNFCCC, an acronym for the English United Nations Framework Convention on Climate Change*) concluded in Paris.

The goal, which was attained, was to achieve the signing of an agreement to govern the post-2020 period. This agreement, adopted by *Decision 1/CP21*, defines as a long-term goal the containment of temperature increase well below 2 °C and the pursuit of efforts to limit the increase to 1.5 °C above preindustrial levels.

The *Paris Agreement*, which entered into force on November 4, 2016, and applies from 2021, is part of the broader framework defined by the *2030 Agenda for Sustainable Development* and complements the Agenda's goals, starting with Goal 13—"Combat *climate change*." Specifically, the *Paris Agreement* details the contents of subgoal 13.2 of the *2030 Agenda*, which calls for *integrating climate change measures into national policies, strategies and planning*.

Then on November 12, 2021, the XXVI Conference of the Parties (*COP26*) of the *United Nations* Framework Convention on Climate Change (*UNFCCC*) concluded in Glasgow, where nations adopted the *Glasgow Climate Pact*, with the goal of turning the 2020s into a decade of climate action and support.

The decision package consists of a number of items, including strengthening efforts to build resilience to climate change, reduce greenhouse gas (GHG) emissions, and provide the necessary funding for both measures.

The nations reaffirmed their duty to fulfill their commitment to provide $100 billion a year from developed countries to developing ones. They also agreed to work collectively to narrow the gap between existing emission reduction plans and what is needed to reduce emissions so that the global average temperature increase can be limited to 1.5°.

For the first time—this, in my opinion, is an important fact—nations are being called upon to gradually reduce coal-generated energy and inefficient fossil-fuel subsidies.

Coming to the European framework, after the presentation of the Communication on the *Climate- Energy Framework 2030*, the European Council, on October 23–24, 2014, approved the Conclusions containing the new targets for the period 2021/2030, which constitute the EU's nationally determined contribution (*NDC*).

Central to the new *Climate-Energy Framework 2030* was a Europe-wide greenhouse gas reduction target of 40% compared to the year 1990. The conclusions include binding EU-wide targets for final energy consumption from renewable sources and an *indicative* energy-efficiency *target*, and they stipulate that the GHG target be split between the emission trading scheme (ETS) sectors, governed by *Directive 2003/87/EC*, and the non-ETS sectors, at, respectively, 43% and 30% below 2005 levels.

A number of legislative measures have been passed to achieve these goals, including the revision of the ETS Directive (*Directive No. 2018/410/EU*), the new regulation for non-ETS sectors (*Regulation No. 2018/842/EU*), as well as the so-called LULUCF Regulation (*Regulation No. 2018/841/EU*) on the inclusion of greenhouse gas emissions and removals resulting from land use, land-use change, and forestry. Also mentioned are the Energy Efficiency *Directive (EU) 2018/2002* (energy efficiency in 2030 at 32.5%) and the Renewable Energy Sources *Directive (EU) 2018/2001* (share of energy from RES in 2030 at 32%).

But it was in November 2019 that the European Parliament declared a climate emergency, asking the Commission to ensure that all proposals have the goal of limiting global warming to below 1.5 °C and reducing greenhouse gas emissions. Thus, in December of the same year, the Commission presented its *strategic communication on the European Green Deal* to achieve climate neutrality by 2050, and the Council, in its conclusions of December 12, 2019, determined that all EU policies and legislation should be consistent with this goal, which was subsequently enshrined in European climate legislation (*Regulation (EU) 2021/1119)*, which introduced an additional target by 2030, a 55-percent reduction in emissions compared to 1990.

On June 24, 2021, Parliament passed the *European Climate Act*, which makes legally binding the goal of reducing emissions by 55% by 2030 and climate neutrality by 2050. This will enable the EU to move closer to achieving the post-2050 negative emissions target, confirming *leadership* in the fight against climate change.

These measures should facilitate the transposition of the goals into law and result in greater benefits for cleaner air, water, and soil; cheaper energy bills; restored homes; improved public transportation and increased charging stations for electric cars; decreased waste; healthier food; and improved health for present and future generations.

The strategy that Europe is aiming for in raising global standards and creating opportunities will also benefit businesses. More jobs are estimated to be created in the renewables sector or in research for energy efficiency in buildings.

This interim target was accompanied by a package of legislation known *as* Fit for 55, which includes *13 related legislative reforms and six proposed climate and energy bills.*

Against this backdrop, in the wake of the global Covid-19 pandemic, the Next Generation EU (NGEU, also called the European Union Recovery Instrument), a European Union (EU) economic recovery package, was launched to help EU member states recover from the pandemic. Approved by the European Council on July 21, 2020, and adopted on December 14 of the same year, the facility is worth 750 billion euros (806.9 in current prices), will operate from 2021 to 2026, and will be linked to the 2021–2027 budget of the EU's multiannual financial framework (MFF).

The Plan is divided into six Missions, which represent the "thematic" areas of intervention, of which the one dealing with the Green Revolution and Ecological Transition is the primary item.

If the decarbonization process represents a path that involves the abandonment of fossil sources, consumption efficiency, complete energy supply from renewable sources, and the reconversion of so-called *energy-intensive* companies or those whose *core business* is centered on the processing and distribution of fossil sources, it seems clear that, where energy is to be acquired exclusively from a renewable energy system (RES), it is necessary to necessarily guarantee certain, speedy, and streamlined authorization procedures for the construction of plants.

On the other hand, it is unthinkable to believe that the transition from fossil to renewable will take place, albeit rapidly, without a transitional phase, in which inevitably gas, at least natural gas, biogas, and green gas, will have to play a "bridging" role that, in limiting emissions, can guarantee that energy requirement, which, pending the realization of renewable plants and technical solutions for the feeding of clean energy into the national power grid, is necessary for the maintenance of the economic and social development of the country.

I recall that in March 2019, during the hearing in the House Committee on Productive Activities, on the occasion of the cognitive investigation on the prospects for the implementation and adjustment of the national energy strategy to the National Energy and Climate Plan for 2030, the chief executive officer (CEO) of Terna explained, with respect to the targets provided in the National Integrated Energy and Climate Plan (PNIEC), which reported, as an estimate at the end of 2030, an assumed contribution of renewable energy production of about 55% on an annual basis, that this target will produce effects on the balance of the national electricity grid.

Renewables, as is intuitive, operate at full capacity, mainly solar, throughout the day. Taking April 2018 as a reference and comparing energy demand with renewable production, renewables cover some, but not all, of the energy demand during the day, i.e., from 7–8 am to 7 pm.

Dr. Ferraris hypothesized then: in a hypothetical April 2030, with all renewables in operation, there will be a phenomenon that needs to be taken into account, namely, that renewables will exceed, throughout the day, demand, resulting in a situation where during the day there will be *overgeneration*, an excess of renewables availability over demand.

Unless a way is found to store this potential, we risk being inefficient and not using the full potential of RES plants, which with so much effort and I still do not know how timely we are building.

Therefore, work needs to be done on developing energy storage capacity. Today, the available technologies are still hydro, that is, water understood as pumping (which are gas-fired) and the use of electrochemical batteries, a technology that is evolving, but still does not allow for the size levels to be reached to store the amount of energy assumed in the *chart* for 2030 and, I would add, much less for 2050.

Regarding, then, the streamlining of authorization procedures for the construction of RES plants, it must be acknowledged that, especially in view of the commitment of the dedicated resources of the National Recovery and Resilience Plan (PNRR) and the dedication devoted to the issue by the Draghi government and then Minister Cingolani, much has been done, although, in view of the different and fragmented competencies of the regions and local authorities on these matters, much should still be done.

With four very important measures enacted by the Draghi government, the simplification process I mentioned was initiated:

- Decree Law No. 77 of May 31, 2021, commonly referred to as *simplifications*
- Decree Law No. 4 of January 27, 2022, which contains, among other things, the first *regulations to contain the effects of price increases in the electricity sector*
- Decree Law No. 17 of March 1, 2022, known as the *Energy Decree Law*
- Decree Law No. 50 of May 17, 2022, which contains, among others, *urgent measures on national energy policies*

With these measures, to which Parliament has made a positive and decisive contribution, one of the key *milestones* included in the national recovery plan (NRP), namely, *the entry into force of a legal framework for the simplification of authorization procedures for the construction of onshore and offshore renewable energy facilities—M2C2-6*(M), was first implemented.

I would like to recall, with some immodesty, my contribution during the House consideration of the law converting the *simplification* decree. On that occasion, three amendments of mine were approved by the commissions: the first, which provided that, in the context of projects already authorized, design variants related to changes without significant environmental impacts, the simplified authorization procedure should be applied; the second, which provided for the application of the municipal simplified authorization procedure for the installation of accumulators where the RES production plant was already existing or authorized; and the last, but perhaps the most important, which stipulated that, for all RES plants, built in the implementation of the PNIEC in public utility expropriation proceedings, the regions were obliged peremptorily to express their agreement within 30 days of the successful conclusion of the service conference.

On the *Energy DL*, then, work was done while waiting for the adoption of the DM on "eligible areas," also approving a regulation with my first signature, which allowed the application of simplified procedures to those plants that, having started the process, were not found to be in areas defined as unsuitable by their regions; in addition, the power for plants in eligible areas for the purpose of applying simplified procedures was raised to 10 MW; and, finally, the procedures for the installation of ancillary works on plants already in operation were streamlined.

With the publication of Legislative Decree No. 199 of November 8, 2021, implementing *Directive (EU) 2018/2001 of the European Parliament and of the Council of December 11, 2018, on the promotion of the use of energy from renewable sources* and Legislative Decree No. 210, transposing *Directive (EU) 2019/944 (Markets Directive)* has been completed, and, the next steps, which are to provide the regulatory implementation of the reform, are being finalized and three important measures will, therefore, have to be issued, taking into account the necessary interlocution with the European Commission to define state aid schemes:

- The ministerial decree for the establishment of uniform principles and criteria for the identification of suitable surfaces and areas for RES facilities
- The ministerial decree to support sources and technologies that are not mature or have high operating costs
- The initiation of procedures for the development of storage capacity

Regarding the first, we should be in the home stretch, although the drafts are circulating just as I write this contribution, which I do not want to comment on precisely because drafts, at the very least, seem to appear to be inconclusive and certainly not very courageous.

A separate chapter deserves consideration of natural gas, biogas, and green hydrogen as "bridge" fuels toward climate neutrality.

Personally, I believe that instead of putting the question of which energy source is the best at the center, it would be more useful to ask what the best formula is for integrating the different energy sources at hand to achieve that functional mix to attain the set goals.

In fact, I do not think that there is a single source of energy that can ferry us to climate neutrality: the most fruitful way forward is through cooperation between different energy sources working together for the welfare of people and the preservation of the future of the planet, without forgetting the economic sustainability of the process.

This position is relatively new since until a few years ago, it was widely believed that, in order to reduce emissions, the way forward was to abandon gas in favor of electricity obtained through RES. More recently, however, more and more parties, including institutional ones, have realized and stated that, according to their assessments, electricity alone will not be sufficient to achieve the intended goals.

The industry association *Eurelectric* itself, which represents the European electricity industry, has estimated that electricity in 2050 will be able to cover 38–60% of

Europe's needs—a big step in the direction of decarbonization, especially when comparing these figures with those for fossil-fuel energy use in the 1990s—but it is unrealistic to imagine a scenario in which electricity alone can meet the transportation, air conditioning, and industrial production needs of the entire EU.

Added to this are additional problems related to the costs of creating infrastructure for distribution, transportation, and, above all, as we have already mentioned, the storage of such large quantities of electricity or the decommissioning of existing and functioning gas networks or even the need to respond to the needs of companies that operate with processes at very high temperatures, the so-called *energy-intensive ones*.

Problems also arise on the transportation side; while it is certain that more and more electric vehicles are being used for private use and local transport, it is difficult to imagine relying on this source for heavy transport. *(But then will electric really be the future of transport?)*

Finally, it should not be forgotten that electricity generation through hydropower systems, in order to give sufficient guarantees in terms of supply and demand balance and also in terms of maintaining the balance of power grids, mentioned above, requires the use of turbines for pumping, which, in most cases, are gas powered, and currently, about one-third of gas in Italy is used in thermal power plants to produce electricity (in 2020, out of about 70 billion total cubic meters used, 25 are used for this purpose).

For all these reasons, I remain convinced that, precisely in order to hit the climate neutrality goals by 2050, a form of integration, at least in the transition phase, between electricity (which can support, as mentioned, up to a maximum of 60% of requirements) and gas, especially in the form of so-called green gases (e.g. biomethane and green hydrogen), cannot be overlooked.

Under this scenario, Europe's need for natural gas between now and 2050 would be dramatically reduced, and the existing infrastructure could also be effectively and easily converted for green gas distribution. This combination will make it possible to achieve climate neutrality at the lowest possible cost through the integration of electricity from RES and green gas.

This approach, which appears to be the only one that is practically feasible, could guarantee concrete savings in economic terms as well; in fact, it is estimated that by proceeding in this direction, the EU will be able to save 80 billion euros annually on gas imports, 12 billion on oil imports, and 1.7 billion on coal imports.

In conclusion, the whole complex system of the process that is to lead Europe, and not only Europe, toward climate neutrality (it is only worth mentioning here the *Corporate Sustainability Reporting* Directive (CSRD) and the recently proposed *Corporate Sustainability Due Diligence* directive (CSDD), which will progressively lead a good fraction of companies operating in the territory of the Union to take a proactive attitude towards the transition to sustainable economic development, introducing new transparency obligations that presuppose the adoption of a supply chain approach), while having to move ahead quickly with respect to global, European and national objectives, it cannot disregard, and therefore it is right to recall, a concept expressed in the Commission's Work Program for 2023, that the exceptional set of circumstances that Europe is going through can only be addressed collectively, that is, through united action, giving continuity to the approach implemented during the Pandemic and the aggression against Ukraine.

Precisely with a view to this desirable collective action, without going so far as to reach the positions of some anti-Europeans who go so far as to pit our interests against those of other continents, anachronistically dividing the world into blocs in the global era, we must, however, also ensure that, on the issue of energy, Europe does not in the future exchange its dependence on Russian gas for dependence on Chinese REEs (*rare earth elements*), which today, it must also often be said, are derived from illegal mining, common in rural China, known to release toxic waste into water resources.

That is why this approach must also prefigure a strengthening of European competitiveness within—yes, a just transition and a cooperative external dimension and also one that is particularly attentive to safeguarding European assets and values and those of its member states.

In other words, the multiplicity of crises that we have experienced and are still experiencing, which we might call "polycrisis," while not questioning green goals, but, I would add, also digital and social goals, which are inevitably interconnected, must necessarily see public decision-makers devote extreme attention to the *becoming of European processes aimed at* their achievement. It is necessary, therefore, in the midst of an initiated, timetabled, and inescapable path, to insist on the crucial dimensions (institutional, *governance*, internal market, foreign policy) that are capable, within this path, of strengthening the resilience and strategic autonomy of the productive fabric of the Union in general and of the member states in particular.

Italian Parliament, Rome, Italy
6 October 2023

Silvia Fregolent

Foreword

Green Conservatism

When Roger Scruton published his book *Green Philosophy* in 2011, he was already one of the most prominent conservative authors in the West. At that time, he moved to the United States, working at the American Enterprise Institute in Washington, D.C., where he wrote his book devoted to the environment as seen from a conservative perspective. Environmental issues were beginning to enter the media and political debate with increasing frequency, though not nearly as pervasive as they are today. However, Scruton had felt the need to tell *another* view of the environment as seen through the eyes of a conservative. This was not new from a cultural point of view, but it was necessary to vindicate the existence of a tradition of green conservatism that had been all but obscured by an ideological and radical approach to environmental issues. Scruton, in his works, draws on the tradition of Anglo-Saxon conservationist thought by taking up Edmund Burke's vision of the world conceived as a relationship between past, present, and future generations, an intergenerational bond that also applies when it comes to nature. It is indeed our task to cherish what we have inherited from those who came before us in order to pass it on to those who will come after us. Building on Scruton's thought, it is necessary today to ask what *green conservatism* consists of and what its salient features are by distinguishing between a *pars destruens* and a *pars construens*.

In the first case, in light of the drift taken by radical environmentalism in recent years, it is impossible not to reject positions, proposals, directives, and, more generally, a precise ideological vision. Current environmentalism, as Giulio Meotti writes in his book *The Green God. Echolatry and Apocalyptic Obsessions*, has taken on a dogmatic character typical of traditional religions that therefore cannot be questioned.

Yet a mistake that often occurs when talking about the environment from a conservative perspective is to dwell on the critical part without devoting attention to the necessary proposals for an alternative ecologism to the ideological one. Is a different ecological transition possible? If so, under what conditions?

First of all, we need to promote a different approach not only in content (local before global, identity, protection of the weakest and the productive classes, man conceived as an ally and not an enemy of nature) but also in vocabulary and terminology. Striking is the frequency with which the word environment (and environmentalism) is used and the paucity of the use of the word ecology (and ecologism) and even less of the word nature.

If we refer only to the environment, we risk erasing the presence of man and concretize an approach that tends to minimize (or even erase) human presence, a view contrary to the Christian approach based on the concept of creation that holds man and nature together as part of a single whole. It is no coincidence that even the term nature has now taken a back seat to the environment, but what we must cherish is, *first and foremost*, the nature that surrounds us, its rules, and its times, respecting what we have been given.

The relationship between man and nature must be based on harmony and respect, which the ancient Romans called *genius loci*, the spirit of man, his soul, identity, and *sacredness* without which there can be no true love for the earth and nature. A *sacredness* that unites nature and literature united by the sense of beauty as evidenced by Pier Paolo Pasolini's verses dedicated to the divine right "defend, preserve, pray" and Gabriele D'Annunzio's pages with his descriptions of nature. To separate nature from the concept of beauty is to fail to understand its deeper meaning and therefore to be unable to act to preserve and guard it.

Thus, we come to the first point of a conservative approach to environmental issues that is able to combine necessary environmental protection with local identities and traditions. This means an environmentalism that starts from the local even before the global by having small communities at heart. It is about the principle of subsidiarity according to which the closer a power is to the citizen, the more it is possible to control its effects, the opposite of a dirigiste vision that imposes behaviors and rules from above, as is the case today on *green* issues by the European Union. Changing our habits and lifestyles, one of the mantras of current environmentalism, does not mean questioning age-old customs or characteristic features of our identity. It is a diriment point that on the other hand harkens back to the concept of "permanent principles" at the heart of Prezzolinian thought.

The second point of green conservatism is to achieve an ecological transition that does not leave behind the weaker classes. This may sound like an approach closer to a progressive sensibility, but in reality, those who care most about the needs of the people who are most at risk of suffering the consequences of the ecological transition today are conservatives.

The third point, closely related to the second, is to safeguard and protect domestic enterprises and businesses, particularly in strategic sectors.

Finally, here is a warning on a key issue: energy security. The war in Ukraine testified how relying on a single supplier for more than 40% of gas supplies (as in the case of Italy), and with even higher percentages for other European nations, was a mistake. It is important for Italy and Europe to develop its own supply chain, particularly on renewables, to ensure a safe ecological transition.

There is no doubt, however, that the elaboration of thought and the proposals made by green conservatism must be received by the conservative political world, which cannot make the mistake of not devoting the necessary attention to such a fundamental issue as the environment. This is especially true with regard to the younger generation—predominantly postideological—to whom it is necessary to advance an alternative environmental proposal to the ideological and radical one prevailing today.

Rome, Italy
6 October 2023

Francesco Giubilei

Preface

Despite EU and international efforts, biodiversity loss and the degradation of ecosystems continue at an alarming rate, harming people, the economy, and the climate.

The study on biodiversity cannot be limited to legal and regulatory dimensions; an interdisciplinary approach is necessary to understand the complexity of the phenomenon and thus to identify preventive protection systems that are effective.

For this reason, the volume takes an integrated multidisciplinary analytical approach, examining some of the most relevant profiles of the biodiversity issue within Europe, the United States of America, and China. Examining biodiversity in any one social or political context is difficult enough; examining it in two is more than twice as difficult. Indeed, comparative work, particularly in the context of biodiversity, requires both a broad lens to recognize common themes and shared challenges that span cultures and geographies.

It is therefore difficult for any one voice or perspective to provide insights from all of these vantage points. The transnational analysis of biodiversity is therefore well suited to a collection of narratives that, together, provide insights into the challenges and opportunities of contemporary biodiversity studies.

The essays collected here provide such a narrative. They describe how biodiversity in Europe, the United States, and China is addressed. They highlight some of the important gains that have been made and explain how some of them can be models for further development.

Each chapter in this collection shines a spotlight on one section of the tapestry of biodiversity. Individually, the chapters provide moments of profound insight and lucid analysis. Together, the threads of these narratives weave a cohesive story of the regions of the world most responsible for biodiversity threat and with the most power and resources to change the course of global biodiversity governance.

Rome, Italy — Giovanni Antonelli

Contents

Tackling the Unprecedented Biodiversity Loss: The International Law Response

Valériane Thool

Abstract Today, the loss of biodiversity is unprecedented. The latest Intergovernmental Science-Policy Platform on Biodiversity and Ecosystem Services (IPBES) report shows that more than one million species worldwide are threatened with extinction. Yet, international law has been addressing the issue of biodiversity for more than 30 years. While international law was limited to adopting treaties that focused their scope of application on well-defined species or territories, 1992 marked the adoption of the first universal and global instrument on biological diversity. Far from being an instrument of protection, the United Nations Convention on Biological Diversity was born out of the emergence of issues of conservation, exploitation and sharing of biodiversity, against a backdrop of North-South tensions. The Convention quickly evolved from a protectionist approach, thanks to the impetus of scientists, to an instrument of economic development. Today, states are faced with the difficult reality of a major decline in biodiversity, which will have significant impacts on trade, food security and the health of the world population. The last Conference of the Parties to the United Nations Convention on Biological Diversity, held in Montreal under a Chinese presidency, was seen as a major meeting focused on change. This was the watchword and the common thread that guided most of the speeches of the delegations. The Convention, however, is intimately linked to the goals that states are willing to set for themselves. This chapter proposes to review the foundations of international biodiversity law, while showing its limitations and shortcomings. From the Convention on Biological Diversity to the Global Biodiversity Framework for the post-2020 period, states seem determined to tackle the problem head on. With this movement, other instruments have recently been negotiated such as the World Trade Organization Agreement on Harmful Fishing Subsidies (adopted in 2022 at the 12th Ministerial Conference) which aims to find economic solutions to the problem of fish stock loss. States are also negotiating an international treaty, under the auspices of the United Nations General Assembly,

V. Thool (✉)
Faculty of Law, University of Sherbrooke, Sherbrooke, QC, Canada
e-mail: Valeriane.Thool@usherbrooke.ca

G. Antonelli et al. (eds.), *Biodiversity Laws, Policies and Science in Europe, the United States and China*, https://doi.org/10.1007/978-3-031-56218-1_1

aimed at the sustainable management of marine biodiversity outside national jurisdictions, which is not yet regulated.

At the 15th Conference of the Parties on Biodiversity in December 2022, United Nations Secretary-General Antonio Guterres declared that "without nature, we are nothing" and added that "for hundreds of years conducted a cacophony of chaos, played with instruments of destruction."[1] These words relate to the unprecedented biodiversity crisis the world is experiencing today, described by many scientists as the sixth mass extinction of living organisms. Most scientists consider that this erosion is taking place ten thousand times faster than was the case just a few decades ago.[2]

The latest IPBES report shows that over a million species worldwide are threatened with extinction, and 75% of the genetic variability of crop plants has already been lost. Deforestation is the most important factor in the loss of terrestrial biodiversity, with around ten million hectares of forest converted to agricultural land or use. In total, the FAO estimates that 100 million hectares of forest have disappeared in two decades (FAO 2020 report). The FAO considers that 30% of the world's tree species are threatened with extinction, affecting all bird, animal, insect, and plant species living in forest ecosystems.[3]

The loss of marine biodiversity is just as significant. In its 2020 report, the FAO showed that in 2017, 34.2% of the world's fish stocks were overexploited, and that the trend had only increased since then.[4] Several factors are contributing to the decline in marine biodiversity, all of which are directly or indirectly linked to human activities. While ocean acidification, rising ocean temperatures and pollution are important factors, the primary reason for the loss of marine biodiversity is overfishing. The boom in fishing-related technologies, the development of more efficient and enduring fleets enabling ships to stay in the water longer and go further, and the significant progress made in food preservation, are all having a knock-on effect on the state of marine biodiversity.

For these reasons, the United Nations General Assembly has included two general goals relating to biodiversity in its Sustainable Development Goals. Goal 14, entitled "Conserve and sustainably use the oceans, seas and marine resources for sustainable development," sets out a series of targets to be achieved to safeguard the health of the oceans, which is essential to humanity. Goal 15, for its part, aims to "Conserve and restore terrestrial ecosystems, ensuring their sustainable use, sustainably manage forests, combat desertification, halt and reverse land degradation and

[1] UN, "'Without nature, we have nothing': UN chief sounds alarm at key UN biodiversity event," December 6, 2022: https://news.un.org/en/story/2022/12/1131422.

[2] Wilson (1992); Beurier (2017), p. 432, §762.

[3] FAO, Mainstreaming biodiversity in forestry, FAO Forestry Paper no. 188, 2022, p. 175: https://www.fao.org/documents/card/en/c/cc2229en.

[4] FAO (2020), p. 57.

halt biodiversity loss." While these objectives provide guidelines for reducing and restoring biodiversity loss, they are not binding.

International biodiversity law provides a legal framework and establishes mechanisms not only for the conservation and sustainable use of biodiversity, but also for the equitable distribution of the benefits arising from its use. However, the loss of biodiversity is such that it means that all the regulations adopted to date have failed to be effective. The first part will present the international law of biodiversity, and its construction, while exposing certain limits which we consider to be partly responsible for the insufficiency of international law (Sect. 1). The second part will present new international treaties and strategic plans under discussion or recently adopted—adopted with a view to responding to the shortcomings of international law (Sect. 2).

1 International Law of Biodiversity

International biodiversity law is considered being the normative corpus of international law concerning biodiversity. It not only protects identified species or places of importance for the balance of biodiversity; it also regulates certain activities linked to the use of biodiversity. I will present the construction of international biodiversity law (Sect. 1.1) and its limits (Sect. 1.2).

1.1 Building International Law of Biodiversity

International law on biodiversity has developed rapidly since the 1970s, but in a sectoral and sometimes regional manner.[5] States adopted regional treaties to meet local transboundary needs. In other cases, states adopted sectoral treaties, dealing with a specific species or group of species identified on account of its extinction or significant exploitation. This body of legislation has given rise to an abundance of international law on biodiversity and species conservation, but it is also fragmented and lacks a concerted, global response. Spurred on by scientists in the 1980s, but also by the realization that the loss of biodiversity was a growing phenomenon, states began negotiations aimed at an international, legally binding instrument on biodiversity. This approach was crowned with success, as in 1992 the United Nations Convention on Biological Diversity was adopted, not without a few obstacles and disagreements. This section outlines the international law on biodiversity as it has developed over the last decade, starting with the United Nations Convention on Biological Diversity as the cornerstone treaty (Sect. 1.1.1), followed by international law on the biodiversity of wild species (Sect. 1.1.2), international law on biodiversity

[5] Maljean-Dubois (2021), p. 163; Arbour et al. (2016); Gillepsie (2014).

as applied to forests, wetlands, and agriculture (Sect. 1.1.3), and finally international law on marine biodiversity (Sect. 1.1.4).

1.1.1 A Framework Treaty on Biodiversity

At the Rio de Janeiro Conference on Environment and Development, states adopted the United Nations Convention on Biological Diversity.[6] The fruit of a tumultuous negotiation process, but also of the desire to respond to the global challenge of managing biological diversity, the Convention saw its main objectives swing from one vision to another. Indeed, the work of scientists, who presented the first signs of a decline in biodiversity, had initially led the drafters of the first version of the Convention to adopt a protectionist approach to biological diversity. However, the impetus provided by scientists came up against the economic interests of many states, who felt that the Convention should focus more on regulating the exploitation, use and management of biodiversity.[7] Conservationists, who wanted to take advantage of the negotiations to create a new "world environmental order," did not prevail in the negotiations against those who favored a utilitarian approach to biodiversity. This is a first point of divergence between opposing positions. Another point to note is the North-South confrontation between the States Parties. These North-South tensions stem from the economic development issues raised by developing and least-developed countries. Faced with growing reticence on both sides of the Parties, several elements were dropped: the precautionary principle was not included in the Convention's operative provisions and was only mentioned in the preamble; financing issues were postponed until later; and provisions relating to biotechnology were eliminated from the text. It must be said that the outcome of the negotiations disappointed many scientists. The Convention on Biological Diversity was no longer aimed at protecting biodiversity.

Although its content has been characterized as particularly utilitarian, the Convention is nonetheless a framework convention, and above all the most successful binding legal instrument about biological diversity.[8] It is the first international treaty to deal with biodiversity in such a comprehensive way. It contains three objectives: the conservation of biological diversity, its sustainable use and the sharing of benefits arising from the use of genetic resources.[9] It is based on the principle of sovereignty of states over their natural resources—a right that must not create environmental damage in other states or in jurisdictions where no sovereignty exists.[10] The CBD is known for setting out a series of key principles for biodiversity

[6] *Convention sur la diversité biologique*, 5 juin 1995, 1760 RTNU 79 (entrée en vigueur: 23 décembre 1993).

[7] Duchatel and Gaberell (2011), p. 6; Arbour et al. (2016), p. 419.

[8] Campins Eritja and Fajardo del Castillo (2021), p. 2; Michelle Lim (2019), p. 90.

[9] *United Nations Biological Diversity Convention*, Art. 1.

[10] *United Nations Biological Diversity Convention*, Art. 3.

conservation, such as the sustainable use of biodiversity, recognition of the traditional knowledge of indigenous and local communities in the conservation and sustainable use of biodiversity.

While the CBD proclaims broad principles, its corollary is that it does not lay down specific or precise rules on how to proceed with the conservation and sustainable use of biodiversity. In fact, the drafters of the Convention have deliberately used expressions of soft law, such as "as far as possible and as appropriate" or "in accordance with its particular conditions and capabilities."[11] It therefore leaves plenty of scope for improving content and implementation. The main reason for this is the establishment of a Conference of the Parties,[12] which is to meet at regular intervals to adopt protocols supplementing the Convention, on the one hand, and to adopt decisions on how to implement the main thrusts of the Convention, on the other. The main aim of such a Conference of the Parties is to develop the law over time.

The Conference of the Parties therefore has a major role to play. Notably, the Conference of the Parties to the Convention on Biological Diversity has adopted implementation strategies in the form of objectives to be pursued and targets to be achieved. However, the first two strategies, each spanning a decade, failed miserably. The first strategy, called the Strategic Plan 2002–2010, was based on the single objective of significantly reducing the rate of biodiversity loss. This plan was considered too short to meet the objective, but above all it lacked the precision and funding to implement actions aimed at combating biodiversity loss. The States Parties to the CBD have responded to these shortcomings[13] by adopting the Strategic Plan for Biodiversity 2011–2020,[14] adopted in Nagoya. The main objective of this strategy is "to promote the effective implementation of the Convention, through a strategic approach that includes a vision, mission, strategic goals and common objectives, capable of inspiring far-reaching action by all Parties and stakeholders."[15] This strategy is made up of 20 global objectives divided into five strategic goals corresponding to the areas identified (capacity building, safeguards to protect ecosystems, etc.).[16]

Both strategies have failed significantly in the fight against biodiversity loss. And for good reason: not only do scientific reports show that none of the proposed targets have been met, but some have also even been set back.[17] The states themselves have

[11] *United Nations Biological Diversity Convention*, Arts. 5, 6, 7, 8, 9, 10, 11, 14.

[12] *Id.*, Art. 23.

[13] Sandrine Maljean-Dubois (2021), p. 74.

[14] *Plan stratégique pour la biodiversité 2011–2020, incluant les objectifs d'Aichi relatifs à la biodiversité*, UNEP/CBD/COP/DEC/X/2, 27 octobre 2010.

[15] *Id.*, p. 7.

[16] *Id.*, p. 10.

[17] *Global Biodiversity Outlook 5*, Secretariat on Biological Diversity Convention, Montreal, 2020, p. 18. *See also*: Hagerman and Pelai (2016), p. 472.

acknowledged the failure of the strategies.[18] Concerning the strategy that ran from 2002 to 2010, the states noted with concern that "the findings of the third edition of the Global Biodiversity Outlook, which confirms that the 2010 biodiversity target has not been met in its entirety."[19] The reference to the concern of states was the same for the 2010–2020 strategy.[20]

In the meantime, two important protocols have been adopted to complement the Convention. The Nagoya Protocol on Access to Genetic Resources and the Fair and Equitable Sharing of the Benefits Arising out of their Utilization, and the Cartagena Protocol on Biosafety, adopted in 2000. Both deal with subjects that had been relegated to a later date in 1992, in the absence of agreement between states on these sensitive issues.[21]

1.1.2 Protecting Wild Species

In its infancy, international law as applied to biodiversity was generally confined to the conservation of certain wild species threatened with extinction or requiring regulation. The Convention on the Conservation of Migratory Species of Wild Animals (CMS) aims to ensure the conservation of terrestrial, marine, and aerial migratory species throughout their range. It establishes a legal basis for measures to conserve endangered migratory species (listed in Appendix I) and those requiring increased international cooperation (listed in Appendix II).

The Convention on the Conservation of European Wildlife and Natural Habitats (known as the "Bern Convention") was adopted in 1979 and covers a vast list of animal and plant species. It came into being at a time of great concern about the degradation of biodiversity due to increasing urbanization, the intensification of agriculture and the unsustainable exploitation of forests. Essentially, the Convention recognizes the intrinsic value of nature and the importance of preserving essential ecosystems and ecological processes. It establishes measures for the protection of habitats, with a particular focus on Europe's threatened or endangered migratory species. The Bern Convention also includes measures to regulate hunting and environmental education. To ensure that these measures are effective, the Convention promotes international cooperation, since combating the loss of Europe's wild biodiversity requires concerted, collective action.

---

[18] *Decision adopted by the Conference of the Parties to the Convention on Biological Diversity, Review of progress in implementation of the Convention and the Strategic Plan for Biological Diversity 2011–2020 and achievement of the Aichi Biodiversity Targets, CBD/COP/DEC/15/3*, para 5.; Matthieu Wemaëre et al. (2018), p. 2.

[19] *Strategic plan for biodiversity 2011–2020, including the Aichi biodiversity targets*, p. 1.

[20] *Decision adopted by the Conference of the Parties to the Convention on Biological Diversity, Review of progress in implementation of the Convention and the Strategic Plan for Biological Diversity 2011–2020 and achievement of the Aichi Biodiversity Targets, CBD/COP/DEC/15/3*, para 5.

[21] Sandrine Maljean-Dubois (2021), p. 71.

The Convention on International Trade in Endangered Species[22] (CITES), signed in March 1973, applies to endangered species of flora and fauna. Its main aim is to ensure that international trade in animals, plants and products does not threaten the survival of the species in question. The Convention covers over 5500 animal species and almost 30,000 plant species. Like the CMS, it is attached to the United Nations Environment Programme. The contribution of this Convention is to have established a framework obliging Party States to draw up regulations and administrative authorization processes prior to the crossing of borders for live or dead plants and animals whose trade is controlled by trade. In practice, this means that any import, export, re-export, or introduction from the sea of specimens of species covered by CITES must be accompanied by a permit. CITES also applies to trade in products derived from endangered species, such as furs, scales, ivory, trophies, wood, furniture, ready-made meals, skins, and furs. At the 19th Conference of the Parties to CITES in November 2022, states agreed to include some 50 shark species in Appendix II, which targets species that are not necessarily threatened with extinction but whose trade must be avoided. The implementation of CITES is not limited to regulating trade in endangered species: it also involves the collaboration of a large number of institutions, such as Interpol and the United Nations Office on Drugs and Crime.

1.1.3 Biodiversity Law for Forests, Wetlands, and Agriculture

On August 14, 1992, the United Nations General Assembly adopted a non-legally binding but authoritative Declaration of Principles for a Global Consensus on the Management, Conservation and Sustainable Development of All Types of Forests.[23] This declaration comprises a series of 15 principles, which aim to recognize the importance of forests for the equilibrium of ecosystems and local, regional, and global populations, and gives indications on economic issues linked to the exploitation and management of forests (reduction or elimination of tariff barriers and obstacles, environmental benefits and market mechanisms linked to forest products, principle of non-discrimination in forest trade, etc.).[24] In 2021, at COP26 on climate change, 141 states adopted the Glasgow Leaders' Statement on Forests and Sustainable Land Use,[25] the main aim of which is to halt the loss of global forest cover by 2030.

No international treaty regulates forest management and use in a comprehensive way. However, several treaties incorporate protection measures indirectly, such as

---

[22] *Convention sur le commerce international des espèces de faune et flore sauvages menacées d'extinction (CITES)* du 3 mars 1973, Washington, BC, 170, EMuT, 973: 18.

[23] Déclaration de principes, non juridiquement contraignante mais faisant autorité, pour un consensus mondial sur la gestion, la conservation et l'exploitation écologiquement viable de tous les types de forêts, A/CONF.151/26 (vol. III), August 14, 1992: https://www.un.org/french/events/rio92/aconf15126vol3f.htm.

[24] *Id.*, principe 13.

[25] *Glasgow Leaders' Declaration on Forest & Land Use.*

CITES, the United Nations Framework Convention on Climate Change, the International Tropical Timber Agreements of 1983, 1994 and 2006, and the United Nations Convention on Biological Diversity. Some of the existing forest conservation measures stem from regional treaties. The Regional Convention on the Management and Conservation of Natural Forest Ecosystems and the Development of Forest Plantations of October 29, 1993, aims to "promote in Central America national and regional strategies and procedures for the sustainable management of forests, including the establishment of a homogeneous soil classification and the recovery of deforested areas." It should be noted that this treaty only applies to Central American countries.[26] The treaty stipulates that Parties must implement financial and related measures, including mechanisms to guarantee local investment of revenues generated by forest resources, for example. In 2005, a similar treaty was adopted for the forests of Central Africa. The Traité relatif à la conservation et à la gestion durable des écosystèmes forestiers d'Afrique centrale et instituant la commission des forêts d'Afrique centrale (COMIFAC)[27] was adopted by ten states[28] and represents a comprehensive legal framework for consolidating cooperation in the Central African region in the field of forest conservation and sustainable management. Considered to be the Earth's second "lung" after the Amazon rainforest, the forests of Central Africa have seen significant exploitation of their resources, which continues to this day. The United Nations Food and Agriculture Organization estimates that between 1990 and 2020, deforestation caused the destruction of 420 million hectares of forest.[29]

Wetlands are fundamental to the balance of biodiversity in the world. The Ramsar Convention on Wetlands was adopted in 1971 and deals with the conservation and wise use of wetlands.[30] According to the Convention, wetlands include all lakes and rivers, underground aquifers, swamps and marshes, wet grasslands, peatlands, oases, estuaries, deltas and intertidal flats, mangroves and other coastal areas, coral reefs, and all artificial sites such as fishponds, rice paddies, reservoirs and salt marshes.[31] Its main objective is the conservation and wise use of wetlands through local, regional, and national actions and international cooperation, to contribute to sustainable development worldwide. As such, the Convention defines the wise use of wetlands as "the maintenance of their ecological character, achieved through the application of ecosystem approaches in the context of sustainable development." In 1990, the Parties to the Convention adopted Guidelines for the Implementation of

---

[26] Costa Rica, El Salvador, Guatemala, Honduras, Nicaragua, and Panama.

[27] *Traité relatif à la conservation et à la gestion durable des écosystèmes forestiers d'Afrique centrale et instituant la commission des forêts d'Afrique centrale,* February 5, 2005.

[28] Congo, Burundi, Cameroun, Tchad, Democratic Republic of Congo, Gabon, Rwanda, Centrafrican Republic, Guinée équatoriale and Sao Tomé-et-Principe.

[29] FAO. 2022. Summary of The State of the World's Forests 2022. Forestry solutions for green recovery and inclusive, resilient, and sustainable economies. Rome, FAO.

[30] *Ramsar Convention on Wetlands of International Importance especially as Waterfowl Habitat*, 1971.

[31] *Id.,* Art. 1.

the Wise Use Concept, which emphasize the importance of developing programs covering wetland inventory, monitoring, research, training, education, and public awareness, as well as adopting national policies as part of broader initiatives such as national environmental plans. The Convention recognizes the importance of wetlands for biodiversity, as home to a wide range of species. In concrete terms, it commits Parties to designate sites for the Ramsar List and promote their conservation, to cooperate with other Parties and to preserve wetlands.[32] In 2022, the Ramsar list contained 2439 designated wetland sites, corresponding to 254 million hectares worldwide. It is therefore a treaty that directly protects wetlands.

Agricultural biodiversity is essential to humanity: it provides food and income for most of the world's population, as well as being essential in terms of raw materials for clothing, housing, medicines, soil quality and so on. However, like the fishing industry, agriculture has undergone a massive expansion of its farming activities, which have spread over more and more land, causing part of the deforestation. The use of phytosanitary products to eliminate biological damage such as parasites or animal species destroying crops has intensified. These factors contribute directly to the loss of global biodiversity, posing a threat to food security. In addition to the general provisions of the CBD applicable to the agricultural sector, states adopted the Treaty on Genetic Resources for Food and Agriculture ("Seed Treaty") in 2001,[33] which replaces the FAO International Undertaking on Plant Genetic Resources for Food and Agriculture.[34] The objective of the Treaty is "the conservation and sustainable use of plant genetic resources for food and agriculture, and the fair and equitable sharing of the benefits arising out of their use, in harmony with the Convention on Biological Diversity, for sustainable agriculture and food security."[35] The Treaty establishes a multilateral system of access and benefit-sharing for crops. In practice, this means that access is granted via a standard material transfer agreement. Under this agreement, crops become part of an accessible pool of genetic resources made available to the Parties to the Treaty. Agricultural biodiversity is highly sensitive to climate change. This is why the Parties to the United Nations Framework Convention on Climate Change have drawn up a Koronivia Joint Work for Agriculture, on the socio-economic dimension of climate change in the agricultural sector.[36]

[32] *Id.*, Art. 4.

[33] *International Treaty on Plant Genetic Resources for Food and Agriculture,* November 3, 2001.

[34] *International Undertaking on Plant Genetic Resources for food and agriculture*, 1983.

[35] *International Treaty on Plant Genetic Resources for Food and Agriculture,* November 3, 2001, Art. 1.

[36] Koronivia Joint Work on Agriculture: https://www.fao.org/documents/card/en/c/CB5018FR.

1.1.4 International Law on Marine Biodiversity

Marine biodiversity is an inherent component of the balance of the world's ecosystems, but also plays a role in regulating the climate. The oceans cover 71% of the Earth's surface and are home to most of the world's species. Fishing provides over 15% of the world's protein intake, 3 billion people depend on marine resources to meet their needs, and 50% of the world's oxygen comes from the oceans.[37] Several human activities are responsible for an excessive decline in marine biodiversity, starting with overfishing, which not only catches sought-after fish species, but also does not always distinguish between fish species that can be eaten and those that are caught in nets by accident ("bycatch").[38] These activities are subject to fragmented, sector-specific regulations. While the United Nations Convention on the Law of the Sea[39] is the legal foundation for sea-related activities,[40] it was supplemented in 1995 by the Agreement on Straddling Fish Stocks.[41] Some conventions are regional or localized in scope, while others only cover one or more defined species—effectively excluding other species. These include the Convention for the Conservation of Anadromous Fish Stocks in the North Pacific Ocean,[42] the Convention for the Protection of the Marine Environment and the Coastal Region of the Mediterranean,[43] and the Agreement on the Conservation of Cetaceans of the Black Sea, Mediterranean Sea, and Contiguous Atlantic Area.[44]

These regulations remain insufficient, however, given the observed loss of marine biodiversity. The reason is simple. There are many international treaties with a regional or sectoral focus, but they do not address the issue of marine biodiversity loss in a comprehensive way. Although the Convention on the Law of the Sea was designed to respond to many of the issues identified in the 1970s, it remains a framework convention with general provisions about living resources in the oceans.

---

[37] Peter Thomson, *The Ocean Conference: A Game Changer,* United Nations: https://www.un.org/fr/chronicle/article/la-conference-sur-les-oceans-un-potentiel-de-transformation; Cristiana Pasca Palmer, Marine Biodiversity and Ecosystems Underpin Healthy Planet and Social Well-Being, United Nations: https://www.un.org/fr/chronicle/article/la-biodiversite-marine-et-les-ecosystemes-marins-assurent-la-sante-de-la-planete-et-le-bien-etre.

[38] Beurier (2017), §§748–751; Clare Shine, Nattley Williams et Lothar Gündling (2000); FAO (2021).

[39] *UNCLOS*, 1982.

[40] Moore (2018), p. 21.

[41] *Straddling Fish Stocks Agreement*, December 5, 1994.

[42] *Convention on conservation of Anadromous Stocks in the North Pacific Ocean*, February 11, 1992.

[43] *Convention for the Protection of the Marine Environment and the Coastal Region of the Mediterranean*, Barcelona, February 16, 1976.

[44] *Agreement on the Conservation of Cetaceans of the Black Sea, Mediterranean Sea and Contiguous Atlantic Area*, June, 2001.

1.2 The Inherent Limits of International Biodiversity Law in Responding to Biodiversity Loss

The legal framework for biodiversity contains a series of binding and non-binding legal instruments. The preceding paragraphs have provided an overview of international biodiversity law, which is by no means exhaustive, but which is failing to address the widespread and massive loss of biodiversity worldwide. There are several reasons for this lack of effectiveness. We have identified two major ones, which will be the subject of further developments: the institutional landscape for biodiversity governance is fragmented (Sect. 1.2.1), and procedures for monitoring and controlling the implementation of international biodiversity law are inadequate (Sect. 1.2.2).

1.2.1 A Fragmented Institutional Landscape

International governance of biodiversity suffers from several obstacles. The international organizations involved in biodiversity-related missions are numerous, and their work can tend to overlap.[45] The United Nations Environment Programme, the FAO, the World Maritime Organization, UNESCO, the Secretariat of the Convention on Biological Diversity, the World Intellectual Property Organization, and others have direct or indirect biodiversity-related missions. These missions range from technical and scientific assessments to regulation, monitoring and implementation of laws and actions. Because their work overlaps, we consider that some of the actions undertaken, or negotiations remain limited. This is because, to respect the objectives and missions of each entity, discussions on improving concerted and harmonized action to implement biodiversity conservation tools come up against institutional limits. However, we are increasingly witnessing concerted action between these entities, and a growing involvement of each of them in the debates of the others, to make the processes more effective despite the existence of a fragmented institutional landscape.

1.2.2 Difficulty of Implementation and Follow-Up

Another major obstacle to international biodiversity law responding to the phenomenon of biodiversity loss lies in the difficulties of implementing international law in practice.[46] To reduce the effects of this limitation, states constantly recognize the need for effective international cooperation, based on principles of transparency and accountability. Moreover, states have identified the shortcomings inherent in the

[45] *See*: Hufty (2001); Millet Smallwood et al. (2022).

[46] Maljean-Dubois (2021), p. 460.

implementation of international law: implementation mechanisms, financing and follow-up are inadequate.[47] If all States Parties to international biodiversity treaties are to implement them effectively, it must be recognized that the means of implementation vary according to each state's level of development. To this end, international cooperation must focus above all on the sharing and transfer of techniques.[48] Moreover, one of the key issues in implementing international law to combat biodiversity loss is financing. This is a fundamental implementation tool, which is sorely lacking. Least-developed countries, small island developing states, and developing countries bear the brunt of the consequences of biodiversity loss and lack the means to implement the concerted actions defined at multilateral level. Financing is therefore a key element in the implementation of international provisions for the conservation and sustainable use of biodiversity. Finally, monitoring and follow-up of actions is another major obstacle. Many states lack the human, technical and financial resources to carry out controls. This is particularly the case for sustainable fishing, which remains minimal given that many developing countries do not have the capacity to control the catches that take place in their waters. Some countries have forests so vast and dense that controls on the capture of wild animals, the extraction of genetic resources or the exploitation of forest resources are virtually impossible.

Yet, despite the existence of the United Nations Convention on Biological Diversity and its additional protocols, the loss of biodiversity is increasing, and the pace is accelerating. There is a growing need not only to take measures to conserve biodiversity, but also to strengthen the implementation of international biodiversity law.

2 A New Era in International Biodiversity Law?

The last decade has been marked by a collective awareness of the massive decline in biodiversity, initiated in particular by the media coverage of certain critical situations affecting marine and terrestrial biodiversity. Faced with this serious situation, several initiatives devoted to biodiversity-related activities have been launched or are in preparation, with the aim of improving the response of international law to the major crisis of the rapid decline in biodiversity and reversing the trend. This section presents the BBNJ Agreement (Sect. 2.1), the Pollution Treaty (Sect. 2.2), the Global Biodiversity Framework 2022–2030 (Sect. 2.3), and the World Trade Organization Fisheries Subsidies Agreement (Sect. 2.4).

[47] Millet Smallwood et al. (2022).

[48] Sandrine Maljean-Dubois (2021), p. 461.

2.1 *The Marine Biodiversity Agreement Outside National Jurisdictions*

After 20 years of negotiations under the aegis of the United Nations General Assembly, the states have adopted an Agreement on the Conservation and Sustainable Use of Marine Biodiversity beyond National Jurisdiction relating to the United Nations Convention on the Law of the Sea. The Agreement was formally adopted on June 4, 2023, at a final meeting of the negotiating states.[49] The Agreement applies to sones outside the national jurisdiction of states, i.e., on the high seas and in the zone (seabed and subsoil).[50] In fact, international regulation of biodiversity on the high seas and in the zone has been lacking until now, as the Convention on the Law of the Sea is inadequate.[51]

The Agreement contains four main sections. Firstly, an important part is devoted to marine genetic resources and benefit-sharing issues.[52] Until now, the use and exploitation of genetic resources on the high seas and in the Area were not subject to any specific regulations. Thus, these activities were subject to the principle of freedom set out in Article 87 of the Convention on the Law of the Sea.[53] The Agreement already recognizes that these activities are for the benefit of all mankind, and a series of measures place equity at the heart of activities linked to genetic resources, such as the fair and equitable sharing of monetary and non-monetary benefits.[54] A second section is devoted to area-based management tools, and specifically to marine protected areas.[55] The key element here is the need to conserve specific areas of recognized biological importance. A mechanism for electing these areas has been put in place. The third part deals with environmental impact assessments.[56] States are obliged to set up such impact studies to measure potential impacts on the marine environment. Finally, the fourth part concerns capacity building and the transfer of marine technology, which is intended to support developing states in implementing the Agreement.[57]

[49] *Agreement under the United Nations Convention on the Law of the Sea on the conservation and sustainable use of marine biological diversity of areas beyond national jurisdiction,* Art. 3.

[50] *UNCLOS*, Art. 1, para 1 (1).

[51] Gjerde et al. (2022), p. 1; Delfour-Samama (2022).

[52] *Agreement under the United Nations Convention on the Law of the Sea on the conservation and sustainable use of marine biological diversity of areas beyond national jurisdiction,* Art. 9 and following.

[53] *Id.,* Art. 87.

[54] *Agreement under the United Nations Convention on the Law of the Sea on the conservation and sustainable use of marine biological diversity of areas beyond national jurisdiction* Art. 11 bis para 1.

[55] *Agreement under the United Nations Convention on the Law of the Sea on the conservation and sustainable use of marine biological diversity of areas beyond national jurisdiction,* Art. 17 and following.

[56] *Id.,* Art. 27 and following.

[57] *Id.,* Art. 40 and following.

2.2 *Pollution Treaty*

Every year, between 4.8 and 12.7 million tons of plastic are dumped into the oceans. This phenomenon has a chain of consequences: waste is visible on land and in the sea, and this creates so-called "invisible" waste—micro and nano plastics. This in turn has an impact on health, as these plastics find their way into the human body.[58] In terms of biodiversity, plastics are ingested by animals. As a result, an Intergovernmental Committee has been set up under the aegis of the United Nations General Assembly, to negotiate binding measures on the entire plastic life cycle, from the extraction of fossil fuels for production to waste disposal. Several debates are underway, pitting oil producers and consumer countries (Saudi Arabia, China, India, Russia, United States)[59] against the High Ambition Coalition to End Plastic Pollution, which wants to reduce plastic production (59 states, including France and Japan). Several elements are at the heart of the negotiations. These include the elimination of fossil fuel subsidies, more efficient recyclability processes, education for more sustainable consumption, in particular product reuse, and the reorientation of plastic products.[60] To date, there are no international regulations coordinating action on the production, consumption, or waste of plastics, despite the existence of veritable plastic continents in the oceans. This treaty is due to be further negotiated by 2024.

2.3 *Global Biodiversity Framework 2022–2030*

As mentioned above, the strategies adopted by the States Parties to the United Nations Convention on Biological Diversity have failed. It was on this basis that negotiations for the next strategy were conducted. Thus, the strategic plan to 2050, including a mission to reduce biodiversity loss and restore it by 2030, was built on the theory of change, which recognizes the importance of urgent strategic action at global, regional, and national levels to achieve sustainable development and reverse

---

[58] United Nations Program for the Environment, « Plastic Pollution »: https://www.unep.org/fr/pollution-plastique.

[59] Emma Bryce, "First steps agreed on plastics treaty after breakthrought at Paris talk," The Guardian, June 6, 2023: https://www.theguardian.com/environment/2023/jun/06/first-steps-agreed-on-plastics-treaty-after-breakthrough-at-paris-talks; France 24, « À Paris, une « première version d'un traité contre la pollution plastique attendue fin 2023 », June 3, 2023, France 24: https://www.france24.com/fr/plan%C3%A8te/20230603-%C3%A0-paris-une-premi%C3%A8re-version-d-un-trait%C3%A9-contre-la-pollution-plastique-annonc%C3%A9e-pour-fin-2023.

[60] United Nations, « Une réduction drastique de la pollution plastique nécessite des changements profonds », Mai 16th 2023: https://news.un.org/fr/story/2023/05/1135192.

the unprecedented loss of biodiversity.[61] The plan is based on three pillars: means of implementation, an enabling environment, and accountability and transparency.[62]

It was the 15th Conference of the Parties, held in Montreal between December 7 and 19, 2022, that was decisive in enabling the Parties to reach consensus on the content of the strategic plan. They thus adopted the Global Biodiversity Framework 2022–2030, containing 23 targets to be achieved by 2030, not without a few twists and turns. One of the main points of divergence between the states was the question of financing. Developing countries, and especially the least developed countries, were calling for greater funding to enable them to combat biodiversity loss.

However, the content of the Global Framework reveals major advances in the means of action to combat biodiversity loss and restore ecosystems, even if its deployment in practice raises a few questions. First, the famous 30 × 30, which aims to conserve 30% of terrestrial territories and 30% of oceans and seas, has been at the heart of current events and negotiations.[63] The working groups devoted a great deal of time to this target, so important was it to the entire project. Several proposals aimed to conserve 20% or even 10% of territories and spaces. In addition to this target, the Global Framework contains targets in a variety of complementary areas relating to biodiversity, such as agriculture, land restoration, fisheries and forestry, food security, wildlife, biosecurity, etc. One of the most noteworthy aspects of the project is its recognition of the triple global environmental crisis of biodiversity, climate change and pollution. Because they are interrelated, these elements of the environmental crisis are the subject of specific targets, notably target 7 on pollution and target 8 on climate change and ocean acidification.[64]

The participation of the entire population is crucial to restoring biodiversity. The Global Framework therefore includes elements on gender, people with disabilities and indigenous peoples. Targets 22 and 23 aim to ensure gender equality in the implementation of the framework and recognize the rights of girls and women to natural resources. Women, girls, boys, indigenous peoples, and local communities must be involved in decision-making and policy-making processes concerning biodiversity.

---

[61] *Decision adopted by the Conference of the Parties to the Convention on Biological Diversity, Kunming-Montreal Global Biodiversity Framework, fifteenth meeting of the Parties to the Convention on Biological Diversity, CBD/COP/DEC/15/4*, p. 8.

[62] *Recommendation adopted by the working group on the post-2020 global biodiversity framework, CDB/WG2020/REC/5/1*, p. 7.

[63] *Decision adopted by the Conference of the Parties to the Convention on Biological Diversity, Kunming-Montreal Global Biodiversity Framework, fifteenth meeting of the Parties to the Convention on Biological Diversity*, CBD/COP/DEC/15/4, 2022 target 3, p. 9.

[64] *Id.*, targets 7 and 8, p. 10.

2.4 WTO Fisheries Subsidies Agreement

One of the major factors driving and accelerating the decline in marine species stocks is massive subsidies in the fishing industry. These subsidies, which artificially increase profits by reducing the cost of fishing and/or increasing the income received by fishermen, lead to overcapacity and overfishing.[65] The origins of subsidies in the fishing and deep-sea sectors have long echoed the variability in the level of economic development of coastal areas.[66] The first subsidies in this industry were granted to support fishermen and contribute to the economic development of coastal communities, and to combat food insecurity. Subsequently, these subsidies were used to support fishing companies whose revenues were insufficient, by compensating with fuel subsidies, to improve technical equipment for navigation, catching equipment or product packaging.[67] The consequence is simple: the state aid granted was such that the fishing industries were built and developed based on it.[68] They have become dependent on the aid granted.

The fishing industry benefits from government incentives and rebates. It is estimated that each year, 35 billion US dollars are distributed as fishing subsidies throughout the world.[69] It is a fact that this industry has become extremely prolific, if not food-producing. The result? The fishing industry has developed techniques and methods of catching fish that increase fishing capacity and have a direct impact on the state of biodiversity.[70] In response to this situation, in 2021, 296 scientists from around the world published a letter to decision-makers and the World Trade Organization (WTO) to ban harmful fishing subsidies,[71] in direct response to objective 14.6 of the Sustainable Development Goals:

> By 2020, prohibit fisheries subsidies that contribute to overcapacity and overfishing, eliminate those that promote illegal, unreported, and unregulated fishing, and refrain from granting new subsidies, bearing in mind that effective and appropriate special and differential treatment for developing and least developed countries must be an integral part of the World Trade Organization negotiations on fisheries subsidies.[72]

---

[65] World Bank, *The Sunken Billions Revisited. Progress and Challenges in Global Marine Fisheries*, 2017, p. 58.

[66] Schrank (2003), p. 1.

[67] Alice Tipping (2021) "New World Trade Organization Fisheries Subsidies text: It's a balancing act," IISD: https://www.iisd.org/gsi/commentary/new-world-trade-organization-fisheries-subsidies-text-its-balancing-act.

[68] *Id.*

[69] Costello et al. (2020), p. 1391.

[70] *See*: Young (2009); Grynberg (2003); Skerritt and Sumaila (2021).

[71] Sumaila et al. (2021).

[72] Organisation des Nations Unies, "SDG14: Aquatic Life," target 14.6.

After more than 20 years of negotiations, WTO Members have finally reached an agreement on the elimination of harmful fisheries subsidies.[73] The WTO Fisheries Subsidies Agreement[74] was adopted on June 17, 2022, and is the WTO's first-ever agreement on environmental issues.[75]

There are a number of important points to bear in mind regarding the content of the Agreement. The Agreement prohibits subsidies that contribute to illegal, unreported, and unregulated (IUU) fishing, or to fishing-related activities that support IUU fishing.[76] Accordingly, no member shall grant or maintain such subsidies to any vessel or operator engaged in fishing activities. To this end, three actors may determine that a vessel or operator is engaged in IUU fishing: the coastal member, for activities carried out in areas under its jurisdiction; a state or flag member for an activity carried out by vessels flying its flag; or by a regional fisheries management organization.[77] The activity must be positively determined to contribute to IUU fishing, i.e., the entity must have made a final determination and must have listed the vessel or operator involved on an IUU list.[78] Importantly, developing and least-developed countries are exempt for a period of two years.[79]

Secondly, the Agreement prohibits the granting of subsidies that contribute to the overexploitation of fish stocks, unless the subsidy contributes to restoring the stock to a sustainable level.[80] No member may therefore grant such aid. The Agreement also sets out what is to be considered an overexploited stock. This is the stock recognized as such by the coastal member in whose region the fishing takes place, or by an authorized Regional Fisheries Management Organization.[81] Here again, developing and least-developed countries are exempt for a period of two years from the entry into force of the Agreement.[82]

Finally, the Agreement contains other prohibitions on the granting of subsidies harmful to fishing. Article 5§1 states that no subsidies may be granted to fishing activities on the high seas outside the jurisdiction of a Regional Fisheries Management Organization.[83] Furthermore, members must show moderation in granting

[73] WTO, "Les efforts des Membres de L'OMC aboutissent à un ensemble de résultats sans précédent dans le domaine du commerce à la CM12," June 17, 2022, en ligne: https://www.wto.org/french/news_f/news22_f/mc12_17jun22_f.htm; WTO, Note d'information sur l'état d'avancement: December 10, 2021: en ligne: https://www.wto.org/french/thewto_f/minist_f/mc12_f/briefing_notes_f/bffish_f.htm.

[74] *Agreement on Fisheries Subsidies*, WT/MIN(22)/W/22, June 17, 2022.

[75] *Id.*

[76] *Agreement on Fisheries Subsidies,* Art. 3.

[77] *Id.,* Art. 3.2.

[78] *Id.,* Art. 3.3.

[79] *Id.,* Art. 3.8.

[80] *Id.,* Art. 4.1.

[81] *Id.,* Art. 4.2.

[82] *Id.,* Art. 4.4.

[83] *Id.,* Art. 5.1.

subsidies to vessels not flying their flag,[84] or when no information is available on the state of the stock.[85]

3 Conclusion

As can be seen, international biodiversity law has developed in an abundant manner, albeit without any logical interconnection or efficiency. This law has developed on the basis of certain demands from developing states, calling for greater equity in the measures adopted with regard to biodiversity. This situation has created North-South divergences that have not ceased to this day. The most important thing to remember about international biodiversity law is that it has not been effective enough in combating biodiversity loss. In response, states have sought to adopt more effective international treaties and action plans to fill the gaps identified. These international treaties have yet to come into force. Let us hope that when they do, the content of these instruments will enable us to respond to the biodiversity crisis.

References

Arbour J-M et al (2016) Droit international de l'environnement, 3e éd. Yvon Blais, tome 1

Beurier J-P (2017) Droit international de l'environnement. Pedone, Paris

Campins Eritja M, Fajardo del Castillo T (eds) (2021) Biological diversity and international law. Challenges for the post 2020 scenario. Springer, Cham, Switzerland

Costello C et al (2020) Ambitious subsidy reform by the WTO presents opportunities for ocean health restoration. Sustain Sci 16(4):1391

Delfour-Samama O (2022) La protection de la biodiversité en haute mer, une urgence écologique. spécial:HS21 Revue juridique de l'environnement 133

Duchatel J, Gaberell L (eds) (2011) La propriété intellectuelle contre la biodiversité? Géopolitique de la diversité biologique. Edition Centre Europe – Tiers monde (CETIM), Genève

FAO (2020) The State of World Fisheries and Aquaculture 2020. FAO, Rome, p 57

FAO (2021) Déclaration sur la durabilité de la pêche et de l'aquaculture du comité des pêches. FAO, Rome

Gillepsie A (2014) International environmental law, policy, and ethics. OUP, Oxford

Gjerde KM et al (2022) Getting beyond yes: fast-tracking implementation of the United Nations agreement for marine biodiversity beyond national jurisdiction. Ocean Sustain 1(1):1–8

Grynberg R (2003) WTO fisheries subsidies negotiations: implications for fisheries access arrangements and sustainable management. Mar Policy 27(6):499

Hagerman SM, Pelai R (2016) "As far as possible and as appropriate": implementing the Aichi biodiversity targets. Conserv Lett 9(6):469–478

Hufty M (2001) La gouvernance internationale de la biodiversité. Études internationales 32(1):5–29

Lim M (2019) Biodiversity 2050: can the convention on biological diversity deliver a world living in harmony with nature? Yearb Int Environ Law 30(1):79–101

---

[84] *Id.,* Art. 5.2.

[85] *Id.,* Art. 5.3.

Maljean-Dubois S (2021) Le droit international de la biodiversité. RCADI, Brill, p 407
Millet Smallwood J et al. (2022) Global biodiversity governance: what needs to be transformed? In: Visseren-Hamakers IJ, Kok MTJ (eds) Transforming biodiversity governance. Cambridge University Press, pp. 43–66
Moore NJ (2018) The United Nations convention on the law of the sea: one of the greatest achievement in the international rule of law. In: Nordquist MH, Moore JN, Long R (eds) Legal order in the World's oceans. UN convention on the law of the sea. Brill, Leiden
Schrank WE (2003) Introducing fisheries subsidies. Technical Paper 437. Food and Agriculture Organization, p. 52
Skerritt DJ, Sumaila RU (2021) Assessing the spatial burden of harmful fisheries subsidies. Final report. The Fisheries Economic Research Unit, Oceana
Sumaila R et al (2021) WTO must ban harmful fisheries subsidies. Science 374:6567
Wemaëre M et al (2018) Les options juridiques pour l'accord international sur la biodiversité en 2020: une première exploration. IDDRI
Wilson EO (1992) Diversity of life. W.W. Norton, p 424
Young MA (2009) Fragmentation or interaction: the WTO, fisheries subsidies, and international law. World Trade Rev 8(4):477

The Loss of Biodiversity as a Serious Environmental Threat: The Need for a New Legal Paradigm

Maria Vittoria Ferroni

Abstract The starting point of this legal research is the assumption that the loss of biodiversity is the environmental threat that, together with climate change, is looming on the planet, since the two phenomena are intrinsically linked and correlated. A scientific study showed that human societies might have already exceeded some of the planetary limits by placing themselves in a danger zone. At a global level, there has been an awareness of the emergency linked to the speed of the rate of biodiversity loss (which has increased in recent years) also deriving from a legal approach to the protection of biodiversity which is mainly voluntary and not binding on the states. For the effective protection of biodiversity, a crucial point seems to be the search for new legal instruments to ensure the effectiveness and efficiency of protection. In December 2022, 'The Kunming-Montreal Global Biodiversity Framework' was adopted, which has the goal of protecting at least 30% of land and marine areas by 2030 and restoring degraded ecosystems. This agreement marks a crucial change for an effective protection of biodiversity on a global level, even if it seems to have introduced only procedural obligations (and therefore does not appear to be a binding global agreement).

At a European level, until the Green Deal, the protection for biodiversity has been ensured through general rules of soft law, accompanied by a sectoral discipline of hard law through the Birds Directive and the Habitats Directive (as transposed in the domestic legislation).

Starting from the Green Deal, awareness has been gained from the emergency linked to the loss of biodiversity (moreover synergistic with the mitigation of climate change) and of the necessity to change the protection paradigm moving from a soft law approach to general rules, binding for all Member States. An important milestone is the very recent 'Nature Restoration Law', which has been approved by the European Parliament on february 2024 and that provides binding obligations for all Member States, as well a support for the fight against the loss of biodiversity, not only from the protected areas but also from cities and other areas not protected.

M. V. Ferroni (✉)
Department of Political Sciences, Sapienza University of Rome, Rome, Italy
e-mail: mariavittoria.ferroni@uniroma1.it

G. Antonelli et al. (eds.), *Biodiversity Laws, Policies and Science in Europe, the United States and China*, https://doi.org/10.1007/978-3-031-56218-1_2

1 Introduction

The acceleration of biodiversity[1] loss rate influences the balance of the entire planet because, according to the concept of reticularity and interconnection, each species plays a role, and their disappearance threatens the entire ecosystem. In other words, the loss of biodiversity is an indicator of the decline of ecosystems and ultimately of the human health to which it is linked. Furthermore, biodiversity plays a central role in the mitigation of climate change, being that the two phenomena are intrinsically linked and correlated. Human domination of the Earth and its natural resources has increased dramatically over the past century, substantially altering natural ecological processes over three-quarters of the Earth's surface. Human-induced changes to ecosystems and the extinction of species have been more rapid in the past 50 years than at any time in human history. Today, around one million of animals and plant species are already threatened of extinction.

Furthermore, the global rate[2] of species extinction is already at least tens to hundreds of times higher than the average rate over the past ten million years and is accelerating. A scientific study showed that human societies might have already exceeded some of the planetary limits (Rockström et al. 2009; Steffen et al. 2015; Wang-Erlandsson et al. 2022)[3] by placing themselves in a danger zone. This could lead, if not quickly reversed, to the sixth largest extinction event in the history of life on Earth, caused by the impacts of human activities on the planet. According to this study, the most serious and alarming data would concern biodiversity. In fact, the species are becoming extinct at a fast rate, something which has never occurred before. Assuming as a measure of the loss of biodiversity the annual number of extinct species per million (E/MSY) and agreed as the planetary limit the threshold of 10 E/MSY (and an area of uncertainty that would range from 10 to 100 E/MSY), the current rate of extinction would go well beyond the limit of 100 E/MSY, namely, it would be more than ten times higher than the planetary limit. This limit, without

[1] The legal definition of biodiversity is provided for in the 1992 Rio Convention on Biological Diversity as (Art. 2) 'the variability of living organisms of any source, including, inter alia, terrestrial, marine, and other aquatic ecosystems, as well as the ecological complexes of which they are part; this includes diversity within each species, between species, and of ecosystems. Biodiversity includes the state of fauna and flora, forests, but also urban and peri-urban greenery and agricultural areas.

[2] IPBES' Report, available at https://www.un.org/sustainabledevelopment/blog/2019/05/nature-decline-unprecedented-report/.

[3] The Planetary boundaries' theory, in its latest update to 2022, has shown that, with respect to nine macro-processes (1 climate change, 2 change in the integrity of the biosphere and loss of biodiversity; 3) interference with the biogeochemical cycles of nitrogen and phosphorus; (4) depletion of the ozone layer; (5) ocean acidification; (6) water use (7) land use and deforestation; (8) chemical pollution; (9) the spread of aerosols and dust in the atmosphere), six of the nine planetary limits have already been exceeded by humankind. The theory of planetary boundaries (PB) and safe operating space (SOS) was formulated with the publication in Nature in 2009 of a study by a group of 29 eminent scientists led by Johan Rockström. The study was updated in 2015 by W. Steffen, and, lately in 2022.

massive course corrections, will lead to a rate of extinction that will exceed 1000 E/MSY by the end of the century (Rockström et al. 2009), jeopardising the very survival of humanity.

The objective of this chapter is to investigate and verify whether a political and legal paradigm shift is taking place at an international and European level to reverse the loss of biodiversity, which is also essential for the mitigation of climate change. A crucial point seems to be the application of more binding legal instruments to ensure the effectiveness and efficiency of the protection. Moreover, the support of the judges could also help to establish more binding and uniform rules for the protection of biodiversity between the various states. The paradigm shift appears to be linked to the transition from soft law rules to legally binding hard law rules, as it has been noted in recent years that the voluntary approach to restoring and protecting biodiversity has not resulted in a satisfactory outcome. The Kunming-Montreal agreement (which will be examined), being an international agreement, seems to have assumed a more determined position, but has not introduced rules that lead to sanctions in the event of non-compliance with them (therefore its implementation is left to the voluntary of individual states).

Europe, with the Green Deal, seems to have seriously joined the paradigm shift as it has introduced binding rules with special regulations on which we will focus.

Considering that biodiversity includes the state of fauna and flora, forests, but also urban and peri-urban greenery, agricultural areas, and other areas present in the cities (for example, military servitude and confiscated areas from organised crime), the centrality of the transformation and regeneration of cities will be recalled, as a support for the fight against the loss of biodiversity and climate change. In fact, as will be further illustrated, the areas protected or to be protected and restored in the coming years alone are not sufficient to reverse the course of biodiversity loss and the fight against climate change. Therefore, it will be necessary to expand the increase in biodiversity or its regeneration to other areas, including urban ones.

2 The International Convention on Biological Diversity

The protection of biodiversity, with reference to its impact on the entire planet, has been regulated in the legal context by a multilevel framework divided into an international and a European framework. At an international level, several conventions have followed one another over the years, including: the 1971[4] Ramsar

[4]The Ramsar's Convention on Wetlands of international interest signed in Ramsar (Iran) on February 2, 1971 and enforced by Italy adopting the Presidential Decree no. 448 of March 13, 1976 and with the following Decree no. 184 of February 11, 1987. It was considered one of the most important international treaties on biodiversity and the aims are to halt the worldwide loss of wetlands and to conserve, through wise use and management, those that remain.

Convention (Iran) on Wetlands; the 1973[5] Washington Convention on International Trade in Endangered Species of Wild Fauna and Flora; the 1979;[6] Bonn Convention on Migratory Species; and the 1979 Bern Convention,[7] all of which aim, in various respects, to protect biodiversity but with the limitation of being sectoral. The Convention considered most important for the protection of biodiversity is the Convention on Biological Diversity (CBD), which was concluded in Rio de Janeiro from 3 to 4 June 1992.[8] The Convention entered into force on 29 December 1993 and has been ratified by most states. The purpose of this Convention was to extend and focus international cooperation on the environmental issues of a global nature, such as climate change, biodiversity loss and deforestation (Marchisio 2008). The aim was to create an *umbrella convention* that could bring together the efforts of sectoral Conventions. This is a framework convention to enable further agreements to be concluded. Once global objectives have been set, the Parties as provided for in Article 6 shall adopt strategies, plans, and programs to conserve and use biodiversity sustainably. According to this provision, the European and the National Strategies on Biodiversity were issued. That is to say, the provisions of the Convention are characterised by their open nature, because they allow Parties to identify the most appropriate measures to fulfil their general obligations. The Convention on Biological Diversity is the main legal framework of reference for the protection of biodiversity at an international level.

3 The Conference of the Parties: Kunming's Agreement—Montreal

The executive body of the Convention on Biological Diversity is the Conference of the Parties (COP).[9] This is the most relevant body of the Convention, consisting of all governments that have ratified the Treaty, which meets every two years to review

[5]The C.I.T.E.S., an acronym derived from the initials of Convention on International Trade of Endangered Species (more precisely Convention on International Trade in Endangered Species of Wild Fauna and Flora) also known as the Washington Treaty signed in Washington on 3 March 1973 and ratified by Italy with the Act. no. 874 of 19 December 1975.

[6]Convention on the Conservation of Migratory Species of Wild Animals, signed in Bonn on 23 June 1979, ratified in Italy by Law no. 42 of 25 January 1983. It is considered a framework convention on the protection of migratory species, which provides for the support of concerted research activities and the monitoring of endangered migratory species.

[7]Bern Convention, Convention on the Conservation of Wildlife and Natural Habitats in Europe of 19 September 1979, ratified in Italy by Law no. 503 of 5 August 1981.

[8]Convention on Biological Diversity (Convention on Biological Diversity) signed in Rio de Janeiro on 5 June 1992, within the framework of the United Nations Conference on Environment and Development (UNCED).

[9]The purpose of the Conference of the Parties is to coordinate and implement the proper functioning of the Convention and it is vested with various powers: to adopt protocols, amendments, establish subsidiary bodies, working groups, and examine technical and scientific opinions.

progress, set priorities and commit to work plans, and which has set targets over the years for global biodiversity protection. In particular, in 2010, during the Nagoya Conference, the Aichi Biodiversity Targets were established, which were not achieved (as verified in 2020). Consequently, the 75th Session of the United Nations General Assembly (UNGA 75)—Summit on Biodiversity—sought to provide policy direction and impetus on the development of the post-2020 Global Framework for Biodiversity. Also, at a European level, in the Resolution of the European Parliament of 16 January 2020 (on the 15th meeting of the Conference of the Parties to the Convention on Biological Diversity (COP 15) the adjective 'unprecedented' was used to define the destructive action of man on nature. Accordingly, the aforementioned European Resolution insists that the European Union encourages, during COP 15 in Kunming in China, a global project on biodiversity, to abandon voluntary commitments and propose an ambitious and inclusive strategy for 2030 that will establish legally binding objectives. This will include specific targets for the protection of at least 30% of land and sea areas; and the restoration of damaged ecosystems.

On 15 October 2021, the first part of COP15 (which was to be held in Kunming in China but, due to the pandemic, at a distance) was concluded. After the failures of the last decades (just think of the previous 20 Aichi Targets that had to be achieved by 2020) a fast and effective response was requested because humanity is dangerously approaching the '*point of no return*'. The main achievement during this first part of the conference was the *Kunming Declaration*, in which countries committed to negotiating an effective global framework for biodiversity post-2020 in 2022. In December 2022, the second part of COP 15 was held in Montreal, during which 'The Kunming-Montreal Global Biodiversity Framework' for this decade, was adopted. The agreement sets out four goals and 23 targets to be achieved by 2030 to halt and reverse biodiversity loss. In the agreement, recalling the reports of the *Intergovernmental Science-Policy Platform on Biodiversity and Ecosystem Services* (IPBES) it was observed that the rate of biodiversity extinction is accelerating at a pace of ten to one hundred times that of the last ten million years, and about one million species are at risk of extinction. The goal is to reduce the rate of extinction and the risk of it tenfold by 2050. In the final agreement, the conservation target of 30% of terrestrial and marine areas by 2030 was included, although the numerical target of one billion hectares was removed. The target (referred to as 30 × 30) envisages doubling the conservation of terrestrial areas under the Aichi Targets (17%) and tripling that of marine areas (10%), where some believe it will become the guiding target for biodiversity (similar to the Paris Agreement's goal, that aims to limit global warming to 1.5 °C). Regarding the objective of the protection of 30% of the areas, it is not clear whether the 30% should be calculated on a global scale or concerning each State Party to the Convention on Biodiversity. In Europe, it was referred to every state. Furthermore, questions are being raised about the type of areas to be included in the 30%. If it certainly includes protected areas to reach 30%, it is believed that areas of organic agriculture, urban forests, or (as in Canada) military easements could also be included. In Italy, the possibility of also including areas confiscated from organised crime is being tested (Ferroni 2023).[10] Scientists believe that achieving an effective 30% in good conservation status globally will bring 90% of habitats back to balance. However, what emerges from the Agreement is that if the role of protected areas is very important, they are not the solution alone.

It is also necessary to insist on the restoration of degraded ecosystems,[11] intended as a reduction of pressures on nature. The goal is to restore 30% of degraded terrestrial, aquatic, and marine ecosystems, by 2030. In this direction, the agreement sets out to eliminate or reform the nature-damaging subsidies of around USD 500 billion per year, by 2030 (even if there are no references to specific industrial sectors) and increase incentives for the conservation and restoration of biodiversity. Furthermore, the agreement has also introduced the indication of reducing by 50% the risks arising from pesticides by 2030. However, gradual elimination has not been foreseen but only a reduction of the overall risk, concerning at least half of the dangerous substances (that does not seem satisfactory for the effective protection of biodiversity).

The implementation of the measures provided for in the agreement must be accompanied by spatial planning that considers biodiversity, reaching by 2030 almost zero loss of areas of high importance for biodiversity. Furthermore, the agreement recognised the interconnections between biodiversity and health, considering the one-health approach and control of wildlife trade was insisted on to avoid virus spillover. In addition, it was also underlined, on the one hand, that the expansion of protected areas must take place while respecting the rights of indigenous people and local communities. On the other hand, the expansion of protected areas will not be sufficient, as it will also have to act on over-consumption (but the target to reduce the consumption and production footprint by 50% within 2030 was removed, leaving a reference to the need for a reduction but without a numerical target. The reference to sustainable diets was also removed).

A specific target (Target 12) concerns the central role of urban centers in the fight against the loss of biodiversity and climate change by introducing urban planning that includes biodiversity, which will lead to a percentage increase (in Europe already quantified as we will observe) of green areas and urban forests in cities.

The financial profile (Target 19) is a sensitive issue because the lack of adequate financial funds was one of the main causes of the failure of the targets (Aichi targets) for the 2010–2020 decade. Regarding the financial resources to be made available for the protection of biodiversity, at least 200 billion dollars per year should be invested by the end of the decade, for national and international funding related to biodiversity. Funding could come both from the states and from private entities. Some African States (Congo, Cameroon, Uganda, and Namibia) have expressed

---

[10]In this regard, in Italy, the law of 7 March 1996 no. 109 provides for the reuse of assets confiscated from the mafia by citizens, citizens' associations, third-sector subjects.

[11]The implementation of the measures provided for in the agreement must be accompanied by spatial planning that considers biodiversity, reaching by 2030 almost zero loss of areas of high importance for biodiversity.

disappointment with the agreement as it was not accompanied by the financial means necessary to effectively implement the planned measures. Consequently, approximately 20 billion dollars a year (until 2025) and 30 billion dollars, by 2030 will have to be invested to help the less developed countries but still rich in biodiversity. For this reason, there has been a commitment to create a new global biodiversity fund. The delicate point of this agreement seems to foresee only procedural obligations through the reporting systems required by the Global Diversity Framework. However, there do not appear to be binding obligations and redress measures in the event of non-compliance with the substantive objectives established in the agreement.

To achieve an effective protection and restoration of biodiversity on a global scale, it would be desirable both to create a global organism for the political direction and administrative management of interventions on the matter, and an international court endowed with sanctioning powers against the defaulting states. As it will be seen, Europe has decided to modify the regulatory paradigm with which to protect and restore biodiversity, introducing—also under the Kunming-Montreal agreement—binding hard law legislative measures.

4 The Protection of Biodiversity in Europe through the Habitat Directive and the Directive for the protection of Birds

Starting from the international protection of biodiversity, in Europe different strategies have been adopted:

- On the one hand, the European strategies on biodiversity (upon the Convention of Rio in 1992 which established the conclusion of further agreements and strategies) have established a series of principles, objectives, and activities, but they do not present a sanctionary policy that has effectively performed a real deterrent effect (acts of soft law) and of which the objectives up until the last strategy for 2030 have been partially achieved.
- On the other hand, the sectorial binding rules of hard law, of which some have been enacted even before the Convention of Biodiversity in 1992.

Starting from the sectorial rules, these are the Birds Directive and the Habitat Directive (as transposed into internal regulations). These are Directive 79/409/EEC of 2 April 1979 on the conservation of wild birds (recodified by Directive 2009/147/EC[12]) and Directive 92/43/EEC of 21 May 1992 (on the conservation of natural

[12] The Wild Birds Directive in its original version dates to 1979 and was therefore a precursor to the 1992 Rio Convention. Directive 79/409/EEC of 2 April 1979 was replaced by Directive 2009/147/EC of 30 November 2009. The 1979 directive was taken over in 2009 with an update of the lists of protected species and some slight modifications. Migratory birds represent a common heritage of the European peoples and their effective protection is a transnational priority, to be carried out based

habitats and of wild fauna and flora (Ferroni 2015). More recently, Regulation (EU) No. 1143/2014 was adopted, laying down provisions to prevent and manage the introduction and spread of exotic species invasive[13] as well as for the protection of the marine environment, Directive 2008/56/EC (Marine Strategy Framework Directive (MSFD)), which provides for an integrated approach and includes all other instruments and directives that act on the marine environment. Another protection instrument for biodiversity is EU- CITES Regulation 338/97, which implemented the Convention on International Trade in Endangered Species of Wild Fauna and Flora within the European Union.

The protection of biodiversity through the above-mentioned directives (Habitats and Birds) is based on the conservation of hot spots, i.e. identified and protected sites. More specifically, the 'Habitats' Directive 92/43/EEC of 21 May 1992 (on the protection of natural habitats and of wild fauna and flora) defines an overall framework aimed at ensuring the maintenance or restoration, at a favourable conservation status, of natural habitats and species of wild fauna and flora of Community interest through the establishment of a coherent ecological network of special areas of conservation (SACs) called *Natura 2000*. The European ecological network '*Natura 2000*' is thus the main instrument for the protection of biodiversity in Europe, with the aim of maintaining the habitats and species identified in the annexes to the directives in a satisfactory state. That is, in order to ensure the maintenance, or the restoration, at a satisfactory state of conservation of natural habitat types and the habitats of protected species, the directive constitutes a coherent European ecological network of 'special areas of conservation', i.e. areas that the directive requires the Member States to designate by their own measures, called *'Natura 2000'*, formed by the sites where the natural habitat types listed in Annex I and the habitats of the species listed in Annex II are found, which also includes the special protection areas provided for in the Birds Directive (Art. 3, para 1). In addition, the *Natura 2000* network also includes special protection areas classified under the Birds Directive

---

on a coherent network of sites and initiatives, in particular by protecting sites of international importance for the conservation of migratory birds. The scope of the Directive is not only birds, their nests and eggs, but also their habitats, as the European legislator is well aware of the close and inescapable link between the effective protection of birds and that of their habitats. To guarantee the effective protection of the animals covered by the Directive article 5 provides for a protection regime with a general prohibition of killing and capture. Exceptions to this general prohibition are made for the cases expressly provided for by the hunting ban (Art. 7), which can, however, be provided for and implemented in proportion to the size of the population, and the so-called 'derogations' which are subject to a series of peremptory conditions set out in Article 9.

[13]Regulation (EU) no. 1143/2014 of the European Parliament and of the Council of 22 October 2014 laying down rules to prevent and manage the introduction and spread of invasive alien species (OJ L 317 4.11.2014, pp. 35–55) sets out the rules to prevent and manage the introduction and spread of invasive alien species in the EU. Invasive alien species (IAS) are defined as: plants or animals that have been transported outside their natural ecological range by humans (intentionally or unintentionally). These species, according to the regulation, cause considerable ecological and economic damage due to their invasiveness (Art. 3). The European legislation aims to minimise and mitigate the negative effects of invasive alien species on EU biodiversity and ecosystems (Art. 1).

(SPAs) that are designated directly by the Member States.[14] In 2014, the European Commission launched a review of the adequacy of the rules to protect biodiversity, later published on 16 December 2016.[15] In general terms, the review established that the effective achievement of the objectives of the European regulatory framework is closely linked to the substantial improvement of its implementation by the Member States.[16]

Therefore, according to the Commission, its effectiveness and efficiency must be improved. In more detail, according to the audit, the main factors behind the shortcomings in implementation include limited resources, poor implementation, insufficient integration of nature-related objectives into other policy areas (i.e. agriculture), inadequate knowledge and access to data, communication issues and low stakeholder involvement.

5 The European Green Deal and the Shift of the Political and Legal Paradigm for the Protection of Biodiversity

The European Green Deal, starting from the European's Commission communication on 11 December 2019,[17] has initiated a political and regulatory process directed to influence in a significative way the protection of the environment in the European Union. The European Commission (Chiti 2022) seems to have identified a new political objective: the ecosystems' sustainability or sustainability of biodiversity. Moreover, this has been formulated in the 'European Union's Strategy on Biodiversity for 2030' (Ferroni 2022)[18] according to which the sustainability of biodiversity requires two complementary interventions: the protection of Nature and its restoration. In particular, the new Biodiversity Strategy (approved in May 2020 by the EU Commission together with the Farm to Fork Plan) in view of the failures of previous interventions, aims to achieve a share of at least 30% of Europe's protected land and

[14] Article 4 of the Directive regulates the procedure by which Member States identify and notify 'Sites of Community Importance' to the Commission, which in turn draws up a list of them, where the Member States are called upon within six years to designate these sites as Special Areas of Conservation by establishing priorities according to the importance of the sites for the maintenance or restoration, at a favorable conservation status, of one or more natural habitat types in Annex I or one or more species in Annex II and for the coherence of Natura 2000 (Art. 4 par. 4).

[15] Commission staff working document fitness check the EU Nature Legislation (Birds and Habitats Directives) Directive 1147/EC of the European Parliament and of the Council of 30 November 2009 on the conservation of wild birds and Council Directive 143/EEC of 21 May 1992 on the conservation of natural habitats and of wild fauna and flora.

[16] Commission Staff Working Document SWD (2016) 472 final, 16 December 2016, Monitoring the Adequacy of EU Nature Legislation (Birds and Habitats Directives) http://ec.europa.eu/environment/naturellegislation/fitness_check/index_en.htm.

[17] Communication of the European Commission UE COM (2019) 640, final, 11 December 2019.

[18] In the same directions there are the New European Strategy for the Forests for 2030 and the European Strategy for the soil for 2030.

marine areas, by leveraging existing Natura 2000 sites (which under the Habitats Directive and the Birds Directive are the main instrument of biodiversity protection in Europe: special areas of conservation and special protection areas) while ensuring stricter protection of areas particularly rich in biodiversity and with a high climatic value (e.g. forests). Efforts also appear to be aimed at improving the level and effectiveness of protection in other policy areas related to protected areas (e.g. agricultural areas) of which knowledge and adequate access to data must be implemented; as well as adopting a series of concrete actions to rehabilitate, recover and restore degraded ecosystems in the European Union by 2030. The protection and structural and functional restoration of ecosystems requires, according to the Strategy, a change in the European legislative and socio-economic environment through the introduction of a new European framework for biodiversity governance, including a clear definition of obligations and timelines, and a system for monitoring commitments to ensure that Member States integrate them into national policies.

The political objective appears to be legalised with:

- The regulation of the European Parliament and the Council of the 18th June 2020 n. 852, about the institution of a panel that favours sustainable investments and modifies the UE 2019/2088 regulation (taxonomy regulation). The latter has established that to determine the eco sustainability of an economic activity to which direct the funds, there are six environmental objectives[19] among which the protection and restoration of biodiversity and the ecosystems;
- The European law on climate (Regulation No. 1119/2021), directly applicable and binding for all Member States in which it is stated that the restoration of ecosystems must contribute to 'maintaining, managing and enhancing natural wells and to promote biodiversity, counteracting, at the same time, climate change'. In other words, both the European Strategy on Biodiversity for 2030 and the European norm on climate (European Parliamentary Regulation and Council 119/2021) identify nature as a vital ally in the fight against climate change since the protection and restoration of biodiversity on terrestrial and marine areas will be determinant for the reduction of emissions and the adaption to these climate changes. Such regulation determines the passage in Europe from a soft law approach to a hard law one, with direct obligations intended for every Member State.

The legalisation of the sustainability of biodiversity or of the ecosystems in the regulations aforementioned appears to be the expression of a shift in the paradigm in Europe, which started from the Green Deal (Chiti 2022). The protection and restoration of biodiversity no longer represent an objective internal to the market but an external one. Therefore, this new objective does not shape the market, but it

[19]The six objectives established in Article 9 of the European Parliament regulation and of the Council of the 18 June 2020, no. 852 are: the mitigation of climate change, the adaptation to climate change, a sustainable use of water and the protection of these and of the marine resources, the transition towards a circular economy, prevention and reduction of pollution and protection and restoration of biodiversity of the ecosystems.

operates as an external limit because it redefines sustainability as the duty to protect and restore the integrity of ecological systems, which come before the economic and social needs. There would be a hierarchy having at the apex sustainability or the health of biodiversity. The ecologic primacy would be a valid alternative to the building of environmental protection in the European legal order, concentrated on sustainable development. The aforesaid reconstruction could also lead to a rethinking of the sustainable development principle (Chiariello 2022).

The integration of the centrality of sustainability and biodiversity implies a process of change and evolution in the European Union's juridical system, which moves towards regulatory instances that are not traceable to the full ratio of the economic European Constitution concerned mainly with sustainable development (the pillars upon which the European Economic Constitution is built today: economic integration, competition law, economic and social regulation sealed by the sustainable development principle).

In the European Constitution, only one refers to the environment minus all the explicit references to the categories of ecology as a science (whilst many Green Deal acts refer to concepts taken from ecology, highlighting the presence of an 'existential menace' to which one must put forth mindful protection and not just a 'risk for the development') while the word 'nature' is not found (Monteduro 2022).

6 The Nature Restoration Law

On 22 June 2022, the European Commission presented a new proposal for a regulation on nature restoration with legally binding objectives for member states. The objective was to restore at least 20% of terrestrial and aquatic surfaces by 2030, with an extension (by 2050) to all ecosystems in need of restoration. The aforementioned proposal concerned not only protected areas but ecosystems as a whole, including agricultural land and urban areas. The proposed regulation has set the political objective of sustainability and biodiversity of ecosystems for all European states, as expressed in the European Green Deal and in particular in the European Biodiversity Strategy for 2030. The law for the restoration of nature has been approved by the European Parliament on 27 February 2024. The adoption of a European regulation directly applicable to the Member States will produce a change in the paradigm of protection and restoration of biodiversity which, at least in Europe, will be implemented by binding hard law acts. To achieve the objectives set by the EU, by 2030 member states will have to restore the good health status of at least 30% of the habitats covered by the new law: forests, prairies and wetlands, rivers, lakes and coral reefs. This percentage will then rise to 60% by 2040 and 90% by 2050.

The regulation, strictly linked to the fight against climate change, seems to aim at the restoration and protection of the ecosystems of greater support to absorb the carbon. These are the so-called nature based solutions such as forests, peat bogs, damp areas, and marine prairies. The regulation contains seven targets for the different habitats: (Article 4) restoration of terrestrial ecosystems, coastal and of fresh water; (Article 5) restoration of the marine ecosystems; (Article 6) restoration of the urban ecosystems; (Article 7) restoration of the natural connectivity of rivers and of the natural functions of the relative flood plains; (Article 8) restoration of the pollinators' population; (Article 10) restoration of forest ecosystems; (Article 10 bis) planting of three billion trees by 2030, ensuring species diversity and prioritising native tree species. Member States are expected to prepare binding national plans restoration plans by carrying out prior monitoring and pre-research to identify the restoration measures needed to meet the objectives and obligations related to the seven targets.

The plans must also indicate the expected time for the actuation of the restoration measures and the estimate of the necessary funding, and where foreseen, the indication of subsidies that negatively affect the fulfilment of obligations of the regulation. In the plans, the Member States also indicate the synergies with climate change, the adaption of the latter, and disaster prevention, as well as a panoramic view of the interactions with the National Plans on energy and climate.

The historic approval by the European Parliament of the law for the restoration of nature on 27 February 2024, even with amendments and derogations from the initial proposal that postpone to after 2030 the control of some binding obligations, seem to determine in Europe a radical shift of the paradigm from an anthropocentric approach (expressed in the European Constitutions, even if, for example, in Italy the new Article 9[20] of the Constitution was recently approved, which refers to the protection of the biodiversity and ecosystems) towards an eco-centric[21] approach, already present for instance in Ecuador's Constitution and also in Bolivia (Amirante 2022). These have placed the commitment to the relationship between man and nature at the centre of their constitutional framework.

[20] The Article 9 of the Constitution was amended with Constitutional Law No. 1 of 11 February 2022 which added a new paragraph to Article 9 of the Constitution: 'Protect the environment, biodiversity and ecosystems, also in the interest of future generations. State law regulates the methods and forms of animal protection'.

[21] The Constitutions that would best express this approach would be Ecuador and Bolivia which place the relationship between man and the environment at the centre. The preamble to the Constitution of Ecuador celebrates the reference to Mother Earth (la Pacha Mama) and to nature, of which we are a part, and which is vital for our existence and declares the objective of establishing a new form of coexistence in diversity and in harmony with nature. In the Bolivian Constitution, the reference to Mother Earth (Pacha Mama) is already present in the preamble and the conservation of the environment represents an essential purpose and function of the state for the well-being of current and future generations. Other Latin American Constitutions oriented in this sense are those of Guyana (amended in 2001), of the Dominican Republic (2010), of Nicaragua (2014), of Cuba (2019).

7 The Challenge of the Restoration and Protection of Biodiversity in Cities

The application of biodiversity does not only include the natural protected areas and forests, but to reach the objectives set by the European strategy for Biodiversity for 2030,[22] it is crucial to insist on strengthening the greenery in urban areas and the reduction and restoration of degraded urban green areas. Cities are therefore also protagonists of the challenge aimed at reversing the rate of loss of biodiversity together with the challenge of climate change, through the reinforcement of the greenery in urban areas. The European Commission has as an objective to increasing public green spaces in the cities, as a tool for mitigating climate change. The importance of urban green infrastructures has been underlined by the European Biodiversity Strategy for 2030 which considers them nature's benefits to people. Promoting whole eco-systems, green infrastructure and nature-based solutions should be systematically integrated into urban planning, as well as into the design of buildings and their relevance.

To bring back nature in the cities and reward the community's actions, the Commission is calling on European cities of at least 20,000 inhabitants to elaborate urban greenery plan, including measures to create woodlands, parks and gardens accessible and rich in biodiversity, vegetable gardens, green roofs and walls, tree-lined streets, lawns and hedgerows and which also help improve links between green urban spaces, eliminate the use of pesticides. To make the work easier to the cities, the European Commission created an EU Urban Greening platform in 2021, as part of a new 'Green City Accord'[23] with the cities and mayors and in close coordination with the European Agreement of Mayors. Also, the nature restoration law prevails that the urban ecosystems represent about 22% of the terrestrial surface of the Union and it is here that the majority of the EU citizens live. The Nature Restoration Law calls for a strengthening of urban green spaces that provide essential ecosystem services, including the reduction of the risk of natural disasters (considering 43).

As a result, more actions are called for to ensure that urban green spaces are no longer at risk of degradation and are indeed being restored and expanded (with particular attention to trees) by better integrating green infrastructure and nature-based solutions into urban planning and incorporating green infrastructure, such as green roofs and walls, in building design (considering 44). In particular, Article 6 of

---

[22] See: European Strategy for biodiversity for 2030 'Greening urban and peri-urban areas: Parks and gardens, green roofs and allotments are all urban green spaces that offer not only multiple benefits to city dwellers, but also opportunities for businesses and a haven for flora and fauna. They reduce air, water and noise pollution, protect against floods, droughts and heat waves and preserve the link between man and nature'.

[23] The Green city accord, officially launched on 22 October 2020, at the end of the XVIII edition of the European Week of Regions and Cities, is an initiative of the EU Commission which mayors of European cities can join, to make their cities better places where to live. In fact, it is a movement of European mayors who believe in a paradigm shift and who have decided to align themselves with the parameters set by EU environmental laws.

the nature restoration law (Restoration of urban ecosystems) establishes that by 2030 Member States shall ensure, by 2030, that there will not be any net loss of urban green spaces or urban tree coverage, with regards to 2021 levels, in all cities, small towns and suburbs. This progress will be measured every six years after 2030.

8 Conclusions

In the last years, a shift in paradigm, related to the protection and restoration of biodiversity, seems to have taken place both at an international and European level, through:

- the adoption in December 2022 of the 'Kunming-Montreal Global Biodiversity Framework' that has set itself as the objective of protecting at least 30% of the terrestrial areas, and the restoration of the degraded ecosystems;
- the approval by the European Parliament in February 2024 of the 'Nature Restorations Law' that provides for more binding obligations for all Member States and a support for the fight against the loss of biodiversity, not only through the protected areas but also through the green urban spaces of the cities and to other types of areas.

Therefore, it seems that the emergency linked to a strong acceleration of the loss rate of biodiversity (that affects the mitigation of climate change) has, first of all, convinced Europe to change the paradigm of protection, moving from a soft law approach to general hard law rules, as it appears from the Nature Restoration Law (and already earlier with the European Climate Law of 2021). Furthermore, to achieve the protection and restoration of a sufficient quantity of areas, cities have been involved requesting a strengthening of green urban areas. The hope is that this binding approach, with the necessary economic compensations, will be implemented at a global level in the awareness of the reticularity and interconnection between all living beings present on planet Earth.

References

Amirante D (2022) Costituzionalismo ambientale. Atlante giuridico per l'Antropocene, Il Mulino

Chiariello C (2022) La funzione amministrativa della biodiversità nella prospettiva dello sviluppo sostenibile. Editoriale Scientifica

Chiti E (2022) In motu. L'Unione Europea e la trasformazione della costruzione giuridica della sostenibilità. La riforma costituzionale in materia di tutela dell'ambiente, Atti del Convegno 28 gennaio 2022, AIDAMBIENTE, pp. 184–209

Ferroni MV (2015) La protezione degli animali nell'ambiente. In: Dell'Anno P, Picozza E, Tutele parallele norme procedurali, Trattato di diritto dell'ambiente, CEDAM, pp. 447–496

Ferroni MV (2022) La perdita della biodiversità, gli strumenti di tutela ed il codice dell'ambiente. Rivista quadrimestrale diritto dell'ambiente 1:133–134

Ferroni MV (2023) The Re-use of assets confiscated from organized crime: how to make the informal formal. In: Ferroni MV, Galdini R, Ruocco G (eds) Urban informality. A multidisciplinary perspective. Springer, pp. 67–77

Marchisio S (2008) Il diritto internazionale dell'Ambiente. In: Cordini G, Fois P, Marchisio S (eds) Diritto ambientale. Profili internazionali, europei e comparati, Torino, Giappichelli, p. 10

Monteduro M (2022) Riflessioni sulla "primazia ecologica" nel moto del diritto europeo (anche alla luce della riforma costituzionale italiana in materia ambientale). In: La riforma costituzionale in materia di tutela dell'ambiente, Atti del Convegno 28 gennaio 2022, AIDAMBIENTE, pp. 245–246

Rockström J, Steffen W, Noone K, Persson Å, Chapin FS, Lambin E, Lenton TM, Scheffer M, Folke C, Schellnhuber H, Nykvist B, De Wit CA, Hughes T, van der Leeuw S, Rodhe H, Sörlin S, Snyder PK, Costanza R, Svedin U, Falkenmark M, Karlberg L, Corell RW, Fabry VJ, Hansen J, Walker B, Liverman D, Richardson K, Crutzen P, Foley J (2009) Planetary boundaries: exploring the safe operating space for humanity. Ecol Soc 14(2):39

Steffen W et al (2015) Planetary boundaries: guiding human development on a changing planet. Science 347(6223):736 ss. https://www.science.org/doi/10.1126/science.1259855

Wang-Erlandsson L et al (2022) A planetary boundary for green water. Nat Rev Earth Environ 3: 380–392. https://doi.org/10.1038/s43017-022-00287-8

Ecosystems: Biodiversity, Climate, Agriculture, Markets: A New Holistic Approach from the European Union

Maura Mattalia

Abstract Biodiversity is a key feature of an ecosystem, i.e. a complex network of interrelated organisms whose diversity becomes an element of resilience and good functioning of the system itself. The preservation of ecosystems and their biodiversity has become a key and transversal element of many European Union policies, which likewise figuratively take on the structure of an ecosystem. So, agricultural policy, agri-food market regulation, climate protection regulation and competition policy are intertwined. The specialty of sector's rules does not exclude a holistic view of the production chain, the preservation of the countryside and the interactions between the different players involved, starting with the producer and ending with the consumer. This approach is reflected in the collective interests and the planet's own health and takes on specific and recurring legal regulatory patterns of economic activities affecting biodiversity, climate, environment, nature and health. This contribution offers an interpretation of such a European "ecosystem" of legal sources, focusing on those legal provisions in which the protection of biodiversity takes on greater significance and highlighting its transversal nature in the most recent implementations of European agri-food policies.

1 Introduction

"Eating is an agricultural act":[1] this slogan summarizes the connection between food and agriculture, but it is self-evident how this link is also inseparable from the environment. In fact, within the complex framework of European Union agri-food law, the protection of the ecosystem represents a central concept.[2] The connection between this fundamental issue of the policy of the European Union is translated into

[1] Wendell (2015).

[2] Passalacqua (2022).

M. Mattalia (✉)
Università degli Studi di Torino, Turin, Italy
e-mail: maura.mattalia@unito.it

G. Antonelli et al. (eds.), *Biodiversity Laws, Policies and Science in Europe, the United States and China*, https://doi.org/10.1007/978-3-031-56218-1_3

legal provisions of difficult interpretation, when considering the interests at stake, the fast-occurring changes that involve the environment—especially climate—and society, and the difficult balance of different and contrasting issues emerging from the heterogenous composition of the Union.

The contribution intends to focus on this connection between food, agriculture, and environment, analyzing their correlation and the legal provisions that stress their relevance as a system, though providing for a critical analysis of flaws and inconsistencies that still are at the core of the Union institutions' attention.

In particular, the contribution will analyze the system of legal sources in European Union environmental law (para 2), with reference to their evolution in time, which is strictly linked to the evolution of the Union itself from an organization born to challenge the economic issues of the II world war to the foundation of a European Union that looks out for individual freedoms, social rights, and sustainable development. Particular attention will be drawn to the Common Agricultural Policy (para 3), in which firstly the attention for environmental protection has developed, becoming sustainability nowadays a structural element of such policy.

A quick look must also be necessary on the legal models set to achieve goals related to the protection of the environment, biodiversity and sustainability, consenting their coexistence with other provisions supporting the economy related to food and agriculture and in general with the fulfillment of public interest as a not easy with competition (para 4). Thus, before concluding the analysis (para 6), a focus will be proposed on the Green Deal, as a policy that protects biodiversity and the environment intending to assimilate and match the mentioned opposite interests regarding the European policies' system (para 5).

2 Ecosystem and System of Legal Sources in European Union Environmental Law

Even though food, agriculture and environment are nowadays considered intertwined, the Treaty establishing the European Economic Community (EEC) of 1957 did not originally include provisions for environmental protection in its original formulation.[3] To address this gap in the absence of a specific legal basis, the Community resorted to Articles 114 of the Treaty on the Functioning of the European Union (TFEU, formerly Article 94 of the EC Treaty, previously Article 100 of the EEC Treaty) and 352 of the TFEU (formerly Article 308 of the EC Treaty, formerly Article 235 of the EEC Treaty), respectively related to the approximation of national legislations and the so-called "flexibility clause." A particular focus on ecological matters first emerged at political level during the Paris Summit of 1972,

[3] This paragraph presents an overview on the evolution of the European Policies, on which: Bruno (2017); Canfora (2021), pp. 425–430; Cavallo Perin (2022), pp. 24–46; Manservisi (2018); Passalacqua (2022).

followed by the First Environmental Action Program of 1973. During this phase, the Court of Justice played a significant role by identifying environmental protection as an "imperative requirement," capable of justifying the adoption of national derogations to fundamental freedoms, while reserving the task of reviewing the conformity of Member States' choices with the interests of the European Union.

Environmental protection only became one of the objectives of the European Economic Community with the Single European Act of 1986, which came into effect in 1987. The Single European Act, partially endorsing the practice that had developed up to that point, introduced a new Title VII, dedicated to the Environment, in Part II of the EEC Treaty, consisting of three articles: 130R, 130S, and 130 T. It also inserted a new provision concerning the approximation of provisions (Article 100A of the EEC Treaty, later Article 95 of the EC Treaty, now Article 114 of the TFEU), which recognized the environment as a goal to be considered in the establishment of the internal market.

With the Treaty of Maastricht of February 7, 1992 (entered into force on November 1st, 1993), the environment became the object of a specific community policy, broadly identified in Article 3, letter K, of the Treaty on European Union (TEU). The relative discipline has changed compared to the Single European Act, also to consider new developments and orientations in international law. Thus, to complete the principles of Article 130R, both the principle of a high level of environmental protection and the "precautionary principle" were included, the latter being considered as an obligation to refrain from activities for which there is a lack of scientific certainty regarding the absence of serious risks to the environment.

The Amsterdam Treaty of October 2nd, 1997 (entered into force on May 1st, 1999), primarily brought procedural changes to environmental regulation, which were renumbered as Articles 174–176 of the EC Treaty (formerly Articles 130R of the EEC Treaty, now Articles 191–193 of the Treaty on the Functioning of the European Union, TFEU). The cooperation procedure was replaced by the co-decision procedure (now the ordinary legislative procedure). However, unanimity voting was retained for the so-called sensitive sectors.

Article 174 of the EC Treaty (now Article 191 of the TFEU) broadly outlined the goals of safeguarding, protecting, and improving environmental quality, safeguarding human health, cautious and rational use of natural resources, and promoting international measures to address environmental issues at regional or global level.[4] The Community aimed to achieve a high level of protection, committing itself under Article 174(3) of the EC Treaty (now Article 191(3) of the TFEU) to consider, among other instances, the socioeconomic development of the European territory as a whole and the balanced development of individual regions.

Among the significant novelties introduced by the Treaty of Amsterdam with implications for environmental matters, there was a modification of the discipline, aimed at harmonizing national legislations for the purpose of achieving the internal market (formerly Article 95, now Article 114 of the TFEU). The provision

[4]Porchia (2014), pp. 153–220.

repeatedly emphasized the environment as a value to be protected at the highest level within the framework of harmonization regulations (Article 95(3), now Article 114(3) of the TFEU) and as a ground for derogation that could justify the maintenance or introduction of national provisions that deviated from community rules, the latter subject, however, to thorough scrutiny by the Commission.

The Treaty of Amsterdam introduced a reference to the principle of sustainable development in the preamble, among the goals of the Union (Article 2 of the Treaty on European Union, now Article 3 of the Treaty on European Union) and in the list of tasks assigned to the Community (Article 2 of the EC Treaty). The Treaty also provided for the need to integrate requirements related to environmental protection into the definition and implementation of community policies and actions (Article 6 of the EC Treaty, now Article 11 of the TFEU). The inclusion of the integration principle among the general provisions, not just in the environmental title, qualified the principle as a guiding criterion for community action as a whole.[5]

To facilitate the practical application of Article 6 of the EC Treaty, the European Council in 1998 launched the so-called Cardiff Process on the integration of environmental instances into various Union policies. An environmental impact assessment declaration was also attached to the final act of the Intergovernmental Conference, establishing the Commission's commitment to accompany legislative proposals that significantly affect the environment with "impact studies." Finally, the Treaty of Amsterdam provided for the establishment of a Cohesion Fund to provide financial contributions for environmental projects (Article 161(2) of the EC Treaty, now Article 177(2) of the TFEU).

The Treaty of Lisbon strengthens the legislation dedicated to environmental protection. Leaving aside the rebounds and effects of the general rules on the institutional architecture of the Union, it is important to note that, according to Article 3, no. 3, of the Treaty on European Union (TEU), the Union establishes an internal market with a complex character inspired by a logic that is not exclusively economic. In this context, the Union strives for the sustainable development of Europe, based, among other things, on a high level of protection and improvement of the quality of the environment.[6]

Article 11 of the Treaty on the Functioning of the European Union (TFEU) (formerly Article 6 of the EC Treaty) reaffirms that the needs related to environmental protection must be integrated into the implementation of European Union policies and actions, also with the aim of promoting sustainable development. Following the reform adopted in Lisbon and the subsequent elimination of the pillars, this provision is destined to create an obligation that applies to all activities of the Union institutions and all policies and forms of cooperation provided for in the Treaties, including the areas of Foreign Policy and Judicial Cooperation in Criminal Matters.[7]

---

[5]Porchia (2014), pp. 153–220.

[6]Passalacqua (2022).

[7]Nascimbene (2012).

Turning to specific provisions, Article 191, no. 1 of the TFEU broadly defines the goals of the Union environmental policy. Firstly, it contributes to the safeguarding and protection of the environment and, in an active sense, aims to allow the improvement of environmental quality. These goals are flexible and capable of adapting to new developments and different protection needs. They are also broad, as they cover the protection of nature, landscapes, and animals. Measures aimed at improving the environment directly or indirectly can be adopted based on Article 191, no. 1, first dash, which includes measures related to access to environmental information as an example of indirect contributions.

The term "environment" is understood in a broad sense, and it is not explicitly defined in the Treaty. It includes human health and the cautious and rational use of natural resources.[8] The jurisprudence of the Court of Justice, from its early judgments, has highlighted the connection between the environment and human health, stating that, in case of uncertainties about human health risks, institutions can adopt protective measures without waiting for the full demonstration of their severity.[9] The notion of health protection should be understood in broader sense than "public health." Article 191 of the TFEU, second dash, allows for action even when it involves the interests of certain individuals or specific groups, always with due regard to the principle of subsidiarity. Moreover, this reference should be considered limited to human health, as animal welfare and the protection of flora are covered by the first dash of Article 191 of the TFEU.

The Union also intends to promote international measures aimed at solving environmental problems at regional or global level, confirming an already established practice. A significant part of environmental policy is aimed at protecting the environment outside the Union's territory, a focus also confirmed in the new Action Plan that aims to "enhance the effectiveness of Union action in addressing environmental challenges at regional and global levels."[10] An expansive interpretation of Article 191 allows the Union to pursue extraterritorial protection goals, provided it acts in accordance with the principles of international law.

Returning to the goals, the new Article 191, as reformed by the Treaty of Lisbon, also explicitly refers to the need for the European Union to challenge climate change, a purpose that thus takes on an autonomous dimension.[11] Environmental protection continues to represent a value to be safeguarded within the framework of legislation harmonization (Article 114 of the Treaty on the Functioning of the European Union, formerly Article 95 of the EC Treaty). In particular, when proposing measures for the harmonization of provisions related to the functioning of the internal market, the Commission relies on a high level of protection, considering, in particular, any new

[8] Dell'Anno (2022).

[9] Fisher et al. (2013).

[10] Communication from the Commission to the European Parliament, the Council, the European Economic and Social Committee and the Committee of the Regions, A new Circular Economy Action Plan for a cleaner and mor competitive Europe, COM/2020/98 final.

[11] Porchia (2014), pp. 153–220.

developments based on scientific findings (Article 114, no. 3, of the Treaty on the Functioning of the European Union). Environmental protection requirements also affect other closely related sectors, particularly the energy sector and civil protection.

With regard to the energy sector, under Article 194 of the Treaty on the Functioning of the European Union, the Union, while considering the need to preserve and improve the environment, aims, among other things, to promote energy saving, energy efficiency, and the development of renewable energies in a spirit of solidarity among Member States.

In the field of civil protection, "the Union encourages cooperation between Member States in order to enhance the effectiveness of systems for preventing and protecting against natural or man-made disasters" (Article 196 of the Treaty on the Functioning of the European Union).

The scale of the mentioned goals and the complexity of the structure and actions arranged by the European Union suggest the opportunity to refer to a plurality of environmental policies rather than a single environmental policy.[12]

The worsening climate emergency has inevitably led to a change in fundamental needs that require protection. This change is reflected in the importance of environmental interests, which, emerging from their previous sectoral context, are taking on an increasingly central role among the interests that public institutions must safeguard. The protection of environmental interests is no longer aimed at ensuring that economic activities do not excessively compromise environmental needs; it goes beyond, demanding an absolute priority, especially in the face of the imminent threat posed by climate change. This protection is no longer just a marginal "consideration" in development policies but becomes an imperative necessity.

3 Sustainability in the Common Agricultural Policy (CAP)

Unlike environmental matters, the European Union has established the Common Agricultural Policy (CAP) since its foundation, recognizing the crucial importance of the agricultural sector in ensuring fair and sustainable development among its member countries.[13]

The significance of agriculture as a source of livelihood led European communities to allocate a substantial portion of their resources to the agricultural sector, making it the foremost among the community policies.[14] To this day, it remains one of the most considerable components of the Union's budget. The concept of a common policy in the agricultural sector has been in place since the Treaty of

[12] Dell'Anno (2022).

[13] On the Common Agricultural Policy, in particular: Borghi (2021), pp. 93–99; Bruno (2017); Canfora (2021), pp. 425–430; Cavallo Perin (2022), pp. 24–46; Ciatti Càimi (2022); Costato (2021), pp. 3–11.

[14] Cavallo Perin (2022), pp. 24–46.

Rome (Articles 2, 3 letter d), TFEU), with historically significant integration processes that posed challenges similar to those encountered during the unification of Italy.

The original objective of the CAP (1962)—to provide the citizens of the European Union with affordable food and ensure a fair standard of living for farmers—faced a crisis 20 years later (1984). This crisis arose because agricultural enterprises' production increased to a level that exceeded the demand for food, necessitating corrective measures to align production levels with market demand. In the 1990s (1992), the CAP further evolved, shifting from market support to support for producers. Price support was reduced and replaced with direct subsidies to farmers, encouraging them to adopt more environmentally friendly practices.

A new reform of the CAP (2003) severed the link between subsidies and production, allowing subsidies even in the case of land "resting." As a result, farmers could now receive a unified income support, provided they protected agricultural lands and met specific criteria related to the environment, animal welfare, and food safety.[15]

Community policies complement the European integration process, which is complementary and opposite to the elimination of obstacles to integration through the removal of barriers to the movement of goods, people, services, and capital, and through the creation of a competitive market. The underlying rationale of the Common Agricultural Policy (CAP) was to centralize aid from the Member States after introducing agricultural products to the free movement of goods. The initial interventions of agricultural policy were indeed based on the free movement of agricultural products, achieved by removing trade barriers and establishing common market organizations (CMOs) to regulate agricultural products and their prices, as it was impossible to leave the agricultural sector to the "laissez-faire" rules. The CAP was further reformed to strengthen the competitiveness of the agricultural sector, promote innovation, and support sustainable agriculture for rural growth and employment (CAP 2014–2020), with direct payments becoming the main intervention tool.[16]

In the agricultural sector—following the Lisbon Treaty—the discipline and administrative decisions of economic policy fall under concurrent European competence, which finds its substantive boundaries defined by the Treaty (Articles 38–44, TFEU), with authorization for Union intervention and then Member States to the extent that the Union has remained silent in whole or in part.

In the years 2021–2022, prolonged negotiations and the pandemic led to the adoption of a transitional regulation to ensure the continuation of support to farmers. Policies related to agriculture and the trade of agricultural products have also been an important lever for the protection of additional interests in recent years. They are now among the objectives of the CAP for 2023–27 with the approval of the Next Generation EU: action to challenge climate change, environmental protection,

[15] Mattalia (2023), pp. 339–371.

[16] Mattalia (2019), p. 103; Mattalia (2023), p. 339.

preservation of landscapes and biodiversity, promotion of knowledge and innovation, protection of food quality and health. To pursue these goals, two instruments are available: either offering an advantage to those who want to work towards achieving a result, or prohibiting activities that would lead to a certain result without explicit permission. The first group of instruments consists, as mentioned, of incentive measures.

The New Delivery Model, which the European Commission has devised, is based on the creation of a single National Development Plan. The Plan is structured around nine strategic objectives, grouped into three overarching goals (economic, environmental, and social), and a cross-cutting objective on knowledge and innovation. This new model grants greater autonomy to Member States to respond more effectively to specific national needs and implement their strategies more freely, as well as allowing for a shift from a compliance-based approach to a results-oriented approach.[17]

The Reform Regulations of the CAP, which came into effect on January 1st, 2023, have emphasized the need to: "a) promote a smart, competitive, resilient, and diversified agricultural sector that ensures long-term food security; b) support and enhance environmental protection, including biodiversity, and action on climate and contribute to the achievement of the Union's environmental and climate objectives, including commitments made under the Paris Agreement; c) strengthen the socio-economic fabric of rural areas" (Article 5 of Regulation (EU) 2021/2115).

These regulations have introduced innovative institutional arrangements, including the provision for a National Strategic Plan, and require the adoption of shared choices to avoid potential conflicts, such as those that have characterized the relationship between the Italian State and Regions regarding the environment and natural resources over the past 20 years.[18]

However, over the past decade, the progressive integration of environmental concerns into agri-food regulations seems to have led to a significant imbalance in favor of the environment,[19] as is evident in the direction of the CAP for 2023–2027. In this regard, it seems to be enough the mere reference, by way of example, to eco-schemes, which were introduced to replace greening and outlined a system mandatory for Member States and only apparently voluntary for agricultural producers. These appear to aim, along with other measures, at selecting agri-food producers by providing payments not to farmers as such but as compliant with environmental and market obligations.

Nevertheless, while sustainability represents the key to understand the importance of the environment in agriculture, as evidenced by well-defined incentive policies within the Common Agricultural Policy (CAP), by prohibitions that have restricted the use of certain products in agricultural activities, and by the cessation of imports of products linked to deforestation, as well as by choices made by

---

[17] Cavallo Perin (2022), pp. 24–46.

[18] Ibidem.

[19] Costato (2021), pp. 3–11.

agricultural and industrial entrepreneurs interested in creating entirely sustainable production chains and informing consumers through specific environmental declarations (green claims) accompanying products in the market, it is equally true that this balance may require reconsideration in light of recent historical events.[20]

Recent food crises, stemming from the spread of COVID-19 and subsequently the Russo-Ukrainian conflict, have brought the issue of food security to the forefront. This term refers to the assurance of a strategic supply of food resources, a problem that was thought to be resolved through market globalization, leading European institutions to primarily focus on food safety, with attention to production quotas, planting rights, and transformation constraints, while assigning agriculture the role of guardian of environmental resources and a key player in the fight against climate change.

The risk of insufficient access to food and the awareness of not having achieved food self-sufficiency have led to a change of course. Derogations from the obligation to set aside land in so-called "ecological focus areas" have occurred. A European Regulation has been issued requiring an urgent action plan from the European Union to ensure food security both within and outside the Union, bringing both food security and economic sustainability back into the spotlight, aspects that had largely been neglected in previous strategic documents.

In this context, it seems reasonable to assert that the current crisis has acted as a brake on globalizing trends and the predominance of environmental interests. However, it does not seem possible to completely revert, disregarding the knowledge gained in environmental protection in the agri-food chain. On the contrary, this knowledge should push towards forms of sustainability certification. A suggestion in this regard comes from the wine sector, in which were recently approved guidelines for a sustainability certification system in the production chain.[21]

We are going through a transitional period that could represent an opportunity to reconsider the issue of food security while balancing the interests at stake. At the same time, it might be an opportune moment to develop mandatory environmental regulations for agri-food chains, rather than relying solely on voluntary and loosely binding applications.

The new course of the Common Agricultural Policy reflects the transition from a food crisis to an environmental one. Moving from a phase where every effort in agriculture was directed towards achieving maximum economic productivity for the enterprise to one where the construction of sustainable development becomes essential, it emerges a conceptual and regulatory framework that is no longer solely aimed at supporting income in agriculture but is geared towards promoting socially responsible development capable of influencing market mechanisms to steer them towards a balance based on the maximization of a well-being function that includes ethical, social, and environmental values.

---

[20] Ciatti Càimi (2022).

[21] Costato (2021), pp. 3–11.

The reform of the CAP, the Common Fisheries Policy (CFP), and the use of existing tools such as the European Agricultural Fund for Rural Development (EAFRD) and the Research and Innovation (R&I) area play a fundamental role in supporting the transition to sustainable food systems while ensuring decent living conditions for farmers, fishermen, and their families. The Farm to Fork and Biodiversity strategies encompass a range of initiatives under the framework of the European Green Deal, aimed at creating a production model capable of ensuring the security and resilience of the EU's agri-food system. These objectives are intended to be achieved by implementing the following measures by 2030: a 50% reduction in the use of agrochemicals and antimicrobials in animal farming; the development of organic cultivation areas to cover 25% of the total agricultural land; a 50% reduction in nutrient losses and a 20% reduction in the use of chemical fertilizers; dedicating 10% of land areas to biodiversity development.

The link between climate change and agriculture is complex and interconnected. Climate change negatively impacts agriculture through reduced productivity and increased risks to food security. At the same time, agricultural activity itself contributes to climate change through greenhouse gas emissions, creating a cycle of negative interdependence.

To address this challenge and build sustainable agriculture for the future, interventions are needed both on the supply and demand sides of food products.

On the supply side, a key strategy is the reduction of greenhouse gas emissions through the optimization of soil management practices and the improvement of livestock techniques. Additionally, it is important to outline adaptation strategies that mitigate the impact of climate change. These strategies should include plans and actions aimed at minimizing the negative effects of climate change on agriculture.

In the context of resilient agriculture, it is crucial to assess the environmental impact in terms of carbon emissions, land use, and the relationship between resource consumption and nature's capacity to regenerate them. This involves measuring the impact generated by food production and consumption on the environment.[22]

Actions to reduce carbon emissions, promote carbon sequestration in vegetation, develop sustainable energy sources such as bioenergy, and manage soils sustainably are all important for making agriculture more resilient. Forest protection and the adoption of appropriate agronomic practices are also part of this approach.

However, aspects related to food processing, storage, transportation, and preparation should not be overlooked. These processes also influence the climate impact of agricultural production and must, therefore, be considered in the overall assessment of agricultural sustainability.

In summary, the goal of building agriculture for the future requires an integrated vision that considers both aspects of agricultural production and those related to the food chain to reduce environmental impact and mitigate climate change.

The interconnection between food consumption and strategies to address climate change is evident. Among the actions aimed at reducing emissions associated with

[22]Manservisi (2018).

food production, one of the key mitigation measures is reducing the demand for products with a high environmental impact. This translates into promoting the consumption of local products, reducing and challenging food waste.

It is important to note that economic strategies aimed at mitigating and adapting to climate change, influencing production patterns and organizational structures, represent only part of the solution regarding climate change and the creation of resilient agriculture.

The economic context is directly related to the protection of climate-related rights, such as the right to food, water, and food security. It is known that climate change can affect the availability of food in terms of quantity and quality, access to food, and the financial resources needed to obtain it, in response to price fluctuations caused by global warming, while also jeopardizing the stability of the food system itself.

The increasing variability of weather conditions, along with the rising frequency and severity of extreme atmospheric events, leads to fluctuations in agricultural production and jeopardizes food supply stability. These changes are accompanied by the spread of pests and the proliferation of disease vectors, which are influenced by ecosystem changes. Economic adaptation and resilience strategies must, therefore, address the issue of food security. In pursuit of significant goals, it must be considered that certain studies conducted so far highlight that the implementation of measures envisaged by the Farm to Fork and Biodiversity strategies will lead to a significant reduction in the productive capacity of European agriculture, resulting in an inevitable increase in EU imports from other countries and a significant rise in consumer prices for food products.

The relationships between actions to address climate change and food security, as recognized in the Paris Agreement and incorporated into EU Regulation no. 2021/2115, are closely connected to the guarantee of rights. These rights include the consumers' right to sufficient food supplies at affordable prices for all citizens, regardless of their situation, during the transition to sustainable food systems. Furthermore, the prerogatives of producers for adequate income are also involved, achieved through improvements in production technologies, trade and inventory management systems, and the implementation of appropriate policies to address the damages caused by climate and environmental risks.[23]

Furthermore, it is essential to consider the impacts of climate emergencies on rights within the scope of agricultural development, in line with the objectives of the Common Agricultural Policy (CAP). Article 39 of the Treaty on the Functioning of the European Union (TFEU) sets specific goals for the CAP, including production, social, and market-related objectives. However, climate change can threaten the achievement of these goals, endangering food supply security, market stability, the livelihoods of farming communities, agricultural productivity, as well as fair prices for consumers.

[23] Popovski and Allaoui (2019).

From a broader perspective, the European Economic and Social Committee has put forward the proposal to start a discussion on the creation of a European Charter of Climate Rights. This Charter should establish the rights of European Union citizens and nature in response to the challenges posed by climate crises.

In summary, climate change is undeniably a matter of rights that require legal protection.

4 In Particular: The Relationship Between the Common Agricultural Policy and Competition, Beyond Public Interest

The four freedoms provided for in the TFEU define the discipline of the internal market (Article 26, § 2, TFEU), in which the treaty also encompasses agriculture (Article 38, § 1, section 2, TFEU). This is not the case for the competition rules, which depend on choices made by the European legislator (Article 42, § 1; Article 43, § 2, TFEU).

This issue is of theoretical importance as it clarifies that there is no coincidence between the scope of application of the detailed provisions on competition (concentration, abuse of dominant position, prohibition of agreements and State aid) and the rules protecting the freedoms of movement of goods, capital, services, and persons, even though both are in the Treaty on the Functioning of the European Union.[24]

A market exists as soon as a plurality of individuals aspiring to exchange compete for the possibility to exchange. Whether they are spatially gathered in the local market, in the high-traffic market (fair), or in the market of traders (stock exchange) represents only the most consequential form of market formation, the only one that allows the full development of the specific market phenomenon: bargaining.[25]

The prevailing definition of the "internal market" today assumes meanings that were once associated with other designations ("common market" or "single market"), so much so that they can be considered notions that belong to essentially equivalent concepts.

The internal market is not the sum of the markets of individual Member States, as the scope of European regulation in this regard is the entire territory of the Union, regardless of the nationality of those operating within it.

Within the internal market, the free movement of goods (Articles 28 to 37 TFEU), services (Articles 56 to 62 TFEU), capital (Articles 63 to 66 TFEU), and persons (Articles 49 to 55 TFEU) defines "a space without internal borders" (Article 26, § 2 TFEU), a regulation of the internal market that is complemented by the regulation of the customs union (Articles 30–37 TFEU).

[24] Passalacqua (2022).

[25] Russo (2021), pp. 12–24.

The creation of a single market must be accompanied by the maintenance of a competitive environment among businesses; therefore, competition itself is not an inherent value but also a tool for the achievement of further social objectives. Hence, the reference to the "social market economy" is common.[26]

Agriculture and the trade of agricultural products have been included in the internal market (Article 38, TFEU) since its establishment, resulting in the application of the mentioned freedoms of movement of goods, services, persons, and capital.

This discipline has been tempered by the European Union's recent focus on values protected through the definition of sustainable development in Europe and a social market economy (Article 3, § 3, TFEU). The freedom of movement in agriculture is affirmed regardless of the establishment of a common market organization, as has been the case for certain commodity sectors not subject to the CMO discipline or during the initial accession period of new Member States that are not immediately subject to the CAP.

Sustainable development is "development that meets the needs of the present without compromising the ability of future generations to meet their own needs."[27] New theories in this regard emphasize the concept of an economy no longer based solely on labor and capital but on an ecologically oriented economy. In the context of sustainable or ecologically oriented agriculture, capital is defined as the collection of pre-existing natural assets (seas, rivers, lakes, forests, flora, fauna, and territory), their reasonable utilization (fishing, hunting, cultivation), and the enhancement of the landscape heritage.[28]

The term "social market economy" is used to emphasize that the Union pursues both economic and social goals, striving to balance the protection of the market and individuals. These are rights that derive from the Treaty provisions, whether related to the free movement of goods, persons, services, and capital or rights related to promoting employment, improving living and working conditions, and providing adequate social protection. These rights promote social dialogue, the development of human resources for a high and sustainable level of employment, and the fight against exclusion (Article 151, § 1, TFEU).[29]

---

[26] Costato (2021), pp. 3–11.

[27] Piccari (2017).

[28] Salzman and Thompson (2013).

[29] Passalacqua (2022).

5 Integrated Instruments for Biodiversity Protection: The Green Deal and Sustainability of the Supply Chain

For 70 years, Europe considered peace, as well as food security, as something taken for granted. The recent food crises, triggered by the spread of the COVID-19 pandemic and subsequently exacerbated by the Russian-Ukrainian conflict, have brought the importance of food security back into the political agenda. This issue, once primarily considered a European concern, is now recognized as a global problem. This change in perspective has occurred even though Europe has faced periods of oversupply in the past. The disruption of supply chains, caused by logistical problems and a shortage of raw materials, has highlighted the limits of globalization and the role of international markets in ensuring the basic needs of European populations and, consequently, their food sovereignty.

A cultural, social, and certainly political and legal change has materialized through the European Green Deal. This integrated strategy aims to achieve an economic, energy, and environmental transition by 2050 with the objective, among others, of completely eliminating greenhouse gas emissions within the European Union. It was adopted on December 11, 2019, as the first significant result of the Von Der Leyen Commission. Furthermore, the Green Deal is an integral part of the Commission's strategy to implement the United Nations' Agenda 2030 and its Sustainable Development Goals (SDGs). Within the Green Deal, the Commission intends to redefine the macroeconomic coordination process of the European Semester to incorporate the United Nations' sustainable development goals, with the aim of placing sustainability and citizens' well-being at the center of economic policy and making the Sustainable Development Goals the focal point of the European Union's policy and interventions.

Within this initiative, the European Commission assigns a primary role to agriculture, which is one of the key sectors to address in order to effect a genuine change from the models that the Union has pursued towards sustainability over the last 30 years. The European Green Deal represents an opportunity to reconcile our food system with the planet's needs and to respond positively to Europeans' demand for healthy, fair, and environmentally friendly food products. One of the objectives of this strategy is also to make the European Union's food system a global standard for sustainability. The transition to sustainable food systems requires a collective approach involving public authorities at all levels of government, private sector actors throughout the entire food value chain, non-governmental organizations, social partners, and citizens. A sustainable food system will be crucial in achieving the climate and environmental goals of the Green Deal and, at the same time, in increasing the income of primary producers and strengthening the competitiveness of the European Union.

In this perspective, the Green Deal draws attention to labor law related to the ecological transition. Between labor protection and environmental protection, ethical-legal conflicts often arise, such as the conflict between the right to employment, sustainability policies, and environmental conservation. The sustainability-oriented approach in this vision undoubtedly represents added value because it incorporates not only environmental and economic aspects but also social and labor-related ones. Therefore, considerations regarding social protection, working and housing conditions for workers, as well as health and safety protection, will play a fundamental role in building fair, robust, and sustainable food systems.

It is evident that this transition must be supported by a Common Agricultural Policy focused on the Green Deal, aimed at helping farmers improve their environmental and climate performance through a more results-oriented model, better data management and analysis, strengthened mandatory environmental regulations, new voluntary measures, and increased investment in green and digital technologies.[30] At the same time, it is essential to ensure an adequate income that allows farmers to support their families and deal with various crises. The European Commission's proposal focuses on creating economic opportunities for farmers and effectively improving their position in the food chain. The planned measures include a combination of voluntary and mandatory initiatives that bring benefits for the environment and climate, better integration of support for agricultural income and rural areas with the adoption of sustainable models and practices, as well as actions to promote knowledge, innovation, and technology (including digital) to support this ambition.

The need to improve the efficiency and effectiveness of direct payments, through better targeting and distribution of income support to farmers in need who contribute to achieving environmental objectives, rather than simply favoring entities and companies that own agricultural land, remains a crucial element for the future Common Agricultural Policy. In the European document, the choice of a development model based on a sustainable social market economy is clear and the environment is no longer seen as a cost but as an opportunity.

While it is undeniable that agriculture will play a decisive role, according to the text of the Green Deal, the long-term strategy for integrating the regulation of the agricultural sector into this transition process still appears to be not fully defined, especially concerning the blurred overlap between the innovative Farm to Fork strategy and the framework of the new Common Agricultural Policy in some cases.

The latter, through eco-schemes, improved conditionality, climate investments, income support distribution, and support for "genuine" farmers, will be essential in helping the European Union achieve the Green Deal's objectives in terms of economic, social, and environmental sustainability. This is because it will incentivize, empower, and support European farmers in addressing climate change, preserving the environment, and transitioning to more sustainable and resilient food systems.

The European Commission has presented the "Farm to Fork Strategy," along with the "Biodiversity Strategy for 2030." These strategies are an integral and fundamental part of the legislative proposal of the "Green New Deal," which aims to address the climate crisis and guide the transition to sustainable and climate-neutral models

---

[30] Cavallo Perin (2022), pp. 24–46.

by 2050. Farm to Fork was included by the European Commission in the Green Deal in May 2020 and embraces a comprehensive concept of agricultural sustainability that clearly indicates how the farm-to-fork strategy should be directed toward a fair, healthy, and environmentally respectful food system. The text explicitly underscores that "people are increasingly concerned about environmental, health, social, and ethical issues, and now more than ever are seeking value in food products." Among the new objectives aimed at "building a food chain that works for consumers, producers, the climate, and the environment," there is an emphasis on the need to preserve "the economic affordability of food while generating a fairer economic return throughout the supply chain." The goal is to make food more sustainable, improve its economic accessibility, and enhance the competitiveness of the EU supply sector through the promotion of fair trade and the creation of new business opportunities. In this context, the new objectives of European policy stand out to ensure not only the integrity of the single market but also health and safety at work. The convergence between the fundamental right to work and environmental protection is realized through an ecological transition that leads to an employment transition. This means that the "greening" strategy, aimed at environmental protection, not only does not have negative impacts on employment but actually contributes to its improvement.

In particular, by adopting this perspective, businesses can contribute to enhancing human well-being and social equity while concurrently reducing environmental risks and resource depletion. Enterprises can reap economic benefits from improved environmental performance, including energy savings, reduced resource and raw material costs, and minimized environmental risks. Thus, the transition to an economy based on renewable technologies can support employment by creating new career opportunities, replacing traditional roles with new skills derived from the emerging economy, and facilitating the adaptation of market-driven skill demands. This holds particularly true for emerging sectors related to the transition to a low-carbon economy and eco-industries. All these factors will prompt businesses to modify their production, organizational, and communication processes, necessitating additional professional training geared towards the green economy and environmental competencies.

Finally, it is important to emphasize that there is no predefined model for "green jobs," but rather a general framework that encompasses all activities aimed at developing an economy that values human capital and social well-being without jeopardizing natural capital. Agriculture plays a strategic role in this context, as it is involved in challenges such as distributed energy generation, biomass utilization, and the reduction of the use of biocides and pesticides, which are crucial for the environment and overall sustainability. Therefore, the agricultural sector can play an even more significant role in creating "green jobs" and implementing sustainable solutions for the benefit of the environment and employment.

Rising agricultural prices and the risk of inadequate supply for industry and distribution have prompted European institutions to reassess the situation. Temporary derogations from cultivation obligations in ecologically sensitive areas have been granted to address these challenges.

The reemergence of food security issues brings to the forefront of political and scientific debate the principles of food sovereignty, as defined in the Nyéléni Declaration, and food democracy.

The Farm to Fork Strategy represents a long-term, comprehensive, ambitious plan aligned with the Sustainable Development Goals of the 2030 Agenda. With reference to the three Ps: "People, Planet, and Prosperity," this strategy aims to promote fair, healthy, and environmentally respectful food systems through 27 ambitious actions. The transformation towards sustainable and inclusive food systems requires a reformulation of the entire production chain, from product origin to the final consumer.

Both community strategies share goals to be achieved by 2030, such as a 50% reduction in pesticide use and associated risks, a 20% decrease in fertilizer use, allocating one-quarter of agricultural land to organic farming, and replacing chemical fertilizers with organic ones derived from plant and agricultural residues. Additionally, the F2F strategy commits to reducing antimicrobial use in agriculture and aquaculture by 50%, reducing nutrient losses by 50% without compromising soil fertility, and cutting the use of the most dangerous pesticides by 50%. Consumer and retail sector food waste will also be reduced by 50%.

The Farm to Fork strategy includes initiatives to ensure fast broadband Internet access in all rural areas by 2025 to promote digital innovation and the use of artificial intelligence and precision agriculture. A crucial aspect concerns food sales and marketing practices by producers and retailers. Labeling and product certification are another key point. The Commission will assess options for indicating animal welfare on labels to convey value along the food chain in the context of improving animal welfare.

6 Conclusion

The proposed analysis has drawn the attention to the environment in the European agri-food system, underlining the existence of a broad sense of "environment," though not defined in the European Treaties, and including human health and a wise and rational use of natural resources. It has also stressed the connection between biodiversity, environment, and human health, taking into account the Union institutions' measures to precautionary protect such values.

The evolution of the European Union and its policies, connected with the severe alteration in the fundamental needs of society and environment, has resulted in a protection of the latter as an absolute priority not only related to the exercise of economic activities such as agriculture. The European Union is clearly set for sustainable development, where the environment is considered as an opportunity and not anymore as a cost.

The sustainability of the European agri-food system, in the comprehensive sense previously mentioned, entails the overall ability of this system to pursue environmental and climate neutrality while maintaining the capacity to provide food to the population residing in the European Union. This implies ensuring that food is both materially and economically accessible, so that its cost is proportionate to available income. Moreover, the capacity to provide food also entails the system's ability to withstand the impacts of destabilizing factors, some of which may be of a conjunctural nature (such as nearby armed conflicts within the Union, which we hope are temporary but could have long-term economic and geopolitical effects) and others tend to become structural (such as climate change).

Sustainability, therefore, represents both a long-term action to counter climate change and the ability of the food production system to adapt and survive this phenomenon. However, structural challenges appear to hinder the realization of this desired flexibility and "adaptability capacity."

References

Borghi P (2021) Le linee guida europee. In: Borghi P, Canfora I, Di Lauro A, Russo L (eds) Trattato di diritto alimentare italiano e dell'Unione Europea. Giuffrè Lefebvre, pp. 93–99

Bruno F (2017) Il Diritto Alimentare nel Contesto Globale: Usa e Ue a Confronto. Cedam

Canfora I (2021) La Politica della qualità dei prodotti agroalimentari dell'Ue. In: Borghi P, Canfora I, Di Lauro A, Russo L (eds) Trattato di diritto alimentare italiano e dell'Unione Europea. Giuffrè Lefebvre, pp. 425–430

Cavallo Perin R (2022) voce Agricoltura. Enciclopedia del Diritto: 24–46

Ciatti Càimi A (2022) Corso di diritto agrario. Zanichelli Editore

Communication from the Commission to the European Parliament, the Council, the European Economic and Social Committee and the Committee of the Regions, A new Circular Economy Action Plan for a cleaner and mor competitive Europe, COM/2020/98 final

Costato L (2021) Agricoltura e prodotti agroalimentari nel TFUE. In: Borghi P, Canfora I, Di Lauro A, Russo L (eds) Trattato di diritto alimentare italiano e dell'Unione Europea. Giuffrè Lefebvre, pp. 3–11

Dell'Anno P (2022) Diritto dell'ambiente. Cedam

Fisher E, Lange B, Scotford E (2013) Environmental law: text, cases, and materials. Oxford University Press

Manservisi S (2018) Nuovi profili del diritto ambientale dell'Unione Europea. Tra evoluzione scientifica e sviluppo sostenibile. Aracne

Mattalia M (2019) I principi d'amministrazione pubblica in agricoltura tra libertà di circolazione, innovazione sociale e regolazione. Edizioni Scientifiche Italiane

Mattalia M (2023) L'incentivazione pubblica. Dir. Amm. 2:339–371

Nascimbene B (2012) Studi su ambiente e diritto. Il diritto dell'Unione europea. Cacucci

Passalacqua M (2022) Diritti e mercati nella transizione ecologica e digitale. Cedam

Piccari P (2017) Società sostenibili e processi trasformativi. Franco Angeli

Popovski V, Allaoui M (2019) The implementation of the Paris agreement on climate change. Routledge

Porchia O (2014) Le politiche dell'Unione europea in materia ambientale. In: Ferrara R, Sandulli MA (eds) Trattato di diritto dell'ambiente, Le politiche ambientali, lo sviluppo sostenibile e il danno. Giuffrè Lefebvre, pp. 153–220

Russo L (2021) Mercato agroalimentare e concorrenza. In: Borghi P, Canfora I, Di Lauro A, Russo L (eds) Trattato di diritto alimentare italiano e dell'Unione Europea. Giuffrè Lefebvre, pp. 12–24

Salzman J, Thompson BH Jr (2013) Environmental law and policy. Foundation Press

Wendell B (2015) Mangiare è un atto agricolo, Lindau

Natural Capital and Ecosystem Services—Legal Aspects

C. Colognese and N. Granato

Abstract Ecosystem services are defined as the conditions through which "natural ecosystems, and the species that make them up, sustain and fulfill human life" (R. Costanza). In other words, they are "benefits people obtain from ecosystems" (Reid et al.). Strictly linked to ecosystem services, natural capital can be defined as the world's stocks of natural assets. Although these notions are the results of ecological and economic reflections, natural capital and ecosystem services are gaining more and more consideration in European and Italian legislation. On that basis, we will describe the legal framework and modes of applications that can be pointed out nowadays. In particular, we will focus on Payments for Ecosystem Service, or "PES programs," which is the specific kind of contract in which landowners or communities are remunerated for managing their land to produce one or more ecosystem services. Indeed, more and more frequently PES are chosen as a valid option to safeguard biodiversity. Furthermore, we will discuss the possibility to consider as Payments for Ecosystem Services some juridical instruments—already in force—with the same "ratio" but traditionally not included in "PES programs," also with reference to the opportunities offered by EU environmental policies to protect nature and in particular on the PNRR.

1 Introduction

The environmental crisis casts a shadow of uncertainty over the fate of our planet, signaling an urgent call for attention, action, and accountability. As human activities continue to unfold with staggering intensity, the Earth's ecosystems face unprecedented challenges, pushing the delicate balance of nature to its limits.

The environmental crisis encompasses a broad spectrum of interconnected issues, from climate change and biodiversity loss to deforestation, pollution, and resource depletion. The signs of this environmental crisis are all around us—from soaring

C. Colognese (✉) · N. Granato
Sapienza University of Rome, Rome, Italy
e-mail: chiara.colognese@uniroma1.it; nicola.granato@uniroma1.it

G. Antonelli et al. (eds.), *Biodiversity Laws, Policies and Science in Europe, the United States and China*, https://doi.org/10.1007/978-3-031-56218-1_4

global temperatures and extreme weather events to the depletion of vital natural resources and the loss of biodiversity. The consequences of these actions are far-reaching and affect every aspect of human life, from our health and well-being to our economies and social stability.

In this context, it is important also for the jurist to ask the question of what legal instruments can help in the—always more necessary—ecological transition.

We believe that the concepts of ecosystem services and natural capital can be a good weapon in this regard, enabling the introduction of ecological stability needs within public policies, along with assessable economic parameters.

For these reasons, it was decided to focus on the legal relevance of the concepts of ecosystem services and natural capital, along with their potential.

In particular, in the first part of the chapter, an attempt will be made to outline the cultural and scientific context in which thoughts on ecosystem services and natural capital have arisen. A reference to ecological and economic sciences will then be essential to fully understand the scope of these concepts.

Before then addressing the issue of the legal relevance of ecosystem services and natural capital, some questions will be asked about the relationship between biodiversity and ecosystem services, highlighting their naturally close connection. We will then reflect on the current relationship between science and law, identifying some critical issues along with some future potentials.

Moving then to a more purely legal reflection, in the second part of the chapter, the talk will start with a much-needed account of the current regulatory framework for ecosystem services and natural capital, and then focus on one of the clearest applications of the concept of ecosystem services: Payments for Ecosystem Services (PES). These will be studied in their essential elements, seeking to identify differentiation from other instruments, referred to as "PES-like," which, while lacking some of the basic elements of traditional PES, respect their *ratio*.

Finally, we will ask, at this time of strong legislative activism toward an ecological transition, what are the opportunities offered by the European Union's environmental policies to protect nature and in particular the National Recovery and Resilience Plan.

2 Ecosystem Services and Natural Capital: Concept and Frameworks

The concept of ecosystem service has as its premise in that of "ecological function," a notion explored in the ecological sciences, capable of encompassing all those activities performed by nature that do not necessarily entail a utility for man. They are aimed at maintaining the dynamic equilibrium of the ecosystem to which they belong, through exchanges of energy and matter between individual units.

According to Cardinal,[1] *"Ecosystem functions are ecological processes that control the fluxes of energy, nutrients and organic matter through an environment."*

Within the more general category of ecosystem functions, studies in the non-ecological sciences have focused more on ecosystem *services*, i.e., as a first approximation, those ecosystem functions that provide direct or indirect benefits to human beings. Ecosystem services, therefore, unlike ecosystem functions, only exist if they contribute to human well-being and could not be defined independently of this.[2]

More precisely, the term *"nature's services"* first appeared[3] in the academic literature in a paper published in the journal *Science* in 1977 by ecologist Walter Westman entitled *"How Much Are Nature's Services Worth?,"* while the term—used synonymously—*"Ecosystem Services"* was employed a few years later by ecologists Paul R. Ehrlich and Harold A. Mooney in the well-known article "*Extinction, Substitution, and Ecosystem Services.*"

It was towards the end of the 1980s that the concept of services provided by nature became increasingly popular: the reasons for the affirmation of this notion are to be found in the increasingly evident ecological degradation, in the increased awareness of the functioning mechanisms of ecosystems and, finally, in the emergence of a new discipline capable of creating a link between ecological and economic reflections, which had hitherto been parallel but distinct.[4]

As far as the definition of ecosystem services is concerned, we can now state that there seems to be a general consensus in the literature on what can be defined as the "core" of the definition of ecosystem services, the result of the reception of the first and most important studies on the subject, namely the article *"The value of the world's ecosystem services and natural capital"* published in 1997 by the economist Robert Costanza,[5] at the same time as the volume *Nature's Services: Societal Dependence On Natural Ecosystems*[6] written by the environmental scientist Gretchen Cara Daily. Ecosystem services are thus considered as "those ecological features, functions, or processes that directly or indirectly contribute to human well being, i.e., the benefits that individuals derive from the functioning of ecosystems."[7]

---

[1] Cardinale et al. (2012), pp. 59–67.

[2] Braat (2014).

[3] However, the idea that "natural systems provide benefits that support human well-being is as old as humans themselves." Costanza et al. (2017).

[4] *Passim*, ibidem.

It was the economist Robert Costanza who, in the 1990s, founded a new strand called *"ecological economics," which was able to* combine the needs of the two disciplines considered.

[5] Costanza et al. (1997), pp. 253–260. The article is considered the founding act of the new discipline that aims to integrate ecological considerations within an economic context called *"ecological-economics."*

[6] Daily (1997).

[7] Costanza et al. (1997).

With respect to the hard core of the definition, there have been several proposals or attempts from the scientific literature to define more precisely the boundaries of a definition that can appear vague.

Some scholars limit the concept of ecosystem service to those ecosystem functions that bring a benefit *perceived as such* by humans.[8] This seems to align with the traditional method of economic analysis, which is accustomed to assessing in strictly anthropocentric terms the benefits and "profits" that can benefit the individual.

Others have emphasized the distinction between "intermediate" and "final" services with respect to the welfare of populations.[9]

Still others have studied ecosystem services by focusing on their spatial characteristics, including in the assessment categories that describe the relationship between the services produced and the place where these services insist. In this sense, ecosystem services have been divided between "*in situ,*" where services are produced and benefits are realized in the same place; "*omnidirectional,*" where benefits are produced in a single place, but benefits are projected into the surrounding area without a precise orientation; "*directional,*" where the production of services benefits a specific place due to the direction of the flow of services.[10] Considering ecosystem services from this perspective could be useful when assessing the quality or type of ecosystem service provision in a given territory, given the possibility of better visualizing the spatial distribution of benefits.

It is generally accepted, however, that ecosystem services can be distinguished into four different categories. This distinction was proposed by the *Millennium Ecosystem Assessment*[11] and later adopted by TEEB (*The Economics of Ecosystems and Biodiversity project*).[12] Ecosystem services could then be subdivided into:

---

[8] Potschin and Haines-Young (2017).

[9] If we consider, for example, the benefit of a food product such as fruit, food production is the final service, while pollination is the intermediate service. This distinction should not be understood in a rigid sense since services are often "a function of the perspective of the beneficiary." Kerry Turner et al. (2008). For example, the water regulation services provided by a vegetation-rich zone could be considered as an end service by those interested in a constant supply of water, but considered as an intermediate service by those interested in the end service of clean water (for whom the end service is the benefit of drinking water). Indeed, we can say that "ecosystems are multidimensional and the distinction between direct and indirect contributions to human well-being is complex and not yet fully understood." Costanza et al. (2017), p. 6.

[10] *Passim*, Kerry Turner et al. (2008), p. 8.

[11] The Millennium Ecosystem Assessment (MEA), in Italian, the "Millennium Ecosystem Assessment," is a UN-funded research project, active from 2001 to 2005 with the contribution of more than 1360 experts from all over the world with the aim of assessing the consequences of ecosystem change in relation to human wellbeing and providing the scientific basis for the actions necessary for the conservation and sustainable use of ecosystem services. More information can be found at the institutional website https://www.milleniumassesment.org.

[12] TEEB (The Economics of Ecosystems and Biodiversity) is an international initiative with the objective of "*making nature's values visible,*" *so* that the value of ecosystem services can be taken into account in decisions. Again, more information can be found on the institutional website https://teebweb.org/. The results of the study are discussed in more detail in the next chapter.

- *provisioning* services: these are those services that are essentially the products obtained from ecosystems (food, fresh water, firewood, but also genetic resources and chemicals).
- *regulating* services: these are those services that enable the regulation of various natural phenomena, e.g., the function of flood control, regulation of the water cycle, regulation of gas cycles or even pollination and climate control. They tend to be perceived less immediately by the community.
- *cultural services*: these are those services capable of guaranteeing a cultural identity to the territory, scientific or aesthetic cues or even just recreational-tourist or spiritual or religious ones. They are all those non-material benefits of the ecosystem that risk overlapping with the concept of landscape. Ecosystem services can thus be the "result of ecological, social and cultural processes and their interactions and, especially in cultural landscapes, some Ses are the result of a historical co-evolution of uses, rules of use, social norms and natural processes."[13]
- *supporting services*: these are those services that are necessary for the production of all other ecosystem services and constitute the basic ecological processes such as soil formation, nutrient cycling, and the provision of habitat for living species. The TEEB actually replaced this category with that of "*habitat or refugia services*" to highlight the importance of these services in providing a refuge for migratory species and for the protection of the gene *pool* (e.g., natural habitats enable natural selection processes to preserve the viability of the gene pool of such a species).[14]

In any case, regardless of the due consideration of the different ways in which the notion of ecosystem services has been conceived, it is in the opinion of the writer that there is no single classification system for ecosystem services that can be adequate in every context and for every purpose.[15] However one classifies them, it is important to note that ecosystem services have a public value because they provide the inhabitants of a territory with very often irreplaceable benefits, some of which are of global interest, such as the maintenance of the chemical composition of the atmosphere, while others depend on the proximity of inhabited areas, such as soil consolidation.[16]

This is the background to Robert Costanza's seminal work, *"the value of the world's ecosystem services and natural capital": the* first organic attempt to use economic methodologies to assess the annual flow of the main ecosystem services provided by natural capital globally. An initial estimate of the monetary value of the flow of benefits provided by ecosystems is 33 trillion dollars annually, later

---

[13] Santolini and Morri (2010), p. 3.

[14] Costanza et al. (2017).

[15] See, in this sense, Kerry Turner et al. (2008).

[16] Santolini and Morri (2010), 3.

increased to between 125 trillion and 145 trillion dollars annually in subsequent work in 2014.

The conceptual assumption for quantifying the concept of ecosystem service in economic terms is to consider it as coming from nature as natural capital.[17] Accordingly, ecosystem services would be "flow of services produced by the stock of natural capital." Natural capital includes the entire stock of natural assets—living organisms, air, water, soil and geological resources—that contribute to providing goods and services of direct or indirect value to humans, and that are necessary for the survival of the very environment from which they are generated, subject to economic valuation. Just as the future returns associated, for example, with a capital asset define the value of the investment in the property, similarly, the present value of the flow of ecosystem services also defines the value of the stock of natural capital from which they are generated.

The use of the ecosystem services methodology is to provide a tool for internalizing the assessment of ecosystem services in public decision-making processes, thus overcoming the under—or non-assessment—of these services. Furthermore, this methodology has the merit of being characterized by a unitary and tendentially all-encompassing vision of the human-nature relationship, so that it can constitute a useful conceptual tool for improving the application of the instruments through which environmental policies are implemented.

The criticism that can be levelled at this method lies in the possible interpretation of ecosystem services "as a one-way, utilitarian type of relationship,"[18] with the risk of underestimating the complexity and balance of the environment. On the contrary, I believe that such a method might be able to consider more deeply the relationship between Man-Nature and, more specifically, the "duties of care that people have in relation to the non-human world."[19] More problematic is the consideration that it would be difficult to develop an "objective way of assessing the benefits of ecosystem services."[20] In this regard, it is possible to say that since the publication of the Millennium Ecosystem Assessment in 2005, considerable conceptual and methodological progress has been achieved, although some difficulties certainly remain.

---

[17] The concept of natural capital arises in a context in which traditional economic categories appeared increasingly inadequate. See Costanza R., *Ecosystem services in Theory and Practice*, in Potschin et al. (2016), p. 15: "Our traditional concepts and models of the economy were developed in the empty world. The conventional view of the economy is based on a number of assumptions about the way the world works, what economy is, and what economy is for. In this 'empty world' context, built capital—the houses, cars, roads, and factories of the market economy—was the limiting factor. Natural capital-our ecological life support system-and social capital-our myriad relationships with each other-were abundant. It made sense, in that context, not to worry too much about environmental and social 'externalities'. [. . .] But in the new full world context, we have to think differently about what the economy is and what it is for if we are to create sustainable prosperity."

[18] Ibid., p. 7.

[19] Ibidem.

[20] Potschin et al. (2016), p. 13, "Not least because of the difficulties of disentangling the contributions made by natural and human capital in the production of many services."

2.1 The Link Between Biodiversity and Ecosystem Services

One of the fundamental prerequisites for the proper performance of ecosystem functions is biodiversity, currently one of the aspects most challenged by the ecological crisis we find ourselves in.[21]

The assumption that we must always bear in mind is that we still do not know enough about the structure and functioning of ecosystems to be able to predict the extent to which they may be able to tolerate a loss of biodiversity while continuing to provide the ecosystem services on which we depend.[22] Uncertainty therefore remains regarding the specific link between ecosystem services,[23] resulting in particular from "mismatches between ecosystem functions measured and final ecosystem services; mismatches between study considerations and management conditions; insufficient consideration of all functions upon which a service depends; insufficient integration of multiple potentially critical components of biodiversity; confounding environmental factors; trade-offs between the positive and negative effect of changes in biodiversity on various ecosystem functions that underlie ecosystem services; contact-dependent patterns; different scales between studies linking biodiversity and both the management and delivery of services."[24]

Once this aspect has been clarified, it is evident how the variety of living forms provides, first and foremost, services directly to human beings: think of the genetic heritage that could become the basis for new pharmaceutical or technological products,[25] or the "food safety" service that guarantees the variability of seeds and species that are used for food, as well as the ability to limit the transmission of certain diseases from animal species to humans (so-called zoonoses).[26]

More generally, we can state that a great diversity of species and organisms is a condition for maintaining the vitality of ecosystems and their ability to perform their functions.[27] Studies are now unanimous in pointing out that the loss of biodiversity

---

[21]Scholars who have focused on the topic of ecosystem services have understood the close link between biodiversity and ecosystem services early on. The literature on the subject is vast, we only mention Schulze and Mooney (2012); Loreau et al. (2002); Mace et al. (2012).

[22]For most of the species we have recorded *"we know little or nothing about the roles they play in maintaining the ecosystems of which they are part."* May (2011), pp. 346–350.

[23]It could be argued that for most ecosystem services the relationship between biodiversity and ecosystem services remains unknown, while for those for which such a relationship is known, it may also be negative, or ambivalent. Balvanera et al. (2016), p. 56.

[24]Ibid., p. 48.

[25]Biodiversity is defined as a "precious resource of genetic novelties," which could be the starting point for future discoveries, "so let us not burn the books before we have read them." May (2011).

[26]This is referred to as the "dilution effect," whereby the risk of a disease decreases as the diversity of the set of animal potential disease vectors increases. Furthermore, studies show how the loss of biodiversity increases disease transmission. Balvanera et al. (2016), p. 52.

[27]This is a correct statement, although necessarily an approximation: in fact, ecologists have more accurately stated that for some ecosystem services there is sufficient evidence to show that biodiversity has a direct impact (with regard to "*provisioning services,*" intra-species genetic

increases the fragility of ecosystems, "reducing their resilience, i.e. their ability to withstand stressful situations without shifting to a completely different organisational state, and thus maintaining the same structures, processes, and functions."[28] If we assume, in fact, that the diversity of species in an ecosystem corresponds to the complexity of the interactions between them, then the alteration of biodiversity produces changes in the stability of the ecosystem,[29] the reduction in the functionality of habitats as well as their possible progressive dystrophy, i.e., a loss of functions, usually preceded by the disappearance of key species, as well as their disappearance.[30]

In other words, according to a reconstruction carried out by scholars, the relationship between biodiversity and ecosystem services would be "*multilayered,*"[31] to the extent that biodiversity is able to play three different roles in relation to ecosystem services. A distinction should therefore be made between those situations in which biodiversity can perform the function of a "regulator" of fundamental ecosystem processes, those in which biodiversity itself is characterized as an ecosystem service, and those in which it has the value of a good. Thus with regard to the regulating function, we think of different nutrient cycles in the soil, favored by a

---

diversity increases crop yields; tree species diversity increases timber production within plantations; fish species diversity is associated with greater stability of fisheries; with regard to "*regulating services,*" tree species diversity increases resistance to invasion by exotic species, as well as decreases the incidence of pathogens"); for other ecosystem services such as carbon sequestration from the atmosphere, on the other hand, the data have shown mixed results, casting doubt on the influence of biodiversity *per se* in this activity in the long term. Cardinale et al. (2012), pp. 59–67.

[28] The concept of vulnerability is linked to territorial resilience. The quantity and quality of ecosystem services that a territory can offer nowadays depends on its spatial planning, which can contribute positively or negatively to the development of resilient territories: spatial planning decisions, in fact, influence and can irreversibly modify ecosystem structures and processes. For example, there is already evidence of how sealing of urban soils can aggravate the impacts of climate events, cumulatively to other negative effects, such as increased water and air pollution and increased health risks for citizens (the greatest damage from flood events occurs in urban areas with poor drainage surfaces, just as in several European cities a significant increase in mortality has been ascertained in recent years due to the association of heat waves with the 'heat island' phenomenon, caused by impermeable and thermo-absorbent surfaces). In relation to the latter phenomenon in particular, "the semi-natural or artificial areas of so-called urban greenery can provide significant ecosystem services, mitigating heat waves and thus helping to regulate the local microclimate and limit the number of 'tropical nights' in cities." *Passim*, Santolini et al. (2012), p. 60.

[29] Specific studies on the relationship between biodiversity and ecosystem stability have been conducted since the 1950s. See, for example, the reflections of Odum (1953); MacArthur (1955); Elton (1958). There is also talk of a specific "insurance value" of biodiversity that "helps minimise the costs of various unpredictable events." Tilman (1997).

[30] Cardinale et al. (2012), pp. 59–67, "Meta-analyses published since 2005 have shown that, as a general rule, reductions in the number of genes, species and functional groups of organisms reduce the efficiency by which whole communities capture biologically essential resources (nutrients, water, light, prey), and convert those resources into biomass."

[31] Mace et al. (2012).

greater diversity of the biological component;[32] with regard to biodiversity as an ultimate ecosystem service, on the other hand, we think for example of the genetic diversity of "*wild crop relatives,*" which is fundamental for the fortification and improvement of strains used in agriculture, as well as for species used in breeding; finally, as far as biodiversity itself having the function of a commodity, we think of the cultural value, which passes through the appreciation of wild life forms, spiritual, religious educational and recreational.[33]

Studies on the subject have highlighted three different ways in which greater biodiversity can lead to greater ecosystem services and vice versa.

First, the so-called "complementary effect" was identified, whereby complementary differences between species, in combination with spatial heterogeneity, could lead to the effect that the community as a whole provides a higher rate of ecosystem services than would be the case if it were simply the sum of its components. Second, the so-called "selection effect" was identified, whereby predominance by species providing particularly high rates of ecosystem services could lead to a positive "diversity effect" on average. Thirdly, scholars have discussed the "insurance hypothesis," according to which asynchronous responses of species to environmental fluctuations could lead to a greater and more stable provision of ecosystem services in mixed crops than in monocultures.[34]

In any case, regardless of the role to be attributed to biodiversity in relation to ecosystem services, its function with respect to the overall resilience of the ecological system has been highlighted by the theorization developed by the *Stockholm Resilience Centre*. This have calculated nine "*planetary boundaries,*"[35] i.e., boundaries within which the human species should remain in order to continue to develop and prosper.[36] It is precisely for the loss of biodiversity (along with the extent of nitrogen use) that it has been estimated that we are already in an area of high risk, while for two others, climate change and earth systems change, we are in an area of increasing uncertainty.

[32] "Ecosystem processes generally depend on the right combination of biotic and abiotic components. However, sometimes what matters is not just the presence of a particular component or its quantity, but its diversity and variety," ibidem.

[33] Not to mention the fact that "the same component of biodiversity may be linked in very different ways to multiple ecosystem services." Consider the example of fish: "fish are widely recognised as food, a 'provisioning service' with a direct market value. However, fish also provide indirect benefits or regulating services, like biological control. Specifically, experiments have highlighted the importance of fish predation in regulating invasive species like zebra mussels. Concurrently, the presence of fish, such as in crowded streams during spawning, can also be a highly valued cultural service." Balvanera et al. (2016), p. 47.

[34] Ibid., p. 48.

[35] Rockstrom et al. (2009).

[36] The value of the study can be attributed to the fact that for the first time, quantitative *threshold levels* have been identified linked to nine macro-processes (*large-scale Earth-system processes*) that disrupt the fundamental ecological systems supporting life on Earth. See, for a legal perspective, Monteduro (2014).

2.2 Science and Legal System

It should be clear at this point how the science of ecosystem services is "truly transdisciplinary,"[37] as are many contemporary sciences. It appears to stand at a crossroads between ecological science, economics, and law.

From the perspective of the jurist, it therefore seems appropriate to ask what is the role of science, and ecology in particular, in relation to law.[38]

The relationship between law and science has in fact been discussed extensively in various areas of law and from many angles,[39] but with regard to environmental law it takes on a particular value.

Anticipating the conclusion to be reached, it is in the writer's opinion that it is necessary to go beyond the mere interdisciplinary contamination between legal and ecological science.[40]

From the very beginnings of the formation of a branch of law that we can define as "environmental," environmental law has been considered a "dynamic" law ("the environment moves, changes, mutates over time, we find ourselves regulating or managing an object that is constantly changing") and a technical one ("environmental protection cannot be done without having an adequate stock of technical knowledge and therefore technical-scientific instruments, and, above all, without ensuring that the instruments provided today can be continually adapted as technical-scientific progress is made"[41]), to such an extent that the environment is not considered a

---

[37] Potschin et al. (2016), p. 5. That is an important characteristic of this "post- normal science," that makes it different from more traditional ones.

[38] A specular debate has been going on for some time in the scientific sphere, thus from the point of view of the scientist, in order to be able to answer the question "what role does law play for science?" See, in this regard, Lubchenco (1998). The author reflects on the responsibility of the scientist to offer the right tools to policy for "more enlightened decisions," "the current and growing extent of human dominance of the planet will require new kinds of knowledge and applications from science-knowledge to reduce the rate at which we alter the Earth systems, knowledge to understand Earth's ecosystems and how they interact with the numerous components of human-caused global change, and knowledge to manage the planet."

[39] One might think in particular of criminal law and the role of technical expertise within the phase of evidentiary instruction, also in relation to the concept of judge *peritus peritorum*. But also to all the questions that the law has to resolve in relation to, among others, genetic engineering, nanotechnology, synthetic bioethics and health-epidemiological issues.

[40] In the same perspective, see Monteduro (2014); Zanini (2019).

On the lack of such an approach in the early years of the development of environmental law, see Caravita (2005): "in environmental matters there has long been a lack of reference to the data and elaborations of ecology, that is, of the science that studies the real living conditions of organisms from the point of view of the interrelations between organisms and the environment, with the consequent use of those elaborations to construct legally significant notions on them."

On the contrary, a part of Italian doctrine shows some perplexity about the possibility of law being able to integrate its categories with those of ecology in a coherent manner, given the structural diversity. See Plinio (1994).

[41] Cecchetti (2012), p. 354.

"legally indeterminate concept" but rather a "scientifically determined legal concept."[42]

While acknowledging the diversity of the methods, vocabulary, and categories of the two disciplines, we believe, as mentioned above, that this relationship should not be limited to contamination and dialogue,[43] but that, on the contrary, some of the scientific theories outlined above should be introduced into the jurist's own reflection. First and foremost, the theory of *planetary boundaries:* in identifying the thresholds beyond which the stability of the ecosphere would be undermined,[44] the jurist should also see drawn the boundary within which "human conduct is constrained in order to be carried out safely"[45] and the "complex of constraints that cannot be abrogated by any human law," on pain of their very possibility of being carried out.[46] In other words, given the relevance of scientific acquisition, such as to call into question life itself, the presupposition of every right and every juridicality, the scientist would come to define both the "material" limit within which human action is compatible with its development (or, at least, its survival) and the limit of the "juridically possible," thus drawing the "space of the practicability of the intervention of law,"[47] whose task is to regulate the performance of such actions. In this perspective, any other interest, even legally relevant, would be recessive compared to the need, which would stand above, almost like a "super-right," to place itself within the operational space considered safe for humanity.[48]

If the assumption, in these terms, would become that of the "clear prevalence of the dimension of extra-legal knowledge that is indispensable for the evaluation of the facts to be regulated and consequently for the interpretation and application of the legal discipline,"[49] it would, however, be necessary to "identify new methods and

---

[42] Morbidelli (1996), p. 1163.

[43] "The capillarity of relations between the scientific and legal systems is also visible in the places and actors involved. Scientists and lawyers have reciprocally colonised their respective places of expertise. Scientists (together with engineers and technologists) are present as experts in courts of law or in parliamentary hearings, work as officials in agencies or authorities for the regulation of *science-based* activities, are members of ethics or *policy advice* committees, claim intellectual property rights in patent offices, and direct institutes or research programmes dedicated to scientific-legal issues. Jurists, for their part, not only support scientists in the above-mentioned activities, but are directly involved in laboratory activities, not only to ensure their correctness and safety from the point of view of the rules, but also to grasp 'in the field' the emergence of new norm-relevant situations." Tallacchini (2012).

[44] In the authors' words, we would be facing a situation of "*risk of deleterious or even catastrophic environmental change at continental to global scales.*" Rockstrom et al. (2009).

[45] Monteduro (2014).

[46] Ibidem.

[47] Ibidem.

[48] Such a theoretical perspective is based on the concept of "*rule of* ecological law," an "ecological legality," analyzed in particular by US doctrine. See, for all, Garver (2013), p. 316.

[49] Grassi (2012).

procedures to enable a correct and democratic relationship between science and law."[50]

In fact, the question posed in this way would risk posing a problem of the democratic nature of the law, with the scientific parameter becoming a de facto normative parameter. There would thus be a risk of attributing the same value to a scientific rule, identified through the methods recognized by the scientific community, based on theoretically reproducible evidence and experiments, with a legal rule, which under the Constitutions of European countries, can only be set by the legislator, the expression of popular sovereignty.

This is a remarkable argument, considering that it relates to the very foundations of the entire legal system. It could be overcome by stating that it is not intended to recognize the value of a legal norm *to* scientific acquisitions *tout court*. More precisely, if the latter remain strong guiding notions for the legislator, which he should dutifully take into account in the exercise of his legislative function, in respect of the jurist in general they should assume the value of a guiding parameter when interpreting the legal norm.[51]

In applying this perspective, one could rethink legal categories of environmental law that have become traditional. Think for instance of the concept of sustainable development, based on the equal consideration and balancing of economic, social, and environmental needs. According to part of the doctrine,[52] the scientific assumption recognizing the need not to exceed certain thresholds would lead one to replace such a reconstruction with one "in concentric circles, in which economic needs are subservient to (and thus inscribed within) social needs and the latter are in turn subordinate to the ecological limits of the planet identified by planetary boundaries."[53]

Another applicative example of this theoretical construction can be found in the extrapolation, from ecological sciences, of a series of so-called ecojuridical principles, i.e., capable of transposing and rendering normative parameter the scientific laws of ecosystem functioning.[54] The strong point of this new tendency is to entrust the construction of principles not so much to the legislator, but to the interpreters, consisting of both doctrine and jurisprudence, forcing the latter to a continuous dialogue with science in order to correctly identify their content. Specifically, the principle of non-regression, the principle of resilience, the principle of ecological integrity, and the principle of ecological proportionality have been considered "ecojuridical principles."

In other terms, used mainly in philosophical literature, such a relationship between science and law can be considered one of "co-production," thus

[50] Ibidem.

[51] As if the regulations were to be "ecologically oriented."

[52] See Monteduro (2014).

[53] Ibidem.

[54] Zanini (2019).

emphasizing their "mutual interaction and legitimisation."[55] The theory of "co-production" stands in contrast to the theory of the "separation" between science and law, which instead remains "anchored to the fundamental conceptual and systemic differences that separate science and law; to the radical otherness between scientific and normative discourses; and to a (purported) liberal-democratic vision of the scientific community, according to which the freedom of science demands its exemption from the rules of society."[56] On the contrary, the theory of co-production, while not denying "the conceptual distinction between descriptions and prescriptions," wants to highlight "the continuity of interactions when their languages meet (instead of stopping at their abstract forms of validation)": it is recognized that increasingly, "the relationship between the factual moment and the normative moment appears to be reversed: not only is the knowledge that becomes the object of norms not at all external to the normative fabric, but the potential normative qualifications are anticipated already in the elaboration of scientific methodologies."[57] In other words, normativity "already pervades the choice of knowledge and the modes of legal translation."[58] According to this peculiar perspective from the philosophy of law, therefore, this would be a way of extending "democracy and its guarantees to science as well."

3 European and Italian Legal Framework

References in European and Italian legislation to ecosystem services and natural capital continue to multiply.

[55] Tallacchini (2012).

[56] The issue is addressed here from a legal philosophy perspective, for which "the background of the relations between science and law is linked to the theorisation of what is the proper place of science in society, i.e. whether science should be thought of outside any legal-political control or whether it cannot escape the dynamics of democratic control." Tallacchini (2012), p. 317.

Manifestations of the separatist approach can be found in the "view of 'technical standards' as neutral normative containers with respect to knowledge produced by external expertise; (. . .) the image of the judge applying and not interpreting the law that still persists in specialised areas of law (as, for example, in the courts of the European Patent Office, (. . .) the 'technical standards' as a 'legal instrument' are not a 'legal instrument' but a 'legal instrument'.) separatism also underlies the so-called law-lag argument, the accusation that legal instruments are structurally inadequate to keep up with science, which should evolve in the absence of external constraints." Ibid., p. 318.

[57] "Even the '*Whereas*' (or 'recitals'), the initial 'narrative' sections of conventions, recommendations, laws and regulations that are supposed to 'describe' the general background of regulation—normative-substantive (context and reasons for intervention, existing regulatory provisions) and normative-procedural (bodies, committees heard and involved, distribution of regulatory competences) —are less and less representable as the mere preamble to the following normative section (the articulate). The articulate re-proposes in prescriptive language what has been normatively defined by the apparently descriptive language of the 'recitals'." Ibidem.

[58] Ibidem.

As far as European law is concerned, we have a first rather vague description of ecosystem services in the European Regulation 2020/852/EU, which aims at "establishing a framework for supporting sustainable investments" in Article 2, no. 14, according to which ecosystem services are "the direct and indirect contributions of ecosystems to the economic, social, cultural and other benefits that people derive from those ecosystems." More generally, references to ecosystem services in European legislation are mostly contained in all those acts aimed at protecting biodiversity (think of the EU Biodiversity Strategy 2030). It is noticeable how the two concepts are very often placed side by side. A similar argument must be made with regard to references to Natural Capital, for which the EU's 7th Environment Action Programme (EAP) is the most explicit reference aimed at preserving Europe's natural capital ("Living well within the limits of our planet"): the first priority objective to be achieved by 2020 is thus defined, "to protect, conserve and enhance the Union's natural capital."

We therefore limit ourselves to providing the general impression that there is a lack of real specific legislation at the European level to regulate ecosystem services and natural capital. These, on the contrary, are increasingly mentioned but in a fragmentary way, and frequently within sources aimed at protecting biodiversity or sector regulations.

The situation does not seem to have changed much as a result of the new growth strategy outlined in the European Green Deal and confirmed with the national Recovery and Resilience mechanisms (in Italy, embodied in the National Recovery and Resilience Plan, the so-called PNRR):[59] while representing an opportunity to speed up a green and ecological transition in Italy, too little attention still seems to be paid to the dimension of ecosystem services and their evaluation.

As far as purely domestic legislation is concerned, the tendency to have fragmentary regulations at the expense of an organic framework is confirmed.

Considering the topic of natural capital specifically, the establishment of the Natural Capital Committee by Law 221/2015 should be highlighted. It has two main tasks: to produce an annual report on the state of the country's natural capital in which ex ante and ex post assessments of the effects of public policies on natural capital and ecosystem services are expressed; promote the adoption by local authorities of environmental accounting systems by preparing environmental budgets.

On the other hand, with regard to ecosystem services, the most important reference can be found in Article 70 of the aforementioned law, which provided

[59] In the aftermath of the crisis caused by the Coronavirus pandemic, the European Commission proposed the Next Generation EU in May 2020 in order to support the recovery of the eurozone. The package "provides for the allocation of 750 billion in loans and grants, of which around 90 per cent is earmarked for the recovery and resilience facility. Each EU Member State that wished to apply for a financial contribution had to submit a plan for recovery and resilience to the Commission, setting out a programme of reforms and investments inter alia consistent with the challenges and priorities identified in the European Semester and the Council's recommendations. Italy, together with Spain, is the beneficiary of the largest share of funds, amounting to EUR 191.5 billion." Lazzari (2021), p. 1.

for a delegation to the Government for the introduction of remuneration systems for ecosystem and environmental services. It was worded as follows: "The Government is delegated to adopt, within six months from the date of entry into force of this law, without new or greater burdens for the public finance, one or more legislative decrees for the introduction of a system of payment for ecosystem and environmental services (PSEA)." It was thus supposed to outline an organic discipline on payment systems for ecosystem services, but the implementing discipline was never issued within the time limits set by the delegation.

Hints of ecosystem services can also be found in the legislation on Governance in relation to the National Recovery and Resilience Plan: Decree-Law No. 77 of 31/05/2021 (Governance of the National Recovery and Resilience Plan and initial measures to strengthen administrative structures and speed up and streamline procedures), Art. 35 bis (measures for simplification and promotion of the circular economy in the forest-wood sector), c. 4-quinques: "the stipulation of forest agreements in the national territory is promoted, as instruments for the development of networks of enterprises in the forest sector, in order to enhance the public and private areas with an agroforestry vocation as well as for the conservation and provision of ecosystem services provided by forests." These agreements are therefore negotiation tools used to build synergies and promote the circular economy of the forest-wood sector.

Other references can be found in the Ministry of Ecological Transition's Regulation of Organisation, Prime Minister's Decree No. 128 of 29/07/2021, Art. 8, which states that "the Directorate General for European and International Activities (AEI) performs the functions falling within the Ministry's competence in the following areas: participation of the Ministry in the processes of defining European policies and legislation and international agreements for the protection and enhancement of the environment, including natural habitats, the sea, *biodiversity and ecosystem services*, ..."

Or, again, we find a reference in the preamble of the Ministerial Decree of 10/03/2020 regarding the Minimum Environmental Criteria for the management service of public green areas and the supply of green care products: "deemed it appropriate to proceed with the revision of the decree of 13 December 2013 due to the evolution of the legislation that has intervened in the meantime on the *protection of natural capital and the value of ecosystem services and the need to adopt a systemic*, integrated approach addressing the management of public green areas within a strategic vision of the role that the same can have for the urban environment and for the community."

In all these cases, it can be seen that ecosystem services are "postulated," i.e., given as assumptions, and never described.

We can also find a partially more defined discipline in relation to Payments for Ecosystem Services, the so-called PES. In addition to the already mentioned reference contained in Article 70 of Law 221/2015, which has not been realized, we can identify cases in which the legislator has taken up the PES system but from a sectoral perspective.

Consider, for example, the case of the "Testo Unico in materia di Foreste" (consolidated text on forestry, Legislative Decree No. 34 of 3 April 2018): in Article 7, paragraph 8, it is provided that the regions promote payment systems for ecosystem and environmental services generated by sustainable forest management. They are conditional on the assumption of specific environmental commitments and aim to support owners, managers, and beneficiaries of services in the definition and monitoring of contractual agreements.

The forest heritage lends itself perfectly to the PES system, not only because of the multiplicity of services offered but also because of the ownership characterization of this resource in Italy, which is mostly held by individual owners and enterprises.

It should also be noted how the ability of forest ecosystem services to be evaluated in economic terms lends itself not only to the production of positive effects as regards the better quantification of possible environmental damage and compensatory activities, but also to the planning activity of a vast area. In fact, the administration's better knowledge of the greater or lesser ecosystem relevance of a given forest area allows it to quantify the environmental impact of certain works or interventions more effectively.

In addition to this, and a few others,[60] explicit references to PES, some scholars have pointed out that other environmental transactions are also very reminiscent of the geometry of PES, although they are regulated by Italian law under different names such as river contracts or lake contracts.[61]

Opening our gaze and looking at the discipline of ecosystem services and natural capital from a greater distance, it is possible to argue that the main reference standard for understanding the relevance of these concepts in the Italian legal system remains that on environmental damage. Article 300 of the Consolidated Text on the Environment (Legislative Decree no. 152 of 2006) states that "environmental damage is any significant and measurable deterioration, direct or indirect, of a natural resource or of the utility provided by it." It thus transposes Article 2 of Directive 2004/35/EC, according to which "environmental damage is the measurable deterioration of natural resources or resource services." On the basis of this legislation, it is possible to understand what the legislator considers to be the constituent elements of the

[60] We can also find legal experiments of PES in the agricultural sphere, especially linked to the rural development plans developed by the regions. These are the so-called agri-environmental payments, which are defined as payments made annually to compensate for additional costs and income foregone resulting from environmental commitments.

Some scholars believe that agri-environmental measures, directed at the production of raw materials, do not necessarily coincide with PES, which are explicitly aimed at the production of ecosystem services. However, it is not possible to omit the fact that, "if agro-ecosystems arise from land conversion processes put in place to respond to a food need, the ecosystem service in this context will always be the indirect benefit of a productive end." Chiariello (2022).

[61] River and lake contracts are both consensual instruments between subjects with responsibilities in water management and use. They are voluntary instruments of strategic and negotiated planning that pursue the protection, the proper management of water resources and the enhancement of river territories together with the safeguard against hydraulic risk, contributing to local development.

environment in the legal sense: this is therefore made up of both "natural resources" and the "*services* of these resources," in fact, ecosystem services. It is precisely these latter that make it possible to have a more modern vision of the environment, no longer and not only understood as the sum of several natural resources, considered separately from each other, but understood as a connected system. In this way, it is possible for the jurist to consider the connecting elements between resources that have hitherto been ignored or not sufficiently considered.

That the environment should be considered as a *system* is even clearer today in Italy thanks to the recent constitutional reform.[62] The current Article 9 of the Italian Constitution now sees, in its last paragraph, the phrase: "(The Republic) protects the environment, biodiversity and ecosystems, also in the interest of future generations." It is precisely by virtue of this first reference to ecosystems in the Italian Constitution that it is possible to firmly maintain that today the environment must be protected above all in its ecosystem integrity, that is, in the quality and quantity of its ecosystem services.

Constitutional reform was anticipated in Italy by the positions expressed on several occasions by the Constitutional Court. There are many rulings in which the "judge of laws" invited us to look at the environment as a "system." Let us consider, for example, sentence 378/2007, in which it is stated that "The object of protection, as is also evident from the 1972 Stockholm Declaration, is the biosphere, which is taken into consideration, not only for its various components, but also for the interactions between them, their balances, their quality, the circulation of their elements, and so on. Which is necessary, in other words, to look at the environment as a 'system' considered in its dynamic aspect, as it really is, and not only from a static and abstract point of view." Or, again, sentence 105/2008, "A characteristic feature of woods and forests is that of expressing environmental multifunctionality, in addition to an economic-productive function. It can therefore be said that on the same visual asset, woods and forests, there are two legal assets: an environmental legal asset with reference to the environmental multifunctionality of the forest, and a patrimonial legal asset with reference to the economic productive function of the forest itself."

In conclusion, we can say that the regulation of ecosystem services and natural capital, although having developed in recent years, still leaves its greatest potential untapped. In fact, ecosystem services, biodiversity and natural capital can play the role of a perfect creative laboratory for the development of new and updated instruments.

[62] Constitutional Law of 11 February 2022, No. 1. This reform is particularly important because for the first time the Italian legislature decided to amend the first articles of its Constitutional Charter, called "Fundamental Principles."

4 Payments for Ecosystem Services (PES)

In this section of the chapter, the aim is to focus the study on payment systems for ecosystem services (PES), from an international and national perspective. As already considered in the previous pages, the global economy is highly dependent on the health of natural ecosystems and in general on the functions generated by nature.[63] International scientific studies have long consolidated this assumption by focusing concern on three macro-risks defined as "global": environmental degradation, ecosystem collapse and biodiversity loss.[64] According to recent data provided by the World Economic Forum 2023 (WEF), "the world is experiencing a catastrophic decline in biodiversity (. . .) Not only is this an environmental disaster, but it can also lead to financial ruin: $44 trillion is moderately or highly dependent on nature and its related services." There, the Global Risks Report identifies anthropogenic activity as the main cause of this degradation, estimating that it "has wiped out 83% of wild mammals and half of all plants, and has also severely altered three-quarters of the ice-free land and two-thirds of marine environments. Finally, one million species are threatened with extinction in the coming years."[65] Interesting is the WEF's definition of *global risks* as "the possibility of an event or condition occurring that, if it did, would have a negative impact on a significant portion of global GDP, population or natural resources."[66] The equipe of experts that led the study also identifies biodiversity loss and ecosystem collapse as the most rapidly deteriorating global risks over the next decade.[67] The snapshot to be drawn is clearly alarming and portrays the connection of a series of natural factors in continuous degradation that have and will have serious repercussions on our economy and obviously on life on the planet.[68]

---

[63] The centrality of this assumption is well described in Chiti (2022), pp. 469–470, *cit.*, "Ecosystem sustainability is an essential element of the overall strategy through which the Union wants to achieve climate neutrality. (. . .) The sustainability of ecosystems coincides with their resilience and integrity. (. . .) A system is resilient when it has the capacity to continuously provide certain services and products due to its condition. Understood in this sense, the resilience of ecosystems presupposes their integrity."

[64] *Cfr* the valuable study by Steffen et al. (2015).

[65] World Economic Forum (2023), *The Global Risks Report 2023,* 18th Edition, Insight Report. Consider that by 2010, UNEP's "Dead planet, living planet" report estimated that natural ecosystems provide human beings with services worth around 72 billion dollars annually.

[66] Ibid., p. 14. The Global Risks Perception Survey (GRPS) identifies "Energy supply crisis;" "Cost-of-living crisis;" "Rising inflation;" "Food supply crisis" and "Cyberattacks on critical infrastructure" as among the top risks for 2023 with the greatest potential impact on a global scale.

[67] Ibid., p. 32. Over the next ten years, the interaction between biodiversity loss, pollution, natural resource consumption, climate change and socio-economic factors will form a dangerous mix: the collapse of ecosystems will have far-reaching economic and social consequences.

[68] Ibid., p. 32. "Nature loss and climate change are intrinsically interlinked—a failure in one sphere will cascade into the other, and attaining net zero will require mitigatory measures for both levers (. . .) Land-use change remains the most prolific threat to nature, according to many experts. Agriculture and animal farming alone take up more than 35% of Earth's terrestrial surface and are the biggest direct drivers of wildlife decline globally."

The ongoing trend of such degradation also affects the stock of natural capital that provides and ensures the bundle of ecosystem services outlined in the preceding pages. However, it is precisely on this last aspect that we need to take a step back to shed light on the comparison between ecosystem services and the recent notion of nature's contributions to people. A respected scientific contribution in 2018 began to popularize the notion of *Nature's Contribution to People* (NCP), which is based on the concept of ecosystem service popularized by the MEA, but as put into practice by IPBES, differs from it in several ways.[69] First, the NCP approach recognizes culture as having a central role in defining and understanding all the links between nature and people. Second, the use of the NCP emphasizes and elevates the role of indigenous and local knowledge in understanding nature's contribution to people. The IPBES defines NCP as "all the contributions, both positive and negative, of living nature (diversity of organisms, ecosystems, and their associated ecological and evolutionary processes) to people's quality of life."[70] However, if in the context of IPBES by now the notion of NCP has been assimilated and has also found space and centrality in the latest reports of the international organization,[71] in 2018 Diaz's article provoked several reactions, including some criticism based on the usefulness of such a paradigm shift and whether it would be useful scientific progress in contexts other than IPBES.[72] The Intergovernmental Science-Policy Platform on Biodiversity and Ecosystem Services has identified 18 categories of partially overlapping NCP, among which are *material contributions* that are substances or other material elements that come directly from nature and directly support people's physical existence and material goods. The second category of *non-material contributions* are the effects of nature on the subjective or psychological aspects underlying people's quality of life. Again, *regulatory contributions* are functional and structural aspects of ecosystems that modify environmental conditions and/or regulate the generation of the first two categories of contributions.[73] The importance of nature's contributions to people has prompted economists to develop various market and non-market valuation methods to measure the value of many NCP, outlining advantages and disadvantages. If on the side of advantages, studies such as those of the TEEB, US EPA *et similia* recognize the relevance of entrusting an economic valuation to the services offered by nature, on the side of disadvantages, it is interesting to elaborate on two profiles. The first leads to the risk that economic

[69]Diaz et al. (2018).

[70]IPBES (2017), *Report of the Plenary of the Intergovernmental Science-Policy Platform on Biodiversity and Ecosystem Services on the work of its fifth session*, Bonn, Germany, available at: https://www.ipbes.net/events/ipbes-5-plenary.

[71]IPBES (2019b), p. 10, "Nature embodies different concepts for different people, including biodiversity, ecosystems, Mother Earth, systems of life and other analogous concepts. Nature's contributions to people embody different concepts, such as ecosystem goods and services and nature's gifts. Both nature and nature's contributions to people are vital for human existence and good quality of life."

[72]For further discussion, see Peterson et al. (2018); Braat (2018), pp. A1–A2.

[73]For more on the list of 18 identified NCP, see IPBES (2019a), p. 346 ff.

valuation methods may privilege the rich over the poor, since monetary valuation depends on the willingness to pay and the latter is, in turn, dependent on the distribution of wealth and income. Second, authoritative scholarship has shown that framing the question in terms of the market and money can influence the way people value nature.[74] Therefore, questioning the applicability of monetary valuations to ecosystem services or, more broadly, to NCP means delving into the object of such an operation: the values of nature. According to the latest IPBES report "it is important to note that the word 'value' means different things, depending on the context. Consequently, it is challenging to identify a general definition of what the 'value(s) of, about or for nature' mean, in a way that it makes sense and is agreeable across all knowledge systems, academic traditions, and lay people's understandings."[75] The necessary implementation, as we will illustrate below, of market mechanisms such as PES should not eliminate from the discussion the heterogeneity of nature values, which cannot be reduced *sic et simpliciter* to a subset of ecological measures and economic growth indicators. In fact, international studies show that international biodiversity policies and databases lack a "diversity of values" approach, favoring the economic approach to implement policies on ecosystem services.[76]

The question of the values entrusted to nature leads to that of its translatability in terms of the responsibility of political decision-makers, social actors, and the role of local communities. The next step in assimilating the ecological functionality of the services provided by the stock of environmental resources constituted by natural capital is to implement instruments, mechanisms capable of valorizing these "contributions," even monetizing what is not usually the subject of either negotiation or payment.[77] Traditional regulatory instruments, well framed in the so-called command and control, do not go beyond the mere management of the natural resource, relying on passive regulation that has moved between zoning, constraints and taxes. In environmental policies *tout court*, it is now advanced in doctrine that these instruments are obsolete, *a fortiori* in those that have as their object the conservation and improvement of biodiversity.[78] In their place, remuneration and compensation instruments are gradually being preferred, suitable for incentivizing actions aimed at enhancing SE through active protection interventions. As has been observed, this is basically "applying typical market instruments to 'market-less' products and services."[79] The value invisibility historically entrusted to natural services leads in the

[74] Falk and Szech (2013), pp. 707–711; Sandel (2012).

[75] IPBES (2022), p. 8.

[76] Ibid., p. 43 ff. For further discussion, see Zisenis (2009), pp. 639–648.

[77] Paletto et al. (2020), p. 282. The conservation and improvement of the services provided by natural ecosystems can be achieved through various environmental policy instruments of different natures, including: regulatory or normative instruments (e.g., protection zones, licenses, permits), market instruments (e.g., eco-taxes, subsidies, contributions) and information and communication tools (e.g., awareness-raising campaigns and processes to involve social actors).

[78] Sanchirico and Siikimaki (2007), pp. 8–10; Pettenella and Secco (2016), pp. 316–325.

[79] Cima et al. (2022), pp. 26–27.

consumer society to a destiny of overexploitation; therefore, what is needed is to implement instruments capable of inducing social actors to recognize an explicit value, including an economic one. In this order of ideas, the market instrument of *Payments for Ecosystem Services* (PES) and *PES-like*[80] fits perfectly. In fact, as early as the 7th EAP of the EU, PES systems were discussed as the instrument of choice for the protection of biodiversity.[81] In generic terms, PES can be defined as that voluntary and conditional agreement between at least one supplier/seller and at least one buyer/beneficiary concerning a specific environmental/ecosystem service.[82] In Wunder's well-recognized definition, the five conditions that make up PES are described, where he notes, first, the voluntary nature of the negotiation transition that distinguishes such instruments from authoritative and command-and-control instruments. Next, the "negotiated" ecosystem service must be well defined and its provider must ensure its provision.[83] In fact, if well identified, ES—necessary for the maintenance of essential conditions for human life—are measurable and thus can be given a monetary value.[84] The purpose of instruments such as PES is to translate "non-monetisable environmental values into real financial incentives for local actors to promote and support the maintenance of the multiple ecological functions provided by biodiversity and natural capital."[85] This transforms, on the one hand, the ES into a market product and, on the other hand, recognizes the right of the provider/producer of the ES to be financially rewarded for the service rendered. Precisely for this purpose, the implementation of PES passes through the contractual instrument, where the local institutions themselves can take on the role of both contractor and promoter.[86] Having defined its structure, the scientific literature has offered several classifications of PES, among which the best known, internationally, is the one that divides pure PES from "PES-like."[87] PES of the first type are those which, conventionally, follow the five conditions theorized by Wunder; in other

---

[80]Paletto A. et al., 302, *cit.* At the terminological level, in the international scientific literature on PES, the term Payment for *Environmental Services initially became* widespread, the first three publications of which date back to 2000, while only later did the term *Payment for Ecosystem Services become* established thanks to the 2005 work of Salzman (2005), pp. 870–961.

[81]EU Decision of the European Parliament and of the Council of 20 November 2013, No. 1386, "Living well within the limits of our planet," in particular priority VI, para 77 and para 83, point VIII.

[82]Wunder (2005); Wunder (2015), 234–243; Chiariello A.M., 423 ff., *op. cit.*

[83]Ibid., p. 3.

[84]Lalli (2017), p. 55.

[85]Chiariello (2022), p. 423, *cit.* The author goes on to state that PES systems are based on economic advantages for operators who can offer, maintain and enhance specific SEs, so as to push them towards voluntary adherence to incentive mechanisms proposed by the competent authorities, thus facilitating a realignment of public interest with private interest.

[86]Cafagno (2021), p. 867.

[87]See Pagiola et al. (2005), pp. 237–253; Engel et al. (2008), pp. 663–674; Baggethun et al. (2010), pp. 1209–1218. PES-like measures of public funding programmes that provide rewards and subsidies to support activities with positive environmental externalities that ensure the maintenance of ecosystem structure and function over time may be considered PES-like.

words, whose transition is intentional, has a well-determined ES as its object, and its supply is guaranteed over time. The main distinguishing criteria with PES-like, of which there are an increasing number, is the lack of the element of voluntariness of the transaction, which is instead framed in a mandatory regulatory framework. Examples of PES-like in the Italian context are to be found in the old surcharge to produce hydroelectric energy or in Art. 24 of the Galli Law (no. 36/1994) on the subject of rules on the pricing of drinking water consumption. Still other PES-like forms have been activated through forest-environmental payments within the last Rural Development Plans (RDPs).[88] At the national level, a second classification of PES divides them into two broad categories. The first includes those remuneration systems that follow the Italian and American example, which are purely negotiated and result in a series of voluntary market transitions between stakeholders.[89] The second, on the other hand, concerns those payments that can be imposed "for services produced by ecosystems consisting of assets owned or managed by a public body."[90] The last classification we review relates to the different role played by public entities and divides PES systems into four categories. In addition to the first two treated categories of pure PES and PES-like, this subdivision includes remuneration schemes for environmental compensation aimed at offsetting a negative impact on the environment and PES for economic compensation aimed at offsetting the opportunity cost of certain legal restrictions on resource use (e.g., payments in protected areas, hydroelectric levies, etc.).[91]

Given that the aim of current environmental policies, in terms of biodiversity, on the old continent is to implement the PES mechanism, here we ask how a PES-program is constructed. By comparing authoritative doctrines and concrete experiences,[92] the central element is to be entrusted to a thorough cognitive activity of the territory where the ES to be remunerated operates. To clearly define an

[88]Pettanella and Bottaro (2019), pp. 51–52. For a study of the legal experiments of PES in agriculture identifiable in regional RDPs, see De Nuccio (2020), p. 111. "In particular, the agro-climatic-environmental payments provided for in Art. 28 of EU Regulation No. 1305/2013 and measure 10 contained in the 2014/2020 rural development programming are defined as payments made annually to compensate, in whole or in part, for additional costs and income foregone resulting from agro-climate-environmental commitments."

[89]Lalli A., 57, *cit.* The author refers to Art. 36 of Bill No. 119-1004-1034-1931-2012-B on protected areas.

[90]Ibid., p. 58 ff.

[91]Masiero et al. (2017), p. 12 ff.

[92]Cima S. et al., 29 ff., *cit.* Among the various experiences carried out in our territory, we cite that of the ECOPAY2020 project implemented by the Upper Garda Park, which made it possible to start thinking about the development and application of a PES Pesca 4.0. The project, which saw the involvement of various subjects (the Park's Mountain Community, Enel spa, the Unione Pescatori Bresciani, etc.), demonstrated how collaboration and in-depth knowledge of the area are determining factors for the success of similar projects. We would also like to mention here the LIFE+ Making Good Natura Project (2012-2016) that detailed 33 PES schemes in 19 Natura 2000 network sites in seven regions of Italy, the reports of which are available at: http://www.lifemgn-serviziecosistemici.eu/IT/docu/Pages/default.aspx.html.

ecosystem service or a contribution of nature, it is necessary to know the territory of reference, to collect an impressive amount of data on the environmental resources that exist there. Concomitantly, the local dimension and the involvement of local communities are indispensable from a cultural point of view, but also for the legal-economic purpose underlying PES systems.[93] The dissemination of this toolbox also passes through the simplification of complex (natural) processes; if it is assumed that the main beneficiary is Natural Capital, there must also be a beneficial implication for mankind, for the community where the valorization policies are insisted upon, producing benefits both of a value-naturalistic and economic nature.[94]

5 Conclusions

This chapter has attempted to outline the design framework of PES schemes, from structural to governance profiles, passing through the elements that go to make such remuneration systems efficient. As can be researched in the scientific literature, there is no shortage of projects and successful experiences of PES schemes,[95] however, what appears, in the opinion of the writer, to be that these are often 'pilot' projects, difficult to frame in a single organic strategy and highly dependent, in terms of efficiency, on the specific context. In 2016, Robert Brouwer stated that "Despite the global increase in PES schemes, the factors that contribute to the functioning of PES are still poorly understood."[96] To date, some progress can be recorded. First, more weight is given to local communities and indigenous knowledge of the territory. As has been pointed out in doctrine, the balancing of ecological processes and human choices requires a *bottom-up* approach, local territories being the valuable location of ecosystem services and resources. The involvement and responsible participation of the different actors that make up the governance of PES schemes on this profile is rather similar to what happens for instance in river contracts.[97] Second, in recent years there has been an increase in significant economic incentives aimed at the

[93] Diaz S. et al., *cit.*, p. 272. "Providing space for context-specific perspectives recognises that there are multiple ways of understanding and categorising relationships between people and nature and avoids leaving these perspectives out of the picture or forcing them into the 18 generalising NCP categories. The NCP approach thus facilitates respectful cooperation across knowledge systems in the co-construction of knowledge for sustainability."

[94] Brouwer (2016), pp. 549–552.

[95] For a review of the main PES-schemes in the world and in our context, see Lliso et al. (2022), pp. 312–329; Sheng and Han (2022), p. 191; Cafagno M., 868–871, *cit.*; Bosso and Moonen (2017), pp. 67–70; Carrer (2020), pp. 142–144.

[96] Brouwer R., 552, *cit.* "In practice, PES schemes are developed and implemented in a wide variety of shapes and forms, often based on more than a single ecosystem objective. Both the ecological and socio-economic impacts of PES will be directly linked to the institutional design of the schemes. More research is needed in this area."

[97] *Infra*, paragraph no. 2.

conservation and enhancement of biodiversity (e.g., RRF scheme, PNRR,[98] CAP[99]). On this point, in addition to the enactment of the *Biodiversity Strategy for 2030*, the first *Nature Restoration Law*[100] was amended and published on 12 July 2023, which provides for the restoration of 20% of degraded ecosystems by 2030, with the long-term goal of eliminating degraded natural systems before 2050.[101] Given the historicity of such a measure, the interpreter has only to wait for the implementation of reinforcement measures for PES remuneration systems, also in urban contexts, following the example of "green infrastructure."[102] Net of these considerations, it is possible to affirm that the road to success for measures falling within the scope of PES-schemes is still uphill; this, probably because their implementation passes, inevitably, through the awareness, which must mature in potential purchasers, of recognizing the value of the ecosystem service. This awareness, juridical-institutional-social, must reflect its costs, direct and indirect, followed by an adequate quantification of its monetary value, together with conformative processes that highlight the difference between good and service and the frequent incompatibility between use of the good and ecological functionality in support of a targeted management of ES.[103]

[98] In Italy's Resilience Plan, the National Centre for Biodiversity is established in implementation of Mission 4—Component 2—Investment 1.4. to conduct research and promote the development of solutions to monitor, preserve and restore functional biodiversity to counteract anthropogenic impacts, the effects of climate change and to support ecosystem services. The Centre identifies three priority areas for study: The Biodiversity of the Sea; The Biodiversity of Mediterranean Terrestrial Ecosystems; Urban Biodiversity for Wellbeing. See Natural Capital Committee (2022), 34, *Quinto Rapporto sullo stato del Capitale Naturale in Italia*, Rome.

[99] The EU's Common Agricultural Policy (CAP) is a partnership between agriculture and society, and between Europe and its farmers. The CAP 2023-27 entered into force on 1 January 2023. Support for farmers and rural stakeholders across the 27 EU countries is based on the CAP 2023-27 legal framework and the choices detailed in the CAP Strategic Plans, finally approved by the Commission in June 2022.

[100] COM(2022) 304 final, Proposal for a Regulation of the European Parliament and of the Council on the restoration of nature, adopted on 12 July 2023 - P9_TA(2023)0277.

[101] Art. 3, para 3, Nature Restoration Law, "restoration means the process of actively or passively assisting the recovery of an ecosystem in order to improve its structure and functions with the aim of conserving or enhancing biodiversity and ecosystem resilience."

[102] Ibid., considering (43). "Urban ecosystems represent around 22% of the land surface of the Union. (…) As the other ecosystems addressed in this Regulation, urban ecosystems provide important habitats for biodiversity, in particular plants, birds and insects, including pollinators. They also provide many other vital ecosystem services, including natural disaster risk reduction and control (e.g., floods, heat island effects), cooling, recreation, water and air filtration, as well as climate change mitigation and adaptation."

[103] See Santolini et al. (2015), pp. 41–55.

References

Baggethun EG et al (2010) The history of ecosystem services in economic theory and practice: From early notions to markets and payment schemes. Ecol Econ 69(6)

Balvanera P et al (2016) The links between biodiversity and ecosystem services. In: Potschin M, Haines-Young R, Fish R, Turner RK (eds) Routledge handbook of ecosystem services. Routledge Taylor and Francis Group, p 56

Bosso A, Moonen AC (2017) Servizi ecosistemici, le relative forme di remunerazione (PES) e la valutazione non monetaria. Atti di Convegno, La sostenibilità in agricoltura. Una opportunità per i sistemi agricoli e per l'agroalimentare "made in Italy"

Braat LC (2014) The value of the ecosystem services concept in economic and biodiversity policy, chapter 10. In: Jacobs S, Dendoncker N, Keune H (eds) Ecosystem services. Global issues, local practises. Elsevier

Braat LC (2018) Five reasons why the Science publication "Assessing nature's contributions to people" (Diaz et al. 2018) would not have been accepted in Ecosystem Services. Ecosyst Serv 30, Part A

Brouwer R (2016) Payments for ecosystem services. In: Potschin M, Haines-Young R, Fish R, Kerry Turner R (eds) Routledge handbook of ecosystem services, 1st edn. Routledge, pp 549–552

Cafagno M (2021) L'ambiente nei contratti pubblici: due angoli visuali e una morale, Diritto e processo amministrativo, no. 4

Caravita B (2005) Diritto dell'ambiente (Environmental Law), 3rd edn. Il Mulino

Cardinale B, Duffy J, Gonzalez A et al (2012) Biodiversity loss and its impact on humanity. Nature 486:59–67

Carrer M (2020) Servizi ecosistemici. Note per una critica costituzionale. Quaderni amministrativi, no. 3

Chiariello AM (2022) La funzione amministrativa di tutela della biodiversità nella prospettiva dello sviluppo sostenibile (The administrative function of biodiversity protection in the perspective of sustainable development). Editoriale Scientifica

Chiti E (2022) Oltre la disciplina dei mercati: la sostenibilità degli ecosistemi e la sua rilevanza nel Green Deal europeo. Rivista della Regolazione dei mercati 2

Cecchetti M (2012) Contributo alla Tavola rotonda (Roundtable contribution). In: Grassi S (ed) Problemi di diritto costituzionale dell'ambiente (Issues in constitutional environmental law). Giuffrè, Milan, p 354

Cima S, Cau M, Maino G (eds) (2022) Il valore della natura. Esperienze dalle comunità di pratica del bando Capitala Naturale. Quaderni dell'Osservsatorio, no. 41

Costanza R, d'Arge R, de Groot R, Farber S, Grasso M, Hannon B, Limburg K, Naeem S, O'Neill RV, Paruelo J, Raskin RG, Sutton P, van den Belt M (1997) The value of the world's ecosystem services and natural capital. Nature 387:253–260

Costanza R, de Groot R, Braat L, Kubiszewski I, Fioramonti L, Sutton P, Farber S, Grasso M (2017) Twenty years of ecosystem services: how far have we come and how far do we still need to go? Ecosyst Serv 28, Part A:1–16

Daily DC (1997) Nature's services: societal dependence on natural ecosystems. Island Press

De Nuccio A (2020) L'incentivazione economica dei servizi agro-ecosistemici per un nuovo modello di sviluppo nell'ambiente rurale. RQDA 2

Diaz S et al (2018) Assessing nature's contributions to people. Science 359(6373)

Elton CS (1958) The ecology of invasions by animals and plants. Methuen and Co., London

Engel S, Pagiola S, Wunder S (2008) Designing payments for environmental services in theory and practice: an overview of the issues. Ecol Econ 65(4)

Falk A, Szech N (2013) Morals and markets. Science 340

Garver G (2013) The rule of ecological law: the legal complement to degrowth economics. Sustainability 5(1):316–337

Grassi S (2012) Problemi di diritto costituzionale dell'ambiente (Issues in constitutional environmental law). Giuffrè, Milan
IPBES (2017) Report of the Plenary of the Intergovernmental Science-Policy Platform on Biodiversity and Ecosystem Services on the work of its fifth session, Bonn, -Germany, 7-10 March
IPBES (2019a) Global assessment report of the intergovernmental science-policy platform on biodiversity and ecosystem services
IPBES (2019b) Summary for policymakers of the global assessment report on biodiversity and ecosystem services of the intergovernmental Science-Policy Platform on Biodiversity and Ecosystem Services, p. 10
IPBES (2022) Methodological Assessment Report on the Diverse Values and Valuation of Nature of the Intergovernmental Science-Policy Platform on Biodiversity and Ecosystem Services, p. 8
Kerry Turner R, Georgiou S, Fisher B (2008) Valuing ecosystem services. The case of multi-functional Wetlands. Earthscan, London
Lalli A (2017) *I servizi ecosistemici e il capitale naturale: una prospettiva giuridico-istituzionale*. Studi parlamentari e di politica costituzionale, Anno 50:195–196
Lazzari S (2021) The Green transition in the national recovery and resilience plan. Italia Domani, Rivista Quadrimestrale di Diritto dell'Ambiente, 1
Lliso B et al. (2022) Motivational crowding effects in payments for ecosystem services: exploring the role of instrumental and relational values. People Nat 4(2):312–329
Loreau M, Naeem S, Inchausti P (2002) Biodiversity and ecosystem functioning: synthesis and perspectives. Oxford University Press
Lubchenco J (1998) Entering the century of the environment: a new social contract for science. Science 279(5350):491–497
MacArthur RH (1955) Fluctuations of animal populations and a measure of community stability. Ecology 36:533–536
Mace GM, Norris K, Fitter AH (2012) Biodiversity and ecosystem services: a multilayered relationship. Trends Ecol Evolut 27(1)
Masiero M, Leonardi A, Polato R, Amato G (eds) (2017) Pagamenti per servizi ecosistemici. Guida tecnica per la definizione di meccanismi innovativi per la valorizzazione dei servizi idrici e il miglioramento della governance ambientale. Etifor Srl and University of Padua
May RM (2011) Why should we be concerned about loss of biodiversity. Comptes Rendus Biologies 334
Monteduro M (2014) Per una "nuova alleanza" tra diritto ed ecologia: attraverso e oltre le "aree naturali protette" (For a "new alliance" between law and ecology: through and beyond "protected natural areas)," GiustAmm.it, fasc. 6
Morbidelli G. (1996) Il regime amministrativo speciale dell'ambiente (The special administrative regime of the environment). In: Scritti in onore di Alberto Predieri (Writings in honor of Alberto Predieri). Giuffrè, Milan, p. 1163
Odum EP (1953) Fundamentals of ecology. Saunders, Philadelphia
Pagiola S, Arcenas A, Platis G (2005) Can payments for environmental services help reduce poverty? An exploration of the issues and the evidence to date from Latin America. World Dev 33(2)
Paletto A, De Meo I, Morelli S (2020) Sistemi di Pagamento per i Servizi Ecosistemici (PES) analisi della letteratura nazionale e internazionale. L'Italia Forestale e Montana 75(6)
Peterson GD et al (2018) Welcoming different persepctives in IPBES: "Nature's contributions to people" and "Ecosystem services,". Ecol Soc 23(1)
Pettanella D, Bottaro G (2019) Pagamenti per i servizi ecosistemici. I contributi della Gestione Forestale Sostenibile
Pettenella D, Secco L (2016) Strumenti finanziari per l'ambiente: quali rischi? Aggiornamenti Sociali 4/67
Plinio D (1994) Public environmental law and protected natural areas. Il dualismo giuridico dell'ambiente fra tutela comparativa e protezione integrale (The legal dualism of the environment between comparative protection and integral protection). Utet

Potschin M, Haines-Young R (2017) From nature to society. Linking people and nature: Socio-ecological systems. In: Burkhard B, Maes J (eds) Mapping ecosystem services. Pensoft, Bulgaria
Potschin M, Haines-Young R, Fish R, Turner RK (2016) Routledge handbook of ecosystem services. Routledge Taylor and Francis Group
Rockstrom J, Steffen W, Foley JA (2009) A safe operating space for Humanity. Nature 461
Salzman J (2005) Creating markets for ecosystem services: notes from the field. New York Univ Law Rev 80
Sanchirico J, Siikimaki JV (2007) Natural resource economics and policy in the 20th century conservation of ecosystem services. Resources 165:8–10
Sandel M (2012) What money can't buy: the moral limits of markets. Farrar Straus & Giroux
Santolini R, Morri E (2010) Ecosystem services, an old approach for a new vision of environmental goods. Ecoscienza 3
Santolini R, Morri E, Scolozzi R (2012) Sustainable and resilient territories: the ecosystem services perspective. Territory 60
Santolini R, Morri E, Scolozzi R (2015) Mettere in gioco i servizi ecosistemici: limiti e opportunità di nuovi scenari sociali ed economici. Ri-Vista ricerche per la progettazione del paesaggio 9(1–2)
Schulze ED, Mooney HA (2012) Biodiversity and ecosystem function. Springer
Sheng J, Han X (2022) Practicing policy mobility of payments for ecosystem services through assemblage and performativity: lessons from China's Xin'an River Basin Eco-compensation Pilot. Ecol Econ 191
Steffen W et al (2015) Planetary boundaries: guiding human development on a changing planet. Science 347(6223)
Tallacchini M (2012) Scienza e diritto. Prospettive di co-produzione. (Science and Law. Prospects of co-production). Rivista di filosofia del diritto, Fasc. 2
Tilman D (1997) Biodiversity and ecosystem functioning. In: Nature's services. Societal dependence on natural ecosystems. Island Press
World Economic Forum (2023) The Global Risks Report 2023, 18th Edition, Insight Report
Wunder S (2005) Payments for environmental services: Some nuts and bolts. CIFOR Occasional Paper No. 42
Wunder S (2015) Revisiting the concept of payments for environmental services. Ecol Econ 117
Zanini S (2019) La tutela dell'ecosistema, tra scienza e diritto (Ecosystem protection, between science and law). Rivista AIC (Associazione Italiana Costituzionalisti), no. 3
Zisenis M (2009) To what extent is the interdisciplinary evaluation approach of the CBD reflected in European and international biodiversity-related regulations? Biodiver Conserv 18

Sustainable Development and Biodiversity: Hype or Hope?

Pierluigi Montalbano and Carlo Palleschi

Abstract The notion of sustainable development implies, by construction, a deep engagement with Nature: what we take from it, how we transform it and return to it, and what we will leave of it to the next generations. An essential component of Nature is biodiversity, which increases Nature's productivity and resilience to shocks, and thereby reduces risks to the ecosystem services on which we rely for our sustainable development. Biodiversity is being lost worldwide at unprecedented rates, jeopardizing the contribution that natural capital can give to economic growth and livelihoods. From an economic standpoint, this is a pivotal issue which requires a deep reflection on how to address biodiversity for achieving sustainable development. Can economies grow indefinitely by accumulating produced and human capital at the expense of biodiversity, or there are boundaries posed by Nature? The answer to this critical question depends to a great extent upon the substitutability assumed between different categories of capital, as well as on how humans—and thus economies—are conceived in relation with Nature. Framing biodiversity within this theoretical framework and in relation with natural capital as an enabling asset means acknowledging the contribution of biodiversity to sustainable development as well as its role in influencing the value of assets in the core accounts. Overall, a path towards a more sustainable future requires a forward-looking approach, which involves anticipating the nature and consequences of major socioeconomic changes, both before and as they unfold, and adopting a proactive planning guided by such analysis. To this end, a throughout analysis of four key megatrends (demographic changes, urbanization, climate change, and technological change) is proposed in the final section of this work for the benefit of policymaking.

P. Montalbano (✉) · C. Palleschi
Department of Social Sciences and Economics, Sapienza University of Rome, Rome, Italy
e-mail: pierluigi.montalbano@uniroma1.it; carlo.palleschi@uniroma1.it

G. Antonelli et al. (eds.), *Biodiversity Laws, Policies and Science in Europe, the United States and China*, https://doi.org/10.1007/978-3-031-56218-1_5

1 Introduction

From an economic perspective, biodiversity can be defined as an enabling asset that supports the efficient functioning of natural capital and influences its resilience and ability to deliver goods and services to business and society. Put simply, greater biodiversity generally results into a higher quantity, quality, and resilience of ecosystem and the services they provide; with lower degree of biodiverse, natural systems can still yield ecosystem goods and services but they are generally fewer, of lower quality, and more vulnerable to shocks. Healthy and diverse ecosystems are better equipped to withstand environmental disturbances such as climate change, extreme weather events, and natural disasters. In other words, biodiversity could be seen as an indicator of the condition and the resilience of natural capital (CC and CCI 2020). Drawing an analogy with human society, we could say that biodiversity in an ecosystem resembles the diversity of human talents in economics. From a financial perspective, just as diversity within a portfolio of financial assets reduces risk and uncertainty, so biodiversity increases Nature's resilience to shocks, and thereby reduces risks to the ecosystem services on which we rely.

Biodiversity is key for economies in severable tangible ways. Biodiverse ecosystems provide a wide range of essential services that directly support economic activities. For instance, forests offer timber and non-timber forest products, wetlands contribute to water purification and flood control, and coral reefs sustain fisheries and tourism. These ecological services hold particular significance especially for the poorest and most vulnerable, who are typically the most dependent on natural capital for their livelihoods. A vital sector which heavily depends on biodiversity is agriculture, as it relies on diverse ecosystems, species, and genetic resources for crop improvement, pollination services, pest control, and soil fertility. Furthermore, biodiversity-rich support nature-based tourism, generating economic benefits for local communities.

Biodiversity is being lost worldwide at unprecedented rates, jeopardizing the contribution that natural capital can give to economic growth and livelihoods. In recent decades, humanity has been degrading biodiversity at rates far greater than ever before, getting to the point where the demands we make of natural goods and services far exceed the ability to meet them on a sustainable basis (Dasgupta 2021; World Bank 2021a). Land and sea-use change has been identified as the most important direct anthropogenic driver, followed by direct exploitation, climate change, pollution, and invasive non-native species (Ichii et al. 2019). This period in which we live has been defined by some scientists as the "Anthropocene," referring to the current geological age in which human activity has become the dominant influence on the biosphere (Crutzen and Stoermer 2000). As biodiversity loss increases, ecosystem productivity declines at an accelerated rate, leading to abrupt, irreversible change in the ecosystem state. Already, 14 of the 18 assessed categories of ecosystem services have declined since 1970 (IPBES 2019). This means, among others, smaller fish catches, pollinator decline, poorer freshwater quality, and reduced ability of nature to control pathogens and protect economic assets from extreme weather. The most problematic aspect in this regard lies in the fact that ecosystem dynamics are nonlinear and characterized by uncertain degradation thresholds and "tipping points," which are not yet well comprehended. This inherent lack of understanding makes predicting such events particularly difficult, especially when considering vast spatial scales (Lenton 2013).

Against this backdrop, it is crucial to recognize and integrate the value of biodiversity into development models and decision-making processes, as an essential element of natural capital. Now, more than ever, it is of utmost importance to emphasize this significance, particularly considering that the unfolding biodiversity crisis continues to be partially neglected in the development agenda, in part, to data gaps and a limited understanding of the interconnected impacts between nature loss and the global economy. With this purpose in mind, this chapter investigates the contribution of biodiversity to the economies and well-being, as well as the limitations of gross domestic product (GDP) in accounting for the detrimental impact of human activities on the biosphere. Afterwards, it looks at biodiversity and the correlated notion of natural capital in economic development, discussing main implications of main economic models with a special focus on the concept of embeddedness. Finally, advocating for mainstreaming foresight analysis and scenario planning into economic development studies, this chapter focuses on four key megatrends that have the potential to drive biodiversity change: demographic changes, urbanization, climate change and technological change. Proposing this approach, which lies at the crossover between development and foresight analysis, this work seeks to deepen the understanding of how different socioeconomic trends interact and affect biodiversity outcomes under the range of possible futures within the context of an embedded economy.

2 Underestimating What Is Invisible to the Eye

Mainstreaming biodiversity into global development agenda implies acknowledging the essential function and contribution of biodiversity to increasing ecosystem productivity and resilience of natural capital (Kinzig et al. 2002). Functional biodiversity is directly related to the provision of ecosystem services through several channels (Balvanera et al. 2006; Diaz et al. 2007; Isbell et al. 2015). High functional biodiversity, which means a wide range of functional traits and species with different ecological roles, enhances the resilience and stability of ecosystems, ensuring that ecosystems can withstand disturbances and maintain their functioning over time (Naeem and Li 1997; Mace et al. 2012). In turn, this stability provides a more reliable supply of ecosystem services, which can have economic implications for industries relying on those services (Tilman et al. 1998; Gamfeldt et al. 2008). Additionally, functional similarity, where multiple species perform similar ecological functions, provides backup mechanisms for maintaining ecosystem services (Eisenhauer et al. 2023). If one species or functional group is lost or declines, other species with similar traits can compensate, ensuring the continuity of ecosystem services and minimizing potential economic losses.

Increased productivity induced by greater functional biodiversity can benefit sectors like agriculture and forestry by supporting higher crop yields, timber production, and overall land productivity. Functional diversity, particularly of pollinators and natural enemies of pests, plays a crucial role in agricultural systems, leading to improved crop yields and quality (Garibaldi et al. 2013; Klein et al. 2007). Similarly, diverse predator and parasitoid communities help regulate pest populations, reducing the need for synthetic pesticides. These aspects contribute to economic benefits and sustainable agricultural practices. Functional biodiversity also contributes to ecotourism and cultural services, generating economic value through recreational activities, nature-based tourism, and cultural heritage preservation. Diverse and intact ecosystems with rich functional biodiversity attract visitors, create employment opportunities, and support local economies.

Although essential for natural capital and thus for economic development, biodiversity is invisible to the human eye. The invisibility of biodiversity has led to a large underestimation of its value: when something is not easily observable, it becomes challenging to assign a monetary price to it (TEBB 2010). This is what happen with economic systems and metrics used to measure progress, which fail to account for the economic contribution of biodiversity, leading to its underrepresentation in wealth measurements. For instance, GDP, the most common economic indicator, says nothing about a country's natural capital or biodiversity (OECD 2021). GDP could show double-digit growth without indicating whether natural assets have been depleting or whether biodiversity has been degraded. The difficulty in bringing to the surface the fundamental role of Nature has led to unsustainable practices and undervaluation of biodiversity. In the "Anthropocene," economic growth has often come at the detriment of Nature, consequently compromising future prosperity.

To assess the sustainability of growth, *all* the assets that generate income and ultimately well-being should be considered. This means looking not only at the produced and human capital, but also at the natural capital and at the variety within living parts of the natural stock, namely biodiversity. The World Bank has provided a valuable contribution through "The Changing Wealth of Nations" (CWON) (World Bank 2021b) to measure wealth in a more comprehensive approach. CWON estimates wealth data for 146 countries from 1995 to 2018 using five asset classes: produced capital and urban land, non-renewable natural capital, renewable natural capital, human capital, and net foreign assets. Overall, the CWON shows that degrading the value of renewable natural capital has been associated with lower or declining total wealth per capita. For example, in Benin and Madagascar, although human capital increased by 20% from 1995 to 2018, per capita wealth declined or was stagnant over the same period, since renewable natural capital declined by more than 30%. At the same time, it has been shown that protecting and enhancing the value of renewable natural capital is associated with better economic performance overall. So, looking at the wealth through the CWON would avoid the risk of neglecting natural capital in favor of growth, something that would likely exacerbate the negative long-term consequences of short-term gains. Nevertheless, although providing a great contribution to move beyond GDP and while accepting Dasgupta's (2021) definition of biodiversity as an enabling asset, the CWON does not include biodiversity in the wealth measurement, leaving room to further expand natural capital accounting to integrate biodiversity considerations into measures of national performance and policy appraisal.

3 Beyond or Within? An Economic Perspective on Biodiversity

Biodiversity loss, alongside other drivers, is found to be depreciating natural capital (Dasgupta 2021), hindering poverty reduction and sustainable development objectives. Like other forms of capital, natural capital can depreciate over time,[1] and this happens when natural resources are consumed or depleted at a rate faster than they can be naturally replenished or regenerated. Rapid accumulation of physical and human capital, but at the expense of excessive depletion and degradation of natural capital, is far from be sustainable, as it compromises the ability of future generations to meet their own needs (WCED 1987). This is indeed what has been happening. Considering 140 countries between 1992 and 2014, Managi and Kumar (2018) showed that globally produced capital per head doubled and human capital per head increased by about 13%, while the value of the stock of natural capital per head declined by nearly 40%.

From an economic standpoint, this is a pivotal issue which requires a deep reflection on how to address biodiversity for achieving sustainable development. This debate revolves around two interlinked questions: does natural capital depletion jeopardize the future of next generations, or it is possible to compensate them for this loss? Can economies grow indefinitely by accumulating produced and human capital at the expense of biodiversity, or there are boundaries posed by Nature? The answer to these critical questions depends to a great extent upon the substitutability assumed between different categories of capital, as well as on how humans—and thus economies—are conceived in relation with Nature. Framing biodiversity within this theoretical framework and in relation with natural capital as an enabling asset means acknowledging the contribution of biodiversity to sustainable development as well as its role in influencing the value of assets in the core accounts.

In economic thinking, the balance between economic development and environmental concerns has not always resulted in the prioritization of the preservation of natural capital. This is the case of the so-called weak sustainability (Hartwick 1977; Solow 1974), which suggests that depreciated natural capital can be substituted by human-made capital, based on the assumption of limitless substitutability between

[1] Natural capital can either appreciate or depreciate. Since the focus here is mainly on natural depletion, we refer just to the depreciation aspect.

different asset classes. In concrete terms, this means, for instance, that although lands or forests can be converted for agriculture or for built infrastructure as urban areas expand, the economic model is still sustainable, since the decline in one form of capital (natural capital) is offset by gains in others. The consequence of this approach is that, as far as the rents from natural resource depletion are invested in building capital in the rest of the economy, natural capital can be exploited to generate economic output. As a result, aggregate wealth is non-declining even if natural capital is being depleted (Pearce and Barbier 2000; Heal 2000; Arrow et al. 2012). Conversion of land to agriculture, industry, infrastructure, or residential uses implies that the value of the discounted stream of services of converted areas dominates the value of services in the unconverted state (Pezzey and Toman 2002). This approach has clear policy implications, as it can be used to justify natural capital depletion in favor of greater output performances.

When it comes to biodiversity, the concept of weak sustainability can be seen as problematic or limited in its application. It does not reflect the fact that the removal or significant decline of certain species or key components of biodiversity can disrupt ecosystem functioning, leading to negative impacts on ecosystem services and overall ecosystem health, as each species and ecosystem plays unique roles and provides irreplaceable services. Furthermore, weak sustainability may not adequately account for tipping points and ecological thresholds and the potential irreversibility of biodiversity loss (Rockström et al. 2009). These caveats are crucial to be considered also when biodiversity offsets mechanisms are designed, whose main goal is to achieve at least no-net loss in comparison to the baseline situation before the original project is implemented (World Bank 2016). For the reasons stated above, the effectiveness and ecological integrity of biodiversity offsets, as well as their alignment with sustainability principles, are topics of debate and contingent on the design, implementation, and monitoring of offset program.

In contrast to weak sustainability, a more comprehensive and holistic approach has been developed, to account for the unique role of Nature. This is the case of strong sustainability, which goes beyond the notion of substitutability among different forms of capital arguing for the preservation of natural capital—and thus by extension biodiversity—as non-substitutable assets (Neumayer 2003; Dobson 2007). It emphasizes that certain aspects of natural capital, such as ecosystem integrity and biodiversity, are irreplaceable and should be safeguarded for their inherent value. In other words, the elasticity of substitution between produced and natural capital is low—or even equal to zero— making impossible to maintain economic production while depleting natural capital stock and degrading biodiversity. This framework raises the issue of an intrinsic trade-off between biodiversity and economic growth: modern agriculture has enabled us to produce food at rates per hectare unthinkable in the past, but at the expense of biodiversity; croplands are productive, but in mono-crops and without housing crop genetic diversity, let alone diversity of species and ecosystems; land given over to ranching and animal grazing is productive, but mainly in terms of sheep and cattle; plantations of oil palm and soya are also productive, but poor in biodiversity. This theoretical approach emphasizes the need to protect and restore biodiversity for the long-term benefit of both humans and the planet.

The analysis of Nature and its interaction with capital asset management has been addressed by mainstream resource and environmental economics through an approach which is substantially framed within the weak sustainability paradigm. The main argument is that the limits of Nature are irrelevant for economic growth, the biophysical boundaries can be pushed forward by technological progress (Young 1991; Burness et al. 1980), and ecosystem have heterogenous characteristics which provide flexibility for substitution between different types of resources (Solow 1997). This approach is built on the conception of an economy operating outside the environment. An emblematic example of this "outside" approach is pollution, which has been traditionally seen as a mere "externality." To address this issue, solutions have been devised only to internalize the external costs of pollution, by taxing the activity responsible for this negative externality. This is the reasoning behind the well-known Pigouvian tax, which is set at a level that reflects the social cost of the activity, with the aim of incentivizing individuals or businesses to reduce their harmful behavior and adopt cleaner and more efficient alternatives (Pigou 1920). This theoretical framework is reflected in the methodological approach, which is mainly about extending the tools and principles of neoclassical economics to analyze environmental issues (Proops andSafonov 2004; Venkatachalam 2007), and especially to understand how marketed goods are combined within non-market environmental goods (Becker 1965; Domencich and McFadden 1975).

This perspective has been challenged by ecological economics, which gradually gained ground since the 1970s and 1980s advocating for the inherent integration between ecological and economic systems, while acknowledging the interdependencies and feedback loops between them. Unlike resource and environmental economics, economic system is not presented by ecological economics as separate from the environment, but as a sub-system of global ecosystem (Gowdy and O'Hara 1997; Sollner 1997). Recognizing that biodiversity and functioning ecosystems are essential for sustaining human societies and economic activities, ecological economists have advocated for the incorporation of ecological principles and the consideration of ecological limits in decision-making processes to ensure long-term sustainability. In summary, Nature should be therefore protected for its intrinsic value, and not just because instrumental for the welfare of individuals (Daly and Townsend 1993).

Building on a framework familiar with ecological economics, Dasgupta (2021) further expands the concept of strong sustainability, proposing the model of an economy embedded in the environment, and not simply in relation to it. The concept of the embeddedness recognizes that economic systems are embedded within, and dependent upon, the Earth's ecosystems and natural resources. Dasgupta formalizes the embeddedness in the so-called "impact inequality" equation (Eq. 1), which shows the evolution over time of the stock of the biosphere ($\frac{dS}{dt}$ where S is the biosphere stock) as the result of the comparison between the biosphere's regeneration rate (G), which is function of the real accounting value of the stock of the biosphere, and the aggregate demand on the biosphere. This latter is decomposed in two parts: what we extract or harvest from the biosphere *($X = Ny/\alpha_x$)* and the demand we make of the biosphere as a pollution sink *($Z{=}Ny/\alpha_z$)*, where N is global human population, y per capital global GDP, α_x a numerical measure of the efficiency with which the biosphere's goods and services are converted into global GDP, and α_z a numerical measure of the extent to which the biosphere is transformed by global waste products. The X-function records that both production and consumption require the biosphere's goods and services as inputs, while the Z function reflects the fact that waste products, which are inevitably associated with production and consumption, impose a strain on the biosphere. *(X+Z)* is also known as the ecological footprint, which represents the human impact on the biosphere. When humanity's demand exceeds the regeneration rate, the biosphere depreciates, otherwise the biosphere would appreciate. The difference between the biosphere's regeneration rate and our demand has been negative for decades, giving rise to what Dasgupta calls the *impact inequality*. In this regard, it is important to underline that demands have outstripped supply in some ecosystems and geographies but not in others, further affecting the distribution of natural assets.

$$\frac{dS}{dt} = G(S) - \left(\frac{Ny}{\alpha_x} + \frac{Ny}{\alpha_z}\right) \tag{1}$$

The embeddedness in the biosphere, as described in the impact inequality equation above, has clear implications in terms of sustainable development, as it implies that growth is limited within the binding planetary boundaries. From a macroeconomic point of view, this represents a clear departure from mainstream growth theory and neoclassical models by environmental economics, as the embeddedness of economic into Nature places bounds on the extent to which GDP, or wealth, can be imagined to grow (Dasgupta 2021). To be noted that the boundaries imposed by Nature do not perfectly correspond to the well-known limits to growth closely associated with the work of the Club of Rome, which put emphasis on non-renewable resources and their imminent exhaustion (Groom and Turk 2021). The focus provided by Dasgupta (2021) is rather more on the renewable flow of the Net Primary Product (NPP)[2] and the erosion of the stocks (the primary producers and other aspects of natural capital) that underpin NPP.

[2]The NPP is the flow of biomass generated by primary producers (plants, algae, and bacteria), that utilize primary energy sources, such as sunlight, and convert them into chemical energy stored in the form of biomass (Levin 2009). This flow of biomass provides the foundation for higher trophic levels in the ecological hierarchy, including herbivores, carnivores, and decomposers. The flow of NPP into higher ecological structures, such as species and ecosystems, is a crucial component of energy transfer and nutrient cycling. It sustains the diversity and functioning of ecosystems, supporting the growth, reproduction, and survival of organisms at different trophic levels. Using the economic jargon, we could say that NPP is a flow measure (kilograms of biomass per unit of time), like output or income, while primary producers, which ultimately are part of the natural capital, represent the stock from which NPP is generated. Although other more appropriate

4 A Glimpse of the Future: Future Trends on Biodiversity

Embeddedness implies that the underpinning role of biodiversity is strictly intertwined with social and economic systems, which means that the interlink between development and biodiversity has to be assessed in conjunction with mega-trends, namely those large-scale, transformative forces that shape and influence multiple aspects of society, the economy, and the environment. There has been growing awareness that the risks that can permeate economies and societies, and that can turn out to be highly disruptive for Nature, are multiple and diverse. Facing this uncertainty, traditional approaches to risk management consisting of extrapolating historical data and assumptions of normal distributions could be irrelevant for assessing future risks (Bolton et al. 2020). In fact, the status of biodiversity, and thus its contribution as enabling asset to natural capital, depends on multiple various intricate interactions of nonlinear dynamics that are interconnected and influenced by uncertainties. To overcome such constraints of existing and conventional approaches, it would be beneficial to look at major megatrends that have the potential to shape different possible futures in biodiversity. Studying such long-term trends is fundamental to identify critical factors and develop exploratory scenarios that help define the range of potential outcomes for biodiversity conservation and management. In fact, as underlined by the Intergovernmental Science-Policy Platform on Biodiversity and Ecosystem Services (IPBES 2016), "new scenarios of indirect and direct drivers departing from existing global environmental assessment scenarios such as Intergovernmental Panel on Climate Change (IPCC) Shared Socio- economic Pathways (SSPs)/Representative Concentration Pathways (RCPs) and Millennium Ecosystem Assessment (MA) are needed to find a better fit with biodiversity and ecosystem services-specific contexts."

To contribute to this effort, this section provides the analysis of four key megatrends which have, in our opinion, the potential to drive biodiversity and ecosystem changes in the near future: (i) demographic change; (ii) urbanization; (iii) climate change; (iv) technological change. The adoption of the notion of megatrends is instrumental to the attempt to apply concepts of the domain of foresight to economic development studies. This holistic and forward-looking approach has a twofold advantage: on the one hand, a better understanding of how different drivers interact and affect biodiversity outcomes is an essential condition to then move to the design of novel scenarios, as envisaged by the IPBES; on the other hand, the recognition that underlying long-term trends are intimately connected to the functioning and limitations of Nature is a concrete way to account for embeddedness. Each of the four selected megatrends affects the components of the Dasgupta's (2021) inequality equation, determining the impact on the biosphere and thus confirming that future challenges need to be addressed bearing in mind that our

---

measures of functional biodiversity could be used such as species richness or genetic diversity, the NPP, as underlined by Dasgupta (2021), is relevant to capture the contribution of biodiversity to economic growth. In other words, the NPP is the regenerative rate of the stock of natural capital.

economies are embedded within Nature. In what follows, we will go through each of these selected megatrends and clarify how they will actually impact on each component of the Dasgupta's (2021) equation.

4.1 Demographic Change

Demographic change[3] is the most important underlying cause of changing biodiversity (MEA 2005). Growing population enters the inequality equation through *N*, which accounts for the global human population, whose growth indeed affect the demand we make of the biosphere: as population increases, we tend to intensify the extraction of natural resources and rely more heavily on ecosystem services to fulfill our needs for consumption and production (the *X* component of the demand). A growing population requires more resources, such as food, water, energy, and materials, while leading to increased demand for land for housing, agriculture, infrastructure, and resource extraction. This increased demand for resources can lead to overexploitation of natural resources, including forests, fisheries, and wildlife. Unsustainable harvesting or extraction practices can deplete populations of species, disrupt ecosystems, and contribute to biodiversity loss. At the same time, as populations grow, so do the levels of pollution and contamination into ecosystems (the *Z* component of the demand), including air, water, and soil, with adverse effects on biodiversity by contaminating habitats, reducing water quality, harming wildlife, and disrupting ecological processes.

A pivotal pathway through which demographic change affects biodiversity is land conversion. Natural areas, such as forests, wetlands, and grasslands, are converted into agricultural fields or livestock pasture to fulfil growing demands for food, biofuel, and other commodities, and to accommodate expanding markets (Crist et al. 2017; D'Odorico et al. 2018). Consequently, these practices can lead to deforestation, habitat destruction, and amplified water usage for irrigation, all of which have detrimental impacts on biodiversity. This phenomenon accelerated over the last 300 years. Ramankutty et al. (2018) estimated that between 1700 and 2007 croplands expanded from 3 to 15 million km^2 at the expense of forests, whereas pasturelands expanded from 5 to 27 million km^2, mainly replacing grasslands, savannas, and shrublands. Alexandratos and Bruinsma (2012) projected that aggregate agricultural production (of all crop and livestock products) will increase 60% by 2050 compared with a 2005–2007 baseline. Land used for livestock feed also

[3]The latest projections by the United Nations (UNDESA 2022) suggest that the global population could grow to around 8.5 billion in 2030, reach a peak of around 10.4 billion people during the 2080s and then remain at this level until 2100. However, population growth is expected to be uneven. It will stagnate in many advanced economies, whereas the fastest growth will be in the poorest regions, especially in sub-Saharan Africa, where the population will double by 2050. These demographic dynamics are likely to put additional pressure on resources and challenge the achievement of the Sustainable Development Goals (SGDs).

represent a significant driver of land conversion. It has been estimated that approximately 71% of rainforest conversion in South America has been for cattle ranching, and a further 14% for commercial cropping including soya for animal feed (Godfray et al. 2018). To fully harness the potential impact of demographic growth, this latter needs to be explored in combination with increasing standards of living. In recent decades, there has been a significant increase in global consumption, accompanied by a notable geographical separation between production and consumption patterns. This shift has resulted in a situation where commodities are primarily produced in developing tropical countries, which are often rich in biodiversity, to meet the demands of consumers in developed countries. Such unsustainable consumption patterns are exacerbated by the above-mentioned invisibility of Nature, which does not allow for the correct pricing of imported primary goods from distant parts of the world, incentivizing overconsumption (Dasgupta 2021).

An interesting aspect of this analysis refers to the fact that while cropland area is increasing globally in absolute terms, the proportion of land harvested for direct food use crops is actually decreasing and may continue to drop further. Between 1995 and 2010, there was a significant increase in the amount of arable land allocated for the cultivation of biomass used for non-food purposes. While in 1995, the total area of arable land used for this purpose was more than 132 million hectares, in 2010, this figure had risen to over 178 million hectares, indicating a substantial 35% growth within a span of just 15 years (Bruckner et al. 2018). Poore and Nemecek (2018) estimated that non-food agricultural areas account for approximately 13% of overall global agricultural land area. If current trends continue, by 2030, crops harvested for exports, processing, and industry will account respectively for approximately 23%, 17%, and 8% of overall harvested hectares, while crops for direct food use will decrease to approximately 29% of total harvested area (Ray et al. 2022). This would result in the paradoxical situation in which biodiversity conservation is impeded, while substantial progress in ensuring food security remains elusive.

Fostering inclusive economic growth while preserving biodiversity in the context of rapid population growth remains a formidable challenge. The impact of this megatrend on biodiversity is even more worrisome when acknowledged that there is not much that can be done to alter this trend in the near future, since both the size and age structure of the population over the next few decades have been determined by demographic processes that have already taken place in the recent past (UNDESA 2022). This is a key takeaway, which has remarkable implications for biodiversity: while advocating for smaller human populations is still essential to reduce global population at least in the second half of the century (Cafaro et al. 2022), preserving biodiversity in both less developed and more developed countries requires pursuing sustainable economic development models, integrating environmental considerations, encouraging sustainable consumption patterns and investing in human capital development, especially in female empowerment.

4.2 Urbanization

The aggregate demand on the biosphere is impacted not only by the growing aggregate number of global populations, but also by its distribution or, in other words, by population density (Teixidó-Figueras et al. 2016). By looking at the geographical distribution of population, what comes to the fore is the flourishing role played by cities as areas of expanding economic activity and main centers of demand for goods and services. The importance of urbanization as a mega-trend shaping our societies and economies is clear when it looks at projections. By mid-century, roughly two thirds (68%) of the world's population will be living in urban areas: the global urban population is projected to grow by 2.5 billion urban dwellers between 2018 and 2050, reaching 6.68 billion urban dwellers in 2050, with nearly 90% of the increase concentrated in Asia and Africa (UNDESA 2019). Although not directly displayed in the inequality equation, urbanization amplifies both the X and Z components of the aggregate demand.

Expected urban expansion, driven by growing populations and internal migration, threatens habitats in biodiversity hotspots and contributes to carbon emissions associated with tropical deforestation and land use change (Seiler 2001). The expansion of cities, exacerbated by urban sprawl and poor urban planning, has happened mostly replacing diverse and complex habitats with buildings, roads, and infrastructure, leaving little space for native species to thrive. Additionally, as urban areas expand, they create a patchwork of fragmented habitats surrounded urban infrastructure (Haddad et al. 2015; Taubert et al. 2018). This is compounded by the fact cities tend to be preferentially located in places of high endemism such as on coastlines, rivers, and islands (McDonald et al. 2008; Elmqvist et al. 2013). Overall, it is estimated that future urban expansion will lead to 11–33 million hectares of natural habitat loss by 2100 under the SSP scenarios, reducing local within-site species richness by 34% and species abundance by 52% per 1 km grid cell, and 7–9 species may be lost per 10 km cell (Li et al. 2022). According to Seto et al. (2012), considerable loss of habitats will take place in regions that were relatively undisturbed by urban development in 2000: the Eastern Afromontane, the Guinean Forests of West Africa, and the Western Ghats and Sri Lanka hotspots.

Also, the impact of urban expansion on species loss is not evenly distributed (McDonald et al. 2018). The greatest challenge in global biodiversity conservation lies in the least developed countries, mainly in sub-Saharan African countries, which are indeed those that are likely to be most affected by urban expansion (Li et al. 2022). In fact, patterns of urbanization between the more developed regions and the less developed regions present striking differences: while just under half of the population of the less developed regions currently lives in rural areas, the urban population of these regions has been growing and will continue to grow considerably faster than that of the more developed regions (Fig. 1). By 2050, with 5.6 billion urban dwellers, the less developed regions are projected to have 83% of the world's urban population (UNDESA 2019). This is another key takeaway which has strong implications when it comes to unpack the link between sustainable development and

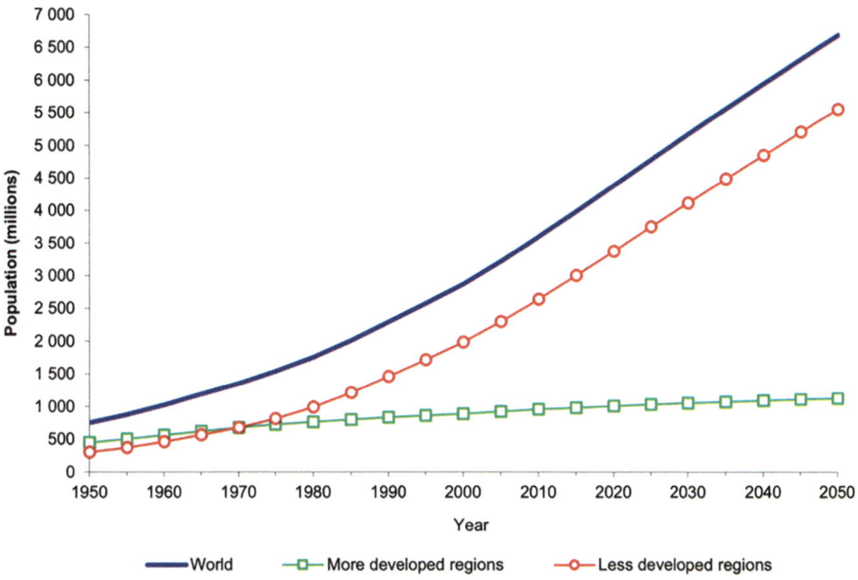

Fig. 1 Estimated and projected urban populations of the world, the more developed regions and the less developed regions, 1950–2050. Source: UNDESA (2019) Copyright © 2019 by United Nations, made available under a Creative Commons license CC BY 3.0 IGO: http://creativecommons.org/licenses/by/3.0/igo/

biodiversity: the impact of urban expansion on biodiversity is expected to be most acute in less developed areas, where it is more difficult to adopt sustainable urban management policies, due to lack of institutional capacity and higher investment gap in biodiversity conservation. Therefore, to mitigate the amplifying impact of urbanization on the aggregate demand for the biosphere, it is vital to keep a strong focus on urbanization in less developed countries, promoting sound urban planning, upscaling targeted investments, and fostering smart and green urban growth, while harnessing the pro-poor benefits of urban agglomerations.

4.3 *Climate Change*

Climate change contributes to the loss of biodiversity. Although land-use remains the main driver of biodiversity decline, climate change, through elevated CO_2, rising temperatures and changing precipitation patterns, is increasingly disrupting terrestrial, marine and coastal ecosystems, altering habitats, and impacting the survival and reproductive patterns of many species (WMO 2022). It can lead to shifts in species distributions, increased extinction risk, and the loss of ecosystem services (Costello et al. 2022). It is estimated that climate change could overtake land-use change as the leading cause of biodiversity loss by 2070 (Newbold 2018). At the same time, biodiversity loss has implications for climate change, as land and ocean ecosystems—and the biodiversity they contain—are natural carbon sinks, providing so-called nature-based solutions to climate change (UNEP and IUCN 2021). These climate-induced ecological changes alter the biosphere's aggregate supply represented by *G(S)* in Eq. (1). Biodiversity can be impacted by climate change not only through these direct ecological effects, but also through indirect effects arising from shifts in human pressures driven by the changing climate. In the light of this, we could consider climate change as a multiplier of the impact of other megatrends, thus not only affecting the supply side of Eq. (1) but also amplifying the underlying dynamics which determine the demand side.

An important channel of this indirect mechanism is the impact of climate change on displacement and increased mobility, which, in turn, have implications for patterns of urbanization and population density, and thus for biodiversity. As environmental conditions deteriorate in rural areas due to climate hazards and worsening climate conditions, farmers and rural communities are often compelled to migrate in search of better living conditions and opportunities (Clement et al. 2021). Being income diversification one of the most effective adaptation practices, this could lead to rapid urbanization of developing contexts, whose expansion could be fueled by the well know Todaro Paradox (Todaro 1976). Additionally, the movement of people and goods associated with increased mobility can introduce non-native species to new areas, disrupting local ecosystems and biodiversity. It is crucial to consider the complex interactions between climate change, displacement, urbanization, and biodiversity loss in order to develop effective strategies for conservation and sustainable development.

Changing climate conditions also give rise to shifts in agricultural practices, such as changes in crop types or land-use intensification, which in turn can lead to habitat loss and fragmentation, affecting both wild species and ecosystem services. This dynamic needs to be framed in conjunction with the need to produce higher yields to accommodate growing population and overconsumption patterns. The alteration of climatic variables is expected to cause changes in the areas suitable for cultivating for various staple and cash crops (Yadav et al. 2010), increasing the anthropogenic pressure on previously uncultivated areas. For instance, developed nations are likely to observe a significant expansion of suitable arable land towards higher altitudes, presenting the potential for increased production if these lands are cultivated (Fischer et al. 2002). Furthermore, the decline in pollination services caused by climate change is anticipated to have a detrimental impact on crop production, leading to a potential rise in the usage of fertilizers and pesticides (Raven and Wagner 2020). While these practices aim to maximize agricultural productivity, they can have negative impacts on biodiversity.

Therefore, mitigating against the worst effects of climate change will have substantial benefits for biodiversity, and avoiding biodiversity loss will have in turn a positive effect on climate change. Within this context, the most critical challenge ahead is to ensure food security in the face of climate change amid increasing demographic pressure and changing consumption patterns, while protecting and restoring biodiversity. Integrating sustainable agricultural approaches, such as agroecology, conservation agriculture, and diversified farming systems, can support food production while promoting biodiversity conservation and ecosystem health.

4.4 Technological Change

Technological progress is a megatrend that holds an immense transformative potential, capable of significantly altering the dynamic between humanity and the natural world. It has long been argued in mainstream economics that technological advancements can increase the efficiency of our utilization of the biosphere, particularly by minimizing the damage to ecosystems resulting from extraction of provisioning services. In fact, technology plays a pivotal role in facilitating the provision of ecosystem services, transforming agriculture and food production systems, and leading to increased productivity and efficiency of soil use. A foresight report produced by the Food and Agriculture Organization (FAO 2022) stressed the potential of cell-based food production technology, as various methodologies are now well characterized and sufficiently matured to initiate production and commercialization of cell-based food products in some parts of the world. Another example of pro-efficiency applied technology is hydroponics, a method of growing plants in a water-based, nutrient-rich solution, without the use of soil. This is a potentially useful tool to overcome some of the challenges of traditional agriculture in the face of freshwater shortages, climate change and soil degradation (FAO 2020). Moreover, hydroponics is instrumental for delivery nutrients in vertical farming that aims to reduce the pressure on traditional agricultural land by using soil-free growth systems in tightly controlled environments. The environmental benefits of reducing inputs and land-use through vertical farming could be substantial (Beacham et al. 2019). At the same time, the successful and safe implementation of these alternative techniques by both household and small or large-scale farmers necessitates the acquisition of specific knowledge and skill development.

Technology has also a huge potential in reducing the impact of waste and pollution from consumption and human activities, enabling more efficient waste management processes, and thus reducing the impact on Nature (Umar et al. 2021; Yu et al. 2021). These include waste-to-energy systems, recycling technologies, and improved landfill management techniques. For example, advancements in recycling technologies allow for better sorting and processing of recyclable materials, reducing the amount of waste (Fletcher et al. 2021; Di Foggia and Beccarello 2021). Another effective approach to mitigate the harmful impact of human activities on ecosystems and biodiversity involves substituting degradable waste for persistent pollutants, which involves using alternative materials or substances, such as biodegradable plastics or green cleaning products, that can break down in the environment through natural processes (Kumar et al. 2021). Another key area where technology can produce disruptive changes is the energy field. Contributing to transitioning away from fossil fuels, technological advancements can still boost the adoption of renewable energy sources such as solar, wind, and hydroelectric power, overcoming bottlenecks and practical and cost-benefit concerns which hamper their large-scale application.

Within the impact inequality, technology raises the efficiency indexes α_x and α_z, thus contributing to reducing the overall impact of the aggregate demand for the biosphere. This means that in theory there would be the chance to make global population (N) or global output per capita (y), or both, grow, provided that α_x and α_z increase correspondingly, producing a neutral impact on natural capital. Such conceptualization has remarkable implications in framing biodiversity concerns in economic growth models, as it seems suggesting that technology can enable humanity reducing their impact on Nature despite growing population and overconsumption patterns. Contemporary growth models (Romer 2011) propose that ongoing scientific and technological progress holds the promise of sustaining a perpetual increase in the global production of final goods and services. The literature discussing the economics of climate change (Stern 2006; Nordhaus 2007; Lomborg 2013) has gone as far as suggesting that by investing in clean energy sources within the coming years, we could potentially experience unlimited and sustained economic growth. Dasgupta (2021) on the contrary, argues that such approach on sustainable development assumes humanity to be external to Nature. He concludes that the global output of goods and services has inherent limitations, making economic growth an inevitably bounded concept. Regardless of these divergences, technological progress keeps playing a crucial role in addressing the question of how sustainable development can be harmonized with biodiversity.

5 Conclusions

Preventing biodiversity loss goes beyond conservation and restoration efforts; it involves achieving green, inclusive, and resilient development. Understanding the interplay between biodiversity and sustainable development is indispensable to determine whether economies can continue to grow indefinitely by prioritizing the accumulation of produced and human capital at the expense of biodiversity, or if there are inherent limits imposed by nature that need to be recognized.

Taking a forward-looking approach, it is important to couple the aforementioned analysis with robust scenarios related to the key drivers and common transmission channels of biodiversity loss. The intrinsic interconnectedness between biodiversity, demographics, urbanization pressures, climate change, and technological advancements should be acknowledged. Urgent actions are required to address these intertwined challenges, which may necessitate structural changes in our production and consumption patterns.

Framing biodiversity within sustainable development models, strategies, and policies is not merely hype; it is neither just a hope; it is an imperative. However, it is crucial that this recognition is translated into concrete action. Acknowledging the embeddedness of our economies and developing new narratives that align economic growth models with biodiversity conservation is a necessary step, but it must be complemented by consistent and effective policymaking.

References

Alexandratos N, Bruinsma J (2012) World agriculture towards 2030/2050: the 2012 revision. ESA Working paper No. 12-03

Arrow K, Dasgupta P, Goulder L, Mumford K, Oleson K (2012) Sustainability and the measurement of wealth. Environ Dev Econ 17(3):317–353

Balvanera P, Pfisterer AB, Buchmann N, He JS, Nakashizuka T, Raffaelli D, Schmid B (2006) Quantifying the evidence for biodiversity effects on ecosystem functioning and services. Ecol Lett 9(10):1146–1156

Beacham AM, Vickers LH, Monaghan JM (2019) Vertical farming: a summary of approaches to growing skywards. J Horticult Sci Biotechnol 94(3):277–283

Becker GS (1965) A theory of allocation of the time. Econ J LXXV:493–517

Bolton PM, Despres LA, Pereira da Silva F, Samama, Svartzman R (2020) The Green Swan: Central Banking and Financial Stability in the Age of Climate Change. Working Paper 5, Bank for International Settlements and Bank of France, Basel, Switzerland

Bruckner M, Giljum S, Fischer G, Tramberend S, Börner J (2018) The global cropland footprint of the non-food bioeconomy

Burness S, Cummings R, Morris G, Paik I (1980) Thermodynamics and economic concepts as related to resource-use policies. Land Econ 56:1–9

Cafaro P, Hansson P, Götmark F (2022) Overpopulation is a major cause of biodiversity loss and smaller human populations are necessary to preserve what is left. Biol Conserv 272:109646

Capitals Coalition (CC) and Cambridge Conservation Initiative (CCI) (2020) Integrating biodiversity into natural capital assessments

Clement V, Rigaud KK, de Sherbinin A, Jones B, Adamo S, Schewe J, Sadiq N, Shabahat E (2021) Groundswell part 2: acting on internal climate migration. World Bank, Washington, DC

Costello MJ, Vale MM, Kiessling W, Maharaj S, Price J, Talukdar GH (2022) Cross-Chapter Paper 1: Biodiversity Hotspots. In: Pörtner H O, Roberts DC, Tignor M, Poloczanska ES, Mintenbeck K, Alegría A, Craig M, Langsdorf S, Löschke S, Möller V, Okem A, Rama B (eds) Climate change 2022: impacts, adaptation and vulnerability. Contribution of Working Group II to the Sixth Assessment Report of the Intergovernmental Panel on Climate Change. Cambridge University Press, Cambridge

Crist E et al (2017) The interaction of human population, food production, and biodiversity protection. Science 356:260–264

Crutzen PJ, Stoermer EF (2000) The "Anthropocene,". Glob Change Newslett 41:17–18

D'Odorico P et al (2018) The global food-energy-water nexus. Rev Geophys 56:456–531

Daly HE, Townsend KN (eds) (1993) Valuing the earth: economics, ecology, ethics. The MIT Press, p 387

Dasgupta P (2021) The economics of biodiversity: the Dasgupta review. HM Treasury, London

Di Foggia G, Beccarello M (2021) Designing waste management systems to meet circular economy goals: the Italian case. Sustain Prod Consump 26:1074–1083

Diaz S, Lavorel S, de Bello F, Quetier F, Grigulis K, Robson TM (2007) Incorporating plant functional diversity effects in ecosystem service assessments. Proc Natl Acad Sci 104(52): 20684–20689

Dobson A (2007) Environmental sustainability: an introduction. Routledge

Domencich T, McFadden DL (1975) Urban travel demand: a behavioral analysis, p. 215

Eisenhauer N, Hines J, Maestre FT et al. (2023) Reconsidering functional redundancy in biodiversity research
Elmqvist T, Fragkias M, Goodness J, Güneralp B, Marcotullio PJ, McDonald RI, Parnell S, Schewenius M, Seto KC, Wilkinson C (2013) Urbanization, biodiversity, and ecosystem services: challenges and opportunities, global assessment, pp. 175–251
Fischer RA, Santiveri F, Vidal IR (2002) Crop rotation, tillage and crop residue management for wheat and maize in the sub-humid tropical highlands I. Wheat and legume performance. Field Crop Res 79:107–122
Fletcher CA, Clair RS, Sharmina M (2021) A framework for assessing the circularity and technological maturity of plastic waste management strategies in hospitals. J Clean Prod 306:127169
Food and Agriculture Organization (FAO) (2020) The State of Food and Agriculture 2020. Overcoming water challenges in agriculture
Food and Agriculture Organization (FAO) (2022) Thinking About the Future of Food Safety – A foresight report
Gamfeldt L, Hillebrand H, Jonsson PR (2008) Multiple functions increase the importance of biodiversity for overall ecosystem functioning. Ecology 89(5):1223–1231
Garibaldi LA, Steffan-Dewenter I, Winfree R, Aizen MA, Bommarco R, Cunningham SA, Kremen C (2013) Wild pollinators enhance fruit set of crops regardless of honey bee abundance. Science 339(6127):1608–1611
Godfray HCJ, Aveyard P, Garnett T, Hall JW, Key TJ, Lorimer J, Pierrehumbert RT, Scarborough P, Springmann M, Jebb SA (2018) Meat consumption, health, and the environment. Science 361(6399)
Gowdy J, O'Hara S (1997) Weak sustainability and viable technologies. Ecol Econ 22:239–247
Groom B, Turk Z (2021) Reflections on the Dasgupta review on the economics of biodiversity. Environ Resour Econ 79:1–23
Haddad NM et al (2015) Habitat fragmentation and its lasting impact on earth's ecosystems. Sci Adv 1:e1500052
Hartwick J (1977) Intergenerational equity and the investing of rents from exhaustible resources. Am Econ Rev 67:972–974
Heal G (2000) Nature and the marketplace: capturing the value of ecosystem services. Island Press
Ichii K, Molnár Z, Obura DO, Purvis A, Willis K (2019) IPBES Global Assessment on Biodiversity and Ecosystem Services – Chapter 2.2 Status and Trends – Nature (draft)
Intergovernmental Science-Policy Platform on Biodiversity and Ecosystem Services (IPBES) (2016) The methodological assessment report on scenarios and models of biodiversity and ecosystem services. In: Ferrier S, Ninan KN, Leadley P, Alkemade R, Acosta LA, Akçakaya HR, Brotons L, Cheung WWL, Christensen V, Harhash KA, Kabubo-Mariara J, Lundquist C, Obersteiner M, Pereira HM, Peterson G, Pichs-Madruga R, Ravindranath N, Rondinini C, Wintle BA (eds) . IPBES Secretariat, Bonn
Intergovernmental Science-Policy Platform on Biodiversity and Ecosystem Services (IPBES) (2019) In: Díaz S, Settele J, Brondízio ES, Ngo HT, Guèze M, Agard J, Arneth A, Balvanera P, Brauman KA, Butchart SHM, Chan KMA, Garibaldi LA, Ichii K, Liu J, Subramanian SM, Midgley GF, Miloslavich P, Molnár Z, Obura D, Pfaff A, Polasky S, Purvis A, Razzaque J, Reyers B, Chowdhury RR, Shin YJ, Visseren-Hamakers IJ, Willis KJ, Zayas CN (eds) Summary for policymakers of the global assessment report on biodiversity and ecosystem services of the intergovernmental science-policy platform on biodiversity and ecosystem services. IPBES Secretariat, Bonn
Isbell F, Craven D, Connolly J, Loreau M, Schmid B, Beierkuhnlein C, Hector A (2015) Biodiversity increases the resistance of ecosystem productivity to climate extremes. Nature 526(7574):574–577
Kinzig AP, Pacala SW, Tilman D (2002) The functional consequences of biodiversity: empirical progress and theoretical extensions. Ecol Lett 5(3):293–301

Klein AM, Vaissière BE, Cane JH, Steffan-Dewenter I, Cunningham SA, Kremen C, Tscharntke T (2007) Importance of pollinators in changing landscapes for world crops. Proc Royal Soc Biol Sci 274(1608):303–313
Kumar R, Verma A, Shome A, Sinha R, Sinha S, Jha PK, Kumar R, Kumar P, Shubham DS et al (2021) Impacts of plastic pollution on ecosystem services, sustainable development goals, and need to focus on circular economy and policy interventions. Sustainability 13(17):9963
Lenton TM (2013) Environmental tipping points. Ann Rev Environ Resour 38:1–29
Levin SA (2009) The Princeton guide to ecology. Princeton University Press
Li G, Fang C, Li Y et al (2022) Global impacts of future urban expansion on terrestrial vertebrate diversity. Nat Commun 13:1628
Lomborg B (2013) How much have global problems cost the world?: A scorecard from 1900 to 2050. Cambridge University Press, Cambridge
Mace GM, Norris K, Fitter AH (2012) Biodiversity and ecosystem services: a multilayered relationship. Trends Ecol Evolut 27(1):19–26
Managi S, Kumar P (2018) Inclusive wealth report 2018: measuring progress towards sustainability. Routledge
McDonald RI, Kareiva P, Forman R (2008) The implications of urban growth for global protected areas and biodiversity conservation. Biol. Conserv. 141:1695–1703
McDonald RI, Güneralp B, Huang CW, Seto KC, You M (2018) Conservation priorities to protect vertebrate endemics from global Urban expansion. Biol. Conserv. 224:290–299
Millennium Ecosystem Assessment (MEA) (2005) Ecosystems and human well-being: synthesis; a report of the millennium ecosystem assessment. Island Press
Naeem S, Li S (1997) Biodiversity enhances ecosystem reliability. Nature 390(6659):507–509
Neumayer E (2003) Weak versus strong sustainability: exploring the limits of two opposing paradigms. Edward Elgar Publishing
Newbold T (2018) Future effects of climate and land-use change on terrestrial vertebrate community diversity under different scenarios. Proc Royal Soc B 285(1881):20180792
Nordhaus WD (2007) A review of the stern review on the economics of climate change. J Econ Liter 45(3):686–702
OECD (2021) Biodiversity, natural capital and the economy: a policy guide for finance, economic and environment ministers, OECD Environment Policy Papers, No. 26
Pearce DW, Barbier EB (2000) Blueprint for a sustainable economy. Earthscan
Pezzey JCV, Toman MA (2002) Progress and problems in the economics of sustainability. international yearbook of environmental and resource economics 2002/2003: A survey of current issues: 165 232
Pigou AC (1920) Economics of welfare. Macmillan Press, London, p 876
Poore J, Nemecek T (2018) Reducing food's environmental impacts through producers and consumers. Science 360(6392):987–992
Proops JLR, Safonov P (eds.) (2004) Modelling in Ecological Economics. Edgar Elgar, Cheltenham, p. 20
Ramankutty N, Mehrabi Z, Waha K, Jarvis L, Kremen C, Herrero M, Rieseberg LH (2018) Trends in global agricultural land use: implications for environmental health and food security. Annu Rev Plant Biol 69:1–27
Raven PH, Wagner D (2020) Agricultural intensification and climate change are rapidly decreasing insect biodiversity. Proc Natl Acad Sci USA 2021 118:e2002548117
Ray DK, Sloat LL, Garcia AS, Davis KF, Ali T, Xie W (2022) Crop harvests for direct food use insufficient to meet the UN's Food Security Goal. Nat Food 3(5):367–374
Rockström J, Steffen W, Noone K, Persson Å, Chapin FS, Lambin E, Lenton TM, Scheffer M, Folke C, Schellnhuber H, Nykvist B, De Wit CA, Hughes T, van der Leeuw S, Rodhe H, Sörlin S, Snyder PK, Costanza R, Svedin U, Falkenmark M, Karlberg L, Corell RW, Fabry VJ, Hansen J, Walker B, Liverman D, Richardson K, Crutzen P, Foley J (2009) Planetary boundaries: exploring the safe operating space for humanity. Ecol Soc 14(2):32

Romer D (2011) Endogenous growth. Advanced macroeconomics, 4th edn. McGraw-Hill, New York, pp 101–149
Seiler A (2001) Ecological effects of roads: a review. Introd Res Essay 9:1–40
Seto KC, Güneralp B, Hutyra LR (2012) Global forecasts of Urban expansion to 2030 and direct impacts on biodiversity and carbon pools. Proc Natl Acad Sci, pp. 16083–16088
Sollner F (1997) A reexamination of the role of thermodynamics for environmental economics. Ecol Econ 22:175–201
Solow RM (1974) Intergenerational equity and the exhaustible resources. Rev Econ Stud (Symposium on the Economics of Exhaustible Resources) 41:29–46
Solow RM (1997) Reply: Georgescu-Rogen versus Solow/Stiglitz. Ecol Econ 22:267–268
Stern N (2006) The economics of climate change: the stern review. Cambridge University Press, Cambridge
Taubert F et al (2018) Global patterns of tropical forest fragmentation. Nature 554:519–522
TEEB (2010). The economics of ecosystems and biodiversity: ecological and economic foundations
Teixidó-Figueras J, Steinberger JK, Krausmann F, Haberl H, Wiedmann T, Peters GP, Duro JA, Kastner T (2016) International inequality of environmental pressures: decomposition and comparative analysis. Ecol Ind 62:163–173
Tilman D, Lehman CL, Bristow CE (1998) Diversity-stability relationships: statistical inevitability or ecological consequence? Am Nat 151(3):277–282
Todaro MP (1976) Urban job creation, induced migration and rising unemployment: a formulation and simplified empirical test for LDCs. J Dev Econ 3:211–226
Umar M, Khan SA, Muhammad Zia-ul-haq H, Yusliza MY, Farooq K (2021) The role of emerging technologies in implementing green practices to achieve sustainable operations. TQM J
United Nations, Department of Economic and Social Affairs (UNDESA) (2019) World Urbanization Prospects: The 2018 Revision (ST/ESA/SER.A/420)
United Nations Department of Economic and Social Affairs (UNDESA) (2022) World Population Prospects 2022: Summary of Results. No. 3
United Nations Environment Programme (UNEP) and International Union for Conservation of Nature (IUCN) (2021) Nature-based solutions for climate change mitigation. Nairobi and Gland
Venkatachalam L (2007) Environmental economics and ecological economics: where they can converge? Ecol Econ 61(2-3):550–558
World Bank (2016) Biodiversity offsets: a user guide. World Bank
World Bank (2021a) Unlocking nature-smart development: an approach paper on biodiversity and ecosystem services. World Bank
World Bank (2021b) The changing wealth of nations 2021: managing assets for the future. World Bank, Washington, DC
World Commission on Environment and Development (WCED) (1987) Our common future. Oxford University Press
World Meteorological Organization (WMO) (2022) State of the Global Climate 2021
Yadav SS, Redden R, McNeil DL, Patil SA (2010) Climate change and management of cool season grain legume crops. ICRISAT 4:1–460
Young JT (1991) Is the entropy law relevant to the economics of natural resource scarcity? J Environ Econ Manage 21:169–179
Yu Z, Khan SAR, Umar M (2021) Circular economy practices and industry 4.0 technologies: a strategic move of automobile industry. Bus Strategy Environ 31(3):796–809

Biodiversity and Environmental Impact from Climate Change: Causes and Consequences

Federica Villa, Marta Cimatti, and Moreno Di Marco

Abstract The Intergovernmental Panel on Climate Change reports that current global warming is unprecedented in the past 2000 years, and atmospheric CO_2 levels are the highest in at least 2 million years. Such profound alteration of the global climate is exacerbating the effect of direct human pressure on biodiversity. Climate change affects human activities and, consequently, land-use change, for example forcing the shifting of crops to newly suitable areas (e.g., at higher latitudes and higher altitudes). Land-use change acts synergistically with climate change in altering the distribution and abundance of wildlife, with cascading effects on ecosystems, for example in terms of pest species and pathogens arrival. Thus, the combined effects of climate and land-use change pose high risk to global biodiversity, with a high projected increase in global extinction rates which already largely surpass the rates registered from the fossil record. The projected decline of biodiversity compromises ecosystem functioning and, consequently, the provision of Nature's Contributions to People (NCP)—the contributions of nature to people's quality of life. However, several studies show that bold climate policies (compliant with the Paris Agreement) can largely reduce such risks. Reversing biodiversity decline is still possible, combining international abatement of carbon emissions with actions that limit habitat loss and degradation, such as the establishment of protected areas and the definition of sustainable land-use policies. Analyzing scenarios of future environmental change can guide the definition of strategies to safeguard biodiversity and NCP, but this requires a paradigm shift from the "business-as-usual" approach, built on the intense use of fossil fuel and natural resources, to a greener socio-economic growth which aims at achieving ambitious biodiversity targets.

F. Villa · M. Cimatti · M. Di Marco (✉)
Department of Biology and Biotechnologies "Charles Darwin", Sapienza University of Rome, Rome, Italy
e-mail: federica.villa@uniroma1.it; marta.cimatti@uniroma1.it; moreno.dimarco@uniroma1.it

G. Antonelli et al. (eds.), *Biodiversity Laws, Policies and Science in Europe, the United States and China*, https://doi.org/10.1007/978-3-031-56218-1_6

1 Introduction

The evidence of rapid human-induced global warming is now undeniable as the ongoing changes in climate are much faster than those recorded in the pre-industrial era. The concentrations of well-mixed greenhouse gases have risen since 1750 due to anthropogenic activities (IPCC 2021). In particular, carbon dioxide (CO_2), methane, and nitrous oxide concentrations have rapidly continued to rise since 2011 (IPCC 2021). According to the Sixth Assessment Report of the United Nations' Intergovernmental Panel on Climate Change (IPCC), atmospheric CO_2 levels in 2019 were the highest in at least 2 million years. Additionally, the global surface temperature and the global mean sea level have risen dramatically in recent decades compared to pre-industrial levels. Every region of the world is now coping with weather extremes due to human-induced climate change. In fact, the frequency of heatwaves, droughts, and floodings have globally increased in most inhabited areas since 1950 (IPCC 2021).

In 2015 member states of the United Nations Framework Convention on Climate Change met in Paris to agree on an international treaty to curb greenhouse gas emissions and climate change. The main objective of the so-called Paris Agreement was *"to hold the increase in the global average temperature to well below 2 °C above pre-industrial levels and pursuing efforts to limit the temperature increase to 1.5 °C above pre-industrial levels."* Defining strategies to achieve the Paris commitments requires the analysis of scenarios, i.e., coherent, plausible, and integrated description of several potential future states of the human-environment system (Nakićenović et al. 2000). Scenarios are frequently used in climate change studies to examine long-term socio-economic and environmental effects of anthropogenic activity (van Vuuren et al. 2014). Since 2006, a process has begun to define a new set of common global scenarios focusing on climate change impacts, mitigation, and adaptation capacity (van Vuuren et al. 2014). These scenarios result from the integration of two main elements, the Shared Socioeconomic Pathways (SSPs) and the Representative Concentration Pathways (RCPs) thus, producing several SSP-RCP combinations. SSPs describe alternative futures in which societal trends (including demographics, economics, technologies, and governances) obstruct or favor climate change mitigation and adaptation to varying degrees (O'Neill et al. 2017). RCPs represent possible future pathways for atmospheric concentrations of greenhouse gases and pollutants (van Vuuren et al. 2011). The RCPs are distinguished by the different radiative forcing values—measures of the alteration in the energy balance between incoming and outgoing radiation from the atmosphere compared to pre-industrial levels—reached in 2100 (Myhre et al. 2014; Westphal 2021).

Each scenario combination projects a different temperature and greenhouse gas increase. For example, the most optimistic scenario (SSP1 associated with RCPs 1.9 and 2.6), is based on sustainable growth and the idea of "Taking the Green Road," and would fulfill the commitment set under the Paris Agreement of minimizing global warming to 1.5 °C or 2 °C above pre-industrial levels. Nevertheless, there is a high probability that the 1.5 °C and 2 °C global warming thresholds will be breached throughout this 21st century if greenhouse gas emissions are not drastically reduced (IPCC 2021). Indeed, according to the worst-case scenario (SSP5 associated with RCP 8.5), based on a "business-as-usual" approach to socio-economic growth and with the global economy still largely relying on fossil fuel, global warming can more than double the Paris Agreement limitations, reaching an increase of >4 °C by 2100.

2 Environmental Impacts of Climate Change

2.1 *Extreme Aridity and Megafires*

During the past 50 years there has been an increase in the frequency and magnitude of extreme events, such as floods, droughts, and megafires which cause widespread adverse impacts on nature and people (Carnicer et al. 2022; Fischer and Knutti 2015; He et al. 2019; IPCC 2014, 2021, 2022; Ummenhofer and Meehl 2017). In particular, extreme heat events (heat waves) and heavy precipitation events became more intense and frequent, while cold events (cold waves) became less frequent (IPCC 2007, 2014, 2022; Carnicer et al. 2022). Compound extreme events (such as simultaneous heatwaves and droughts) have also increased their frequency since 1950 (Sutanto et al. 2020). This is because rainfall events are interspersed with long dry periods, during which high temperatures promote intense evapotranspiration and a decline in low or medium precipitation. As a recent example, between September 2019 and January 2020 south-eastern Australia experienced the most destructive bushfire season ever recorded (Abram et al. 2021; Boer et al. 2020; Lindenmayer et al. 2020), with more than 10 million hectares burnt (Walter et al. 2020). Due to the effect of fire, 33 people died and 3000 houses were destroyed (Walter et al. 2020), while there were about 10 million people exposed to heavy smoke (Bowman et al. 2020; Walter et al. 2020).

More than 21% of Australia's temperate deciduous and mixed forest biome burnt in a single megafires season, which corresponded to the global highest percentage of any continental forest biome destroyed by fire (Boer et al. 2020). In these areas, the impact on biodiversity has been dramatic, with an estimated 3 billion vertebrates perishing because of the fires (van Eeden et al. 2020). Specifically, 70 taxa of vertebrates (many already endangered) had more than 30% of their habitat significantly damaged by fires (Ward et al. 2020). This bushfire crisis can be seen as an emblematic example of climate change consequences, which has induced a compound fire weather with low precipitation and extremely high temperatures. However, land-use change has also contributed to the severity of these events. Between 1996 and 2018, the forestry industry in Australia removed 161 million cubic meters of natural forest (Commonwealth of Australia 2018). These logging practices leave a lot of debris on the ground, which constitutes fuel for the rapid expansion of fires (Raison and Squire 2008). In addition, deforestation influences the composition of tree communities making them more flammable: tree ferns and other typical rainforest elements that are less flammable give way to large areas with a few short-statured and highly flammable trees (Taylor et al. 2014). Thus, many Australian forests have become progressively more prone to fires, with a self-reinforcing loop that makes them contribute to the direct microclimatic conditions that further increase fire risk, such as higher ground temperatures and dryness (Boer et al. 2020; Lindenmayer et al. 2020).

2.2 Land Use and Climate Change

Currently, climate and land-use changes are the two major causes of environmental alteration. They are closely interconnected as the effects of one alter those of the other. The effects of land-use change (i.e., the conversion of natural land for human activities) on climate change are direct, by removing stored carbon from natural vegetation and releasing it in the atmosphere, and indirect, by altering the ability of natural systems to retain water and regulate temperature (Dale 1997; Dale et al. 2011). On the other hand, climate change is affecting human activities and consequently also land use. For example, climate change makes some areas impossible to cultivate, while it induces an increase in the crop yields of other lands causing a spatial shift in the areas dedicated to agriculture (Dale 1997). Furthermore, rising sea levels due to global warming are inducing a major loss of many coastal areas, with direct impact on the commercial and industrial activities located there which are now gradually moving (and impacting) new areas at higher elevations (Dale 1997).

Besides, given lack of climatic adaptation, climate change could substantially enhance the effect of land-use change on biodiversity loss, becoming the greatest risk driver for the environment in the coming future (Newbold 2018; Di Marco et al. 2019; Pereira et al. 2020). For instance, under different SSP-RCP scenarios, the synergistic effect of climate and land-use changes on the persistence of biodiversity will be far larger than the effect of land use alone (Di Marco et al. 2019; Newbold 2018). Synergetic mitigation of climate change and land use will both be necessary to conserve biodiversity in the near future.

2.3 Spread of Pathogens, Invasive Alien Species, and Pests

Climate change has an impact on every aspect of biodiversity and species can respond to it in several ways. Species can cope with climate change by moving to areas with more suitable climatic conditions. Some studies predicted that many species' geographical ranges—the extent of their geographic distribution—will shift by at least 100 km in the coming century (Chen et al. 2011; Burrows et al. 2014). However, this process can also affect invasive alien species, pests, and pathogens, leading to a series of cascading effects that compromise both ecosystem equilibrium, socio-economic development, and human health. Changes in climate can facilitate alien species invasion, altering the environment and making it more suitable for them. It can also induce species to move to non-native habitats, and modifies species hierarchies in ecosystems, resulting in the emergence of new dominating species with potential invasive traits (Masters and Norgrove 2010). For example, a recent study projected the impact of climate change on mammal–virus associations, and predicted that mammal range shifts will double the potential interaction between viral hosts species, with a risk of rapid increase of interspecific viral sharing and potential transmission to humans (Carlson et al. 2022). In this context, the role of invasive alien species—non-native species that damage the new environment where they have been introduced—may also be crucial for pathogens to spread, because they can bring new parasites into the colonized environment, increasing zoonotic risks. Several cases of association between the presence of invasive alien species and the incidence of zoonoses have often been observed, especially during the last decades. For example, invasive rats played a crucial role in spreading plague (Kosoy et al. 2015), introduced raccoons from North America facilitated outbreaks of West Nile virus in Europe (Beltrán-Beck et al. 2012), and invasive mosquitoes have aided in the transmission of chikungunya and dengue fever (Medlock et al. 2012). In fact, a recent work by Zhang et al. (2022) showed that the number of zoonotic events rises with increasing abundance of alien zoonotic hosts, and also found that global transformations, such as climate change, land-use change, and biodiversity loss, could exacerbate these processes.

Climate change is also a key determinant of the abundance and distribution of pest species. The outbreak of desert locusts (*Schistocerca gregaria*) can be considered an emblematic case of food insecurity associated to how pests respond to climate change. This species has a dual biology, as it can change from being sedentary and solitary to becoming gregarious and migratory. During the dry season, nymphs (immature individuals) with a green coloration live a solitary life. With the arrival of heavy rains and the consequent growth of vegetation, they mature and begin to mate. When the number of individuals is such as to lead to overcrowding, close physical contact triggers a cascade of metabolic and behavioral changes that result in the transition from the solitary to the gregarious form. The coloration changes from green to yellow-black in nymphs, and from brown to yellow-black in adults, and locusts aggregate in swarms that begin to migrate long distances. The gregarious stage of locusts reproduces much faster, can live at much higher densities (thousands of times higher than the solitary state), and can easily colonize new areas through wind transportation. They can easily destroy large extensions of crops in a matter of days.

In May and October 2018, two extreme weather events, cyclones Mekunu and Luban, occurred in the south of the Arabian Peninsula, the breeding ground of locusts, and brought heavy torrential rains (FAO 2020). This allowed the perfect conditions for desert locusts to breed for nine months, increasing their number by about 800,000% (FAO 2020). This uncontrolled reproduction led to the formation of numerous swarms, which in 2019 invaded the Indo-Pakistan border, Somalia, and Ethiopia (FAO 2020). In 2020, swarms of desert locusts continued to spread until they invaded Kenya, Uganda, Sudan, and Eritrea. The invasion also persisted in

2021 in Ethiopia, Kenya, Somalia, Tanzania, and Eritrea (FAO 2021). This locust upsurge had a devastating impact on crop fields and pastures and forced 42 million people, living in countries already troubled by droughts, wars, and high nutritional costs, to deal with food insecurity (FAO 2020). Since January 2020, the Food and Agriculture Organization of the United Nations collaborated with governments and other partners to implement a short, medium, and long-term emergency control system on over 2 million ha of land in the Greater Horn of Africa and Yemen (FAO 2021). These control efforts, which involved the use of pesticides, aerial operations and the monitoring of the environment and locust populations, began to show initial successful results in 2021, but it was not until early 2022 that the locust plague in the Horn of Africa was brought to an end.

3 Scenarios of Climate Change Impact on Biodiversity

Life on the planet has faced dramatically different climatic conditions through geological eras, but these changes have exerted their effects over hundreds of thousands, sometimes millions, of years. The recent acceleration in global climate change (Loarie et al. 2009) casts doubts about the ability of species to adapt to environmental change happening at a much faster pace than before. Land-use change—the modification of natural environments for human purposes—and overexploitation—the excessive extraction of natural resources—have been the main drivers of global biodiversity decline in the past decades (Maxwell et al. 2016). Yet, many have argued that future biodiversity loss will be mainly driven by the direct or indirect effects of climate change (Newbold 2018; Di Marco et al. 2019).

Analysis of the fossil record indicates strong effect of climate change even in recent geological times, as species have responded to change in climatic conditions by altering their distribution, their ecological niches—the breadth of environmental conditions they are able to tolerate—and even disappearing from several areas (Di Marco et al. 2021; Pineda-Munoz et al. 2021; Mondanaro et al. 2021). Not every species has suffered from climate change, as so-called "climate exploiters" can benefit from alteration of climate conditions towards more suitable environments. For example, the coyote—a widespread Northamerican canid—had a relatively narrow distribution during the mid-Pleistocene (ca. 6000 years ago) but, thanks to climate change and a reduction in the distribution of the gray wolf, occupies a much larger area and can experience a broader set of climatic conditions today (Fig. 1a) (Di Marco et al. 2021). Other mammal species were instead unable to tolerate significant change in climatic conditions, such as the Ethiopian wolf—an endangered and range-restricted African canid. This latter species has suffered a reduction in its distribution due to climate change (Fig. 1b).

In general, when climate instability (i.e., the change in climatic conditions) resulted in a >30% loss of suitable climatic conditions within a species' distribution range, most species have shown a reduction in their climatic niche ("niche shrink")

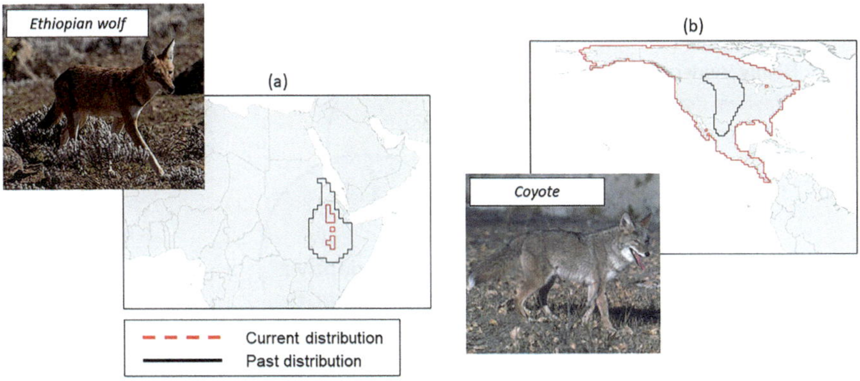

Fig. 1 Change in the distribution and climatic niche of two wild canids, the coyote (Canis latrans) and the Ethiopian wolf (Canis simensis) over the course of 6000 years. While the Ethiopian wolf has suffered a large reduction in its distribution, the coyote has expanded it over time. Distribution data sourced from Faurby et al. (2018), photo credits: (**a**) Charles J. Sharp (CC-BY 4.0); (**b**) California Department of Fish and Wildlife from Sacramento, CA, USA (CC-BY 2.0)

and geographic distribution (Di Marco et al. 2021). A reduced climate niche is often associated with a reduced ability to adapt to changing conditions, as species living in a more homogeneous environment often show lower genetic diversity (Hanson et al. 2017). Similar large-scale analysis for groups other than mammals are less easy to perform due to more limited fossil records, but an analysis of European plants found that species have largely contracted and expanded their range in response to climate change (Maiorano et al. 2013).

While these changes have manifested over long periods in the past, rapid acceleration of climate change means species might need to adapt to a global warming which is between 1.5 °C and 4.5 °C above pre-industrial levels by the end of the century (i.e., over the course of just 250 years). Such change in global mean temperature translates into much higher local-scale effects in some areas, with acceleration in the frequency and magnitude of extreme events (Murali et al. 2023; see also Sect. 2.1). Many of these consequences can be minimized by limiting global warming to 1.5°, as proposed under the Paris Agreement, but the world is not on track to achieve such commitment (Matthews and Wynes 2022). Additionally, even that value would carry some risk to global biological systems. It is thus essential to estimate what level of risk abatement can be achieved by limiting global warming to within Paris' limits.

A comprehensive attempt at measuring climate risk for biodiversity under Paris-compliant vs other scenarios was made by Warren et al. (2018). They found a high risk of decline for vertebrate (e.g., birds), invertebrate (e.g., insects), and plant species due to new climate conditions within their distribution range by 2100. The authors found high levels of global warming (leading to 4.5 °C above pre-industrial levels) would determine a proportion of species at risk of >40% for vertebrates and >60% for plants and insects. However, they also found that limiting warming to 2 °

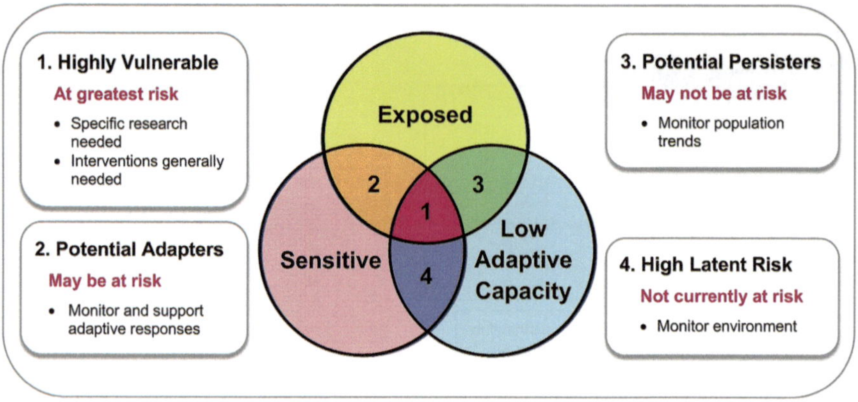

Fig. 2 Combinations of the three dimensions of climate change vulnerability: sensitivity, exposure, and adaptive capacity. Species in different conditions, according to these three dimensions, have different conservation needs. Source: Foden et al. (2013), licensed under CC BY 4.0

C (the less ambitious target set under the Paris Agreement) would lower this risk to 8–18% species, and limiting warming to 1.5 °C would further lower the risk to only 4–8% of species (depending on the group). Yet, those estimates refer to only one element of climate vulnerability, that of "exposure" to climate change, but disregards the elements of sensitivity and adaptive capacity (Fig. 2; Foden et al. 2013).

More recent work considered some of those additional elements, and also included the potential indirect effect of climate-mediated land-use change on biodiversity. Results on vertebrate species (Newbold 2018) confirm a much higher risk under a high-emission scenario compared to a scenario that stays within 2 °C global warming. Results on plant species (Di Marco et al. 2019) have found high risk even under a 2 °C scenario, but still substantially lower than a 4.5 °C scenario (16% extinction risk vs 21%). Results on mammal species—a group of endotherms with presumably lower climate sensitivity compared to other groups—have also considered the possibility for species to tolerate certain levels of climate change based on evidence from the past 6000 years (Mendez Angarita et al. 2023). Out of 63 biomes analyzed—i.e., biogeographical units defined by similar internal physical and biological conditions—six were identified as being of high importance for mammalian biodiversity and facing significant risk under a 4.5 °C scenario. Instead, none of these biomes would face significant climate risk under a 1.5 °C scenario.

4 Climate Change Consequences on Nature's Contribution to People

Healthy ecosystems and rich biodiversity support human life and well-being. Ecosystems perform a myriad of services that make our planet a habitable place. However, anthropogenic climate change and increasing extreme weather events are now affecting most biological and ecological processes on Earth, weakening the structure, functioning, and resilience of ecosystems. The projected decline of biodiversity from climate change affects ecosystem functioning and, consequently, the provision of different Nature's Contribution to People (NCP), threatening sustainable and equitable development (Arneth et al. 2020; Runting et al. 2017). NCP are defined as all the contributions, both positive and negative, of living nature to people's quality of life (Brauman et al. 2020; Díaz et al. 2018). These contributions help addressing important societal challenges such as climate change, food and water security, or the risk of natural disaster, simultaneously providing human well-being and biodiversity benefits. There are 18 NCP categories (Díaz et al. 2018, 2019) organized in three partially overlapping groups (Table 1): regulating, material, and nonmaterial.

Regulating contributions are especially important as they outline the role of ecosystems and their biological constituents in affecting good quality of life, as well as the production of material and non-material contributions. Regulating NCPs include critical ecosystem services such as pollination, regulation of water quality and quantity, regulation of climate and air quality and detrimental organisms. Yet regulating NCP face high risk of decline from climate change. Over the past 50 years fourteen of the eighteen categories of NCP declined, and only material NCP have increased due to faster human consumption of natural resources (Díaz et al. 2019). Importantly, the declining trend of regulating and non-material NCP reflects that of biodiversity, meaning these two processes are progressing in parallel. This requires a better understanding of the relationships between biodiversity and human pressure, as well as a new understanding of conservation measures that will be effective at maintaining both NCP and biodiversity in a rapidly changing environment.

4.1 *Climate Risk for Regulating NCP*

4.1.1 NCP 1 Habitat Creation and Maintenance

The creation and maintenance of natural habitat (NCP 1) has been largely impacted by human exploitation of natural resources, and is further affected by climate change effects on species and ecosystems (Adhikari et al. 2022; Díaz et al. 2019). To cope with climate change, terrestrial species have been reported to be moving poleward and to higher elevations (Bellard et al. 2012), while aquatic species are moving deeper and to higher latitudes (Brito-Morales et al. 2020). Climate change also

Table 1 Global trends in the capacity of nature to contribute to good quality of life from 1970 to the present. Fourteen of the 18 categories of Nature's Contributions to People show a decline. Half of the 18 categories show consistent patterns globally, whereas the other half show declines in some regions and gains in others

Nature's Contribution to People	Type	50-year global trend
1 Habitat creation and maintenance	Regulating	Decreased
2 Pollination and dispersal of seeds and other propagules	Regulating	Decreased
3 Regulation of air quality	Regulating	Decreased
4 Regulation of climate	Regulating	Decreased
5 Regulation of ocean acidification	Regulating	Stable
6 Regulation of freshwater quantity, location, and timing	Regulating	Decreased
7 Regulation of freshwater and coastal water quality	Regulating	Decreased
8 Formation, protection, and decontamination of soils	Regulating	Decreased
9 Regulation of hazards and extreme events	Regulating	Decreased
10 Regulation of detrimental organisms and biological processes	Regulating	Decreased
11 Energy	Material	Mixed trend
12 Food and feed	Material	Mixed trend
13 Materials and assistance	Material	Mixed trend
14 Medicinal, biochemical, and genetic resources	Material	Decreased
15 Learning and inspiration	Non-Material	Decreased
16 Physical and psychological experiences	Non-Material	Decreased
17 Supporting identities	Non-Material	Decreased
18 Maintenance of options	Non-Material	Decreased

determines ecosystem-wide consequences, such as decline in biomass production and changes in vegetation structure (Svenning and Sandel 2013). Furthermore, extreme weather events over the past two decades, coupled with other factors such as deforestation and fires, have had pervasive and long-lasting impacts on forest structure and function, affecting water and carbon cycles (IPBES 2019). Thus, climate change is foreseen to exacerbate the impacts of other anthropogenic pressures such as land-use change, predominantly through habitat loss, and fragmentation which pose an even more severe threat to ecosystems, reducing the availability of areas with suitable climatic conditions for species, including areas that have not yet been converted to human use (Mantyka-Pringle et al. 2012).

4.1.2 NCP 2 Pollination and Dispersal of Seeds and Other Propagules

Pollination (NCP 2) is the most studied NCP worldwide (Breeze et al. 2016), as 75% of our food crops and nearly 90% of wild flowers depend at least to some extent on animal pollination. Thus, the loss of both wild and domestic pollinators has dramatic consequences for food production (Klein et al. 2007). Changes in pollinator health, diversity and abundance generally resulted in localized decreases in pollination of pollination-dependent crops. The decline in pollination by wild pollinators in general follows the decline in their habitat. Thus, land-use-driven changes to landscape structure coupled with climate change might lead to reduced diversity of plant-pollinator communities, dominated by highly mobile, habitat generalist species (Hegland et al. 2009; Parmesan 2007; Settele et al. 2016). Furthermore, the rate of climate change, especially under moderate and extreme emission scenarios, is projected to overtake the maximum distance that many pollinator groups can disperse or migrate. Thus, declines in pollinator diversity have been recorded and are expected to continue globally. Currently, 16.5% of vertebrate pollinators are threatened with global extinction (IPBES 2016) while populations of European bees and butterflies are declining by 37% of bees and 31% respectively.

4.1.3 NCP 3 Regulation of Air Quality

Air quality depends on the percentage of pollutants present in the atmosphere such as particulate matter, black carbon and ozone, and nature (above ground and below ground vegetation) contributes to the regulation of air quality (NCP3) by sequestering these emissions. Nevertheless, nature's contribution to controlling and preventing air pollutant emissions is undermined by fires, deforestation, and agriculture, while the life cycle of pollutants is also influenced by chemical and meteorological factors such as wind, temperature, precipitation, and solar radiation. Anthropogenic climate change has a significant impact on air quality, while air quality itself can affect climate change and both can directly or indirectly affect human health (Orru et al. 2017). Specifically, climate-driven changes in weather conditions, in particular temperature and precipitation, are degrading the removal processes (dispersion, precipitation) and amplifying the atmospheric chemistry leading to increase ground-level ozone and particulate matter (Giorgi and Meleux 2007). As a result, issues of climate change and future air quality are deeply intertwined. Future air quality is then determined by several factors, including anthropogenic emissions, natural (climate-influenced) emissions, and climate change resulting from changes in emissions of long-lived greenhouse gases (Doherty et al. 2017). An increase in climate variability with a mean shift towards warmer conditions can lead to an increase in extreme seasons (e.g., hot summers) (Schär et al. 2004), like the European summer of 2003, with significant impacts on human health and natural ecosystems (Giorgi and Meleux 2007). Furthermore, hotter and drier climates lead to frequent wildfires and a longer wildfire season, impairing air quality around the globe (Sanderfoot et al. 2022; Vicente-Serrano et al. 2020; Xie et al. 2022). Nevertheless, it is also well recognized that well-developed vegetation structure has the potential to protect soils, prevent airborne dust emissions, and prevent emissions by trapping air pollutants in plant parts. Vegetation also has the ability to trap air pollution on the surface of leaves.

4.1.4 NCP 4 Regulation of Climate

The impacts of climate change are manifested through multiple environmental phenomena besides rising temperatures, such as shifting rainfall patterns, rising sea levels, increasing ocean acidification, and extreme weather events (IPCC 2014, 2022). All these phenomena influence the biological mediated processes that regulate atmospheric processes and weather patterns. The regulation of climate (NCP 4) depends on ecosystems through either sequestration or release of greenhouse gases such CO_2. Consequently, changes in carbon stored in vegetation can potentially mitigate warming caused by increasing concentrations of CO_2 in the atmosphere (Erb et al. 2018; Sierra et al. 2021). Nevertheless, it is increasingly likely that by the end of the 21st century, several ecosystems will include bioclimatic conditions not experienced at present (i.e., "novel" climates) and some of the current climates may disappear (Williams et al. 2007). Furthermore, land use change, particularly deforestation, burning, and conversion to agriculture, is a significant source of CO_2 emissions that almost offset land-based sequestration. Carbon sequestration is spatially heterogeneous with tropical forests playing a main role in CO_2 absorption, first of all the Amazonian rainforest. The world's forests are major sinks of carbon but, as forests are cleared and intensively exploited, their natural contribution to climate regulation is diminishing.

4.1.5 NCP 6 Regulation of Freshwater Quantity, Location, and Timing

Human and terrestrial wildlife survival relies on freshwater supply and the regulation of this contribution (NCP 6) is an essential ecosystem function. Earth's vegetation plays an important role in the water cycle and it regulates and maintains evapotranspiration and precipitation. The water cycle is an extremely complex system based on different processes including precipitation, evapotranspiration, and runoff. Climate warming and land use change such as deforestation and conversion from forest to cropland, enhances evapotranspiration, thereby accelerating the hydrologic cycle. Changes in the spatio-temporal distribution of precipitation and evapotranspiration alter the availability of water (Dezsi et al. 2018; Konapala et al. 2020), and anthropogenic climate change affects the water balance by altering these variables (Guo et al. 2017). Furthermore, the aridity, or the lack of moisture, depends on the same variables and many studies predicted a global terrestrial drying in the future (Lin et al. 2018; Park et al. 2018; Wang et al. 2021).

4.1.6 NCP 8 Formation, Protection, and Decontamination of Soils

Soil systems are dynamic and complex. The soil itself consists of a mineral part and an organic part containing a wide variety of organic compounds, water, and various organisms. Biodiversity contributes to the formation and maintenance of soil structure, decomposition of organic matter and maintenance of moisture and nutrient cycling (NCP 8). But changes in rainfall and wind patterns will lead to an increase in erosion in vulnerable soils causing a decrease of the Organic Matter in the soils, reducing its fertility and biodiversity (Bardgett and Van Der Putten 2014; Bellard et al. 2012). Microbial biodiversity, a crucial ecosystem's component that governs the biogeochemical cycle of elements, is especially vulnerable to these changes (Jansson and Hofmockel 2020).

Climate is an important factor in soil development and a major driver of the processes of soil formation. At the same time, changes in the bio-physical nature of soil, due to rising temperatures, changing precipitation intensity and frequency and more severe droughts, are likely to release substantial amounts of CO_2 and other greenhouse gases. Altered climate will, therefore, have an effect on soil processes, properties, and services it provides like food security, water filtration and carbon storage. Changes in precipitation patterns can also impact soil moisture dynamics, leading to changes in water infiltration, runoff, and water holding capacity of soils (Bates et al. 2008).

Soil, functioning as a carbon sink, is fundamental to regulate atmospheric CO_2 concentration and therefore mitigating global warming (Stockmann et al. 2015). Increasing temperatures will accelerate decay rates, leading to increased carbon dioxide and methane emissions from soil. For example, climate warming accelerates permafrost thaw in northern regions making a lot of soil organic matter vulnerable to microbial decomposition, with huge release in the atmosphere of soil carbon in the form of carbon dioxide and methane with consequent positive feedback to global warming itself (Schuur et al. 2015).

5 Conclusion

Several Earth systems, including climate, are close to surpassing safe planetary boundaries that might trigger important consequences for the biosphere (Cardinale et al. 2012; Armstrong McKay et al. 2022). We are currently facing 1.15 °C global warming which is close to the 1.5 °C bar considered a key tipping point for many climatic phenomena—critical thresholds beyond which the Earth system is abruptly and/or irreversibly altered by global warming (IPCC 2021; Armstrong McKay et al. 2022; WMO 2023). Yet, remaining within the 1.5 °C limit set under the Paris Agreement would substantially reduce climate risk compared to a business-as-usual scenario, which might lead to much higher global warming with many more climatic tipping points triggered.

A recent study by Armstrong McKay et al. (2022) outlined an updated list of climate tipping elements, and global warming thresholds at which these tipping points would probably be prompted. According to their assessment, even if the world complies with the less ambitious Paris Agreement goal of keep global warming below 2 °C, there will still be high risk of ice sheet collapse in Greenland and West Antarctic, a risk of abrupt thawing of the boreal permafrost, and die-off of the low-latitude coral reefs (Armstrong McKay et al. 2022). However, surpassing the 2 °C threshold would trigger many more tipping points, such as: dieback of the Amazon rainforest, loss of mountain glaciers, the abrupt vegetation growth in the Sahel, collapse of Arctic winter sea ice, collapse of the boreal permafrost.

A more recent work by Lenton et al. (2023) quantified the human cost of global warming, demonstrating that climate change has already left more than 600 million people out of the "human climate niche" (i.e., the set of favorable climatic conditions for humans). Current policy trajectories leading global warming to ~2.7 °C could put 22–39% of people outside of the human climate niche. Instead, achieving the Paris Agreement target of limiting global warming to 1.5 °C would halve the amount of people left outside this niche. These outcomes highlight how climate policies can make a significant difference in limiting the human cost of global warming.

The window of opportunity to safeguard both human beings and ecosystems from the climate crisis is rapidly closing (IPCC 2023). Despite the gravity of current climate conditions and the urgency of limiting global warming, the IPCC Synthesis Report approved in March 2023—the last before 2030—launches a message of hope. Limiting global warming to 1.5 °C compared to pre-industrial levels by 2050 will be possible if deep greenhouse gas emissions reductions are implemented in this decade and, specifically, if a global decline in CO_2 emissions to net zero is achieved by 2050 (IPCC 2023). Short-term actions which integrate greenhouse gas mitigation and adaptation measures to promote climate resilient development are needed to reach these goals (IPCC 2023). In fact, increasing international cooperation, suitable access to financial resources, inclusive governance and coordinated policies will be crucial to foster climate resilient development (IPCC 2023). Implementing this strategy in the current decade would significantly reduce the expected damage to human beings and biodiversity, and generate numerous side benefits, particularly for air quality and health (IPCC 2023).

The conservation of biodiversity and the maintenance of healthy natural environments remains the most strategic global investment to achieve international climate commitments. The International Union for Conservation of Nature defined the so-called Nature-Based Solutions as *"actions to protect, sustainably manage, and restore natural or modified ecosystems, that address societal challenges effectively and adaptively, simultaneously providing human well-being and biodiversity benefits"* (Cohen-Shacham et al. 2019). Thus, Nature-Based Solutions can play a key role in reducing climate change effects. For example, promoting the management of working lands and seas lowers greenhouse gas emissions and sequesters carbon while conserving and restoring natural ecosystems helps allow healthy soil and plants, which lowers the likelihood of floods, droughts, and landslides (Seddon 2022).

Yet, to maintain biodiversity contributions to climate regulation, it is paramount to control and reduce the current rates of habitat loss and, consequently, sustainable land-use policies are essential to reverse the trend of biodiversity loss. Leclère et al. (2020) showed that biodiversity trends could turn positive by the mid-21st century if countries implement policies that institute new protected areas, restore degraded areas, and generalize conservation planning at the landscape level. However, not all models investigated in their analysis achieved this outcome, because rising food prices—expected in almost half scenarios—could result in biodiversity loss (Leclère et al. 2020). Instead, limiting land-use change drivers could minimize the environmental effects of the food-provision system (Leclère et al. 2020). A transformation of the food-system and energy system is thus required to bend the curve of biodiversity loss. This transformation requires bold environmental policies (e.g., protected area expansion, reduced use of fossil fuel) to be coupled with deep societal change (e.g., reducing food waste and favoring plant-based diets).

References

Abram NJ, Henley BJ, Sen Gupta A, Lippmann TJ, Clarke H, Dowdy AJ et al (2021) Connections of climate change and variability to large and extreme forest fires in southeast Australia. Commun Earth Environ 2(1):8

Adhikari B, Prescott GW, Urbach D, Chettri N, Fischer M (2022) Nature's contributions to people and the Sustainable Development Goals in Nepal. Environ Res Lett 17(9):093007

Armstrong McKay DI, Staal A, Abrams JF, Winkelmann R, Sakschewski B, Loriani S et al (2022) Exceeding 1.5 C global warming could trigger multiple climate tipping points. Science 377(6611):eabn7950

Arneth A, Shin YJ, Leadley P, Rondinini C, Bukvareva E, Kolb M et al (2020) Post-2020 biodiversity targets need to embrace climate change. Proc Natl Acad Sci 117(49):30882–30891

Bardgett RD, Van Der Putten WH (2014) Belowground biodiversity and ecosystem functioning. Nature 515(7528):505–511

Bates B, Kundzewicz Z, Wu S (2008) Climate change and water. Intergovernmental Panel on Climate Change Secretariat

Bellard C, Bertelsmeier C, Leadley P, Thuiller W, Courchamp F (2012) Impacts of climate change on the future of biodiversity. Ecol Lett 15(4):365–377

Beltrán-Beck B, García FJ, Gortázar C (2012) Raccoons in Europe: disease hazards due to the establishment of an invasive species. Eur J Wildl Res 58:5–15

Boer MM, Resco de Dios V, Bradstock RA (2020) Unprecedented burn area of Australian mega forest fires. Nat Climate Change 10(3):171–172

Bowman D, Williamson G, Yebra M, Lizundia-Loiola J, Pettinari ML, Shah S et al (2020) Wildfires: Australia needs national monitoring agency. Nature 584(7820):188–191

Brauman KA, Garibaldi LA, Polasky S, Aumeeruddy-Thomas Y, Brancalion PH, DeClerck F et al (2020) Global trends in nature's contributions to people. Proc Natl Acad Sci 117(51): 32799–32805

Breeze TD, Gallai N, Garibaldi LA, Li XS (2016) Economic measures of pollination services: shortcomings and future directions. Trends Ecol Evol 31(12):927–939

Brito-Morales I, Schoeman DS, Molinos JG, Burrows MT, Klein CJ, Arafeh-Dalmau N et al (2020) Climate velocity reveals increasing exposure of deep-ocean biodiversity to future warming. Nat Climate Change 10(6):576–581

Burrows MT, Schoeman DS, Richardson AJ, Molinos JG, Hoffmann A, Buckley LB et al (2014) Geographical limits to species-range shifts are suggested by climate velocity. Nature 507(7493): 492–495

Cardinale BJ, Duffy JE, Gonzalez A, Hooper DU, Perrings C, Venail P et al (2012) Biodiversity loss and its impact on humanity. Nature 486(7401):59–67

Carlson CJ, Albery GF, Merow C, Trisos CH, Zipfel CM, Eskew EA et al (2022) Climate change increases cross-species viral transmission risk. Nature 607(7919):555–562

Carnicer J, Alegria A, Giannakopoulos C, Di Giuseppe F, Karali A, Koutsias N, Lionello P, Parrington M, Vitolo C (2022) Global warming is shifting the relationships between fire weather and realized fire-induced CO2 emissions in Europe. Sci Rep 12:8–13. Nature Publishing Group UK. Available from https://doi.org/10.1038/s41598-022-14480-8

Chen IC, Hill JK, Ohlemüller R, Roy DB, Thomas CD (2011) Rapid range shifts of species associated with high levels of climate warming. Science 333(6045):1024–1026

Cohen-Shacham E, Andrade A, Dalton J, Dudley N, Jones M, Kumar C et al (2019) Core principles for successfully implementing and upscaling nature-based solutions. Environ Sci Policy 98:20–29

Commonwealth of Australia (2018) Department of Agriculture and Water Resources Australia's State of the Forests Report 2018

Dale VH (1997) The relationship between land-use change and climate change. Ecol Appl 7(3): 753–769

Dale VH, Efroymson RA, Kline KL (2011) The land use–climate change–energy nexus. Landsc Ecol 26:755–773

Dezsi Ş, Mîndrescu M, Petrea D, Rai PK, Hamann A, Nistor MM (2018) High-resolution projections of evapotranspiration and water availability for Europe under climate change. Int J Climatol 38(10):3832–3841

Di Marco M, Harwood TD, Hoskins AJ, Ware C, Hill SL, Ferrier S (2019) Projecting impacts of global climate and land-use scenarios on plant biodiversity using compositional-turnover modelling. Global Change Biol 25(8):2763–2778

Di Marco M, Pacifici M, Maiorano L, Rondinini C (2021) Drivers of change in the realised climatic niche of terrestrial mammals. Ecography 44(8):1180–1190

Díaz S, Pascual U, Stenseke M, Martín-López B, Watson RT, Molnár Z et al (2018) Assessing nature's contributions to people. Science 359(6373):270–272

Díaz S, Settele J, Brondízio ES, Ngo HT, Agard J, Arneth A et al (2019) Pervasive human-driven decline of life on Earth points to the need for transformative change. Science 366(6471): eaax3100

Doherty RM, Heal MR, O'Connor FM (2017) Climate change impacts on human health over Europe through its effect on air quality. Environ Health 16(1):33–44

Erb KH, Kastner T, Plutzar C, Bais ALS, Carvalhais N, Fetzel T et al (2018) Unexpectedly large impact of forest management and grazing on global vegetation biomass. Nature 553(7686): 73–76

FAO (2020) Desert locust upsurge –Progress report on the response in the Greater Horn of Africa and Yemen (May–August 2020). Rome

FAO (2021) Desert locust upsurge – Progress report on the response in the Greater Horn of Africa and Yemen, May–August 2021. Rome. https://doi.org/10.4060/cb7161en

Faurby S, Davis M, Pedersen RØ, Schowanek SD, Antonelli A, Svenning JC (2018) PHYLACINE 1.2: the phylogenetic atlas of mammal macroecology. Ecology 99(11):2626

Fischer EM, Knutti R (2015) Anthropogenic contribution to global occurrence of heavy-precipitation and high-temperature extremes. Nat Climate Change 5(6):560–564

Foden WB, Butchart SH, Stuart SN, Vié JC, Akçakaya HR, Angulo A et al (2013) Identifying the world's most climate change vulnerable species: a systematic trait-based assessment of all birds, amphibians and corals. PLoS One 8(6):e65427

Giorgi F, Meleux F (2007) Modelling the regional effects of climate change on air quality. Comptes Rendus Geosci 339(11-12):721–733

Guo D, Westra S, Maier HR (2017) Sensitivity of potential evapotranspiration to changes in climate variables for different Australian climatic zones. Hydrol Earth Syst Sci 21(4):2107–2126

Hanson JO, Rhodes JR, Riginos C, Fuller RA (2017) Environmental and geographic variables are effective surrogates for genetic variation in conservation planning. Proc Natl Acad Sci 114(48): 12755–12760

He X, Liang J, Zeng G, Yuan Y, Li X (2019) The effects of interaction between climate change and land-use/cover change on biodiversity-related ecosystem services. Global Chall 3(9):1800095

Hegland SJ, Nielsen A, Lázaro A, Bjerknes AL, Totland Ø (2009) How does climate warming affect plant-pollinator interactions? Ecol Lett 12(2):184–195

IPBES (2016) The assessment report of the Intergovernmental Science-Policy Platform on Biodiversity and Ecosystem Services on pollinators, pollination and food production. In: Potts SG, Imperatriz-Fonseca VL, Ngo HT (eds) Secretariat of the Intergovernmental Science-Policy Platform on Biodiversity and Ecosystem Services, Bonn, Germany, 552 pp. https://doi.org/10.5281/zenodo.3402856

IPBES (2019) In: Brondizio ES, Settele J, Díaz S, Ngo HT (eds) Global assessment report on biodiversity and ecosystem services of the Intergovernmental Science-Policy Platform on Biodiversity and Ecosystem Services. IPBES Secretariat, Bonn, Germany, 1148 pp. https://doi.org/10.5281/zenodo.3831673

IPCC (2007) Climate Change 2007: Impacts, Adaptation and Vulnerability. In: Parry ML, Canziani OF, Palutikof JP, van der Linden PJ, Hanson CE (eds) Contribution of Working Group II to the Fourth Assessment Report of the Intergovernmental Panel on Climate Change. Cambridge University Press, Cambridge, UK, 976 pp

IPCC (2014) Climate Change 2014: Mitigation of Climate Change. In: Edenhofer O, Pichs-Madruga R, Sokona Y, Farahani E, Kadner S, Seyboth K, Adler A, Baum I, Brunner S, Eickemeier P, Kriemann B, Savolainen J, Schlömer S, von Stechow C, Zwickel T, Minx JC (eds) Contribution of Working Group III to the Fifth Assessment Report of the Intergovernmental Panel on Climate Change. Cambridge University Press, Cambridge, United Kingdom and New York, NY, USA

IPCC (2021) Climate Change 2021: The Physical Science Basis. In: Masson-Delmotte V, Zhai P, Pirani A, Connors SL, Péan C, Berger S, Caud N, Chen Y (eds) Contribution of Working Group I to the Sixth Assessment Report of the Intergovernmental Panel on Climate Change. In Press, p. 3949. https://www.ipcc.ch/report/ar6/wg1/downloads/report/IPCC_AR6_WGI_Full_Report.pdf

IPCC (2022) Climate Change 2022: Impacts, Adaptation and Vulnerability. In: Pörtner H-O, Roberts DC, Tignor M, Poloczanska ES, Mintenbeck K, Alegría A, Craig M, Langsdorf S, Löschke S, Möller V, Okem A, Rama B (eds) Contribution of Working Group II to the Sixth Assessment Report of the Intergovernmental Panel on Climate Change. Cambridge University Press, Cambridge, UK and New York, NY, USA, pp. 3–33. https://doi.org/10.1017/9781009325844.001

IPCC (2023) Climate Change 2023: Synthesis Report. A Report of the Intergovernmental Panel on Climate Change. In: Core Writing Team, Lee H, Romero J (eds) Contribution of Working Groups I, II and III to the Sixth Assessment Report of the Intergovernmental Panel on Climate Change. IPCC, Geneva, Switzerland, 36 pp. (in press)

Jansson JK, Hofmockel KS (2020) Soil microbiomes and climate change. Nat Rev Microbiol 18(1): 35–46

Klein AM, Vaissière BE, Cane JH, Steffan-Dewenter I, Cunningham SA, Kremen C, Tscharntke T (2007) Importance of pollinators in changing landscapes for world crops. Proc R Soc B: Biol Sci 274(1608):303–313

Konapala G, Mishra AK, Wada Y, Mann ME (2020) Climate change will affect global water availability through compounding changes in seasonal precipitation and evaporation. Nat Commun 11(1):3044

Kosoy M, Khlyap L, Cosson JF, Morand S (2015) Aboriginal and invasive rats of genus Rattus as hosts of infectious agents. Vector-Borne Zoonotic Dis 15(1):3–12

Leclère D, Obersteiner M, Barrett M, Butchart SH, Chaudhary A, De Palma A et al (2020) Bending the curve of terrestrial biodiversity needs an integrated strategy. Nature 585(7826):551–556

Lenton TM, Xu C, Abrams JF, Ghadiali A, Loriani S, Sakschewski B et al (2023) Quantifying the human cost of global warming. Nat Sustain:1–11

Lin L, Gettelman A, Fu Q, Xu Y (2018) Simulated differences in 21st century aridity due to different scenarios of greenhouse gases and aerosols. Climatic Change 146:407–422

Lindenmayer DB, Kooyman RM, Taylor C, Ward M, Watson JE (2020) Recent Australian wildfires made worse by logging and associated forest management. Nat Ecol Evol 4(7):898–900

Loarie SR, Duffy PB, Hamilton H, Asner GP, Field CB, Ackerly DD (2009) The velocity of climate change. Nature 462(7276):1052–1055

Maiorano L, Cheddadi R, Zimmermann NE, Pellissier L, Petitpierre B, Pottier J et al (2013) Building the niche through time: using 13,000 years of data to predict the effects of climate change on three tree species in Europe. Global Ecol Biogeogr 22(3):302–317

Mantyka-pringle CS, Martin TG, Rhodes JR (2012) Interactions between climate and habitat loss effects on biodiversity: a systematic review and meta-analysis. Global Change Biol 18(4): 1239–1252

Masters G, Norgrove L (2010) Climate change and invasive alien species. UK: CABI Working Paper, 1, 30

Matthews HD, Wynes S (2022) Current global efforts are insufficient to limit warming to 1.5 C. Science 376(6600):1404–1409

Maxwell SL, Fuller RA, Brooks TM, Watson JE (2016) Biodiversity: the ravages of guns, nets and bulldozers. Nature 536(7615):143–145

Medlock JM, Hansford KM, Schaffner F, Versteirt V, Hendrickx G, Zeller H, Bortel WV (2012) A review of the invasive mosquitoes in Europe: ecology, public health risks, and control options. Vector-borne Zoonotic Dis 12(6):435–447

Mendez Angarita VY, Maiorano L, Dragonetti C, Di Marco M (2023) Implications of exceeding the Paris Agreement for mammalian biodiversity. Conserv Sci Pract 5(3):e12889

Mondanaro A, Di Febbraro M, Melchionna M, Maiorano L, Di Marco M, Edwards NR et al (2021) The role of habitat fragmentation in Pleistocene megafauna extinction in Eurasia. Ecography 44(11):1619–1630

Murali G, Iwamura T, Meiri S, Roll U (2023) Future temperature extremes threaten land vertebrates. Nature 615:461–467

Myhre G, Shindell D, Bréon F-M, Collins W, Fuglestvedt J, Huang J, Koch D, Lamarque J-F, Lee D, Mendoza B, Nakajima T, Robock A, Stephens G, Zhang H, Aamaas B, Boucher O, Dalsøren SB, Daniel JS, Forster P et al. (2014) 8 Anthropogenic and Natural Radiative Forcing. 82

Nakićenović N, Alcamo J, Davis G, Vries BD, Fenhann J, Gaffin S, Zhou D (2000) Special report on emissions scenarios: a special report of Working Group III of the Intergovernmental Panel on Climate Change. Cambridge University Press

Newbold T (2018) Future effects of climate and land-use change on terrestrial vertebrate community diversity under different scenarios. Proc R Soc B 285(1881):20180792

O'Neill BC, Kriegler E, Ebi KL, Kemp-Benedict E, Riahi K, Rothman DS, van Ruijven BJ, van Vuuren DP, Birkmann J, Kok K, Levy M, Solecki W (2017) The roads ahead: narratives for shared socioeconomic pathways describing world futures in the 21st century. Global Environ Change 42:169–180. https://doi.org/10.1016/j.gloenvcha.2015.01.004

Orru H, Ebi KL, Forsberg B (2017) The interplay of climate change and air pollution on health. Curr Environ Health Rep 4:504–513

Park CE, Jeong SJ, Joshi M, Osborn TJ, Ho CH, Piao S et al (2018) Keeping global warming within 1.5 C constrains emergence of aridification. Nat Climate Change 8(1):70–74

Parmesan C (2007) Influences of species, latitudes and methodologies on estimates of phenological response to global warming. Glob Chang Biol 13(9):1860–1872

Pereira HM, Rosa IM, Martins IS, Kim H, Leadley P, Popp A et al (2020) Global trends in biodiversity and ecosystem services from 1900 to 2050. BioRxiv:2020–2004

Pineda-Munoz S, Wang Y, Lyons SK, Tóth AB, McGuire JL (2021) Mammal species occupy different climates following the expansion of human impacts. Proc Natl Acad Sci 118(2): e1922859118

Raison RJ, Squire RO (2008) Forest management in Australia: implications for carbon budgets

Runting RK, Bryan BA, Dee LE, Maseyk FJ, Mandle L, Hamel P et al (2017) Incorporating climate change into ecosystem service assessments and decisions: a review. Global Change Biol 23(1): 28–41

Sanderfoot OV, Bassing SB, Brusa JL, Emmet RL, Gillman SJ, Swift K, Gardner B (2022) A review of the effects of wildfire smoke on the health and behavior of wildlife. Environ Res Lett 16(12):123003

Schär C, Vidale PL, Lüthi D, Frei C, Häberli C, Liniger MA, Appenzeller C (2004) The role of increasing temperature variability in European summer heatwaves. Nature 427(6972):332–336

Schuur EA, McGuire AD, Schädel C, Grosse G, Harden JW, Hayes DJ et al (2015) Climate change and the permafrost carbon feedback. Nature 520(7546):171–179

Seddon N (2022) Harnessing the potential of nature-based solutions for mitigating and adapting to climate change. Science 376(6600):1410–1416

Settele J, Bishop J, Potts SG (2016) Climate change impacts on pollination. Nat Plants 2(7):1–3

Sierra CA, Crow SE, Heimann M, Metzler H, Schulze ED (2021) The climate benefit of carbon sequestration. Biogeosciences 18(3):1029–1048

Stockmann U, Padarian J, McBratney A, Minasny B, de Brogniez D, Montanarella L et al (2015) Global soil organic carbon assessment. Global Food Secur 6:9–16

Sutanto SJ, Vitolo C, Di Napoli C, D'Andrea M, Van Lanen HA (2020) Heatwaves, droughts, and fires: exploring compound and cascading dry hazards at the pan-European scale. Environ Int 134:105276

Svenning JC, Sandel B (2013) Disequilibrium vegetation dynamics under future climate change. Am J Bot 100(7):1266–1286

Taylor C, McCarthy MA, Lindenmayer DB (2014) Nonlinear effects of stand age on fire severity. Conserv Lett 7(4):355–370

Ummenhofer CC, Meehl GA (2017) Extreme weather and climate events with ecological relevance: a review. Philos Trans R Soc B: Biol Sci 372(1723):20160135

van Eeden L, Nimmo D, Mahony M, Herman K, Ehmke G, Driessen J et al. (2020) Australia's 2019–2020 Bushfires: The Wildlife Toll Interim Report. WWF-Australia: Ultimo, Australia

van Vuuren DP, Edmonds J, Kainuma M, Riahi K, Thomson A, Hibbard K, Hurtt GC, Kram T, Krey V, Lamarque J-F, Masui T, Meinshausen M, Nakicenovic N, Smith SJ, Rose SK (2011) The representative concentration pathways: an overview. Climatic Change 109(1–2):5–31. https://doi.org/10.1007/s10584-011-0148-z

van Vuuren DP, Kriegler E, O'Neill BC, Ebi KL, Riahi K, Carter TR, Edmonds J, Hallegatte S, Kram T, Mathur R, Winkler H (2014) A new scenario framework for Climate Change Research: scenario matrix architecture. Climatic Change 122(3):373–386. https://doi.org/10.1007/s10584-013-0906-1

Vicente-Serrano SM, Quiring SM, Pena-Gallardo M, Yuan S, Dominguez-Castro F (2020) A review of environmental droughts: increased risk under global warming? Earth-Sci Rev 201: 102953

Walter CM, Schneider-Futschik EK, Knibbs LD, Irving LB (2020) Health impacts of bushfire smoke exposure in Australia. Respirology 25:495–501. https://doi.org/10.1111/resp.13798

Wang X, Jiang D, Lang X (2021) Future changes in Aridity Index at two and four degrees of global warming above preindustrial levels. Int J Climatol 41(1):278–294

Ward M, Tulloch AI, Radford JQ, Williams BA, Reside AE, Macdonald SL et al (2020) Impact of 2019–2020 mega-fires on Australian fauna habitat. Nat Ecol Evol 4(10):1321–1326

Warren R, Price J, Graham E, Forstenhaeusler N, VanDerWal J (2018) The projected effect on insects, vertebrates, and plants of limiting global warming to 1.5 C rather than 2 C. Science 360 (6390):791–795

Westphal MI (2021) Greenhouse gas emissions scenarios: background, issues, and policy relevance. 34

Williams JW, Jackson ST, Kutzbach JE (2007) Projected distributions of novel and disappearing climates by 2100 AD. Proc Natl Acad Sci 104(14):5738–5742

WMO (2023, May 17) Global temperatures set to reach new records in next five years. https://public.wmo.int/en/media/press-release/global-temperatures-set-reach-new-records-next-five-years

Xie Y, Lin M, Decharme B, Delire C, Horowitz LW, Lawrence DM et al (2022) Tripling of western US particulate pollution from wildfires in a warming climate. Proc Natl Acad Sci 119(14): e2111372119

Zhang L, Rohr J, Cui R, Xin Y, Han L, Yang X et al (2022) Biological invasions facilitate zoonotic disease emergences. Nat Commun 13(1):1762

Ecosystem Services and Livestock Systems in Mountain Areas

Bruno Ronchi and Maurizio Ramanzin

Abstract The ecosystem services (ES) conceptual framework defines the contribution of ecosystems to human well-being and is rapidly gaining importance in international and national policies. According to "The Economics of Ecosystems and Biodiversity-TEEB" initiative, ES can be classified into "provisioning," "regulating," "cultural," and "habitat or supporting," which include habitats for species and biodiversity. Humans are an integral component of ecosystems, and the interaction of human activities with the (seminatural) ecosystems' structure and functions is strictly connected with the delivery of the associated services.

Mountain livestock farming systems are highly multifunctional since, through extensive land and livestock management practices, they provide high-quality typical food products but also various non-provisioning services, such as conservation of livestock genetic resources, carbon sequestration, biodiversity conservation, water regulation, protection from fires, pollination, maintenance of cultural landscapes and heritage, space for ecotourism and recreational activities, and others.

In Europe and many areas of the world, the role of livestock systems in the provision of mountain ES is declining due to the concomitant trends toward farming abandonment in marginal areas and the transition to specialized-intensive farming systems in more favorable rural areas. In both cases, the link between agricultural ecosystems and livestock management that allows the delivery of ES, especially non-provisioning, is weakened or disrupted. This is the case of European mountain regions, where, starting from the second half of the 19th century, extensive, grassland-based livestock systems have experienced a massive abandonment, with the result of a strong reduction of traditional, local livestock populations, and loss or degradation of biodiversity, cultural landscape, and cultural heritage. Sustainable management of permanent grasslands and grazing activities is of basic importance to

B. Ronchi (✉)
Tuscia University, Department of Agriculture and Forestry Science, Viterbo, Italy
e-mail: ronchi@unitus.it

M. Ramanzin
University of Padova, Department of Agronomy, Food, Natural Resources, Animals and Environment, Legnaro, Italy
e-mail: maurizio.ramanzin@unipd.it

G. Antonelli et al. (eds.), *Biodiversity Laws, Policies and Science in Europe, the United States and China*, https://doi.org/10.1007/978-3-031-56218-1_7

guarantee the stability of mountain areas and all the ES connected, and new technologies for precision grazing, which open new perspectives for research and management, are rapidly expanding.

When livestock farming systems are managed with unsuitable practices, they may be responsible for ecosystem disservices, i.e., negative impacts on ES. European Environmental policies are tackling important reductions in anthropogenic emissions impacting climate change. Biodiversity and ES indicators should integrate the widespread Life Cycle Assessments of impacts on climate and pollution to develop comprehensive and unbiased evaluation tools for the environmental sustainability of Livestock systems.

The Common Agricultural Policy-EU will include ES in the context of agro-environmental measures. Considering the high variability of rural ecosystems and mountain livestock systems, together with the variability of associated ES, there is a strong need to establish inventories of ES at the regional or local level and to assess their social perception and economic value. This knowledge is necessary to increase society's awareness of the multifunctionality of mountain farming systems and implement fair public payments for ES, subject to the control of measurable and responsive indicators. In addition, it might inform private market initiatives to promote production chains delivering public benefits. This achievement is highly challenging and needs the commitment of the scientific community, stakeholders, and policymakers.

1 Introduction: The Ecosystem Services Framework

The conceptual framework of the Ecosystem Services (ES) was defined by the "Millennium Ecosystem Assessment (MA)" (Millennium Ecosystem Assessment 2005) for linking ecology and nature conservation with economic development. Ecosystems are defined as "*...dynamic complexes of plant, animal, and microorganism communities and the nonliving environment, interacting as functional units...*" and ES as "*... the contributions of ecosystem structure and function (in combination with other inputs) to human well-being...*" Ecosystems can be identified, mapped, and assessed to represent the "natural capital," and their services can categorize the different benefits they may provide to humans. This approach includes natural, artificial, and semi-natural ecosystems, such as those managed by humans for crop and livestock farming. MA classifies the ES into four categories: provisioning services such as food, water, timber, and fiber, etc.; regulating services that affect climate, floods, disease, wastes, water quality, etc.; cultural services that provide spiritual, recreational, and aesthetic benefits; supporting services that do not provide direct benefits but sustain the functioning of ecosystems, such as soil formation, photosynthesis, nutrient cycling, etc. The MA classification of ES has been partially modified by TEEB,[1] CICES,[2] and IPBES,[3] but the conceptual framework did not change. All ES, although with variable priority, are necessary for human well-being. In this respect, ES can be "private" (they are reserved to the tenant of the ecosystem providing them) or "public" (they are available to everyone, and their use by an individual or community does not preclude their use by others) and "marketable" (they can be bought and sold with a clear monetary value) or "non-marketable" (they are not traded and their economic valuation is complex). Provisioning ES are often private and marketable, while non-provisioning ES (regulating, cultural and supporting services) are primarily public and non-marketable. Although these distinctions are not always mutually exclusive (for instance, climate services may be marketed as carbon credits), they are important because public and non-marketable ES, while essential for human well-being and having an (indirect) economic value, are often scarcely perceived and tend to be undervalued by the society. In addition, ES can be "final" (beneficiaries directly use them) or "intermediate" (they contribute to the delivery of a final ES). This distinction is also linked to the beneficiary. For instance, forage production can be viewed as a final ES by the farmer who uses it to feed his livestock and as an intermediate ES by the consumers who eat the meat and milk produced with that forage. Distinguishing between intermediate and final ES helps to avoid double-counting in the valuation of ES, which should focus on the final ES.

The concept of biodiversity is strictly related to that of ES, but they are distinct. Biodiversity is essential to the functioning and resilience of ecosystems and hence supports the variety of services they provide. For this reason, it might also be considered a proxy for supporting ES. In this respect, due to the difficulty of assessing supporting ES, TEEB introduced the ES category "Habitat and supporting," which includes the services "Habitat for species" and "Maintenance of genetic diversity."

2 Livestock Production Systems and ES

Livestock production systems (LPS) can be broadly classified (Steinfeld and Mäki-Hokkonen 1995) into "landless" (that do not directly manage farmland), "mixed" (that manage cropland, possibly but not necessarily in combination with grasslands) and "grassland-based" (managing grasslands as meadows and/or pastures). Landless LPS are typical of industrial poultry and pig production and have little or no direct relation with ES, in contrast with mixed and grassland LPS that are typical (although not exclusive) of ruminant livestock production. A further distinction classifies "intensive" LPS (that keep high-producing breeds at high stocking rates with high

[1] https://teebweb.org.

[2] https://cices.eu.

[3] https://www.ipbes.net.

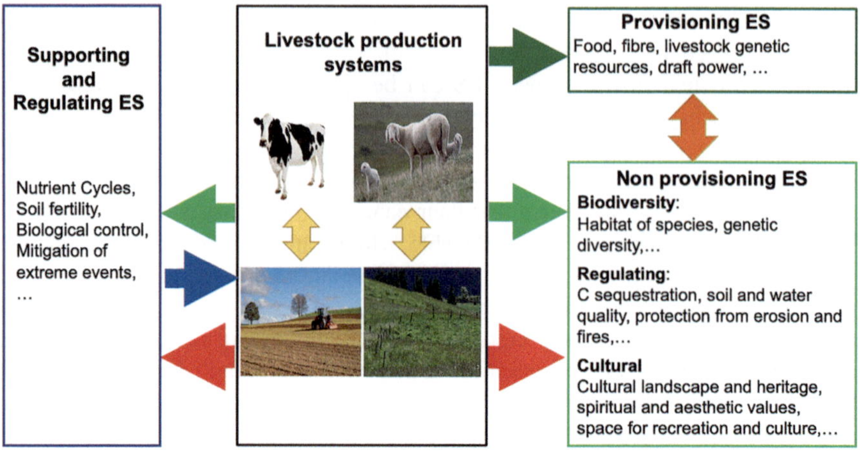

Fig. 1 The flows of Ecosystem Services (ES) and Disservices to and from livestock production systems (LPS): The blue arrow indicates the ES supporting the agroecosystems managed by LS, the dark green arrow indicates the provisioning, marketable ES provided by LS, the light green arrows indicate the contribution of LPS to non-provisioning ES, and the red arrows indicate negative impacts on non-provisioning ecosystem services (Ecosystem Disservices). The yellow arrows indicate the link between livestock and farmland management within LPS, while the orange arrow indicates the general trade-off between provisioning and non-provisioning ES (Graphic designed by the authors)

external inputs, often in confined areas or indoors, to maximize productivity per unit of farmland) and "extensive" LPS (that keep low-producing breeds at low stocking rates with low external inputs, and hence low costs but also low productivity per unit of land). Although there are various intermediate systems, intensive systems are common in mixed LPS and extensive systems in grassland-based LPS. The links between livestock systems, the agroecosystems they manage, and ES is summarized in Fig. 1, expanding from Zhang et al. (2007). The agroecosystems benefit from supporting and regulating ES (nutrient cycles, soil fertility, mitigation of extreme events, pollination, biological control. . .) that sustain forage feeds production for livestock that deliver provisioning, marketable ES as food (meat, milk) but also fiber (wool. . .), livestock genetic resources, draft power, etc. In turn, through land management and grazing practices, LPS contribute to conserving their agroecosystems' functions and productivity, but can also negatively impact them, determining "Ecosystem Disservices (EDS)."

Provisioning ES are often considered the main benefit of LPS. However, the ecosystems they manage, in interaction with the livestock component, may deliver a variety of non-provisioning ES or EDS. In this, mixed, intensive LPS differ from grassland, extensive LPS. Intensive LPS manage mostly cropland to produce the high-energy feeds needed by the highly producing breeds they keep. In contrast, extensive systems manage mostly grasslands and keep less productive, often local breeds. Because of the general trade-off between provisioning and non-provisioning

ES, intensive mixed LPS maximize the delivery of provisioning (food) ES but have a low potential for delivering non-provisioning ES, which can be on the opposite delivered by extensive, grassland ES.

On the other hand, synergies may occur between different non-provisioning ES, for instance, between biodiversity and cultural (landscape and recreation) ES. Therefore, the literature on LPS and ES has mainly focused on grassland-based systems. For a list of ES delivered by livestock farming and their managed agroecosystems, see the reviews of Rodríguez-Ortega et al. (2014); Bernués (2017); D'Ottavio et al. (2017); Leroy et al. (2018); Bengtsson et al. (2019); Zhao et al. (2020); Merida et al. (2022).

In mountain areas, where land morphology and climate constraints are unsuitable for intensive crop agriculture, farming of ruminant livestock, which can transform grasslands and other spontaneous vegetation otherwise unusable by humans into high-quality food or other provisioning ES, is the only form of agricultural activity. Therefore, in the past, mountain ecosystems and landscapes have been shaped by the needs of LPS, which were the basis of local economies. The European socio-economic context has dramatically changed in the last decades, profoundly impacting LPS. While intensive mixed systems now dominate in lowlands, extensive mixed or grassland-based systems are still present in mountain areas (Sturaro et al. 2013) and retain, at least in part, the traditional link with the agroecosystems they manage. In what follows, we will outline the ES and EDS associated with mountain LPS, focusing on European Alpine systems.

3 Mountain LPS and Provisioning ES

Compared to landless or intensive mixed LPS, mountain LPS contribute to a minor proportion of animal-derived foods due to their low share of the total livestock heads and lower productivity.

On the other hand, extensive LPS (and the processing chains to which they are often associated) deliver a rich variety of food products, especially dairy products. When obtained from pasture-based livestock systems, the intrinsic quality of these products is strongly influenced by the grass that transmits to milk (and then to dairy products) specific organoleptic attributes and components of nutritional and bio-medical values. Comparing to products obtained from intensive dairy farming systems, based on the use of cultivated forages, total mixed rations, and on high levels of concentrate feeds, mountain dairy products differ for the following aspects (Martin et al. 2016; Garmendia et al. 2022; Danieli et al. 2022):

- more intense color (in milk and derived products), odor, flavor, and taste;
- different and more complex sensory features linked to pasture botanical composition;
- specific microbiota composition, partially responsible for cheese sensory, or "terroir," properties;

- higher contents of grass-related fatty acids, considered healthier (e.g., vaccenic, rumenic, and α-linoleic);
- higher contents of polyunsaturated fatty acids and conjugated linoleic acid, with higher ratios between polyunsaturated and saturated fatty acids (lower atherogenicity index) which decrease the risk of cardiovascular diseases and diabetes;
- higher antioxidant capacity due to tocopherols (vitamin E), terpenoids and other substances from grass.

For these reasons, and for environmental specificities (soil, climate, vegetation), feeding management, and the traditional manufacturing practices of local processing chains often associated with extensive LPS, the intrinsic quality properties of cheeses and/or dairy products produced in specific mountain areas differs substantially from each other. This variability creates a high richness of typical products (see below for the link with cultural ES).

4 Mountain LPS and Biodiversity

Biodiversity, in terms of genetic diversity, taxonomic richness and habitat diversity, is declining worldwide due to various human pressures driven by economic and social development (IPBES 2019). Biodiversity EDS associated with livestock farming are mainly due to the loss and fragmentation of natural habitats because of deforestation and conversion of (semi)natural habitats into cropland or grassland for animal feeds, particularly in South America, to competition with wildlife, and to excessive or poorly regulated grazing pressure on rangelands (Alkemade et al. 2013), and indirectly to soil and waters pollution due to nutrients excretions (Reid et al. 2009; Pozo et al. 2021). On the other hand, correctly managed, targeted grazing may be beneficial for the conservation of rangelands and specific habitats and their biodiversity (Fraser et al. 2014; Bailey et al. 2019; Öllerer et al. 2019).

In the EU, the interactions of LPS with habitats and biodiversity are double-faced and strictly linked to the recent evolution of livestock farming. During the second half of the last century, agricultural intensification determined an expansion of cropland and a simplification of agroecosystems, which, together with increasingly intensive management practices, has resulted in the degradation, loss, and fragmentation of the natural and semi-natural habitats that were present in, or associated to, traditional mixed agricultural systems (EEA 2020). However, due to environmental and socio-economic constraints, intensification was impossible in mountain areas. The extensive grassland LPS, which had historically shaped the local society, economy, and mountain landscapes and could not be converted into intensive LPS, were massively abandoned. The interruption of grasslands' management allowed their progressive shrub encroachment and natural reafforestation (for examples, see Cocca et al. 2012; Dax et al. 2021), negatively impacting landscape diversity and richness of habitats (ecosystems) and species, which is lower in

Fig. 2 Extensively managed mountain grasslands (here an alpine summer pasture in the Dolomites, Italy; photo: M. Ramanzin) host rich biodiversity, which is exemplified in the picture by the numerous plant species flowering (plant biodiversity), for animals by the bird (*Tordus viscivorus*; vertebrate biodiversity) and for below- and above-ground invertebrates by the earthworm, caterpillar, and the grasshopper in its beak

homogenous forest landscapes than in mixed forest-grassland landscapes. In this respect, we stress the difference between the concepts of "rewilding," when intended as the return to the natural habitats following the interruption of human interference, and biodiversity. Rewilding of mountain grasslands implies their return to forest habitats that humans had previously cut, essentially for obtaining forage. A homogeneous forest landscape, although more "natural," hosts less biodiversity than a mixed forest-grassland landscape. Additionally, in these landscapes, the presence of grasslands (and livestock) contributes synergistically to various regulating and cultural ES (Bengtsson et al. 2019).

In addition to their contribution to biodiversity at the landscape scale, semi-natural grasslands are habitats with high intrinsic biodiversity (Fig. 2) (Habel et al. 2013; Plieninger et al. 2014), are classified as "High Natural Value (HNV) Farmland" by the EU (Keenleyside et al. 2014), and some consist of phytosociological associations listed as "priority habitats" by the "Habitat" directive[4] within the Natura 2000 framework. Therefore, while intensive mixed LPS impacted the biodiversity of lowland areas, the loss of traditional, extensive LPS impacted that of mountain areas (EEA 2020). Kok et al. (2019) recently reviewed the research on the interactions between LPS and European biodiversity. They confirmed these two opposite effects, with negative impacts primarily associated with strictly production-oriented LPS (i.e., mixed intensive systems) and positive effects when livestock farming was also

[4] https://eur-lex.europa.eu/legal-content/EN/TXT/?uri=CELEX%3A01992L0043-20130701.

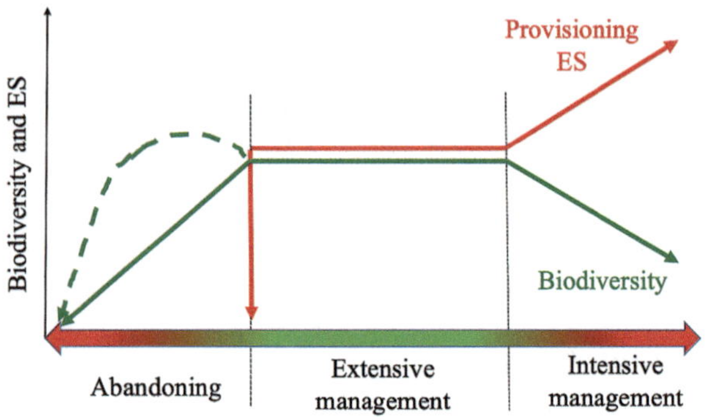

Fig. 3 General relation between management of seminatural grasslands and the associated ecosystem services (ES). Abandoning determines the immediate loss of provisioning ES, and a progressive decline of the specific biodiversity because of shrub encroachment and reafforestation, with a possible increase only during the first stages of the process. Extensive management allows, at a constant level of provisioning ES, to maximize biodiversity. Intensive management, while increasing provisioning ES, implies a decline in biodiversity (Graphic designed by the authors)

conservation-oriented (which can be associated only with extensive grassland systems).

A grassland patch's intrinsic biodiversity value strongly depends on management practices, as exemplified in Fig. 3. The extensive management of semi-natural meadows (low number of cuts, no chemical fertilization, no interventions on sward composition...) and pastures (moderate stocking rate, free or loosely rotational grazing...) creates specific, species-rich phytosociological associations with sward structural diversity, which may be habitat for rare plant and animal species, so maximizing biodiversity. Shifts towards intensive practices (increased use of fertilizers and the number of cuts in meadows, increase in stocking rate in pastures, reseeding...) to increase provisioning ES reduce botanical species richness and degrade habitat functions for plants and animals. High loads of grazing animals may directly impact bird species through trampling or invertebrates with the fecal excretion of residuals of antiparasitic treatments (Vickery et al. 2001; Plantureux et al. 2005; Humbert et al. 2009; Pakanen et al. 2011). The abandoning of grassland management, on the other hand, allows the entry of new species that might improve biodiversity in the short term, but the following shrub encroachment and reafforestation will determine a progressive degradation and finally end up in the loss of the grassland ecosystems and their specific biodiversity.

In general, grazing contributes better to the biodiversity of managed grasslands than cutting and harvesting the grass for hay or silage making because it creates and maintains richer plant communities and heterogenous sward patches, which are attractive for many living species. However, managing pastures to balance the trade-off between provisioning ES and biodiversity is particularly challenging. The main (positive or negative) impacts of livestock on pasture ecosystems consist of influences on sward structure and floristic composition, with cascade effects on

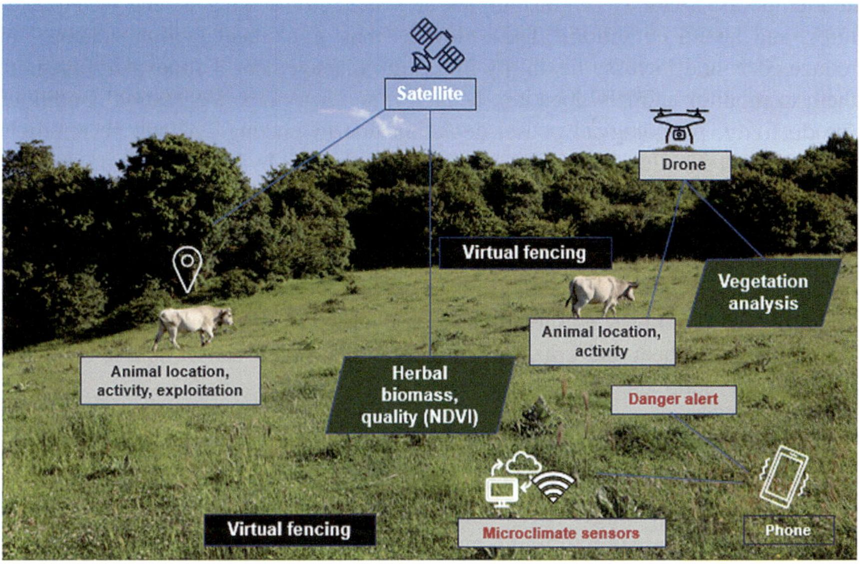

Fig. 4 Schematic representation of technologies available for precision livestock grazing in mountain areas (Photo: Bruno Ronchi; graphic designed by the authors)

living conditions for invertebrates, reptiles, birds, small mammals, and other taxa (Fraser et al. 2022). Many factors mediate the interactions (positive and negative) between sward productivity and structure, plant composition, and grazing livestock. Environmental features (soil, slope, aspect, altitude, climate, season. . .) influence the phytosociological composition, forage value and biomass productivity but also may impose constraints on animals' movement and thermoregulation and limit access to feed resources. In this respect, different livestock categories (species, age, breed, and productivity) have different abilities to move on steep and rough terrain, thermoregulate and fulfil their nutritional requirements with the sward forage value and productivity. Grazing livestock impacts sward through trampling, which may cause soil compaction and erosion, grazing, which selects for plant species more resistant to browsing, and excreta (nutrients) deposition. Farmers implement grazing management (stocking rate, rotational grazing and plots size vs continuum grazing, feed supplementation. . .) to modulate the interactions between the environment and livestock.

Recent technological advances have become available in the last two decades to improve knowledge and monitoring of these interactions to inform grazing management better. Figure 4 offers a schematic overview of the new technologies potentially available for pasture LPS in mountain areas (Ronchi and Primi 2019; Herlin et al. 2021; Aquilani et al. 2022; Horn and Isselstein 2022; Raniolo et al. 2022). Biologging (individual GPS tracking and activity sensors) allows remote monitoring of animal movement and behavior in the pasture area to verify the fine-scale spatial and temporal variability of grazing pressures and activity budgets, energy expenditures, and health conditions. These devices may implement "virtual fencing" to reduce costs and increase flexibility in pasture management. Drones may integrate them to monitor animals' location, behavior, and activities. Vegetation conditions (productivity, phenological phase, depletion due to grazing. . .) may be remotely assessed with satellite imagery or, at a finer spatial scale, by high-resolution imagery with drones; on-site weather stations can monitor climate conditions continuously.

While commercial applications for precision livestock grazing are already available, which may improve the efficiency of management and reduce costs, especially in large-scale pastures or rangelands, these technologies have opened revolutionary opportunities for improving the understanding of the complex interactions between animals, environment and grazing management, and their consequences on grasslands conservation and biodiversity.

One specific aspect of biodiversity that is related to LPS is their role in conserving the diversity of livestock genetic resources, represented by the variety of local breeds and populations. This biodiversity is fundamental for the sustainability and resilience of animal food chains (FAO 2019).

While the conservation of highly productive, cosmopolitan breeds is ensured by intensive LPS, that of local, traditional breeds depends on extensive LPS that make profitable use of their specific adaptations to local environmental conditions, unsuitable for improved breeds. Based on the Domestic Animal Diversity Information System (DAD-IS) of the Food and Agriculture Organisation (FAO), 45% of local breeds/populations are adapted to mountain habitats and climate extremes (Hoffmann 2013). Adaptive traits of these breeds include the ability to walk long distances on rough and steep pastures, excellent grazing ability and efficient use of coarse feed resources, good tolerance to extreme weather and climate conditions, lower vulnerability to diseases, high fertility and longevity, and adaptation to specific local environments. These adaptations create a strong link between the local seminatural agroecosystems and breeds, resulting from a long process of human selection in interaction with the natural constraints and the needs of rural populations. Besides their value of use in extensive LPS, local breeds/populations are important as genetic pools to ensure the long-term sustainability of food systems and resilience to environmental changes, such as climate change (Hoffmann 2013). Due to the historical interaction between livestock systems, breeds, and landscapes, local breeds are also physical expressions of cultural heritage (Hall 2018) and associate with "cultural landscapes" (Porter et al. 2016). Many examples exist worldwide of livestock breeds connected with cultural landscapes, e.g., horses and cattle in Camargue (France); sheep and guanaco in the Patagonian Steppe (Argentina); cattle sheep, and goats in the Samburu highlands of Kenia; horses and camels in semiarid regions of Kazakhstan. Figure 5 shows some examples of Italian mountain areas.

Fig. 5 Examples of cultural landscapes and connected local breeds. Summer transhumance of dairy cows (breeds: Simmental, Alpine Grey) in the Alps (top, photo M. Ramanzin); extensive free-ranging systems of local beef cows (breed: Maremmana) in common lands in Central Italy (mid, photo B. Ronchi); summer transhumance of Podolian cows (breed: Podolica) in the Pollino National Park (bottom, photo B. Ronchi)

5 Mountain LPS and Regulating ES

Managed grasslands provide a significant ES of protection from fires in many regions (Sil et al. 2019). In contrast with intensive cropland, when adequately managed, permanent grasslands contribute to the metabolization of potential pollutants and hence to good quality of surface water, reduce water runoff, and protect soils from erosion (see the review of Zhao et al. 2020). Grassland soils may have carbon stocks much higher than cropland soils and similar to, or even higher than, those of forest soils (Canedoli et al. 2020), especially when extensively managed (Byrnes et al. 2018). Species-rich seminatural grasslands favor pollinators in agricultural landscapes (Hevia et al. 2016; Orford et al. 2016). They may host predator arthropod populations which might improve the biological control capacity of diverse agricultural landscapes. On the other hand, intensive or poor management of grasslands may negatively impact these ES (Byrnes et al. 2018; Nagy et al. 2020) because the complex functions of grasslands ecosystems are more susceptible to human impacts than the simplified ones of cropland of intensive mixed systems.

An EDS commonly associated with LPS is the impact on climate and the quality of air, soil, and water of the emissions of greenhouse gases, reactive nitrogen, and phosphorus compounds (Leip et al. 2015; EEA 2019). We will not address here the ongoing debate on the real impact of livestock farming on such emissions and especially on climate change (Liu et al. 2021; Reisinger et al. 2021), but we argue that, in any case, mountain extensive LPS contribute to the total emissions of the livestock sector much less than intensive mixed LPS, because of the minor share of the total livestock that they maintain. Additionally, extensive LPS need lower external inputs and impact less on the ecosystems they manage thanks to lower emissions per unit of land (Schiavon et al. 2019; Berton et al. 2021). The higher soil carbon stocks of their land may contribute to mitigating climate change impacts. The Life Cycle Assessment (LCA; Hauschild et al. 2018) is the standard approach to assessing human activities' impacts on pollutant emissions. This ISO-standardized methodology is powerful and popular, but it must be used cautiously when comparing different LPS. One critical point is the "functional unit" used to standardize the impact, commonly the unit of product (milk or meat, possibly standardized for fat and/or protein content), and much less frequently the unit of land managed. Because of their higher productivity, intensive mixed LPS have lower emissions per unit of product than extensive, grassland-based ones. However, because of the higher stocking rates and import of nutrients, they have higher emissions per unit of land (Berton et al. 2021). While the emissions per unit of product are indeed relevant for greenhouse gases with a global impact, those per unit of land are more relevant for other compounds, such as nitrogen and phosphorus, that impact especially local ecosystems.

In addition, due to its structure and accounting procedure that have been unable to integrate (satisfactory) estimates of biodiversity and other non-provisioning ES, LCA does not account for the multifunctionality of LPS. This limitation has two consequences. The first is that the allocation of impacts, i.e., the partitioning of the total emissions among the main product and its co-products, considers only marketable products and co-products (for instance, milk and beef in a dairy LPS, provisioning ES). The incomplete allocation does not influence the impact assessments of intensive mixed LPS, which have almost no non-marketable co-products, but introduces a bias in the assessments of extensive, grassland-based LPS because it does not include in the co-products their multiple non-marketable benefits (non-provisioning ES). Considering these benefits as co-products in the allocation of impacts could reduce the emission intensity per unit of marketable products of these systems to values lower than those of intensive LPS (for example, see Kiefer et al. 2015). The second consequence is that, while LCA approaches are very well suited to assess pollutant emissions, they have been unable to integrate estimates of impacts on biodiversity and other non-provisioning ES (McClelland et al. 2018; van der Wilde and Newell 2021). Integrating such evaluations in the conceptual framework of LCA (Rugani et al. 2019) is difficult because of the dichotomy between the accounting for measurable material fluxes (nitrogen, carbon, etc.), which is intrinsic to LCA, and the complexity of assessing non-material benefits as biodiversity and ES.

6 Mountain LPS and Cultural ES

Cultural Ecosystem Services are "*nonmaterial benefits people obtain from ecosystems through spiritual enrichment, cognitive development, reflection, recreation, and aesthetic experiences*" (Millennium Ecosystem Assessment 2005). These benefits are commonly searched for and experienced by people, often without a conscious recognition of their link with ecosystems, and, being linked to human perceptions, vary greatly between cultures and individuals (Milcu et al. 2013).

The cultural landscapes and the cultural heritage of mountain areas have been strongly influenced in the past by the human activities, knowledge, and folklore connected with livestock farming (Plieninger et al. 2006). Recently, these landscapes and heritage have been largely modified and have partially disappeared because of the processes of livestock farming intensification or abandoning. However, part of them is still present where extensive mountain LPS are vital (Fig. 6). They influence local communities' cultural identity and sense of place and can be a source of artistic inspiration, aesthetic appreciation, and recreation. Extensive grasslands, especially in the presence of grazing animals, contribute to the aesthetic quality of the scenery and are highly appreciated (van Zanten et al. 2016). Local breeds also have a cultural value (Gandini and Villa 2003) and are part of the local cultural heritage and identity (Marsoner et al. 2018). Typical food products contribute not only to provisioning ES but are part of culinary traditions and maintain strong links with the local environment, farming systems, and processing chains, which people value. Therefore, the cultural ES of livestock farming are often synergic with other public benefits. Farming and livestock management practices may integrate with agrotourism

Fig. 6 Top: mountain cultural landscape still conserved in South Tyrol (Italy), where the traditional buildings and the conservation of grasslands surrounding the village and connecting the low sides of the valley to the high-elevation pastures reflect the interaction of the needs of livestock farming with the natural resources (photo: M. Ramanzin). Bottom: landscape dominated by the natural reafforestation following the abandoning of farming in central Apennines (Italy), which has lost its cultural identity (photo: M. Ramanzin)

initiatives, and many folkloristic events linked with livestock farming enrich the touristic offer of mountain areas.

7 Mountain LPS Sustainability and ES

Society directly influences the evolution of LPS through the market's demand and price of the provisioning ES they sell and the costs of the external inputs (feeds, energy, etc.) they purchase. Additionally, it acts indirectly through the payments and regulations implemented in agricultural, environmental, and veterinary policies. Agricultural policies should compensate the farmers operating in disadvantaged areas (typically, mountain areas) and reward the non-provisioning ES that the market does not remunerate (La Notte et al. 2015). In addition, together with other policies, they may impose limitations on farming practices. The LPS react to these influences to increase their income by adapting farming practices and managing their agroecosystems to maximize the provision of marketable ES and access to policy payments while complying with regulations (typically, agricultural policies, see below). If society fails to recognize and value specific ES, the market and public policies will not consider them. This lack of consideration is a problem for most non-provisioning ES, which have an indirect economic value and often are not acknowledged by society. In this case, the trajectories of the evolution of LPS will be driven primarily by market demands, and policies will have little effect in compensating for the market limitations. Such failure may result in unwanted evolutions of LPS and their agroecosystems, with losses of ES and release of EDS, as for the abovementioned recent shift of LPS towards intensification or, where not possible, abandoning.

The fragile and unique ecosystems of mountain areas require that the management of human activities adopts action plans recognizing the complexity of ecosystem functioning (Jørgensen et al. 2016), with the evaluation of the stressors affecting ecosystems and how they can be modified by human actions, giving primary importance to the delivery of ES in a framework of "Ecosystem-Based Management" (Farella et al. 2020). We suggest four interconnected steps for ecosystem-based management of LPS. First, there is a strong need to identify and quantify thc ES (and EDS) provided by extensive LPS; second, the social perception and economic valuation of such ES are essential for, third, implementing effective public policies and, fourth, informing private promotion and marketing initiatives.

7.1 Assessing and Valuing the ES

The problem of assessing ES is complex because some may be quantified with biophysical approaches (for example, measuring the biomass of products for provisioning ES, the species richness for biodiversity, the soil C content for climate regulating ES, etc.), while others (especially the cultural ones) require socio-cultural approaches (Plieninger et al. 2015; Small et al. 2017). In addition, proxies and modelling approaches may be used. For example, forage production can be estimated from climate, soil, and land morphology variables (La Notte et al. 2015), or landscape aesthetic value from people's preferences and maps of landscape features (Schirpke et al. 2021). In this assessment process, we emphasize the need to link the ES/EDS to the farming systems and farming management practices delivering them (Santos et al. 2021) and to identify simplified ES indicators at the farm scale. Comparisons of different LPS and implementation of ES in policies need robust but also operational indexing variables.

In addition, ES are context-specific and vary according to the local environmental and socio-economic conditions. For instance, protection from fires and water regulation do not have the same importance in all landscapes, priorities in biodiversity conservation (habitats and species) and perceptions of cultural ES vary locally. In addition, there are synergies and trade-offs between ES. Improving the biodiversity of grasslands may increase regulating ES (waters quality) and cultural ES (diversity and aesthetic quality of the landscape, recreational and touristic value...), while intensive management may reduce them. Because of the specificity of local ES/EDS, these synergies and trade-offs create "bundles" of ES (and EDS) clustered locally (Raudsepp-Hearne et al. 2010). Therefore, ES/EDS should be assessed for the different local contexts.

7.2 *Social Perception and Economic Valuation of ES*

The be valued, ES must be first recognized by society. Understanding the social perception of ES (again, in the local contexts) is necessary to identify gaps in knowledge between different stakeholders. The conceptual framework of ES is still little known, and different stakeholders may have different knowledge biases (for instance, farmers and tourists: Pachoud et al. 2020a). This assessment might enable to address communication of, and education on, the role of farming in delivering public benefits. This information is necessary for society to understand the multifunctionality of LPS and is a preliminary step to their economic valuation. Assessing the economic value of non-marketable benefits is difficult. It requires specific approaches (Liekens and De Nocker 2013). However, it is necessary to design public policies tailored to the local contexts and set payments to farmers objectively justified by the delivered ES and commensurate to their economic value. In this respect, the willingness to pay by the society for non-provisioning ES is higher than the present level of public payments (Bernués et al. 2019).

Quantification and valuation of ES related to LPS are rare in literature due to the difficulties of conducting on-site studies at a territorial scale and measuring environmental and farming parameters. Therefore, it is also difficult to understand the causes of variation in the provision of ES among different LPS and, above all, the trade-offs and synergies between ES and ecosystem components. Table 1 presents a non-comprehensive overview of recent papers analyzing and evaluating ES connected with extensive or semi-extensive LPS in Italian mountain areas.

Table 1 Examples of studies on assessment and/or valuation of ES provided by extensive LPS in Italian mountain areas (Table elaborated by the authors)

Authors	Location	Ecosystem	Livestock system	ES considered	Aim and approach
Bagella et al. (2020)	Sardinia	Mixed cork oak and grassland landscape	Silvopastoral	Plant biodiversity and multiple provisioning, supporting and regulating ES	Biophysical and indicator-based assessment
Faccioni et al. (2019)	Province of Trento	Mountain meadows and pastures	Summer dairy cow farming	Biodiversity (general), regulation (water quality), cultural (landscape); provisioning (variety of cheeses)	Socio-economic valuation
Francioni et al. (2016)	Marche	Permanent pastures	Transhumant sheep grazing	Carbon sequestration	Biophysical assessment
La Notte et al. (2015)	Trentino	Mountain meadows	Cattle farming	Provisioning (forage production)	Modelling assessment
Madau et al. (2022)	Sardinia	Agro-pastoral Mediterranean areas	Extensive dairy sheep farming	Biodiversity and multiple regulation and cultural	Social perception and valuation
Marsoner et al. (2018)	North Italy	Alpine Space regions	Traditional local breeds farming	Potential cultural ES from domestic livestock breeds	Mapping breed/species richness indicators
Montrasio et al. (2020)	Piedmont (Lanzo Valley)	Alpine mountain area	Summer dairy cow farming	Biodiversity and multiple provisioning, regulating and cultural	Social perception
Pornaro et al. (2021)	Eastern Italian Alps	Mountain meadows and pastures	Dairy cow farming	Plant biodiversity	Biophysical assessment
Röhrig et al. (2020)	Umbria, Lazio	Woodland, crop, grassland	Silvopastoral	Biodiversity and multiple regulating	Social perception
Troiano et al. (2021)	Southern Apennines	Mediterranean mountain landscape	Free-ranging transhumant grazing	Plant and arthropod biodiversity, landscape	Biophysical assessment
Zander et al. (2013)	Tuscany, Lazio	Woodland, crop, grassland	Traditional local breeds farming	Multiple cultural	Economic valuation

7.3 Implementing Effective Public Policies and Private Valuation Actions

The European Common Agricultural Policy (CAP) aims to ensure food security and safety, safeguard farmers' income, protect the environment and promote rural development. The last revision (2023–2027) of the CAP has been strongly influenced by the "European Green Deal" (European Commission 2019), a climate pact aiming to transform the EU's economy for a sustainable future by achieving "zero" greenhouse gases net emissions by 2050, decoupling economic growth from the use of resources, and ensuring full people inclusion. At the core of the Green Deal, the "Farm to fork" strategy (European Commission 2020a) aims at a "*fair, healthy and environmentally-friendly food system*", linking farming and food production with the reduction of impacts on climate change and air, soil, water pollution, the conservation of agro-ecosystems functions and biodiversity, and the promotion of healthy diets. An essential part of the Green Deal is also the "2030 Biodiversity Strategy" (European Commission 2020b) that aims to restore European biodiversity and ecosystems, including grasslands, and contains the proposal of a "Nature Restoration Law" that also targets the biodiversity of agricultural ecosystems. To align with the Green Deal, the 2023–2027 CAP revision introduced new forms of "conditionality" (environmentally friendly farming practices) to direct payments to farmers in terms of "good agricultural and environmental conditions" (GAECs) for soil protection and quality, biodiversity, and landscape conservation. Of the direct payments, 25% will be connected to "eco-schemes," mandatory for EU countries but voluntary for farmers, with incentives for climate and environment-friendly practices. The payments in the rural development pillar will be supported with "Agri-environment-climate measures and investments" to improve ecosystem functions, resource use efficiency, and climate neutrality. At least 35% of the funds will be allocated to measures supporting climate, biodiversity, environment, and animal welfare. In these measures, we stress the role of grassland agro-ecosystems. Permanent grasslands depend on LPS for maintenance and cover 34% of the European Union's (28 countries) utilized agricultural area (Eurostat 2020). According to the European Union, permanent grasslands are to be intended as a "*land used to grow grasses or other herbaceous forage naturally (self-seeded) or through cultivation (sown), and that has not been included in the crop rotation of the holding for five years or more, it may include other species such as shrubs and/or trees which can be grazed provided that the grasses and other herbaceous forage remain predominant as well as, where Member States so decide, land which can be grazed and which forms part of established local practices where grasses and other herbaceous forage are traditionally not predominant in grazing areas*" (EU Regulation 1307/2013). The CAP Reform introduced in 2013 supporting measures to contrast the loss and degradation of permanent grasslands (Lostrangio and Clotteau 2021), with the instrument of "green payment," a form of subsidy connected with agricultural practices beneficial for the environment (crop diversification, maintaining permanent grasslands, creating "ecological focus areas"). The

National governments were asked to maintain a minimum proportion of permanent grassland in the total utilized agricultural area. The new CAP 2023–2027 has further emphasized the importance of permanent grasslands for their role in carbon sequestration and the maintenance of biodiversity. Specific permanent grasslands may be classified as "environmentally sensitive," to protect them from inappropriate usage and/or transformation. Farmers, to receive direct payments for grassland protection, will be conditioned by the adoption of GAECs, especially for what concerns environmentally sensitive permanent grassland. Identifying such grasslands based on their biodiversity value and delivery of non-provisioning ES, together with payments fairly supporting the associated management practices, is crucial for implementing effective policies. Due to the diversity of environmental conditions, farming systems, and socio-economic conditions of mountain areas, this identification and the payments must be realized within a general framework but tailored locally. On the other hand, while beneficial practices for biodiversity should be supported, those with potentially negative impacts can be regulated and limited, especially by biodiversity policies within the Natura 2000 network. Additional costs or loss of production for farmers who comply with such regulations should be implemented as incentives and compensation in agricultural policies. For this purpose, a synergy and interchange between agricultural and biodiversity policies at the regional and local scale is needed.

Farmers can also implement private actions to diversify and increase income and add value to their products with market initiatives valorizing the non-provisioning ES associated with productive chains. While certain forms of tourism development may be the cause of the decline of extensive LPS and mountain ES (Muñoz-Ulecia et al. 2021), correct integration of farming with agritourism and/or other touristic events based on cultural ES sustains LPS and may create synergies with other local economic activities (Genovese et al. 2021). Labelling and promoting local products for their "extrinsic" quality, i.e., the territorial specificities of the products and processing chains and the associated ES, can create added value for single farmers or, in a larger context, cooperative processing chains (Pachoud et al. 2020b; Teston et al. 2022). The ES framework can help devise these actions to advertise the public benefits associated with the farming-processing chains correctly and to conserve and promote the local natural and cultural heritage.

8 Conclusions

Livestock production systems are highly diverse regionally and locally, especially in mountain areas. While intensive mixed systems of lowlands deliver almost exclusively provisioning, marketable ES (food), mountain extensive grassland-based systems are highly multifunctional. They maintain seminatural agro-ecosystems of high natural and cultural value. They are strictly connected with landscape diversity, biological diversity, diversity of livestock genetic resources and food products as part of the cultural and natural heritage. Therefore, they are essential for conserving mountain ES which can create synergic interactions between farming and non-agricultural sectors, e.g., tourism, food services, and small industry, and valorize the connection between the local and global social and economic dimensions. Such integration between natural resources and human activities is necessary for local communities' sustainable development and resilience.

On the other hand, if improperly managed, LPS may negatively impact ES and produce EDS, among which climate change impact is currently highly debated. European environmental policies are increasingly committed to reducing such impact from LPS and restoring biodiversity. The LCA assessment procedure commonly used for impacts assessment cannot integrate biodiversity and many non-provisioning ES as impact categories (EDS) and co-products (ES). Evaluation approaches integrating impacts assessed with LCA with assessments of synergies and trade-offs with biodiversity and ES are needed to avoid biased comparisons between LPS and the risk of negative side effects on these ES.

To contrast the decline of mountain LPS and the loss of associated ES, a better market valuation of food products justified by the public benefits associated with production chains, the integration with new tourism activities, and public support from agricultural policies that should evolve from subsidies dispensed generically to effective payments for ES, based on their actual delivery and economic value, are needed. These achievements require an interdisciplinary commitment of the science community to identify reliable and operational indicators and assess their perception and valuation by society, the involvement of all stakeholders to devise locally tailored actions and development plans, and a policy framework supporting them.

References

Alkemade R, Reid RS, van den Berg M, de Leeuw J, Jeuken M (2013) Assessing the impacts of livestock production on biodiversity in rangeland ecosystems. PNAS 110:20900–20905

Aquilani C, Confessore A, Bozzi R, Sirtori F, Pugliese C (2022) Review: Precision Livestock Farming technologies in pasture-based livestock systems. Animal 16:100429

Bagella S, Caria MC, Seddaiu G, Leites L, Roggero PP (2020) Patchy landscapes support more plant diversity and ecosystem services than wood grasslands in Mediterranean silvopastoral agroforestry systems. Agric Syst 185:102945

Bailey DW, Mosley JC, Estell RE, Cibils AF, Horney M, Hendrickson JR, Walker JW, Launchbaugh KL, Burritt EA (2019) Synthesis paper: targeted livestock grazing: prescription for healthy rangelands. Rangel Ecol Manag 72:865–877

Bengtsson J, Bullock JM, Egoh B, Everson C, Everson T, O'Connor T, O'Farrell PJ, Smith HG, Lindborg R (2019) Grasslands—more important for ecosystem services than you might think. Ecosphere:e02582

Bernués A (2017) Animals on the land. Ecosystem services and disservices of grazing livestock systems. In: D'Silva J, Webster J (eds) The meat crisis. Developing more sustainable and ethical production and consumption. Taylor and Francis

Bernués A, Alfnes F, Clemetsen M, Eik LO, Faccioni G, Ramanzin M, Ripoll-Bosch R, Rodríguez-Ortega T, Sturaro E (2019) Exploring social preferences for ecosystem services of multifunctional agriculture across policy scenarios. Ecosyst Serv 39:101002

Berton M, Bovolenta S, Corazzin M, Gallo L, Pinterits S, Ramanzin M, Ressi W, Spigarelli C, Zuliani A, Sturaro E (2021) Environmental impacts of milk production and processing in the Eastern Alps: a "cradle-to-dairy gate" LCA approach. J Clean Prod 303:127056

Byrnes RC, Eastburn DE, Tate KW, Roche LM (2018) A global meta-analysis of grazing impacts on soil health indicators. J Environ Qual 47:758–765

Canedoli C, Ferrè C, El Khair DA, Comolli R, Liga C, Mazzucchelli F, Proietto A, Rota N, Colombo G, Bassano B, Viterbi R, Padoa-Schioppa E (2020) Evaluation of ecosystem services in a protected mountain area: soil organic carbon stock and biodiversity in alpine forests and grasslands. Ecosyst Serv 44(2020):101135

Cocca G, Sturaro E, Gallo L, Ramanzin M (2012) Is the abandonment of traditional livestock farming systems the main driver of mountain landscape change in Alpine areas? Land Use Policy 29:878–886

D'Ottavio P, Francioni M, Trozzo L, Sedic E, Budimir K, Avanzolini P, Trombetta MF, Porqueddu C, Santilocchi R, Toderi M (2017) Trends and approaches in the analysis of ecosystem services provided by grazing systems: a review. Grass Forage Sci 73:15–25

Danieli PP, Lopez A, Bellagamba F, Vetturini T, Bernabucci U, Ronchi B, Moretti VM, Basiricò L (2022) Effects of season and management on fatty acid profile, ACE-inhibitory activity and anti-oxidant properties of Italian Alpine cheeses. Ital J Anim Sci 21:1021–1033

Dax T, Schroll K, Machold I, Derszniak-Noirjean M, Schuh B, Gaupp-Berghausen M (2021) Land abandonment in mountain areas of the EU: an inevitable side effect of farming modernisation and neglected threat to sustainable land use. Land 10:591

EEA-Environmental European Agency (2020) State of nature in the EU. Results from reporting under the nature directives 2013-2018. EEA Report No 10/2020

EEA-European Environment Agency (2019) Annual European Union greenhouse gas inventory 1990–2017 and inventory report 2019

EU (2013) Regulation N° 1307/2013 of the European Parliament and of the Council establishing rules for direct payments to farmers under support schemes within the framework of the common agricultural policy and repealing Council Regulation (EC) N°637/2008 and Council Regulation N° 73/2009

European Commission (2019) The European Green Deal. Brussels 11.12.2019 COM 640 final

European Commission (2020a) A Farm to Fork Strategy for a Fair, Healthy, and Environmentally-Friendly Food System COM(2020) 381 final

European Commission (2020b) EU Biodiversity Strategy for 2030. Bringing nature back into our lives. Brussels, COM(2020) 380 final

Eurostat (2020) Share of main land types in utilised agricultural area (UAA) by NUTS 2. https://ec.europa.eu/eurostat/cache/metadata/en/tai05_esmsip2.htm

Faccioni G, Sturaro E, Ramanzin M, Bernués A (2019) Socio-economic valuation of abandonment and intensification of Alpine agroecosystems and associated ecosystem services. Land Use Policy 81:453–462

FAO (2019) The state of the world's biodiversity for food and agriculture. In: Bélanger J, Pilling D (eds) FAO commission on genetic resources for food and agriculture assessments. Rome

Farella G, Menegon S, Fadini A, Depellegrin D, Manea E, Perini L, Barbanti A (2020) Incorporating ecosystem services conservation into a scenario-based MSP framework: an Adriatic case study. Ocean Coast Manag 193:105230

Francioni M, Toderi M, Lai R, Trozzo L, Foresi L, Sciara F, Avanzolini P, Sedić E, Budimir K, Santilocchi R, D'Ottavio P (2016) Does transhumant sheep provide ecosystem services for climate change adaptation in Mediterranean environment? Option Méditteranéennes 114:103–106

Fraser MD, Moorby JM, Vale JE, Evans DM (2014) Mixed grazing systems benefit both upland biodiversity and livestock production. PLoS One 9:e89054

Fraser MD, Vallin HE, Roberts BP (2022) Grassland-based livestock farming and biodiversity. Animal:16–100671

Gandini G, Villa E (2003) Analysis of the cultural value of local livestock breeds: a methodology. J Anim Breed Genet 120:1–11

Garmendia E, Aldezabal A, Galan E, Andogeni A, del Prado A, Gamboa G, Garcia O, Pardo G, Aldai N, Barron LJR (2022) Mountain sheep grazing systems provide multiple ecological, socio-economic, and food quality benefits. Agron Sustain Dev 42:47

Genovese D, Culasso F, Giacosa E, Battaglini LM (2021) Can livestock farming and tourism coexist in mountain regions? A new business model for sustainability. Sustainability 9:2021

Habel JC, Dengler J, Janišová M, Török P, Wellstein C, Wiezik M (2013) European grassland ecosystems: threatened hotspots of biodiversity. Biodivers Conserv 22:2131–2138

Hall SJG (2018) Livestock biodiversity as interface between people, landscapes and nature. People Nat 1:284–290

Hauschild MZ, Rosenbaum RK, Olsen SI (eds) (2018) Life cycle assessment – theory and practice. Springer International Publishing AG, Switzerland

Herlin A, Brunberg E, Hultgren J, Högberg N, Rydberg A, Skarin A (2021) Animal welfare implications of digital tools for monitoring and management of cattle and sheep on pasture. Animals 11:829

Hevia V, Bosch J, Azcárate FM, Fernández E, Rodrigo A, Barril-Graells H, González JA (2016) Bee diversity and abundance in a livestock drove road and its impact on pollination and seed set in adjacent sunflower fields. Agric Ecosyst Environ 232:336–344

Hoffmann I (2013) Adaptation to climate change – exploring the potential of locally adapted breeds. Animal 7:346–362

Horn J, Isselstein J (2022) How do we feed grazing livestock in the future? A case for knowledge-driven grazing systems. Grass Forage Sci 2(77):153–166

Humbert J-Y, Ghazoul J, Walter T (2009) Meadow harvesting techniques and their impacts on field fauna. Agric Ecosyst Environ 130:1–8

IPBES (2019) In: Brondízio ES, Settele J, Díaz S, Ngo HT (eds) Global assessment report of the Intergovernmental Science-Policy Platform on Biodiversity and Ecosystem Services, IPBES secretariat, Bonn, Germany

Jørgensen SE, Nielsen SN, Fath BD (2016) Recent progress in systems ecology. Ecol Models 319: 112–118

Keenleyside C, Beaufoy GM, Tucker G, Jones G (2014) High nature value farming throughout EU-27 and its financial support under the CAP. Report Prepared for DG Environment, Contract No ENV B.1/ETU/2012/0035. Institute for European Environmental Policy, London

Kiefer LR, Menzel F, Bahrs E (2015) Integration of ecosystem services into the carbon footprint of milk of South German dairy farms. J Environ Manag 152:11–18

Kok A, de Olde EM, de Boer IJM, Ripoll-Bosch R (2019) European biodiversity assessments in livestock science: a review of research characteristics and indicators. Ecol Indic 112:105902

La Notte A, Marongiu S, Masiero M, Molfetta P, Molignoni R, Cesaro L (2015) Livestock and ecosystem services: an exploratory approach to assess agri-environment-climate payments of RDP in Trentino. Land 4:688–710

Leip A, Leach A, Musinguzi P, Davis KF, Yu K, Herrero M, Leip A, Billen G, Garnier J, Grizzetti B, Lassaletta L, Reis S (2015) Impacts of European livestock production: nitrogen, sulphur, phosphorus and greenhouse gas emissions, land-use. Environ Res Lett 10:115004

Leroy G, Baumunga R, Boettcher P, Besbes B, From T, Hoffmann I (2018) Animal genetic resources diversity and ecosystem services. Global Food Secur 17:84–91

Liekens I, De Nocker L (2013) Valuation of ES: challenges and policy use. In: Jacobs S, Dendonker N, Keune H (eds) Ecosystem services. Global issues, local practices. Elsevier, pp 107–119

Liu S, Proudman J, Mitloehner FM (2021) Rethinking methane from animal agriculture. CABI Agric Biosci 2:22

Lostrangio MC, Clotteau M (2021) A review of policy frameworks supporting mountain grasslands in Europe. Palaearctic Grassland 51:17–22

Madau FA, Arru B, Furesi R, Sau P, Pulina P (2022) Public perception of ecosystem and social services produced by Sardinia extensive dairy sheep farming systems. Agric Food Econ 10(19): 1–42

Marsoner T, Vogl LE, Manck F, Jaritz G, Tappainer U, Tasser E (2018) Indigenous livestock breeds as indicators for cultural ecosystem services: a spatial analysis within the Alpine space. Ecol Indic 94:55–63

Martin B, Coppa M, Verdier-Metz I, Montel MC, Joy M, Casasus I, Blanco M (2016) The contribution of mountain pastures to the link to terroir in dairy and meat products. Options Méditerranéennes 116:105–115

McClelland SCM, Arnd C, Gordon DR, Thoma G (2018) Type and number of environmental impact categories used in livestock life cycle assessment: a systematic review. Livestock Sci 209:39–45

Merida VE, Cook D, Ögmundarson Ó, Davíðsdóttir B (2022) Ecosystem services and disservices of meat and dairy production: a systematic literature review. Ecosyst Serv 58:101494

Milcu AI, Hanspach J, Abson D, Fischer J (2013) Cultural ecosystem services: a literature review and prospects for future research. Ecol Soc 18(3):44

Millennium Ecosystem Assessment (2005) Ecosystems and human well-being: synthesis. Island Press, Washington, DC

Montrasio R, Mattiello S, Zucaro M, Genovese D, Battaglini L (2020) The perception of ecosystem services of mountain farming and of a local cheese: an analysis for the touristic valorisation of an Inner Alpine area. Sustainability 12:8017. https://doi.org/10.3390/su12198017

Muñoz-Ulecia E, Bernués A, Casasús I, Olaizola AM, Lobón S, Martín-Collado D (2021) Drivers of change in mountain agriculture: a thirty-year analysis of trajectories of evolution of cattle farming systems in the Spanish Pyrenees. Agric Syst 186:102983

Nagy RK, Bell LW, Schellhorn NA, Zalucki MP (2020) Role of grasslands in pest suppressive landscapes: how green are my pastures? Austral Entomol 59:227–237

Öllerer K, Varga A, Kirby K, Demeter L, Biró M, Bölöni J, Molnár Z (2019) Beyond the obvious impact of domestic livestock grazing on temperate forest vegetation – a global review. Biol Conserv 237:209–219

Orford KA, Murray PJ, Vaughan IP, Memmott J (2016) Modest enhancements to conventional grassland diversity improve the provision of pollination services. J Appl Ecol 53:906–915

Pachoud C, Da Re R, Ramanzin M, Bovolenta S, Gianelle D, Sturaro E (2020a) Tourists and local stakeholders' perception of ecosystem services provided by summer farms in the Eastern Italian Alps. Sustainability 12:1095

Pachoud C, Delay E, Da Re R, Ramanzin M, Sturaro E (2020b) A relational approach to studying collective action in dairy cooperatives producing mountain cheeses in the Alps: the case of the Primiero Cooperative in the Eastern Italians Alps. Sustainability 12:4596

Pakanen VM, Luukkonen A, Koivula K (2011) Nest predation and trampling as management risks in grazed coastal meadows. Biodivers Conserv 20:2057–2073

Plantureux S, Peeters A, McCracken D (2005) Biodiversity in intensive grasslands: effect of management, improvement and challenges. Agron Res 3:153–164

Plieninger T, Höchtl, Spek T (2006) Traditional land-use and nature conservation in European rural landscapes. Environ Sci Policy 9:317–321

Plieninger T, Hui C, Gaertner M, Huntsinger L (2014) The impact of land abandonment on species richness and abundance in the Mediterranean Basin: a meta-analysis. PLoS One 9:e98355

Plieninger T, Bieling C, Fagerholm N, Byg A, Hartel T, Hurley P, López-Santiago CA, Nagabhatla N, Oteros-Rozas E, Raymond CM, van der Horst D, Huntsinger L (2015) The role of cultural ecosystem services in landscape management and planning. Curr Opin Environ Sustain 14:28–33

Pornaro C, Spigarelli C, Pasut D, Ramanzin M, Bovolenta S, Sturaro E, Macolino S (2021) Plant biodiversity of mountain grasslands as influenced by dairy farm management in the Eastern Alps. Agric Ecosyst Environ 320:107583

Porter V, Alderson GLH, Hall SJG, Sponenberg DP (2016) Mason's world encyclopedia of livestock breeds and breeding. CABI International, Wallingford, UK

Pozo RA, Cusack JJ, Acebes P, Malo JE, Traba J, Iranzo EC, Morris-Trainor Z, Minderman J, Bunnefeld N, Radic-Schilling S, Moraga CA, Arriagada R, Corti P (2021) Reconciling livestock production and wild herbivore conservation: challenges and opportunities. Trends Ecol Evol 36: 750–761

Raniolo S, Sturaro E, Ramanzin M (2022) Human choices, slope and vegetation productivity determine patterns of traditional alpine summer grazing. Ital J Anim Sci 21:1126–1139

Raudsepp-Hearne C, Peterson G, Bennett E (2010) Ecosystem service bundles for analyzing tradeoffs in diverse landscapes. Proc Natl Acad Sci U S A 107:5242–5247

Reid RS, Bedelian C, Said MY, Kruska RL, Mauricio RM, Castel V, Olson J, Thornton PK (2009) Global livestock impacts on biodiversity. In: Steinfeld H, Mooney HA, Schneider F, Neville LE (eds) Livestock in a changing landscape, volume 1. Drivers, consequences, and responses. Island Press, Washington DC, pp 111–137

Reisinger A, Clark H, Cowie AL, Emmet-Booth J, Gonzalez Fischer C, Herrero M, Howden M, Leahy S (2021) How necessary and feasible are reductions of methane emissions from livestock to support stringent temperature goals? Phil Trans R Soc A 379:20200452

Rodríguez-Ortega T, Oteros-Rozas E, Ripoll-Bosh R, Tichit M, Martín-López B, Bernués A (2014) Applying the ecosystem services framework to pasture-based livestock farming systems in Europe. Animal 8:1361–1372

Röhrig N, Hassler M, Roesler T (2020) Capturing the value of ecosystem services from silvopastoral systems: perceptions from selected Italian farms. Ecosyst Serv 44:101152

Ronchi B, Primi R (2019) Remote sensing for real time estimate of aboveground biomass productivity in mountain pasture. In "Ruiz R. (ed.), López-Francos A. (ed.), López Marco L. (ed.)". Innovation for sustainability in sheep and goats. Options Méditerranéennens: Série A. Seminaires Méditerranéens 123:385–388

Rugani B, de Souza DM, Weidema BP, Bare J, Bakshi B, Grann B, Johnston JM, Raymundo Pavan AL, Liu X, Laurent A, Verones F (2019) Towards integrating the ecosystem services cascade framework within the Life Cycle Assessment (LCA) cause-effect methodology. Sci Total Environ 690:1284–1298

Santos JL, Moreira F, Ribeiro PF, Canadas MJ, Novais A, Lomba A (2021) A farming systems approach to linking agricultural policies with biodiversity and ecosystem services. Front Ecol Environ 19:168–175

Schiavon S, Sturaro E, Tagliapietra F, Ramanzin M, Bittante G (2019) Nitrogen and phosphorus excretion on mountain farms of different dairy systems. Agric Syst 168:36–47

Schirpke U, Zoderer BM, Tappeiner U, Tasser E (2021) Effects of past landscape changes on aesthetic landscape values in the European Alps. Landsc Urban Plan 212:104109

Sil Â, Fernandes PM, Rodrigues AP, Alonso JM (2019) Farmland abandonment decreases the fire regulation capacity and the fire protection ecosystem service in mountain landscapes. Ecosyst Serv 36:100908

Small N, Munday M, Durance I (2017) The challenge of valuing ecosystem services that have no material benefits. Global Environ Change 44:57–67

Steinfeld H, Mäki-Hokkonen J (1995) A classification of livestock production systems. World Anim Rev:83–94

Sturaro E, Marchiori E, Cocca G, Penasa M, Ramanzin M, Bittante G (2013) Dairy systems in mountainous areas: farm animal biodiversity, milk production and destination, and land use. Livestock Sci 158:157–168

Teston M, Orsi M, Bittante G, Cecchinato A, Gallo L, Gatto P, Macedo Mota LF, Ramanzin M, Raniolo S, Tormen A, Sturaro E (2022) Added value of local sheep breeds in alpine agroecosystems. Sustainability 14:4698

Troiano C, Buglione M, Petrelli S, Belardinelli S, De Natale A, Svenning J-C, Fulgione D (2021) Traditional free-ranging livestock farming as a management strategy for biological and cultural landscape diversity: a case from the southern Apennines. Land 10(957):1–16

van der Wilde CP, Newell JP (2021) Ecosystem services and life cycle assessment: a bibliometric review. Resour Conserv Recycl 169:105461
Van Zanten BT, Zasada I, Koetse MJ, Ungaro F, Häfner K, Verburg PH (2016) A comparative approach to assess the contribution of landscape features to aesthetic and recreational values in agricultural landscapes. Ecosyst Serv 17:87–98
Vickery JA, Tallowin JR, Feber RE, Asteraki EJ, Atkinson PJ, Fuller RJ, Brown VK (2001) The management of lowland neutral grasslands in Britain: effects of agricultural practices on birds and their food resources. J Appl Ecol 38:647–664
Zander KK, Signorello G, De Salvo M, Gandini G, Drucker AG (2013) Assessing the total economic value of threatened livestock breeds in Italy: implications for conservation policy. Ecol Econ 93:219–229
Zhang W, Ricketts TH, Kremen C, Carney K, Swinton SM (2007) Ecosystem services and dis-services to agriculture. Ecol Econ 64:253–260
Zhao Y, Liu Z, Wu J (2020) Grassland ecosystem services: a systematic review of research advances and future directions. Landsc Ecol 35:793–814

EU Soil Strategy for 2030: A Focus on Contaminated Sites and the Case of Italy

Giovanni Savarese and Marco Falconi

Abstract The European Commission has adopted a set of proposals to make the EU's climate, energy, transport, and taxation policies fit for reducing net greenhouse gas emissions by at least 55% by 2030. These ambitious objectives will be achieved within a framework known as European Green Deal. In the context of strategic choices and actions, there is also the EU soil strategy for 2030 which is also a is a key outcome of the EU biodiversity strategy for 2030. The European Commission has recognised how it is important to avoid the risks and impacts that continued soil degradation has on the economy and people's well-being; soils deserve the utmost and urgent attention of governments, parliaments, and public authorities at all levels. Among the various medium-term objectives by 2030, there is the need to make significant progress in the remediation of contaminated sites. This kind of problem is also addressed by EU Action Plan: 'Towards Zero Pollution for Air, Water and Soil'. Contaminated sites are the result of decades of environmental policies with little concern for the environment and directed strong focus on industry and consumption. Many of the contaminated sites in Europe are the product of the industrial activities of the last century. In the absence of specific regulations and policies, profound alterations of ecosystems were produced with particular reference to soil and groundwater. Restoration of these areas is also important to eliminate or reduce soil consumption. Although the 'polluter pays' principle has been in force in Europe in the Treaty on the Functioning of the European Union since the 1970s and in the Directive 2004/35/EC, a common policy for the management of contaminated sites has not yet been identified. Italy began tackling the problem as early as the 1990s with some regional legislation to arrive at the first national legislation in 1999, which provided for the identification of these areas, the definition of reference concentrations, and technical standards for characterisation and remediation. Also with the Italian contribution, more and more works are being done on a network of industry experts to share the best positive and negative experiences. The aim of this

G. Savarese (✉)
Environmetal Specialist, Government authority, Rome, Italy

M. Falconi
ISPRA (Italian Institute for Environmental Protection and Research), Rome, Italy

G. Antonelli et al. (eds.), *Biodiversity Laws, Policies and Science in Europe, the United States and China*, https://doi.org/10.1007/978-3-031-56218-1_8

contribution is to illustrate the European framework in terms of soil protection and remediation of contaminated sites, also reconstructing the historical and legal path of the 'polluter pays' principle and acknowledging the progress that is being made at the EU and Italian national level.

1 Introduction

The greater awareness of anthropogenic impacts on planet earth has recently led to the development of policies and actions of great international scope. The countries of the European Union were among the first, even in recent times, to adopt measures and tools to control anthropogenic impacts and counteract the depletion of natural resources. Among these, to date, the soil is still exposed to numerous risk factors which also undermine the sustainable social and economic development of individual countries. In particular, the issue of contaminated sites has yet to find a common legal framework and an action plan for remediation at European level. The article retraces the fundamental aspects of the European process regarding environmental protection and protection with a historical perspective, focusing attention on soil policies. Regarding contaminated sites, we intend to acknowledge how the state of knowledge has advanced and the recent proposal for a soil directive goes in the right direction. Regarding the management of contaminated sites in Italy, the article intends to illustrate the general guidelines that the country has adopted.

2 The Position of Soil in the Environment, Its Importance and Threats

The natural environment is identified through a multiple variety of elements and depending on the level of detail of the perspective from which it is viewed. A first and broad distinction identifies 4 types of natural contexts: the atmosphere, the hydrosphere, the lithosphere and the biosphere. Each of them has its own characteristics that distinguish it from the others and in each of these contexts characteristic processes (physical, chemical and biological) take place. Furthermore, the way in which each of them interacts with other natural environments takes on particular importance.

The atmosphere, the set of gases that surrounds planet Earth, is made up of nitrogen, oxygen and carbon dioxide, mixed with variable percentages of water vapour. 50% of the mass of gases contained in the atmosphere is found within the first 5 km subaerial of the planet. The fundamental role of the atmosphere is its filtering action against all radiation coming from space, in particular solar radiation; this determines the temperature inside the atmosphere and therefore (for the most part) in planet Earth. A related characteristic is humidity. Temperature and humidity (together with pressure) are the basis of phenomena that have significant impacts on the environment: the action of the wind and atmospheric precipitation, for example, which have direct and generally evident repercussions on the lithosphere and hydrosphere.

The hydrosphere represents the set of all the water present on Earth, on the surface and underground and covers over two thirds of the Earth's surface in most cases (96.7%) made up of the salt waters of the seas and oceans. The interaction of the hydrosphere undoubtedly affects the lithosphere, in particular on the coastal areas where the action of the waves contributes to shaping the coasts but also as an exogenous modelling agent as waterways do with the territory and the emerged continental areas.

The lithosphere is represented by the whole of the earth's crust (a rigid shell whose thickness varies from an average of 35 km under the continents to an average of 6–7 km immediately under the ocean floors) and the first layer of the solid earth's mantle. Of the lithosphere, the continental crust, i.e. the actual earth's surface, is particularly significant. Its evolution, on a planetary scale and in geological times, is strongly conditioned by processes that take place up to the nucleus of the planet and which determine the movement of the continents, volcanic and seismic phenomena but also the morphological modelling of the surface itself through orogenies and the opening or closure of oceans or seas. The mineralogical composition of the lithosphere and its topography has a notable impact, together with factors dependent on the atmosphere and hydrosphere, on how living beings are distributed in time and space in different contexts.

Finally, the biosphere is that part of the Earth in which living organisms are present. In this sense the biosphere is placed at a hierarchically higher level than other environments as it includes them. It is a complex system, which could be divided into a multiplicity of segments, each of which is closely related to the other, which includes biotic factors and biotic factors. In this perspective the biosphere is also referred to as a global ecosystem.

As mentioned, the ecosystem or ecosystems have strong interchange reactions within them and develop an external relationship between them. In this 'natural' multi-relationship framework, the human being is added. Man is evidently capable of influencing the various ecosystem components but is equally dependent on them. It is therefore essential that the relationship between human beings and ecosystems finds a balance. Ecosystems are in fact carriers of the so-called 'ecosystem services' (ES) within natural capital. SEs guarantee human beings their own life cycle: birth, growth and reproduction, death. And this contribution is not only of a biological nature but also of an economic, social, cultural and other benefits nature.

Ensuring a man-nature balance means preserving and developing the natural capital of planet Earth and therefore being able to enjoy the adequate and indispensable ecosystem services offered by the various biotic and abiotic natural components.

Among the various sources of ecosystem services, a central role is played by the soil. Soil is defined as '*the top layer of the Earth's crust situated between the bedrock and the land surface, which is composed of mineral particles, organic matter, water, air and living organisms*'.[1] Soil is a complex ecosystem that plays a fundamental role in many aspects:

- the nutrient cycle ensures soil fertility and the release of the elements necessary for plant growth;
- it is a biological filter and a chemical-physical barrier that counteracts the spread of pollutants. It can store large quantities of water useful for plants and for flood mitigation;
- represents support for plants, animals and infrastructure;
- in addition to representing the largest carbon sink, it regulates the emission of important greenhouse gases (N2O and CH4);
- they are an immense reservoir of biodiversity, representing the habitat for thousands of species, on whose activity the biogeochemical cycles that guarantee life on the planet depend;
- they can be an important source of supply of raw materials.

Soils are one of the main global reservoirs of biodiversity, more than 40% of living organisms in terrestrial ecosystems are associated during their life-cycle directly with soils. These descriptive elements of the soil function can be traced back to the economic concept of natural capital defined as '*stock of natural resources (for example soil, forests and water bodies) that produce a flow of goods or services*' (Costanza and Daly 1992). In particular, according to the Authors, the natural capital of the soil is defined as '*the stock of mass and energy organized together to form the soil*'. Once this capital has been identified, ecosystem services are identified in the flow and transformations that occur in the soil, which are beneficial for humans. Their nature is a function of what is perceived as a benefit for man and therefore subjective. From this perspective it is necessary to distinguish the use of the term 'function' from the term 'service'. Moreover, the terms 'functions' and 'services' are also often confounded. Functions refer to natural biological processes, while services refer to those functions that contribute to human well-being.[2] In soils, ecosystem functions and services result from the interaction of physical, chemical, biological and human factors. In soils, ecosystem functions and services result from the interaction of physical, chemical, biological and human factors.

The ecosystem services that the soil provides to human beings are of different types:

- supply (food and biomass production, supply of raw materials, etc.);
- regulation (climate regulation, carbon capture and conservation, erosion and nutrient control, regulation of water quality, protection and mitigation of extreme hydrological phenomena, etc.);

[1]Munafò, M. (a cura di), 2023. Consumo di suolo, dinamiche territoriali e servizi ecosistemici. Edizione 2023. Report SNPA 37/23.

[2]FAO, ITPS, GSBI, CBD and EC. 2020. State of knowledge of soil biodiversity - Status, challenges and potentialities, Report 2020. Rome, FAO.

- support (physical support for anthropic activities, decomposition and mineralisation of organic matter, species habitat, genetic reserve, biodiversity conservation, etc.);
- cultural (recreational services, landscape, natural heritage, etc.).

It is therefore clear how soil plays a role of central importance not only in the preservation of the ecosystem purely understood as a natural context but also as a fundamental element for the development of human activity at every level. A specific operation to protect the soil from the various threats that weigh on it is therefore necessary. In particular, the following factors are a source of degradation and impoverishment of the resource and related ecosystem services:

1. Changes in land cover: due to the occupation of an originally agricultural, natural or semi-natural surface with an artificial cover which may have a soil waterproofing character in the event that the cover of part of the land and the related soil is permanent.
2. Loss of productivity: it is represented as a change in the productive and biological capacity of the soil, understood as a source of food, fibre and fuel, to support man. Net primary productivity (NPP) is defined as the net amount of carbon assimilated after photosynthesis and autotrophic respiration over a given period of time and is expressed in kg/ha/year.
3. Loss of organic carbon: soil organic matter (SOM) represents the largest terrestrial carbon reserve and is extremely important as a source of nutrients for the plant system which has a direct effect on plant growth thanks to its influence on physical, chemical and biological properties of soil. In equilibrium conditions, the organic substance can give rise to the development of aggregates, of variable size depending on the texture characteristics of the soil, guaranteeing good porosity, which increases the aeration and drainage of the soil. The causes of loss of organic carbon include, among others, deforestation, fires and the removal of plant residues.
4. Loss of habitat quality: in relation to the capacity to maintain biological and genetic diversity.
5. Soil erosion: this occurs when soil loss occurs at a rate greater than its formation. This is a phenomenon naturally present on the earth's surface and of fundamental importance as such for the balance in the continental and submerged crust. The impact of land use at various levels can, however, increase this phenomenon with often irreparable consequences and a prelude to hydrogeological instability.
6. Other factors linked to artificial cover and the presence of areas affected by fire.

Unsustainable agricultural and forestry practices, urban expansion and climate change are the main drivers of land degradation, which according to the recent Intergovernmental Science-Policy Platform on Biodiversity and Ecosystem Services (IPBES) report. have already resulted in loss of ecosystem services in many parts of the world. Urban expansion is accompanied by a greater need for infrastructure (transport, water, waste and electricity), which decreases the long-term availability of productive land resources. During the period 2000–2018, land take concentrated around larger urban agglomerations, with 80% of land taken at the expense of arable land and permanent crops (50%) and of pastures and mosaic farmlands (almost 30%). Equally important is the physical degradation of soils. Soil sealing causes the complete and irreversible loss of all soil functions. Urban expansion and infrastructure consume soils by physical removal or covering them with impermeable (impervious) artificial material (e.g. asphalt and concrete), though only part of the land that is defined as land take is actually sealed.[3]

Another source of threat to the ground is constituted by chemical degradation of soils under intensive land use. Industrial activities, waste disposal and intensive land management have led to the dispersal of contaminants throughout the environment and eventually to their accumulation in soils. Sources of contaminants include the residues of plant protection products, industrial emissions, mineral fertilisers, biosolids (some composts, manures and sewage sludges), wood preservatives and pharmaceutical products. the dominating activities for contamination at local level are municipal and industrial waste sites (37%) together with industrial emissions and leakages (33%).

3 Convergence of Environmental Policies in Europe

3.1 Origin of Programmatic Action and Legal Basis

The countries of the European continent were among the first in the world to attempt to organise a common policy for the management of critical environmental issues deriving from human activity and among the first to identify the need for environmental protection as a founding prerequisite of any other need both on the economic and social plan. The environmental issue is seen as a determining element for full European integration and convergence. The first act of the European Community dates to 1971.[4] The attention of European countries is focused on 5 main objectives:

1. the reduction of the concentration of air and water pollutant
2. the reduction of the caused from industrial processes
3. the initiation of a coordinated research programme on pollutants
4. protection of the natural environment
5. the implementation of the basic studies necessary to obtain a better knowledge of, to define and to solve environmental problems.

[3]The European environment—state and outlook 2020 Knowledge for transition to a sustainable Europe, European Environment Agency, Publications Office of the European Union, 2019.

[4]Community policy on the environment. Information Memo P-24/71, July 1971. First communication of the Commission about the Community's policy on the environment, (doc. SEC (71) 2616 def.

As part of the actions to be undertaken to combat pollution resulting from industrial practices, the agricultural sector was identified as the one capable of negatively impacting the soil. On the other hand, no substantial importance was given to the soil which was still placed as a 'residual' aspect with rural or bucolic connotations. As a subsequent step, in 1972 a document was drawn up from a more operational perspective:[5] also in this case the soil was identified as a transition element between the anthropic component (agriculture, industry, waste) and the natural component to be preserved represented by the groundwater which constitutes the potential target of contamination and therefore the key resource to be preserved.

Another element is structured in a substantially parallel manner which will later become fundamental in the context of European and international environmental policies. In the document produced by the Organization for Economic Co-operation and Development in 1972,[6] the guidelines and general principles for the application of environmental policies in relation to the economy and the international market. In particular, it is in this contest that we find the first internationally documented or at least the most authoritative trace of the 'polluter pays' principle. Measures more specifically aimed at safeguarding the natural environment can be found in the document adopted by the Council of the European Communities in 1973.[7]

In this context, the attention of European countries is focused on the management of waste which is considered '*one of the most harmful sources of pollution, due to the dangers it presents, both for human health and for the environment*'.[8] In particular, emphasis is placed on the need for waste disposal to take place '*without risk to water, air and soil*'. However, these precautions appear, in today's reading, still very far from a real environmental protection policy in a preventive way, recording in the first European Directive on waste[9] a central importance given to the disposal activity via landfill.

In 1987, new objectives were developed and institutionalised towards which the action of European countries was oriented: with the Single European Act, changes were made to the treaty that established the European Economic Community.[10] The

[5]Communication de la Commission au Conseil sur un programme des Communautés européennes en matière d'environnement (Présentée le 24 mars 1972).

[6]OCSE, Recommendation of the Council on Guiding Principles concerning International Economic Aspects of Environmental Policies, adopted by the OECD Council on 26 May 1972 on the proposal of the Environment Policy Committee.

[7]Declaration of the Council of the European Communities and of the representatives of the Governments of the Member States meeting in the Council of 22 November 1973 on the programme of action of the European Communities on the environment Official Journal C 112, 20/12/1973.

[8]Proposal for a COUNCIL DIRECTIVE on waste disposai (submitted to the Council by the Commission) COM(74)1297 final - Bruxelles 10 September 1974.

[9]Council Directive 75/442/EEC of 15 July 1975 on waste Official Journal L 194, 25/07/1975.

[10]Furthermore, the year 1987 was the year in which one of the oldest regulations relating to the remediation of contaminated sites was adopted, that of the Netherlands called the Soil Protection Act.

safeguard and protection of the environment and the guarantee of rational use of natural resources become the legal basis and central elements of the European Community's action.

In the same terms it will then merge into the Treaty on the Functioning of the European Union. It is also important to underline that in 1990 the European Environment Agency[11] will be established, which is recognised as a priority for action in the sectors of activity concerning the '*state of soils, fauna and flora as well as biotopes and the use of land and resources natural*'.

Before entering into the merits of the purely legal steps, first the European Community and then the European Union have given great importance to the adoption of programmatic and operational approaches that would allow them to approach environmental challenges even before identifying a common line. In this sense, the Environmental Action Programmes, summarised below (see Table 1) were very important.

After a long process of discussion, European countries will then arrive at the adoption of a specific directive relating to waste landfills:[12] thus identifying '*through rigid operational and technical requirements*' actions and conditions necessary to combat 'pollution of surface waters, groundwater, soil and atmosphere'. The first directive concerns '*the collection, treatment and discharge of urban wastewater, as well as the treatment and discharge of wastewater originating from certain industrial sectors*'.[13]

European environmental policy will find its greatest expression, for a long period, still in relation to waste management with a series of corrective or integrative interventions[14] of the 1975 directive, until 2008 with the new Directive[15] which contains, in relation to the soil resource, an important new element. In the face of a series of regulatory provisions which until 2008 had applied the principle of

[11] Council Regulation (EEC) No 1210/90 of 7 May 1990 on the establishment of the European Environment Agency and the European Environment Information and Observation Network.

[12] Council Directive 1999/31/EC of 26 April 1999 on the landfill of waste Official Journal L 182, 16/07/1999.

[13] Council Directive 91/271/EEC of 21 May 1991 concerning urban waste-water treatment Official Journal L 135, 30/05/1991.

[14] Council Directive 91/156/EEC of 18 March 1991 amending Directive 75/442/EEC on waste Official Journal L 078, 26/03/1991, Council Directive 91/692/EEC of 23 December 1991 standardizing and rationalizing reports on the implementation of certain Directives relating to the environment Official Journal L 377, 31/12/1991 96/350/EC: Commission Decision of 24 May 1996 adapting Annexes IIA and IIB to Council Directive 75/442/EEC on waste (Text with EEA relevance) OJ L 135, 6.6.1996, Regulation (EC) No 1882/2003 of the European Parliament and of the Council of 29 September 2003 adapting to Council Decision 1999/468/EC the provisions relating to committees which assist the Commission in the exercise of its implementing powers laid down in instruments subject to the procedure referred to in Article 251 of the EC Treaty OJ L 284, 31.10.2003, Directive 2006/12/EC of the European Parliament and of the Council of 5 April 2006 on waste.

[15] Directive 2008/98/EC of the European Parliament and of the Council of 19 November 2008 on waste and repealing certain Directives.

Table 1 Historical examination of the Environmental Action Programmes over time

Period	Content and objectives
1972–1976	• Outline principles of environmental intervention policy by listing • Reduce and prevent pollution and other harmful factors • Improve the environment and living condition • Joint action by Member States within international bodies dealing with ecological problems
1977–1981	• Fundamental principles for a community ecological policy • Reduce pollution and environmental disturbances in general • Protect and rationally manage the territory and natural resources • General actions in favour of the natural environment
1982–1987	• Prevention with the adoption of economic and social measures that prevent the onset of environmental problems • Environmental resources were considered the basis, but also the limit, for further social and economic developments • Integration of environmental requirements in the planning and execution of interventions in many economic and social sectors • Impact assessment as a key tool to ensure such integration
1987–1992	• The establishment of strict environmental standards for non-optional protection purposes is essential • The more punctual application of the 'polluter payment' principle • Wider use of environmental impact assessment procedures • The reduction of pollution and damage, particularly in the areas of air, fresh and marine water and soil pollution
1993–2000	• Legislation to set environmental standards • Economic instruments to encourage the production and use of environmentally friendly products and processes • Horizontal support measures (information, education, research) • Financial support measures (funds)
2001–2010	• Climate change as the main challenge and long-term goal of stabilising greenhouse gas concentrations in the atmosphere • Protect, conserve, restore and develop the functioning of natural systems • Level of quality of life and social well-being for citizens through sustainable urban development • Resource efficiency and better management of resources and waste for the transition to more sustainable production and consumption models
2012–2020	• Protect, preserve and enhance the Union's natural capital • Turn the Union into a resource-efficient, green and competitive low-carbon economy • Improve the knowledge and evidence base for Union environment policy • Secure investment for environment and climate policy and address environmental externalities
2021–2030	• Pursuing a zero-pollution ambition, including for air, water and soil and protecting the health and well-being of Europeans • Protecting, preserving and restoring biodiversity, and enhancing natural capital • Reducing environmental and climate pressures related to production and consumption

preventive action without exceptions whereby every product deriving from an 'industrial' activity had to be included in the rigid waste management schemes, with this directive it is particular attention to the ground. It is thus expected that the '*waste qualification of excavated non-contaminated soils and other material in their natural state used in sites other than those in which they were excavated should be examined based on the definition of waste*'. The objective is to minimise the waste of soil or soil and maximise the possibility that '*uncontaminated soil and other material in its natural state*' can be reused in the same construction activities (see note 15).

The attention of European countries has always been focused on the impact of industrial activities and the need to identify preventive actions and to combat environmental impacts already in the context of the development and operation of production processes. Already from the early 1980s[16] and then in 1996:[17] in this context the concept of 'environmental impact assessment' was developed as a tool to identify, prevent, minimise or mitigate the direct and indirect effects of a project on natural factors and in particular on soil and the concept of 'integrated pollution prevention and reduction' is also defined. This approach will be progressively strengthened until 2008.[18]

The last natural element that was the object of the European Union's attention was water,[19] with particular reference to underground waters, internal waters and marine-coastal waters but in any case, constituting another piece in the environmental protection policy and therefore of the soil and subsoil.

Another fundamental aspect that cannot fail to be recalled is the one added in 2004 with a specific tool for the management of environmental damage and its repair.[20] In particular, the directive looks at the activity that has caused environmental damage or the imminent threat of such damage and considers it financially responsible to induce the operator to adopt measures and develop practices aimed at minimising the risks of environmental damage. Among others, specific damage to the 'land' as a natural resource is identified. Ground effects due to damage or threat

[16]Council Directive 85/337/EEC of 27 June 1985 on the assessment of the effects of certain public and private projects on the environment, Official Journal L 175, 05/07/1985.

[17]Council Directive 96/61/EC of 24 September 1996 concerning integrated pollution prevention and control, Official Journal L 257, 10.10.1996.

[18]Directive 2008/1/EC of the European Parliament and of the Council of 15 January 2008 concerning integrated pollution prevention, and control Official Journal L 24, 29.1.2008 and Directive 2010/75/EU of the European Parliament and of the Council of 24 November 2010 on industrial emissions (integrated pollution prevention and control), Official Journal L334, 17/12/2010.

[19]Directive 2000/60/EC of the European Parliament and of the Council of 23 October 2000 establishing a framework for Community action in the field of water policy Official Journal L 327, 22/12/2000.

[20]Directive 2004/35/CE of the European Parliament and of the Council of 21 April 2004 on environmental liability with regard to the prevention and remedying of environmental damage, Official Journal L 143, 30/04/2004.

must be eliminated or reduced to a level that no longer represents a significant risk of causing adverse effects to human health.

3.2 *Towards to the EU Soil Strategy for 2030*

In 1977, in the European Soil Chart,[21] soil was defined as '*one of humanity's most precious assets*' and through a 12-point programme the conclusion was reached that soil, as a limited and at the same time essential resource, should be managed through conservation measures in the long term which provided for centralised administrative structures, appropriate legislation aimed at the rational and balanced use of the resource and actions for the control of land use techniques also to protect the soil against risks deriving from anthropic activity. Lastly, emphasis was placed on the need to restore natural conditions where necessary.

The Committee[22] follows with concern the reflections of the Commission, which intends to limit itself, in water resources management policy, to regulating procedures and strategies. The Committee believes that it is much more important to introduce concrete standards and limit values at European level. Only in this way can we achieve, on the one hand, uniform environmental quality and, on the other, equal conditions of competition. Soil protection should be given the same importance as environmental and water resource protection. Soil protection takes on particular importance not only to guarantee agricultural production, but also to deal with problems caused, for example, by the introduction of pollutants or erosion.

Nonetheless, the soil issue has always been the most difficult to deal with and consequently it has not yet been possible to achieve the adoption of common European policies on the matter and to date a specific reference directive for soil is still in the process of being developed. proposal. Regarding soil, the principle of subsidiarity has always been asserted as predominant.

Indeed, over time, since 1995 there was already awareness[23] of the phenomena of soil degradation and contamination affected by both physical and chemical phenomena, such as surface erosion (accelerated by changes in land use, by the modification of ecosystems and by loss of biodiversity) and contamination (from acids, heavy metals, pesticides and fertilisers).

However, as previously illustrated, the soil has never really been placed at the centre of technical or political programmatic frameworks, but its protection,

[21] European Soil Charter, Council of Europe, (Ref: B (72) 63), June 1972.

[22] Opinion of the Committee of the Regions on the "Proposal for a Decision of the European Parliament and of the Council on a Community framework for cooperation to promote sustainable urban development" Official Journal C 317, 06/11/2000.

[23] State of the environment report No 3/1995, Report for the Review of the Fifth Environmental Action Programme, Environmental European Agency.

protection and rehabilitation has mostly been managed consequently deriving from the intervention on other sectors: water, waste, industry, natural habitat.

In relatively recent times (2003) reference must be made[24] to the resolution of the European Parliament, which is included in the Sixth Community Action Program on the Environment, in which the Euro community body asks the Commission for the first time to present a 'thematic strategy for soil protection' with the need to preserve the soil from the accumulation of dangerous substances, combat phenomena such as erosion and waterproofing, protect the role of the soil as a resource for ecosystem services and enhance sustainable agri-food production. The prevention, supervision and control of soil pollution require guidelines to which Member States must refer, also with reference to the '*recovery of contaminated soil in urban and semi-urban areas*'.

In a few years (2006) a proposal was made by the European Parliament and the Council for the adoption of a framework for soil protection;[25] the objective is to remedy the lack of specific legislation on the subject also by integrating soil issues into other policies. The proposed directive seeks to dissuade the belief that the principle of subsidiarity prevails over the identification of a unitary reference framework and believes that Member States are not able to independently guarantee the reference objectives, giving the soil a role and significance cross-border, both from a purely physical and geographical perspective but also with reference to the economic balance of the common market within which there is a situation of imbalance in terms of fixed costs since different national regimes correspond to different obligations for economic operators.

The pillars of the 2006 proposed soil directive are very ambitious:

a) the established framework refers to all environmental, economic, social and cultural functions.
b) identification of the areas in which there is risk for different types of phenomena and related preparation of adequate measures.
c) management of soil contamination with the creation of a national inventory for particular types of sites with potentially polluting activities for the soil, identification of a competent authority, measurement of contamination levels, adoption of a national clean-up strategy with scheduling of interventions and measurement of economic funds budgeted.
d) adoption of awareness and communication measures.

This proposal, after a long and troubled process of '*blocking by a minority of member states within the Council*',[26] was definitively withdrawn in 2014.

---

[24] Proposal for a European Parliament and Council Regulation concerning monitoring of forests and environmental interactions in the Community (Forest Focus) (2003/C 20 E/10) COM(2002) 404 final—2002/0164(COD) (Submitted by the Commission on 15 July 2002).

[25] Proposal for a Directive of the European Parliament and of the Council establishing a framework for the protection of soil and amending Directive 2004/35/EC (presented by the Commission), COM(2006) 232 final 2006/0086 (COD), Brussels, 22.9.2006.

[26] See note 31.

After the Paris agreements[27] which constituted a moment of great attention on environmental issues at a global and European level, Europe is moving towards with renewed energy and drive towards the contrast and fight against climate change and towards the adoption of increasingly incisive environmental protection policies and actions. With this perspective, the 'European Green Deal'[28] must be evaluated, defined as 'an integral part of the Commission's strategy to implement the 2030 Agenda and the United Nations sustainable development goals'. Of the over 10 objectives set by the European Green Deal, objective no. 8 '*"zero pollution" for an environment free of toxic substances*' is the one that has the greatest affinity with the protection and restoration of the soil.

Within this reference framework, soil protection finds an immediate place in the EU Biodiversity Strategy for 2030.[29] A more precise definition is given to the EU soil strategy for 2030[30] which aims to achieve the following objectives:

- all EU soil ecosystems are healthy and more resilient and can therefore continue to provide their crucial services.
- there is no net land take, and soil pollution is reduced to levels that are no longer harmful to people's health or ecosystems.
- protecting soils, managing them sustainably and restoring degraded soils is a common standard.

On the same occasion, the Commission also aims at a broader time horizon, that of 2050, with respect to which the main objectives are:

- the achievement of zero net land consumption.
- the reduction of soil pollution to levels no longer considered harmful to human health and natural ecosystems.
- achieve soil-based climate neutrality in the EU by 2035.

In this context, one of the reference objectives is the issuing of a new proposal for a specific directive for the protection of soil, which will be discussed later.

---

[27] In the 2015 United Nations Climate Change Conference, COP 21 or CMP 11 was held in Paris, France, from 30 November to 12 December 2015.

[28] Communication from the Commission to the European Parliament, the European Council, the Council, the European Economic and Social Committee and the Committee and the Committee of the Region, *The European Green Deal,* COM(2019) 640 final, Bruxelles, 11.12.2019.

[29] Communication from the Commission to the European Parliament, the European Council, the Council, the European Economic and Social Committee and the Committee and the Committee of the Region, *EU Biodiversity Strategy for 2030*, COM(2020) 380 final, Brussels, 20.5.2020.

[30] Communication from the Commission to the European Parliament, the European Council, the Council, the European Economic and Social Committee and the Committee and the Committee of the Region, *EU Soil Strategy for 2030 Reaping the benefits of healthy soils for people, food, nature and climate,* COM/2021/699 final, Brussels, 17.11.2021.

4 Contaminated Sites in Europe and the Soil Monitoring Law

4.1 Magnitude of the Phenomenon

Analytical studies concerning the search for the presence of contaminated sites in European countries have been available since the end of the years 1990 (Gundula et al. 2000). In this period, in fact, the evaluation of the environmental impacts of human activity is particularly important if we consider that in 1990 the total waste generated by the 12 European countries amounted to approximately 700 million tonnes of which approximately 69% was delivered in landfill. However, in 1992 approximately 55,000 potentially contaminated sites were identified, mostly attributable to mining activities and the processing of iron and steel, particularly in Northern European countries. The data collected in this phase were consciously greatly underestimated. In fact, in 2014 (with a much greater number of countries), we estimate a much greater presence of contaminated sites equal to 2.5 million potentially contaminated sites of which approximately 14% (340,000 sites) are estimated to be contaminated and in need of remediation measures (Panagos et al. 2013; van Liedekerke et al. 2014). This data is widely confirmed in 2016 (Pérez et al. 2015) and again in 2020 (Payá Pérez and Rodríguez Eugenio 2018). If the ability to frame the problem, collecting information and elements from Member States, consolidates, and refines over time, the research conducted highlights a state of general fragmentation. This phenomenon is constantly traced back to the absence of a European legal basis of reference which allows on the one hand to deal with comparable regulatory and technical systems and on the other to achieve common objectives and strategies. The urgency of adopting a soil protection directive addressing the issue of contaminated sites is therefore highlighted.

4.2 Directive on Soil Monitoring and Resilience

As previously illustrated, the process of convergence of European policies on soil protection has struggled to develop and above all to find a point of arrival. After a 2006 proposal for a directive which was definitively withdrawn in 2014, in 2021 we moved on to a new phase.

Under pressure from a complex system of actions, the European Parliament[31] called the Commission to develop a common legal framework at EU level, in full respect of the principle of subsidiarity, for the protection and sustainable use of land, addressing all the main threats to the soil, underlining the need for a common framework, also provides provisions regarding the mapping of areas at risk and

[31] Soil protection European Parliament resolution of 28 April 2021 on soil protection (2021/2548 (RSP)) (2021/C 506/07).

contaminated, brownfield and abandoned sites, as well as for the remediation of contaminated sites.

These requests are reflected in 2023 with the proposed directive on Soil Monitoring and Resilience (Soil Monitoring Law).[32]

In the published text there are 5 reference pillars:

1. *Definition of soil health and establishment of soil districts*: defining soil health descriptors can have a positive and direct impact on the provision and use of information for further research and development, such as fertility and erosion studies. Soil heath districts can facilitate the engagement of local stakeholders and create a significant incentive towards local participatory approaches for soil management, if the soil health districts are set of a smaller, local size.
2. *Soil health monitoring*: profits indirectly a wide range of ecosystems and the services they provide, such as carbon sequestration, water quality and availability and resilience to natural hazards such as flooding, and basis for biodiversity. Monitoring the health condition of soils across the EU is expected as well to lead to technological development and innovation (productivity and resource efficiency) and stimulate academic and industrial research.
3. *Sustainable soil management*: there is no dedicated soil policy to ensure the sustainable use of all managed soils, even though this would substantially improve the environment, and the quality of natural resources.
4. *Identification, registration, investigation and assessment of contaminated sites*: only accurate identification allows Member States to prioritise remedial actions, to collect funding and to make a planning. Enhanced knowledge of the risks to the environment of soil contamination contributes to the achievement of the water and nature objectives. This pillar could have positive social impacts for EU citizens through a better application of the polluter pays principle, leading to more societal fairness and good administration. It helps to decrease exposure to contamination. Socio-economically disadvantaged households are living closer to contaminated sites due to lower costs of living.
5. *Restoration (regeneration) of soil health and remediation of contaminated sites*: soil restoration results in economic costs and benefits. 60–70% of land is currently unhealthy and underproviding ecosystem services, with a loss that could be quantified at EUR 3.4–292.4 billion for soil contamination and at 16.5–68.8 for the other soil degradation. Soil restoration, that is addressing soil degradation, delivers clear economic benefits for society. The precise costs of remediation are uncertain. The median cost of site remediation is estimated at €124,000 per site with the majority between €50,000 to €500,000 per site. Costs of € 1 billion per annum over a 25-year period could be expected. Soil restoration improves the safety, health, and infrastructure of communities and sustains the livelihood in the surrounding areas, e.g. (agro)tourism, markets, infrastructure.

[32] Proposal for a Directive of the European Parliament and of the Council on Soil Monitoring and Resilience (Soil Monitoring Law), COM (2023) 416 final, 2023/0232(COD), Brussels, 5.7.2023.

The overall vision of the proposed directive is to lay the foundations for homogeneous management of the soil resource at a European level. For this reason, one of the fundamental aspects is the aspect of management and identification of the different types of soil and set measures for monitoring and assessing soil. The greatest weight is not given to the definition of quantitative numerical indicators through which to discretise a '*soil state*' but above all to give rise to the ability to organise a system capable of enhancing and protecting the soil resource. For this reason, the establishment of soil districts and the identification of a specific national authority are first envisaged.

Regarding the risks for human health and the environment of potentially contaminated sites and contaminated sites, a risk-based approach is envisaged for identification, investigation and management of it.

5 The Case of Italy

5.1 The Contaminated Sites Legislation in Italy

Italy has also faced environmental challenges, including soil and groundwater contamination from various industrial activities. Over the years, Italy has developed a comprehensive legal framework to manage and remediate contaminated sites, safeguarding public health and the environment. Before the advent of comprehensive legislation, Italy, like many other countries, grappled with the consequences of industrial pollution. Contaminated sites, often associated with abandoned factories, chemical plants, and hazardous waste disposal sites, posed significant threats to human health and the environment. The absence of clear regulatory guidance and limited awareness of these issues exacerbated the problem.

In 1999, Italy marked a turning point with the issuance of Ministerial Decree 471/99 (aka as DM 471/99). This landmark regulation laid the foundation for managing and remediating contaminated sites. DM 471/99 introduced the National Register of Contaminated Sites, a crucial tool for identifying and cataloguing contaminated areas. The decree also established criteria for site classification with concentration limits set as CLA (Acceptable Limit Concentration) in soil and in groundwater whose exceedance were both the turning point to declare a site as contaminated and the remediation objective. The introduction of DM 471/99 marked a significant shift in Italy's approach to contaminated sites. It recognised the need for a framework to address environmental liabilities and emphasised the importance of public awareness and involvement in the process. This decree had risk assessment just as a residual stage if the remediation targets are not achievable using the Best Available Technologies Not Entailing Excessive Costs.

In 2006, Italy took a substantial step forward with the enactment of Legislative Decree 152/06 (a.k.a. D.Lgsl. 152/06), also known as the Environmental Code. This comprehensive legislation consolidated numerous environmental laws, including those related to contaminated sites, into a single, unified framework. D. Lgsl.

152/06 aimed to streamline and harmonise standards and procedures for site characterisation, risk assessment, and remediation activities. Risk assessment procedure was from this moment at the centre of the management, and necessary to be run to declare a site as 'contaminated' or as 'not contaminated' and to calculate the CSR (Risk Threshold Values) that are the remediation target. It introduced stricter liability provisions, emphasising the 'polluter pays' principle, which held responsible parties financially accountable for cleanup. This consolidation of laws marked a significant milestone in simplifying and strengthening Italy's approach to managing contaminated sites.

In 2015, Italy recognised the specific environmental risks associated with fuel retail outlets and responded with Ministerial Decree 31/2015. This decree introduced tailored regulations to address contamination concerns at these sites. Given the potential for soil and groundwater contamination from petroleum hydrocarbons, DM 31/2015 foresaw a simplified characterisation phase with few Contaminants of Concerns, a simplified risk assessment, and new limits for two gasoline additives, MTBE and ETBE that are very soluble and were found also hundreds of meters from the petrol station. Italy faced a unique challenge with 'orphan' contaminated sites, where the responsible party was either unknown or unable to fund cleanup efforts. To address this issue, Italy introduced the December 29, 2020 Decree. This decree established a fund of 105M€ (now extended to 605 M€) dedicated to financing the remediation of orphan sites, ensuring that environmental liabilities were not left unattended. Italy's commitment to safeguarding the environment extended even when responsible parties were elusive.

The December 29, 2020 Decree marked a significant step in addressing long-standing environmental concerns and preventing further degradation of these sites. While Italy's regulatory framework for contaminated sites has evolved significantly, challenges persist. Coordinating cleanup efforts, particularly at sites with multiple responsible parties, remains complex. Ensuring the availability of adequate funding for remediation continues to be an ongoing concern.

5.2 *Italy's National Interest Contaminated Sites (SIN): A Comprehensive Overview*

Italy bears the legacy of industrialisation, which has left a significant mark on its environment. Over the years, certain areas in Italy have gained national attention due to extensive contamination, earning them the designation of Sites of National Interest (SIN). The Italy's SIN have the characteristic of the complexity of contamination, diverse ownership, types of industries, and the historical origins of pollution, with notable examples including Porto Marghera, Priolo, and Napoli Orientale. Sites of National Interest (SIN) in Italy represent areas where contamination of soil, groundwater, and ecosystems has reached a critical level, necessitating focused efforts to remediate and mitigate environmental risks. These sites are under the coordination of the Ministry of Environment. These sites often have a complex history of industrial activities and pollution, making them unique challenges for environmental management.

Porto Marghera, situated near Venice, is one of Italy's most emblematic SIN. Its history is closely intertwined with industrialisation, dating back to the early 20th century. The site was home to a multitude of industries, including chemical manufacturing, petrochemicals, and heavy machinery production. These activities have left a legacy of soil and groundwater contamination, with hazardous substances like heavy metals, organic compounds, and persistent organic pollutants. The complexity of Porto Marghera's contamination arises from the presence of numerous industrial players and historical pollution dating back to World War II. Cleanup efforts have been hampered by the challenge of allocating responsibility among the various owners and operators, some of whom are no longer in business.

Priolo, located in Sicily, is another prominent SIN in Italy. This site has been a petrochemical hub for decades, hosting oil refineries, chemical manufacturing, and storage facilities. The cumulative impact of these activities has led to widespread contamination, primarily from hydrocarbons, heavy metals (mercury in particular), and volatile organic compounds. The contamination in Priolo is exacerbated by the presence of multiple industrial operators and a historical legacy of inadequate waste management practices. Identifying responsible parties and coordinating cleanup efforts pose significant challenges, given the diversity of industries operating in the area.

Napoli Orientale, on the eastern outskirts of Naples, is a SIN characterised by a complex mix of urbanisation and industrial activities. This region hosts industries ranging from oil deposits to chemical production, all contributing to contamination in various forms, including heavy metals, hazardous waste, and volatile organic compounds. The challenge in Napoli Orientale lies in reconciling urban development with environmental protection. The population density and urban infrastructure add layers of complexity to contamination management efforts. Addressing the pollution in this area requires a balance between safeguarding public health and supporting sustainable urban growth.

Managing SIN presents a myriad of challenges, including the allocation of responsibility among multiple owners and operators, financial constraints, technical complexities, and the need for integrated actions. Coordination among government authorities, businesses, and local communities is essential for successful remediation and environmental restoration.

5.3 SIR: Contaminated Sites of Regional Interest in Italy

Contaminated sites, often resulting from industrial activities, improper waste disposal, or historical pollution, pose significant environmental and public health challenges. In Italy, these sites are categorised as Sites of Regional Interest (SIR), recognising their critical nature within specific regions. This narrative provides a comprehensive overview of contaminated sites of regional interest in Italy, the regional registers known as 'Anagrafi Regionali', and their role in managing and remediating these sites.

Contaminated sites of regional interest (SIR) are areas within Italian regions where soil, groundwater, or environment have been compromised by pollution to a degree that necessitates focused attention. While they may not meet the stringent criteria for national designation, SIRs still represent significant environmental and public health concerns. Each Italian region maintains its own list of SIRs, contributing to a more comprehensive understanding of localised contamination issues.

The management of SIRs relies on the existence of Anagrafi Regionali, or regional registers. These registers serve as vital databases that catalogue and document contaminated sites within specific regions. They are indispensable tools for environmental authorities, government agencies, and environmental professionals. Anagrafi Regionali help maintain an accurate and up-to-date record of contamination issues, which is critical for effective site management and regulatory oversight.

Contaminated sites of regional interest (SIR) in Italy represent a diverse range of environmental and public health challenges. The existence of Anagrafi Regionali has significantly improved the management of these sites by providing comprehensive databases for tracking contamination issues within regions.

Despite the challenges, Italy's dedication to managing SIRs remains unwavering. Regions across the country are making significant progress in characterising, assessing, and remediating contaminated sites to safeguard public health and the environment.

5.4 The Role of ISPRA, ARPA, and SNPA in Contaminated Site Management in Italy

To address the challenge of the management of contaminated sites, various governmental agencies play pivotal roles in coordinating and regulating contaminated site management efforts.

ISPRA, the Italian Institute for Environmental Protection and Research, serves as a central authority in Italy's efforts to manage contaminated sites. It plays a multifaceted role in developing policies, providing scientific expertise, and coordinating activities related to environmental protection. ISPRA actively contributes to the development of national policies and strategies aimed at addressing contamination issues, aligning them with European Union directives and international standards. ISPRA is instrumental in the development and dissemination of risk assessment guidelines. These guidelines provide a standardised framework for evaluating several different issues. The most important are in risk assessment, for determining the background concentration in soil, for the aeriform measurements, as well as the one for remediation technologies. ISPRA oversees the MOSAICO database, a comprehensive repository of data on contaminated sites across Italy. This database is invaluable for tracking contamination issues, assessing risks, and prioritising sites for remediation.

ARPA, or the Regional Environmental Protection Agencies, operate at the regional level, working closely with ISPRA to address contamination within their respective regions. These agencies play a crucial role in implementing national policies and regulations, conducting site assessments, and overseeing remediation activities. ARPA agencies possess in-depth knowledge of local environmental conditions, which is essential for site-specific risk assessments and remediation strategies.

SNPA, the National System for Environmental Protection, operates as an overarching authority responsible for coordinating environmental protection efforts at the national level. SNPA plays a critical role in overseeing the activities of ISPRA and ARPA agencies and ensuring uniformity and compliance with national and EU regulations. National Coordination: SNPA provides strategic guidance and coordinates the efforts of ISPRA and ARPA agencies across Italy. This coordination helps ensure a consistent and unified approach to contaminated site management.

In Italy, the management of contaminated sites involves the coordinated efforts of multiple agencies, with ISPRA, ARPA agencies, and SNPA playing pivotal roles. These organisations work collaboratively to develop risk assessment guidelines, oversee the MOSAICO database. Through their collective efforts, Italy continues to address contamination issues, safeguard public health, and protect the environment, ensuring a sustainable future for all.

References

Costanza R, Daly HE (1992) Natural capital and sustainable development. Conserv Biol 6(1)

Gundula P et al (2000) Management of contaminated sites in Western Europe. European Environment Agency

Panagos P et al. (2013) Contaminated sites in Europe: review of the current situation based on data collected through a European Network, Hindawi Publishing Corporation. J Environ Public Health

Payá Pérez A, Rodríguez Eugenio N (2018) Status of local soil contamination in Europe: revision of the indicator "Progress in the management Contaminated Sites in Europe", EUR 29124 EN. Publications Office of the European Union, Luxembourg

Pérez AP et al. (2015) Remediated sites and brownfields. Success stories in Europe; Report EUR 27530 EN. Joint Research Centre

van Liedekerke M et al. (2014) Progress in the management of contaminated sites in Europe, Report EUR 26376 EN. Joint Research Centre

Predator Law in the United States

John A. Erwin

Abstract Many predators serve as keystone species in their environments, shaping patterns of biodiversity in the ecosystems in which they are found. At the same time, predators are the most likely trophic group to face local extirpation or extinction. Predators have faced a long and arduous road to recovery, and only in the last few decades have populations of these species begun to truly rebound. Yet the more predator populations recover, the greater the pushback to predator recovery. In this chapter, I examine the historic and contemporary law of predator management, specifically focusing on gray wolves, grizzly bears, mountain lions, and black bears. First, I discuss the potential ecological and economic benefits and costs of predator restoration. Then I contextualize trends in predator law through the framing of American predator management in three phases: eradication, conservation, and balance. Specifically, I focus on the difficult and contentious transition from federal to state management, and I explore recent trends in state management of predator populations. Knowledge of state law governing predator populations is of increasing importance to biodiversity legal scholars as recovery of these iconic species will result in a transfer of authority from the federal government back to the states.

1 Introduction

Since time immemorial, predators have occupied a prominent place in our culture. While much of our relationship with Nature is premised on what we can take or extract from it, predators, for much of human existence, were the biological embodiment of Nature reclaiming something from us. As such, wolves, bears, and large cats have long served as antagonists in our tall-tales, fables, folklore, and religions. Few

Special thanks to my research assistants Jack Renaud and Jeannie Regidor and to participants at the FIU/UM 2023 Summer Workshop Series.

J. A. Erwin (✉)
Florida International University College of Law, Miami, FL, USA
e-mail: jerwin@fiu.edu

G. Antonelli et al. (eds.), *Biodiversity Laws, Policies and Science in Europe, the United States and China*, https://doi.org/10.1007/978-3-031-56218-1_9

species have taken on such an oversized culturally symbolic role as wolves and other apex predators (Almarcha et al. 2022). These species have become cultural keystones—with the myriad symbolic meanings we place upon them shaping our own cultural identities (Almarcha et al. 2022).

When European colonists arrived in the "New World," they found a continent blessed, or in their view cursed, with a diversity of large predator species. Some of the species these colonists encountered, were familiar foes—gray wolves and brown bears had already been mostly vanquished across Western Europe by the time Europeans arrived in America (Boitani and Linnell 2015). Mountain lions, black bears, and the more exotic jaguar were new to Europeans, but novelty did not protect these species from prejudicial malice. Colonists sought to dominate and civilize the "wilds;" eradicating large predators was a central tenet of that civilizing process (Goble 1992). This symbolization of "predators as threats" or even "predators as vermin" helped drive predator species to the brink of extinction in the continental United States.

As social mores about the environment and humanity's relationship with nature have changed over the last century, large predators, at least in the eyes of the law, have transformed from pantomime villains into charismatic posterchildren for conservation efforts. Perhaps absence makes the heart grow fonder, but after these species were extirpated across most of their former ranges, our cultural conscience seemed to kick in, driving efforts to conserve and restore predators. In some spheres cultural attitudes shifted. Large predators became symbolically linked with the burgeoning environmental and conservation movements (Almarcha et al. 2022). Many now view these species as majestic and deserving of our protection. For some, predators are emblematic of wilderness or even a broader longing for independence. Few experiences can evoke the feeling of being in "the wild" like the howl of a wolf or the sight of a hulking grizzly bear lumbering in the distance.

Some of this shift was borne out of the burgeoning fields of ecology, wildlife management, and later conservation biology. Despite our contentious relationship with these predators, modern ecology has continuously highlighted their value. Restoring and protecting predators can have significant ecological and economic benefits (Ripple et al. 2014; Raynor et al. 2021). Apex predators have traditionally operated as ecological keystone species, directly and indirectly controlling population sizes of other plants and animals and modulating ecosystem services (Ripple et al. 2014). When these large predators are removed, or subsequently reintroduced, a trophic cascade—a ripple of downstream ecological effects—may occur (Ripple et al. 2016). For example, in the early twentieth century, the removal of predators contributed to irruptions of deer populations across much of the country (Blossey and Hare 2022). Oversized deer populations have caused massive economic and ecological damage and even contributed to the spread of tick-borne disease (Blossey and Hare 2022). Despite our best efforts, human-induced harvest mortality has been incapable of managing many ungulate populations (Blossey and Hare 2022).

As such, the reintroduction and re-establishment of predators is key to re-wilding—conceptually the return of large predators can course-correct ecosystems, directing them back toward a more natural state (Noss and Soulé 1998).

Reintroducing predators back into the ecosystems they once roamed has been shown to cause a cascade, both directly through predation (Ripple et al. 2014) and indirectly by affecting the behavior of prey species, often referred to as the "landscape of fear" (Brown et al. 1999; Laundré et al. 2001). For example, studies following the reintroduction of wolves into the Greater Yellowstone ecosystem found direct effects decreasing populations of coyotes and elk leading to indirect effects on woody plants like birch, pronghorn antelope, birds, small mammals, scavengers, grizzly bears, berry production, and beavers (Ripple et al. 2014). These effects are not solely limited to population sizes of other species; predation can also result in physical and chemical changes to the landscapes where predators are found. The reintroduction of wolves in Yellowstone affected stream morphology (Beschta and Ripple 2012), and a recent study on mountain lions found that predation caused significant effects on nutrient cycling and biogeochemical processes in areas where they hunt (Peziol et al. 2023). There is also evidence that rebounding predator populations can have large scale economic effects. One recent study estimates that, in Wisconsin, wolves have reduced collisions between deer and vehicles by 24%—yielding an economic benefit that is 63 times greater than the cost of wolf predation on livestock (Raynor et al. 2021).

But as our fraught cultural relationship with predators suggests, increasing predator populations and returning them to their former haunts is not without consequence. With the return of predators, old prejudices have risen again, now combined with novel symbolisms. In addition to concerns about depredation, predators have become "biopolitical pawns" (Nie 2001). Predators are proxies and scapegoats in a power struggle between rural and urban communities and local and federal politics (Nie 2001; Almarcha et al. 2022). The needs and nature of these large apex predators often directly conflict with our preferences on the proper use of land. There are economic and cultural costs to growing populations of large predators, and those costs are certainly not distributed evenly amongst all members of society. Wolves, bears, and mountain lions do kill livestock, prized game species, domestic animals, and even humans, and those in the closest proximity to these creatures pay the majority of the costs. Further, predators are returning to landscapes with a far heavier human presence than existed when they were first extirpated; this increased wild-urban interface brings with it an increased chance for conflict (Klees van Bommel et al. 2020). As renowned wolf biologist David Mech once stated: "The wolf is neither a saint nor a sinner except to whose who want to make it so" (Mech 2012). Those in charge of predator management and conservation today must attempt to balance these competing, contradictory symbolic visions of predators held by vocal minorities of the population.

In this chapter, I explore American law as it relates to large mammalian predators. Law is the backbone that supports and structures governmental control over predators and our relationships with them. Much of this chapter deals with legal efforts, both historical and contemporary, to eradicate, manage, restore, or conserve predator populations. Specifically, I focus on law and policy affecting wolves, bears, and large cats. In the United States, there are two recognized wolf species—the red wolf (*C.* rufus) and the gray wolf (*Canis lupus*), as well as a distinct subspecies of the gray wolf known as the Mexican wolf (*C. l. baileyi*). Similarly, there are three bear species in the United States—the grizzly bear (*Ursus arctos horribilis*), the black bear (*U. americanus*), and the polar bear (*U. maritimus*). Finally, though there are a number of smaller cat species found in the United States, I focus on the jaguar (*Panthera onca*), the mountain lion (*Puma concolor*), and the Florida panther (*P. c. coryii*) subspecies.[1] I begin the chapter with a brief history of predator law in the United States, specifically focusing on the different motivations driving broader trends in predator law. I will then discuss contemporary challenges our nation faces in balancing predator conservation and management.

2 History of Predator Policies in the United States

Conceptually, predator policies in the United States can be divided into three phases—with each phase animated by fundamentally different goals and principles. These phases are not truly discrete, with significant temporal overlap occurring across each. From European colonization up through the middle of the 20th century, the aim of predator policy was simple—eradication. Fortunately, despite the best efforts of governments and citizens alike, the ultimate goal of extinction was never completed. The burgeoning environmental movement shifted the national conscience, and conservation and re-establishment of predator populations became the primary focus of predator law and policy. Half a century on, we have reached an inflection point in predator management. Most of these species are no longer at immediate risk of extinction, yet, at the same time, there are valid concerns that if we are not careful we will lose the hard-earned progress that has been made. Our current phase of management is instead focused on balance. State and federal agencies have the unenviable task of balancing wide-ranging and often contradictory interests and values when setting predator management policy. In this manner, a pendulum is an apt metaphor, with predator policy starting at an "eradication" extreme, swinging briefly to the "conservation" apex, and now oscillating back in search of "balance" and equilibrium (Olson et al. 2015).

2.1 *Eradication*

For the vast majority of post-Columbian American history, colonial, state, and federal governments sought to eradicate large predators (Coggins and Evans 1982; Goble 1992; Whiteley 2023). Originally, large predators were targeted specifically in an effort to decrease livestock depredation (Whiteley 2023). Statutes from a number

[1] For clarity, I consistently use the term "mountain lion," though these cats go by a myriad of names including pumas, cougars, catamounts, and panthers.

of states, especially east of the Mississippi River, routinely and explicitly noted the need to protect sheep, or occasionally cattle, as the prime justification for these eradication policies (Whiteley 2023). In later years, as market hunting and widespread conversion of land from wilderness to agriculture decimated wild game populations, the stated rationales for predator removal expanded in an effort to halt this decline of game species (Whiteley 2023). No matter the justification, the goal remained the same—decrease or remove entirely predator populations for our own benefit. Over the eradication phase of predator policy, predator control was accomplished through three primary methods: a bounty system, professional government-sponsored hunters and wildlife professionals, and indiscriminate poisoning and trapping (Coggins and Evans 1982).

European colonists brought their prejudices with them, and bounty systems were established in the colonies as early as 1630 (Whiteley 2023). Bounty systems incentivize the public to take up the state's eradication goal by offering a set monetary payment for proof of each killed animal of a specific species or class of animals. Over the three centuries of predator eradication, bounties had been placed on all of our apex predators: wolves, bears, mountain lions, jaguars, as well as a variety of mesocarnivores and other "noxious" species (Whiteley 2023). Despite their widespread prevalence, these bounty systems were plagued with administrative issues and bogged down by constant litigation (Coggins and Evans 1982). Bounty systems were also notoriously easy to defraud (Coggins and Evans 1982). Payment was supposed to be meted out on a "per 'in jurisdiction' kill" basis, but wily hunters soon worked out a variety of mechanisms to game this system (Coggins and Evans 1982).

While bounty systems worked to weaponize the public at large against predators, governments also began hiring their own professional hunters. As early as 1705, professional wolf hunters were hired by the colonial government in Pennsylvania (Coggins and Evans 1982). State-sponsored hunters were successful at addressing the perverse incentives and widespread fraud associated with bounty systems, and, as a result, predator populations precipitously declined (Coggins and Evans 1982). By the turn of the century, the federal government had become heavily involved with predator eradication. The Biological Survey, and later the Branch of Predator and Rodent Control (PARC), was formed and housed in the Department of Agriculture (USDA), and it provided advice on predator control, including the denning, trapping, and poisoning of wolves and coyotes on national forest lands (Coggins and Evans 1982). In 1931, Congress passed the Animal Damage Control Act, officially authorizing USDA "to conduct campaigns for the destruction or control of" "mountain lions, wolves, coyotes, bobcats, ... and other animals injurious to agriculture, horticulture, forestry, animal husbandry, wild game animals, fur-bearing animals, and birds" (7 U.S.C. 8351 (1931)). PARC undertook massive poisoning schemes on federal lands, using a variety of chemicals such as strychnine, compound 1080, sodium cyanide, and thallium sulfate (Coggins and Evans 1982). PARC also popularized the use of aerial hunting of predators as a more specific and less environmentally detrimental form of predator control (Coggins and Evans 1982). Over the 30 years federal wolfers were in action, they killed over 24,000 wolves (Li 2000).

By the middle of the 20th century, the vast majority of large predator populations in the United States had been eradicated. Red wolves were officially declared extinct in the wild in 1980. Jaguars no longer roamed our borderlands; the last one was shot in Arivaca in 1949 (Babb et al. 2021). Mexican wolves suffered a similar fate, with the latest confirmed kills of Mexican wolves in the United States occurring in the early 1970s. Mountain lions, once the most widespread species with the largest range of any mammal in the Americas, were pushed entirely out of the eastern half of the United States; only a small relict population persisted deep in the swamps of south Florida. Gray wolves and grizzly bears were reduced to just a few small populations isolated in states along the Canadian border.

2.2 Conservation

During the early portion of the 20th century, attitudes about predators began to change. The field of ecology came into its own, highlighting the interconnectedness of the seemingly disparate parts of an ecosystem. Gifford Pinchot and his acolytes reformed the management of natural resources into a professionalized, scientific endeavor, and Aldo Leopold and others worked within that framework to scientize wildlife management (Callicott 1993). Leopold himself famously changed his views on predators after having an ethical awakening while out in the White Mountains. One of the pivotal moments in his seminal *Sand County Almanac* (1949, pp. 129–132) involves Leopold and his companions stumbling across a female wolf and her pups, and "in those days [they] had never heard of passing up a chance to kill a wolf." After "pumping lead into the pack" he watched the "fierce green fire dying in her eyes." Leopold, like many others both past and present, "thought that because fewer wolves meant more deer, that no wolves would mean hunters' paradise. But after seeing the green fire die, [he] sensed that neither the wolf nor the mountain agreed with such a view." The mountain, as Leopold goes onto describe, suffered immensely under the wrath of deer irruptions and nearly unfettered cattle grazing in the wake of the extirpation of wolves.

Accompanying these shifting attitudes and emerging science came a shift in management authority. Wildlife management in the United States had traditionally fallen within the ambit of the states (Freyfogle et al. 2019). Based on common law tradition stretching back through feudal England all the way to Rome, wildlife was the property of the individual states. In 1896, the Supreme Court in *Geer v. Connecticut* (161 U.S. 519 (1896)) held that the states were the sovereign owners of all wildlife within their borders. This sovereign ownership came coupled with a responsibility—the states were expected to act as trustees of wildlife as resources for their citizens (Blumm and Paulsen 2013). In the century after *Geer*, the Supreme Court consistently eroded state supremacy in wildlife management in cases such as *Missouri vs Holland* (252 U.S. 416 (1920)) and *Hughes v. Oklahoma* (441 U.S. 322 (1979)), instead emphasizing the supremacy of the federal constitution.

As state sovereignty began to wane, federal authority over wildlife grew. Each federal attempt at conservation further eroded state authority in favor of federal primacy (Freyfogle et al. 2019). Congress exercised its Treaty Clause powers to protect migratory birds via the Migratory Bird Treaty Act. More relevant for predators, Commerce Clause jurisprudence expanded drastically and was used to justify a variety of federal wildlife-related laws. Wildlife trafficking and illegal trade was prohibited under the Lacey Act of 1900. The conservation of specific species, such as eagles protected under the Bald and Golden Eagle Protection Act, and imperiled species more broadly, under the Endangered Species Act and its predecessor, is justified by Congress's authority to regulate interstate commerce. Further, the federal government also began to exercise authority over its public lands for conservation. The Property Clause gives the federal government near absolute control over federal lands, and, as the Supreme Court held in *Kleppe v. New Mexico* (426 U.S. 529 (1976)), this control extends to wildlife on federal lands.

Over time, the federal government started taking cursory steps to reign in the excesses of its predator eradication policies. The National Park Service (NPS) was the first federal agency to recognize this sea change in our understanding of predator ecology. In 1930, the NPS took the stance that it would not privilege one set of species at the detriment of another, declaring that "no native predator shall be destroyed on account of its normal utilization of any other park animal, excepting if that animal is in immediate danger of extermination, and then only if the predator is not itself a vanishing form" (Coggins and Evans 1982). By the 1960s and 70s, federal reports lead authored by prominent biologists A. Starker Leopold and Stanley Cain argued for major changes in predator management, including curtailing the widespread use of poison (Coggins and Evans 1982). In 1972, President Nixon banned the use of poison for predator control on federal lands (Executive Order 11,643). Similarly, the practice of heli-hunting was restricted by the Airborne Hunting Act of 1971, which banned the use of aircraft "for the purpose of capturing or killing any bird, fish, or other animal" (16 U.S.C. 742j-1 (1976)).

Though it had dabbled with conservation in the past, by the mid-1960s Congress was ready to try its hand with broader biodiversity protection statutes. From the outset, large carnivores were a focal point for federal wildlife conservation. In 1966 Congress passed the Endangered Species Protection Act (ESPA). Shortly afterwards, the Department of Interior issued the first list of endangered species (Wilcove and McMillan 2006). That list included the Florida panther, grizzly bear, red wolf, and timber wolf. Jaguars were first added in 1972, and by 1978 all gray wolves in the continental US were officially listed.

Recognizing that the flawed ESPA was not nearly protective enough, Congress passed the Endangered Species Act of 1973 (ESA). Today the ESA is still the main tool for biodiversity protection in the United States. With the passage of the ESA, Congress recognized that many species were "so depleted in numbers that they [were] in danger of or threatened with extinction" and that these species were of "aesthetic, ecological, educational, historical, recreational, and scientific value to the Nation and its people" (16 U.S.C. § 1531(a) (1973)). As such, the U.S. Fish and Wildlife Service (FWS) was tasked with using "all methods and procedures which are necessary" to recover listed species (16 U.S.C. § 1532(3) (1973)). Once FWS determines that a species is endangered or at risk of becoming endangered, it promulgates a rule officially "listing" the species. Upon listing, FWS is supposed to concurrently list critical habitat for the species and formulate a recovery plan. Listing also triggers the so-called "teeth" of the Act, allowing federal protections for these species to apply. Under Section 9 of the ESA, it is illegal for any individual, whether that person is a private rancher or a paid government hunter, to "take" a listed species; "take" is broadly defined to include actions that "harass, harm, pursue, hunt, shoot, wound, kill, trap, capture, or collect, or to attempt to engage in any such conduct" (16 U.S.C. § 1532(19) (1973)). Further, Section 7 requires that all federal agencies consult with FWS to ensure that their actions do not jeopardize the continued existence of a listed species or adversely modify designated critical habitat. As the Supreme Court would later hold in *Tennessee Valley Association v. Hill* (437 U.S. 153 (1978)), this consultation requirement had the potential to completely derail and block even significant federal projects in the name of endangered species conservation.

Thus, with the passage of the ESA, the "conservation" phase of predator management reached its zenith. Once wolves and other predators were listed, states could no longer authorize the hunting or trapping of these species. Similarly, federal poisoning schemes had to shift focus away from listed species to those that were unlisted, primarily coyotes and other species still considered "varmints" like prairie dogs. Poisoning and trapping schemes that were overly indiscriminate, and thus likely to cause harm to a listed species, have even occasionally been halted by federal courts due to ESA violations.

Ultimately, the stated purpose of the ESA is to recover endangered species to the point at which they no longer need the protection of the federal government. Recovery plans serve as the blueprint the federal government uses when determining how to promote conservation of listed species (Cheever 2001a). These recovery plans have occasionally included suggestions for captive breeding programs, translocations, and ultimately reintroductions of species back into their former ranges.

For wolves especially, federal reintroductions have been critical in restoring wolf populations to their current levels. Red wolves were the first large carnivores successfully brought into a captive breeding and reintroduction program (U.S. Fish and Wildlife Service 2022a). During the 1970s, nearly 400 putative red wolves were brought into captivity. Unfortunately, the vast majority of these animals were deemed to be hybrids between red wolves and coyotes, and only 13 founders contributed to the captive gene pool. Today, a few hundred red wolves exist in various captive bred populations. A series of reintroductions have occurred over the years with varying levels of success, but today between 20 and 30 red wolves are living wild in eastern North Carolina. Mexican wolves have seen a similar, though ultimately more successful, trajectory (U.S. Fish and Wildlife Service 2022b). After a brief "extinct in the wild" phase, wolves from Mexico were used to establish captive populations in the United States. Mexican wolves have now been re-introduced to the mountains on the Arizona and New Mexico border, and between 200 and 300 wolves are established in the wild. The most successful wolf reintroductions occurred in the mid-1990s, when FWS performed their first gray wolf reintroductions into Yellowstone National Park and central Idaho. Much of what we have since learned about the ecological value of wolves has stemmed from monitoring these reintroductions, and today there are well over a thousand wolves in the northern Rocky Mountain region.

Thus far, wolves are the only large predators for which reintroductions have been attempted. FWS and the NPS are currently preparing an environmental impact statement that considers the reintroduction of grizzly bears to the North Cascades in Washington, where the species was functionally extirpated (87 F.R. 68190). Additionally, there have been recent calls from environmental groups pushing FWS to consider reintroducing jaguars to Arizona and New Mexico, but thus far these have fallen on deaf ears (Center for Biological Diversity 2022). Translocation rather than outright reintroduction was used to save the extremely inbred Florida panther when mountain lions from Texas were moved to South Florida to effectuate a genetic rescue (Johnson et al. 2010).

At the same time, successful conservation has allowed predators to begin to naturally repopulate areas they once roamed. Gray wolves have re-established breeding populations in Washington, Oregon, Michigan, and Wisconsin. California now has at least one wolf pack, and wolves have been spotted in Utah, as well. A handful of jaguars have been spotted in Arizona and New Mexico over the last decade. Even without federal protection, mountain lions have begun to spread eastward again, establishing breeding populations in the Midwest, including Nebraska, North Dakota, and South Dakota. Confirmed sightings of mountain lions are becoming increasingly common in pockets of the Northeast, the Great Lakes region, and in Missouri and Arkansas.

3 The Pendulum Swings Back in Search of Balance

As soon as predator populations were no longer on the brink of extinction, the pendulum began to swing back. As predator populations grew, so did the backlash against predator populations; along with that backlash came clamors for increased management. As such, much of the federal conservation response became tempered by this backlash. Conservation efforts, especially reintroductions of predators, need local support to be effective, and the way FWS has sought this local support is perhaps paradoxically by reducing protection for predators. This can be seen over and over again in federal handling of predators, specifically in relation to reintroduction procedures, the continued work of Wildlife Services, and attempts to delist gray wolves and grizzly bears.

3.1 Reintroductions

While wolf reintroductions have on the balance been a success, they also highlight a near immediate backsliding from total conservation to a more balanced, compromise-based approach. Section 10(j) clearly demonstrates this transition. Section 10(j) of the ESA was introduced during the 1982 Amendments, at a time when, a few years after *TVA v. Hill*, endangered species protection had become less politically palatable. As a result, Congress gave FWS wide latitude to reduce normally afforded protection for reintroduced populations in an attempt to balance conservation with negative public sentiment related to the reintroduction. Specifically, Section 10(j) authorizes FWS to create "experimental populations" of threatened and endangered species in an effort to increase the number of populations and spread species back into parts of their former range where they had become extirpated.

Experimental populations must be designated as either "essential" or "non-essential." While this distinction is of legal importance, practically it has not mattered. To date, the Services have never designated an experimental population as "essential" (Cheever 2001b). FWS has maintained that the populations it reintroduces are non-essential in every case because there is a sufficiently sized captive population that will persist even if the experimental population fails completely. As such, even red wolves and Mexican wolves, which were effectively extinct in the wild, have been reintroduced as non-essential experimental populations (Cheever 2001b).

Non-essential experimental populations receive less protection than other populations of an endangered species (Cheever 2001b). For example, FWS does not designate critical habitat for non-essential experimental populations, in an effort to reduce the burden reintroduction plays on private landowners. Non-essential populations are treated as "threatened," rather than "endangered," allowing FWS to issue a special 4(d) rule. These rules can significantly reduce general protections, and they often allow for significant take. Section 4(d) only requires that regulations for threatened species and non-essential populations be "necessary and advisable to provide for the conservation of such species" (16 U.S.C. § 1533(d) (1973)).

As the 8th Circuit held in *Sierra Club v. Clark* (755 F.2d 608 (8th Cir. 1985)), this likely prohibits FWS from transferring management to the states to allow for a sport hunting season, but it does not prohibit removal of depredating animals. For example, under the special rule for the red wolf reintroduction, private landowners are authorized to take red wolves in self-defense or to defend livestock, pets, or other third parties; they may also take red wolves on private land as long as the take is "not intentional or willful" (50 C.F.R. § 17.84(c)). In 2017, FWS tried to further loosen the standards to allow increased take on private lands, but the rule revision was successfully challenged in *Red Wolf Coalition v. FWS* (346 F. Supp. 3d 802 (E.D.N.C. 2018)) and ultimately abandoned. Similarly, the Mexican wolf special rule includes a provision that allow the state game agencies to kill wolves to decrease predation of ungulates or livestock (50 C.F.R. § 17.84(k)). These actions have mired FWS in multiple rounds of litigation, as environmental and animal rights groups have challenged the legality of these take exemptions, among other related issues.

Further, experimental populations are required to be "wholly separate geographically from nonexperimental populations of the same species" (16 U.S.C. § 1539 (j) (1982)). If an experimental population is no longer "wholly separate" then it will cease to be an experimental population and instead would become fully protected. In theory, this provision provides certainty for landowners. If property owners are permitted to take members of the experimental population in certain circumstances, these rules would be impossible to enforce if landowners could not precisely determine that the taken animal is actually a member of the reduced-protection experimental population rather than a fully protected member of the broader species. This provision has, however, frustrated recovery, and FWS has consistently acted aggressively to maintain separation (Cheever 2001b). If the long-term goal is recovery, then maintaining separation in perpetuity is counterproductive, especially as many of these experimental populations have kept their "experimental" label for decades. For the purposes of recovery, gene flow and re-established metapopulations, both of which necessitate connection and intermixing between populations, are necessary.

3.2 State-Sponsored Killings and Depredation

Unrelated to experimental populations, federal and state agencies routinely allow for otherwise protected predators to be lethally removed in efforts to protect livestock and other human interests. For example, the U.S. Forest Service recently authorized up to 72 grizzly bears to be killed as part of a reauthorization of livestock grazing on the outskirts of Yellowstone National Park. The decision was successfully challenged and struck down by the 10th Circuit for violations of the ESA in *Western Watersheds Project v. Haaland* (69 F.4th 689 (10th Cir. 2023)). FWS failed to consider limits for lethal take of female bears, and this oversight would likely contribute to the area functioning as a mortality sink for the species.

While some states have their own agencies, many states and local governments still contract with the federal government for lethal predator control of depredating or nuisance animals (Russell 2015). Though it has changed names and departments numerous times since it was first formed as the Biological Survey, Wildlife Services is the current federal pest control agency. The majority of species killed by Wildlife Services today are either invasive or viewed as damaging to property, such as Canadian geese, prairie dogs, and beavers (Milman 2022). Yet the days of Wildlife Services using professional hunters and poisons to kill predators are not as far in our past as the general public might imagine. Though President Nixon banned poisoning on federal lands, President Regan went on to lift that executive order; today, poisons and snares are still routinely used to kill targeted, and often untargeted, species (Coggins and Evans 1982; Russell 2015). Similarly, though heli-hunting was banned by Congress, prominent loopholes still allow Wildlife Services to use these methods.

Hundreds of black bears, mountain lions, and gray wolves (and tens of thousands of coyotes) are still killed by Wildlife Services each year (Milman 2022). In the last decade, a few lawsuits have been successful at challenging these programs for agency failures to comply with requirements under NEPA to prepare adequate environmental impact statements. Conservation interest groups have used these lawsuits to extract settlement agreements that limit Wildlife Services' ability to lethally take wolves via certain methods and in certain areas (Wild Earth Guardians 2022).

Dealing with depredation is, and will likely always be, one of the central tensions in predator management. There is no getting around the reality that predators do occasionally predate livestock; further there is at least some evidence that the same landscape of fear effects that wolves exert upon wild species indirectly causes harm to livestock (Macon 2020). Ranchers somewhat disproportionately bear the cost of predator conservation. While Wildlife Services, state agencies, and private ranchers still practice lethal removal when authorized, a number of non-lethal techniques have been developed. Some evidence indicates that non-lethal techniques can be more effective than lethal removal. These techniques include: alarms and other scare devices, livestock protection animals, increased human presence on the landscape, removing or spoiling carcasses, and fladry and fencing (Treves et al. 2016). Congress has made money available through Wildlife Services grant funding to help the states develop non-lethal predator control programs. Some areas, such as Marin County in California, have ceased contracting with Wildlife Services entirely, instead adopting cost-sharing programs with a focus on non-lethal, community-based approaches to predator management (Macon 2020).

However, there is evidence that state incentive programs for non-lethal predator control have struggled to entice ranchers to participate. State and federal compensation programs for livestock losses are available throughout the nation, but there is little consensus on the effectiveness of these programs. Ranchers routinely feel they are undercompensated and must go through significant bureaucracy to receive their compensation (Macon 2020). On the other hand, there is significant evidence that livestock depredation funds do not make ranchers more tolerant of predators or predator conservation (Dickman et al. 2011). Moreover, these programs have also been mired in fraud and mismanagement. For example, a USDA whistleblower has claimed that he was wrongfully terminated for attempting to investigate Mexican wolf depredation reports rather than rubber-stamping claims (Roberts 2022). In place of these "pay per kill" programs, there has been at least some clamor for adopting "pay for presence" compensation programs to better incentivize conservation of predators on private lands, and this technique is being trialed as part of the Mexican wolf program (Macon 2020).

3.3 *Delisting and Recovery*

The persistent efforts to remove gray wolves and grizzly bears from the endangered species list through taxonomic and administrative sleights of hand further exemplify the pendulum swing away from conservation. The goal of the ESA is to recover species; once recovered, species are supposed to be delisted, reverting management authority back to the states. A species has recovered when it is no longer endangered or threatened, based on the same amorphous factors used to make that initial designation (16 U.S.C. § 1533(a) (1973)). Further, whether a species remains endangered or threatened is supposed to be considered "throughout all or a significant portion of its range" (16 U.S.C. § 1532(6) (1973)). While these listing and delisting decisions are required to be based on the "best-available science," these decisions have clearly been influenced by predator politics (Doremus 1997).

A quick glance at a current range map shows that neither wolves nor grizzly bears have recovered across their entire range. On the other hand, wolves in the Northern Rockies and Great Lakes areas have far exceeded their original recovery goals. For example, the recovery objectives in the 1987 plan for the Northern Rockies called for a minimum of 10 breeding pairs of gray wolves in each of three separate recovery areas for a minimum of three successive years (U.S. Fish and Wildlife Service 1987). A separate plan for the Great Lakes states was promulgated in 1992 and required a stable population in Minnesota and a second population of wolves in Wisconsin and/or Michigan of at least 100 wolves for five years (U.S. Fish and Wildlife Service 1992). Today, many of these states boast hundreds to thousands of wolves. As such, FWS is presented with a quandary—wolf populations have significantly rebounded in some areas, prompting calls that wolves in these areas are no longer endangered, yet the vast majority of formerly occupied wolf habitat is still devoid of wolves. Further, by removing protection over these rebounded populations, FWS will effectively be limiting future dispersal and the likelihood that wolves repopulate other portions of their former range.

To address this dilemma, FWS has used its authority to designate distinct population segments (DPS) of species as listable entities. FWS is limited to listing "species" under the ESA, but Congress defined species as including subspecies and distinct population segments (DPS) (16 U.S.C. § 1532(6) (1973)). Thus, FWS has consistently tried to carve out a subsection of gray wolves by creating a new DPS, while simultaneously delisting the novel DPS in the same rule. If FWS can separately list regional populations of wolves as separate distinct population segments then each "DPS" becomes a listed "endangered species," and each of these "endangered species" will have recovered across a "significant portion of its range" thus meriting delisting. This is the sleight of hand FWS has tried to pull—by reducing the listable entity to just recovered populations, the agency can delist those populations. The pattern thus far has repeated multiple times over the last two decades. Each time FWS creates a DPS and then delists the novel DPS. This is followed by litigation that almost invariably results in the delisting being vacated and protection under the ESA returning. After a few years FWS tries to fix its mistakes and try again. In the intermediate period, predators are returned to state management, often with severe consequences and high death tolls; this yo-yoing of authority between federal and state agencies has become a recent hallmark of predator law.

This pattern is most pronounced with wolves. Over the years, FWS has created different DPS's centering around the reintroduced wolves in the northern Rocky Mountains and the repatriating wolves in the Great Lakes region. Thus far, FWS has attempted to delist a DPS centered around the Great Lakes region in 2007, 2009, 2011, and again in 2020 (CRS 2022). Each time the rule was vacated by a federal court. Attempts to delist wolves in the northern Rockies has been more successful (CRS 2022). After false starts in 2008 and 2011 (and then the direct involvement of Congress) courts have upheld the creation and delisting of the Northern Rocky Mountains DPS (NRM DPS). As a result, wolves in the NRM DPS—covering Montana, Idaho, Wyoming, eastern Washington, eastern Oregon, and northeastern Utah—are no longer federally protected. In November 2020, in the waning moments of the Trump administration, FWS tried to go a step further, delisting all remaining gray wolves, except for the separately listed Mexican wolf subspecies. Predictably, after nearly a year of litigation, the rule was vacated by the courts; once again the agency was charged with impermissibly manipulating what it considered a "species" in order to reach a delisting (CRS 2022).

Though less pronounced, the delisting of grizzly bears has faced similar issues (Greenwald 2023). Like wolves, grizzly bear populations have successfully rebounded in and around Yellowstone, yet grizzlies are nowhere close to reestablishing themselves throughout the rest of their range. Twice FWS has attempted to create and delist the Greater Yellowstone Ecosystem (GYE) DPS for grizzly bears. Each time the federal courts vacated the ruling. Citing to one of the wolf delisting cases, the district court accused FWS of "real-time balkanization" by attempting to get around examining the species as whole across its whole range by splitting it into separate DPS's (*Crow Indian Tribe v. US*, 343 F. Supp. 3d (2018)). Currently, FWS is examining multiple petitions asking the agency to delist grizzly bears across all or a portion of its range.

4 Permanent Return to State Management

The reality is that wolves and grizzly bears are likely to return to state management at some point in the not-too-distant future. Like black bears and mountain lions, this return will likely expose gray wolves and grizzly bears to sport hunting mortality. Managing the transfer of authority from federal to the state governments, as predator species recover and are removed from the federal endangered species list, is thus critical for the continued persistence of these species. In theory, predators under state control are not at risk of extinction, and at the same time the ESA should act as a backstop to keep states from attempting to eradicate predators. For the five years after delisting, FWS is required to monitor delisted species to ensure they do not become threatened with extinction again (16 U.S.C. § 1533(g) (1973)). Yet listing and delisting can often take a significant amount of time, especially when litigation is involved, and there is legitimate concern that states may backslide on their commitments as soon as they are given the opportunity.

State game agencies operate under the North American Model for Wildlife Conservation (NAM) (Organ et al. 2015). The NAM prioritizes wildlife as a resource, making sustainable harvest the main goal of wildlife management. While some states have their own rare or endangered species protection statutes that cover wolves and grizzlies, most states consider them to be game animals. Whereas the goal of the ESA focuses on the recovery of a species through the increase of current populations and the establishment of new ones, state management instead will use sport hunting as a tool to keep populations within some acceptable population size range based on a much wider range of policy concerns (Organ et al. 2015). For example, predator hunting laws have traditionally been justified under a variety of policy rationales: providing recreational hunting opportunities; reducing human-predator conflict, especially in urban and suburban areas; reducing livestock depredation; increasing population numbers for ungulates and other game species; and, often last and least, preserving predator populations (Laundré and Papouchis 2020).

A return to state management shifts not just authority, but also the incentives affecting that management, the beneficiaries of that management, and the methods in which we may hold managers accountable. When placed under federal management, predators are, in theory, treated as national resources and managed for the benefit of all citizens. Congress, through the ESA, determined that the prevention of extinction benefitted all Americans, and as such conservation was given primacy. Federal managers, though insulated, are only nationally accountable through the President and by Congressional budgetary constraints. State management, on the other hand, is far more responsive to local concerns. Upon delisting, wolves or grizzlies are no longer national resources—instead, they become resources of the state in which they are found. While the "legal fiction of state ownership" was expressly overturned by the Supreme Court, state control over wildlife, now properly subservient to the U.S. Constitution, persists in both practice and narrative. Today, at least 48 states continue to claim ownership of their wildlife (Blumm and Paulsen 2013), and states, as part of their police powers, have the authority to regulate wildlife as long as the state does not violate the federal constitution. State agencies are far more responsive to their constituents; however, they are also far more susceptible to capture (Jacobson et al. 2010). By the nature of their structure and funding, state wildlife agencies disproportionately represent sportsmen and agricultural interests. Significant funding for state game agencies comes from excise taxes levied on sporting equipment and hunting licenses and tags sold. Even the missions of these agencies differ; while FWS primarily oversees endangered species conservation and does not have a federal hunting regime to manage, state agencies often have small or non-existent non-game conservation programs with most of the agency focused on managing harvest.

State control and regulations related to predator hunting vary wildly from species to species and from state to state. For example, mountain lion hunting regulations run the full spectrum (Cooley et al. 2011). Hunting is prohibited, both federally and at the state level, in Florida. Sport hunting is banned by a popular ballot initiative in California, though "problem" lions are still killed by the state agency in response to livestock depredation and other nuisance behavior. Throughout most of the Western United Staes, lion hunting is regulated by state game agencies through the use of hunting permits, bag limits, and open and closed seasons. At the other extreme, Texas, Utah, and Idaho treat mountain lions as non-game animals, allowing year-round hunting with few, if any, limitations or requirements on the number of animals harvested or the methods in which they are harvested. Black bear hunting regulations show a similar diversity; the majority of states now employ a regulated black bear hunting season—though the specifics vary from state to state.

Hunting regulation can be extremely technical and scientific. States generally require hunting licenses for would-be hunters, and states often sell permits allowing individual hunters to take some specified number of animals. States employ quotas to limit the total number of animals harvested in each season; these overall quotas are often accompanied by sub-quotas for different areas within the state, usually called game management units (GMUs). As a sub-quota is met, the state agency will close specific GMUs. States will employ seasons that run between set dates, but these seasons can close early if the overall quota, or all sub-quotas, are met before the end date. Some states also employ bans or limitations on taking females, mothers, and/or kittens/cubs in an attempt to limit population decreases as a result of hunting. Many hunting regulations are focused on banning specific methods that are either viewed as overly harmful or against notions of fair play or ethical values such as: the use of dogs to hunt; bear baiting; aerial hunting; hunting denning animals; and the use of snares or traps.

4.1 Teetering Back Towards the Edge

On the one hand, state management appears to be working. Wolf numbers have been increasing in the three states where state agencies have allowed for harvest (Keiter 2022). Mountain lion and black bear populations generally appear at worst to be stable, and both species have been slowly expanding their ranges. However, recent changes in management might threaten to wipe away much of this progress.

The wake of the most recent wolf delisting in 2020 is perhaps the best example of this phenomenon. Recent events in Wisconsin serve as the canary in the proverbial coalmine—a potential precursor of what is to come if all management of predators is returned to the states. During the brief period in 2021 when gray wolves were removed from the endangered species list, Wisconsin had a calamitous wolf hunt. Going back to 2011, the state of Wisconsin has a statute in place that triggers a mandatory obligation that the Wisconsin Department of Natural Resources (WDNR) "shall allow the hunting and trapping of wolves" once the gray wolf is federally delisted (Treves et al. 2021b). The gray wolf was delisted in November of 2020, and WDNR wanted to wait until the fall to open a wolf hunting season. This decision was successfully challenged by a hunting advocacy group, and WDNR was forced to open a spring season for hunting in February of 2021. The agency set a quota at 119 wolves, explicitly claiming that the "objective is to allow for a sustainable harvest that neither increases nor decreases the state's wolf population" (Treves et al. 2021b). However, hunters drastically exceeded this quota—the agency issued 2380 permits and at least 218 wolves were killed in under three days (Treves et al. 2021b). One study has modeled that this loss, combined with expected cryptic poaching, resulted in a loss of 30% of the wolves in the state (Treves et al. 2021b). Taken in isolation, these losses could likely be replenished within a few years; however, WDNR also planned to offer another hunting opportunity in the fall of 2021 (Treves et al. 2021b). Multiple lawsuits were filed, one by a group of environmental and animal rights organizations and the other by the Chippewa tribes, in an attempt to block this fall hunt. A judge granted a temporary injunction based on WDNR's failure to comply with administrative procedures, and both lawsuits were ultimately dismissed when the federal court relisted gray wolves in early 2022.

The short delisting period also emboldened the Northern Rocky Mountain states, where wolves were already under state control. In 2021, the Montana state legislature expanded wolf trapping and snaring and allowed hunters to each kill an unlimited number of wolves until the area quota had been met (Keiter 2022). The Idaho legislature went even further—allowing up to 90% of wolves in the state to be killed while drastically expanding both the season and methods available for wolf hunting (Keiter 2022). While outright government sponsored bounties for apex predators are no longer in operation, both Idaho and Montana have made overtures at returning to the bounty era. Both states now allow hunters to be reimbursed for their "costs incurred related to hunting or trapping of wolves" (Keiter 2022). At least one private organization now offers up to $1000 "reimbursement" for proof of a wolf kill (Peacher 2019). Idaho Fish and Game Commission has controversially supported this group through grant funding. Further, Idaho's Wolf Depredation Control Board is authorized to hire private contractors to kill wolves once again. The actions of these states has FWS concerned, and the agency is currently revaluating the decision to delist the NRM DPS (86 F.R. 51857).

The increase in wolf hunting is not the only example of overzealous methods of predator control. In Idaho, as of 2021, quotas for mountain lions were removed entirely, allowing both male and females to be taken (Jung 2023). Along those same lines, the legislature in Utah passed a law in 2023 removing closed seasons, allowing lions to be hunted year-round with no bag limits or quotas (Jung 2023). Despite having a paltry double-digit number of lions in the state, in 2024 Nebraska is expanding hunting opportunities into a second region in the state—nowhere else in the country are populations as small as 20 individuals being hunted (Martirosov 2023).

While the ESA might function as a backstop, the states have ample room to erase decades of wolf conservation without hitting that limit. For example, upon delisting, Wisconsin set a population goal that would require a four-fold reduction in population size, down to an intended goal of 350 wolves (Treves et al. 2021b). Critically, some states appear to be setting population targets for wolves based on the minimum threshold to keep the species off the endangered species list. In Idaho, citing back to a 2002 agreement between the state and FWS, the state legislature set a population target of 150 wolves and 15 packs—a target that would see the population reduced by 90% (Keiter 2022). Wyoming also routinely strives to keep its wolf population depressed near the levels it committed to as part of the recovery agreement (Keiter 2022).

The reduction of populations to mere fractions of what there were at the time of delisting is deeply problematic, and this gets at a more fundamental issue with the implementation of "recovery" as a concept. Ultimately the goal of the ESA is to recover listed species to the point in which they are no longer at risk of extinction. The ESA, as currently implemented, is ineffective at restoring broader ecosystem functions by ensuring return of species to all inhabitable portions of their former ranges in ecologically sufficient densities. For wolves especially, if all that is needed for recovery is a minimal number of wolf populations in a handful of states where wolves once roamed, then goals related to restoring ecosystem functions or reducing deer irruptions across the entire country will never be met. Those goals will be placed on state governments, which often have conflicting interests and a preference for reducing predator populations.

The current mosaic of state and federal management also creates complicated spatial dynamics—effectively creating predator zoning. While these predators once lived across the majority of the United States, only a handful of states, where predators have either been reintroduced by the federal government or naturally returned from Canada or Mexico, are charged with having to manage them. Some neighboring states avidly, and legally, work to keep these predators from returning. For example in Utah, where wolves are delisted as part of the NRM DPS in the northeastern corner of the state but remain federally endangered everywhere else, the state legislature authorized the state Department of Wildlife Resources to prevent establishment of wolves outside of the delisted area (Fitzgerald 2022). In 2020, the Utah legislature also passed a resolution prohibiting the "artificial" reintroduction of wolves back into the state (Fitzgerald 2022). Similarly, South Dakota, which holds no known breeding populations, reclassified wolves in 2021 as "predator/varmint." This classification, which attempts to prevent wolves from reestablishing themselves in the state, allows anyone to shoot on sight without restrictions (Fitzgerald 2022).

Even within states, hunting regulations are used to push predators into or out of specific areas. For example, federal national parks have provided protected source populations, but these animals lose protection upon leaving the park boundaries. In Yellowstone National Park, federal protection of wolves has created a safe space for the species (Keiter 2022). For many years, the state of Montana allowed significant wolf harvest on the edges of the park, and only significant public pushback forced the state to change its approach (Keiter 2022). Wyoming offers an even clearer picture of this zoning phenomenon. Wolf management is separated into effectively three different regimes: total protection on certain federal lands such as national parks, regulated trophy hunting throughout the "wolf trophy game management area," and a total lack of protection for wolves across the rest of the state where they are treated as "predatory animals" (Wyoming Game and Fish Department 2022). Wyoming makes it clear that there are some places where wolves are cherished, some where they are tolerated, and many more places where they are an unwelcome nuisance.

4.2 *Range Expansions*

Despite state efforts to curb re-establishment, the natural spread of predators continues to occur, presenting new challenges for unprepared state managers. As predators attempt to return to their former ranges, old problems become new again. Predators are returning to landscapes that look and operate differently than when they were extirpated. Similarly, the people that live in these areas have likely never needed to coexist with large predators. For successful re-establishment to occur, there are certain biological, cultural, and regulatory requirements. Biologically, recolonization of a species requires not only protected corridors between established and reestablishing populations, but also adequate habitat for these populations. Sufficient gene flow is likewise necessary between these existing populations and the recolonizing population. Furthermore, legal protections and management plans need to already be in place for when these organisms arrive and settle down, and state governments must not actively work to prevent this re-establishment.

Part of this process might also include broader changes to wildlife management. For example, the last two wolves documented back in New York have been mistaken for coyotes and shot by hunters (Einhorn 2023). If we are serious about reestablishing wolf populations in the Northeast, coyotes need protection. There is a glut of evidence demonstrating that extensive hybridization between coyotes and wolves occurs in this region. Thus, indiscriminate hunting and trapping of coyotes, in states like New York, poses a significant hurdle for the re-establishment of breeding populations of wolves. Protection of coyotes for the purpose of protecting wolves has been a contentious issue in the past. Federal courts have had to step in and limit certain coyote hunting methods around red wolf reintroduction sites to prevent accidental killings; yet at the same time, FWS has worked to sterilize coyotes in these areas to minimize the risk of genetic swamping in the miniscule red wolf population (U.S. Fish and Wildlife Service 2022a). On the other hand, FWS recently refused to protect coyotes around the Mexican wolf experimental population, citing that they are not easily confused for one another (U.S. Fish and Wildlife Service 2022b).

4.3 *Who Should Decide? How Should Decisions Be Made?*

State management of wildlife highlights difficult questions about democracy versus technocracy. Who should get to decide which species are hunted and which are protected? Who should decide which methods are appropriate for predator management and which are not? Who should set the quotas and population targets for managed species? While these questions may appear scientific, they are ultimately value-based inquiries.

Under federal management these answers are fairly easy—FWS manages predators under the ESA with only the rare direct intervention from Congress. At the state level, this is much more complicated. In general, states have their own dedicated agencies. These agencies range from general environment or conservation agencies to specific wildlife or game agencies. These agencies also tend to have broad discretion over wildlife and are staffed with wildlife biologists and other technical experts. Additionally, some states utilize a board or commission that directs the policy which the rest of the wildlife agency implements and enforces (Freyfogle et al. 2019). However, these boards/commissions are usually filled by political appointment, and there tend to be requirements that a majority of members be hunters or have agricultural backgrounds. Some states do have scientists or even environmentalists on their boards, but these positions are rare and tend to be a minority of each commission. On the other hand, as evidenced above, some state legislatures are directly involved with the more intricate details of wildlife management—even over the protestations of the state wildlife professionals. Moreover, the public at large has also weighed in on proper predator management. For example, popular ballot initiatives in California, Oregon, and Washington have banned mountain lion hunting or hunting mountain lions with dogs (Welch 2014).

No matter who makes the decisions there are ripe grounds for criticism. State agencies and the boards that govern them are criticized as being captured by hunting and agricultural special interest groups and thus generally undemocratic. In my view, this is a valid critique. However, when state legislatures intervene in management, this is often criticized as being unscientific and detrimental to management, and there is ample evidence for this critique as well. The recent wolf hunting fiasco in Wisconsin, where the state legislature and Natural Resources Board acted with flagrant disregard for the recommendations of WDNR, is a perfect example. Ballot initiatives have been especially poorly received amongst agency biologists, and there is at least some evidence that mountain lion ballot initiatives have failed to achieve the desired goals of their supporters (Welch 2014).

In Colorado, a different kind of ballot initiative has sparked difficult questions about the proper decision-makers for wildlife management. In 2020, voters in Colorado were asked to consider Proposition 114—Gray Wolf Reintroduction Initiative. 50.91% of votes were cast in favor of "requiring the Colorado Parks and Wildlife Commission to create a plan to reintroduce and manage gray wolves on designated lands west of the continental divide by the end of 2023." This decision was, and remains, quite contentious. The vast majority of votes in favor came from the urban and populous Front Range, while wolves will be released hundreds of miles away on the Western Slope (CPW 2023). Additionally, the Colorado Parks and Wildlife Commission had been staunchly opposed to the reintroduction for years (CPWC Resolution 16-01). As wolves are still federally protected under the ESA in Colorado, CPW is working with FWS to develop a special 10(j) rule creating an experimental population for the reintroduction.

4.3.1 Dealing with Uncertain Science

Finally, the question of "Who should be in charge of predator management?" is intricately tied to questions about which values deserve primacy when making these decisions. Is it science? Is it economics? What about the pursuit of rural life? Or providing sufficient recreational hunting opportunities? Is the mere knowledge that predators still exist wild and free a legitimate value upon which management decisions can be based? Again, under the federal ESA, Congress has made that decision for the nation—"best available science" is supposed to govern management of endangered species. These other concerns are not supposed to be considered during decision-making. On the other hand, state management is more clearly value-based. State agencies use science when making decisions, but often population targets are set with other priorities in mind.

Difficulties arise when state managers portray their management as solely scientific or try to obfuscate the value-based decisions at the heart of their management. There is a growing body of evidence criticizing the NAM, wildlife agencies, and predator hunting, as "lacking the fundamental hallmarks of science" (Artelle et al. 2014, 2018a, b; Treves et al. 2016; Feldpausch-Parker et al. 2017; Peterson and Nelson 2017). For example, a highly contentious meta-study of mountain lion hunting found that regulations on lion hunting have largely failed to achieve their underlying policy goals: they have not reduced livestock depredation or human-lion conflict and do not increase available ungulate populations (Laundré and Papouchis 2020).

While many of these arguments have been equally criticized by the wildlife managers and other academics (Mawdsley et al. 2018), it is clear that there is still much that we do not have solid, let alone comprehensive, evidence for when it comes to the science of predator management (Blossey and Hare 2022). Comprehensive and controlled experiments are rarely done and often logistically impossible to perform (Erwin et al. 2023). Critically, state agencies must learn to examine their motivations more closely for predator hunting and to be more honest and transparent about those motivations (Treves et al. 2021a). Both science and economics have been wielded like cudgels by the warring pro-hunt and anti-hunt groups, and each side continues to argue that the other is denying scientific reality. State agencies need to be far more transparent about the factors used, and the weight given to each factor, when making decisions related to wildlife management.

5 Conclusion

While predator populations have grown and spread in the last few decades, there is still significant work to be done conserving and restoring these species. This work is, and will likely always be, difficult and contentious; predators will almost certainly continue to divide opinions. Predator management is a difficult mix of biology, economics, politics, and social science, and that is unlikely to change. The pendulum of predator management in the United States has swung from one extreme to the other, but, ultimately, we are still in search of an appropriate balance. We must continue to strive for successful coexistence.

References

Almarcha F, Ferrández T, López-Bao JV (2022) Symbols, wolves and conflicts. Biol Conserv 275. https://doi.org/10.1016/j.biocon.2022.109756

Artelle K, Reynolds JD, Paquet PC, Darimont CT (2014) When science-based management isn't. Science (1979) 343:1311–1313

Artelle KA, Reynolds JD, Treves A et al (2018a) Working constructively toward an improved North American approach to wildlife management. Sci Adv 4:1–4. https://doi.org/10.1126/sciadv.aav2571

Artelle KA, Reynolds JD, Treves A et al (2018b) Hallmarks of science missing from North American wildlife management. Sci Adv 4:1–7. https://doi.org/10.1126/sciadv.aao0167

Babb RD, Brown DE, Culver M et al (2021) Updates of historic and contemporary records of jaguars (Panthera onca) from Arizona. Arizona-Nevada Acad Sci 49:65–91

Beschta RL, Ripple WJ (2012) The role of large predators in maintaining riparian plant communities and river morphology. Geomorphology 157–158:88–98. https://doi.org/10.1016/j.geomorph.2011.04.042

Blossey B, Hare D (2022) Myths, wishful thinking, and accountability in predator conservation and management in the United States. Front Conserv Sci 3:1–11. https://doi.org/10.3389/fcosc.2022.881483

Blumm MC, Paulsen A (2013) The public trust in wildlife. Utah Law Rev 6:1437–1504. https://doi.org/10.2139/ssrn.2189134

Boitani L, Linnell JDC (2015) Bringing large mammals back: large carnivores in Europe. In: Rewilding European Landscapes. pp 67–84

Brown JS, Laundré JW, Gurung M (1999) The ecology of fear: optimal foraging, game theory, and trophic interactions. J Mammal 80:385–399. https://doi.org/10.2307/1383287

Callicott JB (1993) A brief history of American conservation philosophy. Sustainable Ecological Systems: Implementing an Ecological Approach to Land Management Rocky Mountain Forest and Range Experiment Station, Fort Collins, CO (USA) 10–14

Center for Biological Diversity (2022) Petition to reintroduce jaguar (Panthera onca) to New Mexico and designate additional critical habitat in Arizona and New Mexico. https://www.biologicaldiversity.org/species/mammals/jaguar/pdfs/2022-12-12-Center-for-Biological-Diversity-petition-to-reintroduce-jaguars-increase-critical-habitat.pdf

Cheever F (2001a) Recovery planning, the courts and the Endangered Species Act. Nat Resour Environ 16:106–111. https://doi.org/10.2139/ssrn.2536563

Cheever F (2001b) From population segregation to species zoning: the evolution of reintroduction law under Section 10(J) of the Endangered Species Act. Wyoming Law Rev 1:287

Coggins GC, Evans PB (1982) Predators' rights and American wildlife law. Ariz Law Rev 24:821–879

Colorado Parks and Wildlife (2023) Colorado Wolf Restoration and Management Plan, Denver, CO. https://cpw.state.co.us/Documents/Wolves/2023-Final-CO-Wolf-Plan.pdf

Colorado Parks and Wildlife Commission (2016) Resolution 16-01. https://cpw.state.co.us/Documents/WildlifeSpecies/SpeciesOfConcern/Wolf/2016_PWC_Resolution_Wolves_in_Colorado.pdf

Congressional Research Service (2022) U.S. district court vacates gray wolf delisting rule. LSB10697. Prepared by Erin H. Ward

Cooley HS, Bunnel KD, Stoner DC, Wolfe ML (2011) Population management: cougar hunting. In: Jenks JA (ed) Managing Cougars in North America. Berryman Institute Press, Logan, UT, pp 111–134
Dickman AJ, Macdonald EA, Macdonald DW (2011) A review of financial instruments to pay for predator conservation and encourage human-carnivore coexistence. Proc Natl Acad Sci U S A 108:13937–13944. https://doi.org/10.1073/pnas.1012972108
Doremus H (1997) Listing decisions under the Endangered Species Act: why better science isn't always better policy? Wash Univ Law Q 75:1029–1046
Einhorn C (2023) How mistaken identity and one bullet revealed a star predator far from home. New York Times
Erwin JA, Logan KA, Trumbo DR et al (2023) Effects of hunting on mating, relatedness, and genetic diversity in a puma population. Mol Ecol 1–18. https://doi.org/10.1111/mec.17237
Feldpausch-Parker AM, Parker ID, Vidon ES (2017) Privileging consumptive use: a critique of ideology, power, and discourse in the North American Model of Wildlife Conservation. Conserv Soc 15:33–40. https://doi.org/10.4103/0972-4923.201395
Fitzgerald EA (2022) Premature gray wolf delisting. Nat Resour J 62:183–236
Freyfogle ET, Goble DD, Wildermuth TA (2019) Wildlife law: a primer, 2nd edn. Island Press, Washington D.C.
Goble D (1992) Of wolves and welfare ranching. Harv Environ Law Rev 16:101–127
Greenwald N (2023) Recovery of the grizzly bear at the intersection of law and science. Front Conserv Sci 4:1142991. https://doi.org/10.3389/fcosc.2023.1142991
Jacobson CA, Organ JF, Decker DJ et al (2010) A conservation institution for the 21st century: implications for state wildlife agencies. J Wildlife Manag 74:203–209. https://doi.org/10.2193/2008-485
Johnson WE, Onorato DP, Roelke ME et al (2010) Genetic restoration of the Florida panther. Science 329:1641–1645. https://doi.org/10.1126/science.1192891
Jung J (2023) Idaho removed mountain lion quotas. Other states went further. Is the animal in peril?. Idaho Statesman. https://www.eastidahonews.com/2023/07/idaho-removed-mountain-lion-quotas-other-states-went-further-is-the-animal-in-peril/
Keiter RB (2022) Grizzlies, wolves, and law in the Greater Yellowstone Ecosystem: wildlife management amidst jurisdictional complexity and tension. Wyoming Law Rev 22:303–353
Klees van Bommel J, Badry M, Ford AT et al (2020) Predicting human-carnivore conflict at the urban-wildland interface. Glob Ecol Conserv 24:e01322. https://doi.org/10.1016/j.gecco.2020.e01322
Laundré JW, Papouchis C (2020) The Elephant in the room: what can we learn from California regarding the use of sport hunting of pumas (Puma concolor) as a management tool? PLoS One 15:1–26. https://doi.org/10.1371/journal.pone.0224638
Laundré JW, Hernández L, Altendorf KB (2001) Wolves, elk, and bison: reestablishing the "landscape of fear" in Yellowstone National Park, U.S.A. Can J Zool 79:1401–1409. https://doi.org/10.1139/cjz-79-8-1401
Leopold A (1949) A Sand County Almanac. Oxford University Press, New York
Li J (2000) The wolves may have won the battle, but not the war: how the west was won under the Northern Rocky Mountain wolf recovery plan. Environ Law 30:677–700
Macon D (2020) Paying for the presence of predators: an evolving approach to compensating ranchers. Rangelands 42:43–52. https://doi.org/10.1016/j.rala.2020.03.001
Martirosov D (2023) Nebraska expands mountain lion hunting into Niobrara Valley — but not without opposition. Lincoln Journal Star. https://journalstar.com/news/local/nebraska-expands-mountain-lion-hunting-into-niobrara-valley-but-not-without-opposition/article_7e9bba88-0ada-11ee-87fb-8f13de4b5f88.html
Mawdsley JR, Organ JF, Decker DJ et al (2018) Artelle et al. (2018) miss the science underlying North American wildlife management. Sci Adv 4:3–5. https://doi.org/10.1126/sciadv.aat8281
Mech LD (2012) Is science in danger of sanctifying the wolf? Biol Conserv 150:143–149. https://doi.org/10.1016/j.biocon.2012.03.003

Milman O (2022) 'A barbaric federal program': US killed 1.75m animals last year - or 200 per hour. The Guardian

Nie MA (2001) The sociopolitical dimensions of wolf management and restoration in the United States. Hum Ecol Rev 8:1–12

Noss R, Soulé M (1998) Rewilding and biodiversity: complementary goals for continental conservation. Wild Earth 8:19–28

Olson ER, Stenglein JL, Shelley V et al (2015) Pendulum swings in wolf management led to conflict, illegal kills, and a legislated wolf hunt. Conserv Lett 8:351–360. https://doi.org/10.1111/conl.12141

Organ JF, Geist V, Mahoney SP et al. (2015) The North American Model of Wildlife Conservation. The Wildlife Society and The Boone and Crockett Club Technical Review 12-04- December 2012 289–324. https://doi.org/10.7208/chicago/9780226107547.003.0009

Peacher A (2019) State of Idaho funds controversial wolf bounty program. Boise State Public Radio News. https://www.boisestatepublicradio.org/environment/2019-03-28/state-of-idaho-funds-controversial-wolf-bounty-program

Peterson MN, Nelson MP (2017) Why the North American Model of Wildlife Conservation is problematic for modern wildlife management. Hum Dimens Wildlife 22:43–54. https://doi.org/10.1080/10871209.2016.1234009

Peziol M, Elbroch LM, Shipley LA et al (2023) Large carnivore foraging contributes to heterogeneity in nutrient cycling. Landsc Ecol 38:1497–1509. https://doi.org/10.1007/s10980-023-01630-0

Raynor JL, Grainger CA, Parker DP (2021) Wolves make roadways safer, generating large economic returns to predator conservation. Proc Natl Acad Sci U S A 118:1–10. https://doi.org/10.1073/pnas.2023251118

Ripple WJ, Estes JA, Beschta RL et al (2014) Status and ecological effects of the world's largest carnivores. Science (1979) 343. https://doi.org/10.1126/science.1241484

Ripple WJ, Estes JA, Schmitz OJ et al (2016) What is a trophic cascade? Trends Ecol Evol 31:842–849. https://doi.org/10.1016/j.tree.2016.08.010

Roberts S (2022) Cry wolf. In: The Intercept. https://theintercept.com/2022/05/24/mexican-gray-wolf-endangered-wildlife-services-fraud/

Russell AJ (2015) Services gone wild: has Wildlife Services' predator control program gone too far? Villanova Environ Law J 16:123–143

Treves A, Krofel M, McManus J (2016) Predator control should not be a shot in the dark. Front Ecol Environ 14:380–388. https://doi.org/10.1002/fee.1312

Treves A, Paquet PC, Artelle KA et al (2021a) Transparency about values and assertions of fact in natural resource management. Front Conserv Sci 2. https://doi.org/10.3389/fcosc.2021.631998

Treves A, Santiago-Ávila FJ, Putrevu K (2021b) Quantifying the effects of delisting wolves after the first state began lethal management. PeerJ 7. https://doi.org/10.7717/peerj.11666

U.S. Fish and Wildlife Service (1987) Northern Rocky Mountain wolf recovery plan. https://ecos.fws.gov/docs/recovery_plan/870803.pdf

U.S. Fish and Wildlife Service (1992) Recovery plan for the eastern timber wolf. https://ecos.fws.gov/docs/recovery_plan/920131.pdf

U.S. Fish and Wildlife Service (2022a) Draft revised recovery plan for the red wolf (Canis rufus). https://www.fws.gov/sites/default/files/documents/Draft_Revised_Recovery_Plan_Red_Wolf_2022.pdf

U.S. Fish and Wildlife Service (2022b) Mexican wolf recovery plan second revision. https://ecos.fws.gov/docs/recovery_plan/Final%20Mexican%20Wolf%20Recovery%20Plan%20Second%20Revision%202022%20signed_508%20compliant_1.pdf

Welch TM (2014) Can citizens better use the ballot initiative to protect wildlife?: The case of the mountain lion in the west. Colo Nat Resour Energy Environ Law Rev 25:419

Whiteley J (2023) Property in wolves. Cornell Law Rev 108:617–674. https://doi.org/10.2139/ssrn.4186969

Wilcove DS, McMillan M (2006) The class of '67. In: Goble DD, Scott JM, Davis FW (eds) The Endangered Species Act at thirty, vol 1. Island Press, Washington D.C., pp 45–50
Wild Earth Guardians (2022) New legal settlement protects coyotes, wolves in Idaho. https://wildearthguardians.org/press-releases/new-legal-settlement-protects-coyotes-wolves-in-idaho/
Wyoming Game and Fish Department (2022) Wyoming gray wolf monitoring and management: 2022 annual report. https://wgfd.wyo.gov/WGFD/media/content/PDF/Wildlife/Large%20Carnivore/WYWolf_AnnualReport_2022.pdf

Aquatic Biodiversity Management in the United States

Karrigan Börk

Abstract A tremendous number of freshwater fish species, aquatic plants, and aquatic invertebrates are native to North America. The native fish alone number more than 1300 species. But across North America, this biodiversity faces a wide variety of threats, from invasive species to pollution to habitat loss. Freshwater species in the United States are disappearing at a rate two to five times higher than land animals and are the most imperiled species group in the country. This chapter provides background information on the aquatic biodiversity in the United States and the threats it faces, and then discusses the federal major laws and other approaches to mitigating those threats. The two primary laws are the Endangered Species Act, focused on protecting threatened and endangered species, and the Clean Water Act, focused on pollution prevention, wetland protection, and, to a lesser degree, habitat protection. The chapter also reviews other relevant laws and policies, including the Federal Power Act, the Wild and Scenic Rivers Act, federal funding for state aquatic conservation efforts through the Dingell Johnson Act and the Pittman-Robertson Federal Aid in Wildlife Restoration Act, and the Biden Administration's 30×30 initiative.

1 Freshwater Aquatic Biodiversity in the United States

Freshwater ecosystems, found in rivers, lakes, and inland wetlands, cover less than 1% of Earth's surface yet are home to one-third of all vertebrate species and 10% of all species (Strayer and Dudgeon 2010). North America's native freshwater biodiversity includes more than 1300 diadromous or freshwater fish species in 36 families (Darwell and Freyhof 2015; Helfrich and Neves 2019), and roughly 300 species of

I appreciate helpful reviews by Professor Al Lin and Alex Erwin and Dr. Peter Moyle, and helpful research by my research assistant Kayleigh O'Connor.

K. Börk (✉)
University of California, Davis, CA, USA
e-mail: ksbork@ucdavis.edu

G. Antonelli et al. (eds.), *Biodiversity Laws, Policies and Science in Europe, the United States and China*, https://doi.org/10.1007/978-3-031-56218-1_10

native amphibians (Green et al. 2014). Invertebrate species are less well documented, but North America boasts the richest freshwater bivalve biodiversity of any continent, with roughly 350 species of mussels and clams, and myriad other invertebrates (Thorp et al. 2010). This aquatic biodiversity is exceptional; North America has the most biodiverse aquatic fauna in any temperate region in the world (Jelks et al. 2008). The mussel biodiversity is particularly incredible. The Mississippi River basin alone supports 3–4 times as many mussel species as the Amazon-Orinoco or Congo River basins, which support the world's richest freshwater fish faunas. In some parts of the eastern United States, more mussel species can be found in 1 m^2 of river bottom than occur on the entire continent of Europe (Haag and Williams 2014, p. 45).

The continent's biodiversity is distributed unevenly across the landscape. Most North American freshwater aquatic biodiversity is concentrated in the Southeast United States, which hosts almost 80% of freshwater fish species (Page and Burr 2011), 91% of U.S. mussel species, more than two-thirds of North America's species and subspecies of crayfishes, and more amphibians and aquatic reptiles than any other region in the nation, according to the Center for Biological Diversity. This concentration makes the southeastern United States a global "hotspot" for aquatic biodiversity. Even within the Southeast, particular regions host exceptional levels of diversity (Jenkins et al. 2015). According to Helfrich and Neves (2019), the three states with the richest diversity of fish include Tennessee (320 species), Kentucky (246 species), and Virginia (226 species). The American West hosts far fewer aquatic species; four times as many fish species live in the eastern United States versus the West (Helfrich and Neves 2019). For example, California has only 129 native fish species (Moyle et al. 2013) even though the state is larger than Tennessee, Kentucky, and Virginia combined. However, over 80% of these fishes are endemic just to California and, the list include salmon and steelhead species in the western United States that are deemed to be of particular economic and cultural importance and so have been a primary focus of conservation efforts (Male 2014). Many western species are endemics with limited range and an uncertain prognosis.

Native aquatic biodiversity in the United States is in trouble. Declines in fish species are perhaps best documented. The Endangered Species Committee of the American Fisheries Society tracks the status of native North American fishes, and its most recent report paints a distressing picture. As of 2008, 61 species no longer existed in the wild, 280 species were listed as in imminent danger of extinction, 190 species were threatened, and 230 species were listed as vulnerable become threatened (Jelks et al. 2008). In total, the 700 listed fish taxa nearly doubled the organization's 1989 list of imperiled species, and the vast majority of species were in decline (Jelks et al. 2008). The distribution of imperiled species generally parallels the overall distribution of aquatic biodiversity in the United States, with significant concentrations in the Southeast and the mid-Pacific Coast (Jelks et al. 2008). Across North America, Jelks et al. (2008) found that roughly 40% of fish species were in peril. Other studies found that 64% of native freshwater snails were imperiled and 10% were already extinct (Johnson et al. 2013), and 48% of crayfish were imperiled (Taylor et al. 2007). Note that these categorizations and rates differ from those used for formal listing under the U.S. Endangered Species Act, discussed below. Listing is a slower process that generally lags behind scientific measures of imperilment, and the rates of formal listing of these species groups are far lower (1% for crayfishes, 4% for aquatic snails, 5% for fishes, and 28% for mussels) (Haag and Williams 2014).

Mussels, which appear to be more sensitive to changes in their aquatic habitats, face particularly dire challenges. Scientists consider 65% of mussel species imperiled, and 30 species (just under 10% of existing species) are already extinct (Haag and Williams 2014). Because mussels are hard to detect and identify, these are likely under-estimates. Detailed work on a number of watersheds since the 1960s detected huge declines in both the number of mussel species and the number of individuals. However, many of the remaining individuals were old specimens, suggesting that reproduction had dropped to very low levels. For example, "[i]n the Red River, Tennessee, species richness declined 44% between 1966 and 1990, the total number of individuals reported declined 90%." (Haag 2019, p. 44). Other watersheds showed similar results.

Across all the taxonomic groups, the data clearly shows an aquatic extinction crisis (Dudgeon 2019).

1.1 Threats to Biodiversity

North American aquatic species face myriad challenges, and most species are suffering from multiple causes of decline. Generally, the threats to aquatic biodiversity fall under six categories: habitat loss and degradation, water pollution, overexploitation, flow modification, interactions with nonnative species, and climate change (Dudgeon et al. 2006). These categories overlap and may share underlying causes. For example, water infrastructure like dams can directly destroy or degrade habitat, both flooding wetlands, rivers, and streams above the dam and by changing below dam waterway characteristics. Dams also modify flows, which may interfere with fish life cycles or other species needs. Additionally, dams can contribute to thermal or other types of water pollution, as in the Klamath River system in northern California. Finally, as dams alter the characteristics of waterways, they often enable invasion by nonnative species that further challenge the survival of native species through predation or other interactions (Moyle and Mount 2007). Nevertheless, the six categories provide a useful way to understand threats to aquatic biodiversity.

Habitat degradation and loss are the two most prevalent factors leading to species declines, contributing to declines in 92% of species, especially those with a naturally restricted range (72%) (Jelks et al. 2008). It is difficult to overstate the changes to aquatic habitats in the United States since European colonization began. For example, in the coterminous United States, wetland habitat has decreased from approximately 221 million acres to 103 million acres, with six states losing 85% or more of their wetlands and 22 states losing 50% or more (Dahl and Allord 2023). In California's Central Valley, for example, only 5% of historic floodplain wetlands remain, and the loss of this vital habitat factors into the decimation of many California species (Katz et al. 2016). Beyond wetlands, most aquatic habitats have been transformed through water infrastructure, land use changes, and other anthropogenic alterations. Water infrastructure can change and degrade habitat in several ways, such as by altering flows that shape downstream habitat, by flooding upstream habitat, by changing water temperature and quality, and by reducing flows (Moyle and Mount 2007). Land use changes such as "mining, clearing of natural forests for agriculture, urban development, and other intensive land-use practices" cause changes in downstream areas due to sedimentation, and changes in water flow and quality (Walsh et al. 2011). Urban expansion has emerged as a major threat in regions with high freshwater aquatic biodiversity, particularly in the Southeast (Martinuzzi et al. 2014). Although overall figures are hard to determine, studies suggest that 70% of floodplains have poor habitat integrity (Morrison et al. 2023), and "only about 2 percent of the 3.5 million miles of streams in the United States is unaffected by dams, and 18 percent is under the waters of reservoirs" (Graf 2001, p. 5). Across the West, water infrastructure, housing developments, and other anthropogenic disturbances have modified roughly half of river miles and 82% of major rivers (Center for American Progress 2018). Native species often struggle to survive in degraded habitat, and habitat loss is a primary driver of biodiversity loss.

Water pollution takes many forms, from contamination with pollutants from agricultural, municipal, and industrial sources to sedimentation from land use changes to warmer water from power plants or dams. Water quality problems are widespread and difficult to address. The 2017 National Water Quality Inventory (2017) reported:

- 46% of river/stream miles in poor biological condition, due in part to phosphorus and nitrogen loads
- 21% of lakes hypereutrophic, meaning they have extremely high levels nutrients, again largely due to phosphorus and nitrogen
- 18% of coastal/Great Lakes waters in poor biological condition and 14% with poor water quality
- Over half of wetlands impaired by high levels of organic materials, mercury, other metals, or other causes

Degraded water quality often favors nonnative species and can make survival impossible for sensitive native species (Dudgeon et al. 2006).

Water infrastructure for hydropower, water withdrawals, and navigation affects the vast majority of waterways in the United States. Poff et al. (2007) estimate the average density of large dams on larger rivers at one dam for every 48 km of river length. Including smaller, generally unregulated dams drives the total number of dams much higher, to 2.5 million dams in the United States alone (Brewitt and Colwyn 2020). Beyond fragmenting and degrading habitat, these dams also modify flows, both by changing the timing and quantity of flows and often by reducing the total discharge from the waterway (National Academies of Sciences, Engineering, and Medicine 2002). Poff et al. (2007) argue that these dams "have a continental scale effect of homogenizing regionally distinct environmental templates, thereby creating conditions that favor the spread of cosmopolitan, nonindigenous species at the expense of locally adapted native biota" (p. 5732).

Overexploitation is a significant threat to some aquatic species, particularly salmonids (trout, salmon, and whitefish), striped bass, and sturgeons (Walsh et al. 2011). Harvest is generally regulated, which mitigates but does not eliminate the threat of overexploitation for most species.

Nonnative species are a threat to native aquatic biodiversity. Nonnative species enter new waterways either deliberately, through mechanisms like stocking of sportfish or release of baitfish, or through foreseeable mechanisms like transport in recreational watercraft, on equipment, or in ballast water in large ships. Generally, "invertebrate invasions are concentrated in the Great Lakes region, nonindigenous freshwater fish are clustered in the Southeast (Virginia, North Carolina, and Florida) and the Southwest (Nevada, Arizona, Texas, California, Colorado)" (Bobeldyk et al. 2015, p. 367). In the western United States, a study amassing data on 2,113,000 km of streams and rivers found that nonnative vertebrates were present in most streams and constituted the majority of vertebrate species in just over 20% of waterways (Lomnicky et al. 2007). Larger rivers were more likely to have more nonnative species, as were highly modified systems. Introduced species can negatively impact native species in many ways, including through competition, introduction of parasites and diseases, predation, and hybridization (Lomnicky et al. 2007). Native species generally decline after the introduction of nonnative species (Ross 1991), and nonnative species appear to be a primary driver of aquatic biodiversity loss (Panlasigui et al. 2018), especially in degraded habitats.

Finally, climate change constitutes a sixth threat to aquatic biodiversity that will aggravate many of the other threats. Climate change is already affecting most drivers of freshwater ecosystem structure and function, and continued climate change will force changes in most aquatic ecosystems (Reid et al. 2019). The effects of climate change on aquatic ecosystems include increasing air and water temperatures; changes in runoff patterns; increasing extreme flood and drought events; and changes in lake stratification. Each of these effects will shift existing ecosystem conditions, often to the detriment of native species adapted to historic conditions (Moyle et al. 2013; Moyle and Leidy 2023). These changes interact with the threats identified above by accelerating habitat loss and degradation, aggravating the impacts of water pollution, amplifying the impacts of flow modification, and encouraging invasions by nonnative species. Of course, climate change may favor some aquatic species, those that prefer warmer waters or are more able to tolerate degraded conditions, but this is unlikely to benefit overall biodiversity, as these species typically are already well represented and generally less susceptible to threats (Comte et al. 2013).

2 United States Law and Policy Addressing Aquatic Biodiversity

The United States has enacted laws and policies at both the state and federal level to conserve and restore aquatic biodiversity. This overview focuses on the major federal laws that address aquatic biodiversity (the Endangered Species Act, Clean Water Act, the Federal Power Act, Wild and Scenic Rivers Act, the Dingell Johnson Act, and the Pittman-Robertson Federal Aid in Wildlife Restoration Act), mentioning state laws only in passing, due to the fragmented and diverse nature of state laws (National Caucus of Environmental Legislators 2023).

2.1 Endangered Species Act

The Endangered Species Act ("ESA") is a cornerstone of U.S. environmental law. Passed in 1973, the ESA created "an expectation that society will attempt to save all species," (Bork 2021, p. 180) and the ESA continues to motivate most biodiversity protection efforts in the U.S.

The ESA begins with broad language about providing "a means whereby the ecosystems upon which endangered species and threatened species depend may be conserved" (16 U.S.C. § 1531), but the ESA actually focuses almost exclusively on species-level protections. Generally, the ESA's protections apply to species listed as threatened or endangered.

The ESA defines "species" to include "subspecies of fish or wildlife or plants, and any distinct population segment of any species of vertebrate fish or wildlife which interbreeds when mature" (16 U.S.C. § 1532(16)). The National Marine Fisheries Service (for marine and diadromous species) and the U.S. Fish and Wildlife Service (for terrestrial and freshwater species), the two agencies (collectively "the Services") charged with implementing the ESA, have promulgated regulations further defining species. Species may be proposed or listed by the Services themselves or proposed by members of the public, and species listing has generally been driven by public petitions. The Services follow the same process for any proposed change in the status of a species, including listing, delisting, or a change in status between threatened and endangered. In making this determination, the Services are directed to rely only on the best available science. The Services must determine whether the species is "endangered" or "threatened." An "endangered species" is one "in danger of extinction throughout all or a significant portion of its range" (16 U.S.C. § 1532(6)) while a "threatened species" is one "likely to become an endangered species within the foreseeable future" (16 U.S.C. § 1532(20)).

After the relevant Service receives the petition, the Service reviews the petition to see if it "presents substantial scientific or commercial information indicating that the petitioned action may be warranted" (16 U.S.C. § 1533(b); 50 CFR § 424.14). If so, the Service undertakes a year-long process involving public comment and expert review to determine whether to take the proposed action; if the agency determines that listing is appropriate, it will publish a proposed rule for public comment and then, if it still finds that the action is appropriate, it will finalize the rule implementing the proposed action. The Services may also determine that the petitioned action is not warranted, or that it is warranted but precluded by other, higher priority actions, in which case the petition receives ongoing annual review until its ultimate disposition (Alexander 2010). These steps all have binding statutory timing deadlines, added to address the Regan Administration's reticence to proceed with species listing decisions. Finally, the Services are supposed to designate critical habitat and develop recovery plans for the species they list, but these processes are expensive and time consuming, and the Services have often failed to do so (GAO 2017). The recovery plans are not legally binding, further reducing incentives to develop them in the resource-limited Services The Services routinely fail to meet their statutory deadlines, resulting in listing timelines that are more often driven by lawsuits over missed deadlines than by Service priorities or biological needs (GAO 2017), although there is some evidence that the parties bringing the lawsuits have done a good job of prioritizing conservation needs (Biber and Brosi 2010).

Protections under the ESA only begin once the species is listed. Most protections come the ESA Sections 7 and 9. Section 9 prohibits take of "any endangered species of fish or wildlife" (16 U.S.C. § 1538(a)(1)); take is defined broadly to include harm, harassment, or "significant habitat modification or degradation where it actually kills or injures wildlife by significantly impairing essential behavioral patterns" (50 C.F. R. § 17.3 (2019); *Babbitt v. Sweet Home Chapter of Cmtys. for a Great Or.*, 515 U.S. 687, 715 (1995)). Note that plants are not protected from take, although they do receive some minor protections in other ways (Young and Bork 2021). The Section 9 protections for endangered species are strong, barring both direct and indirect take, and violators face both civil and criminal penalties. Species listed as threatened may receive the same protection as endangered species, depending on the applicable regulations promulgated under Section 4(d).

Section 7 of the ESA provides additional protection for listed species by regulating federal agency actions. First, Section 7(a)(1) requires federal agencies to carry out "programs for the conservation of endangered species and threatened species." Some federal courts have read this section to create an enforceable obligation on all federal agencies, although this is generally not viewed as an affirmative obligation (Ruhl 1995). Second, and more importantly, Section 7(a)(2) requires that "[e]ach Federal agency ... insure that any action authorized, funded, or carried out by such agency ... is not likely to jeopardize the continued existence of any endangered species or threatened species or result in the destruction or adverse modification of [critical] habitat of such species" (16 U.S.C. § 1536(a)(2)). Agencies must consult with the relevant Service before undertaking any action that "may affect listed species or critical habitat" (50 C.F.R. § 402.14(a)). In many cases, these consultations result in a formal "Biological Opinion" and an "Incidental Take Statement" (16 U.S.C. § 1536; U.S. Fish and Wildlife Serv. & Nat'l Marine Fisheries Serv. 1998). These binding documents determine whether the federal agency action is likely to violate the law, establish required project mitigation actions, and limit the amount of Section 9 take allowed as part of the agency action. Although Section 7 creates requirements for federal agency actions, many private actions require federal permits, federal funding, or other federal involvement; therefore, Section 7 requirements indirectly apply to these private actions. Examples might include draining a wetland to build a housing development, which may require a CWA Section 404 permit from the U.S. Army Corps of Engineers, or maintaining a state or private hydropower dam, which requires a permit from the Federal Energy Regulatory Commission. For example, perhaps the most famous ESA case of all time, Tennessee Valley Authority (TVA) v. Hill, came from a Section 7 challenge to a dam that would have driven a fish called the snail darter to extinction (437 U.S. 153, 195 (1978)). TVA v. Hill established that the ESA could be used to block federal projects that failed to comply with the law.

The ESA provides a permitting process to allow Section 9 take by non-federal actors that would otherwise violate the ESA, under several provisions in Section 10 (16 U.S.C. § 1539). This includes permits "for scientific purposes or to enhance the propagation or survival of the affected species" (16 U.S.C. § 1539(a)(1)(A)) or for "taking ... incidental to, and not the purpose of, the carrying out of an otherwise lawful activity" (16 U.S.C. § 1539(a)(1)(B)). The first category allows for operation of hatcheries for listed species, among other things. The second category of permits, often termed "incidental take permits," allows nonfederal actors to take listed species provided that the take is incidental, that the actor mitigate the take of the listed species to the maximum extent possible, and that the take "will not appreciably reduce the likelihood survival and recovery of the species in the wild" (16 U.S.C. § 1539(a)(2)(B). The permit applicant meets these requirements through a habitat conservation plan approved by the relevant Service. Many HCPs approved by NMFS address salmonids on the West Coast, while FWS's approved HCPs address a host of different aquatic species nationwide, from toads to snails to turtles to fish. The HCPs are generally available on the Services' websites. A final provision, Section 10(j), allows the Services to reintroduce populations of listed species and designate them as experimental populations, sometimes exempting them from the take protections. This approach has been used for aquatic species like the spring run Chinook on California's San Joaquin River and the Middle Columbia River Steelhead on the Deschutes River, OR. These designations are generally used to make reintroductions politically palatable in the face of opposition to reintroduction efforts (Bork 2019).

Through the Section 7 and 9 protections, the ESA is designed to prevent or reduce new impacts to species, but under current judicial interpretations, it does not directly mandate actions to improve the status of listed species. This creates a tremendous challenge for biodiversity management, because roughly 84% of ESA-listed species are conservation-reliant, meaning they require ongoing human help to avoid extinction (Scott et al. 2010). In response, the Services, environmental non-governmental organizations, and other actors often cobble together management plans that do address these needs through negotiated agreements that are encouraged and enabled by the regulatory backstop (Owen 2023; Bork 2021). These agreements, coupled with the harder limits in the ESA itself, comprise much of the federal biodiversity protection law in the United States. This approach also means that species impacted by expensive and socially important infrastructure projects often get an outsized amount of funding, especially if the species itself is charismatic and of great social value. This is perhaps most notable for Pacific salmonids. From 1994 to 2014, nearly 40% of ESA funding went to six species of Pacific salmon, and in 2011, more funds went to chinook salmon than all other species on the endangered species list (Male 2014). In contrast, only 0.8% of 2014 funds went to 85 species of endangered freshwater mussels (Greenwald et al. 2016). The ESA is a vital tool for conservation, but inadequate funding and a focus on preserving species remnants, rather than recovering species across their range, mean that the ESA alone (at least as currently implemented) will not adequately conserve aquatic biodiversity.

2.2 *Clean Water Act*

Congress passed the 1972 Clean Water Act ("CWA") "to restore and maintain the chemical, physical, and biological integrity of the Nation's waters" (33 USC 1251 et seq.). The CWA relies on two primary regulatory approaches, a discharge ban and state water quality standards.

Citizen Suits and Biodiversity Protection
Lawsuits by individual citizens or environmental groups play an important role in protecting biodiversity in the United States. The ESA and the CWA both authorize citizen suits, both to enforce the acts against violators and to force the government to take action under some provisions of the acts. Some state doctrines, like the public trust, also allow for citizen suits against the state or against individual violators. These citizen suits can ensure enforcement of the law and provide some insulation against administrations that would otherwise choose to weaken environmental protections through agency action (Adelman and Glicksman 2020).

The CWA centerpiece is a broad ban on the unpermitted discharge of any pollutant by any person. This bars the "any addition of any pollutant to navigable waters from any point source" (33 U.S.C. §1362 (12)), including both stereotypical pollutants like chemical wastes and sewage, and dredged spoil and rock, sand, dirt, and other fill materials (33 U.S.C. §1362(6)). The Environmental Protection Agency (EPA) has primary jurisdiction under CWA Section 402 to permit discharge of most pollutants that would otherwise be illegal, but the EPA generally delegates this authority to the states. The Section 402 permits, termed National Pollutant Discharge Elimination System permits (NPDES permits) implement technology-based standards, and thus, the stringency of the permit depends on the nature of the discharge, on whether the source is a new source or an existing source, and on the available technology to treat or avoid the discharge. The permits also contain extensive monitoring and reporting requirements for the discharger, and violation of these requirements is treated as a violation of the act itself for enforcement purposes. For states to have NPDES permitting authority, they generally legislate a state-level version of the Clean Water Act and fund a state agency to implement it. For example, California implements the CWA through its Porter-Cologne Water Quality Control Act (CA Wat. Code, § 13000 et seq.), and the State Water Resource Control Board has primary authority for implementing the state law. In turn, the EPA has delegated significant permitting authority to the state.

The Army Corps of Engineers issues the permits for the discharge of dredge and fill materials, under CWA Section 404, and, with a few exceptions, it has generally not delegated this authority to the states because the states generally have not implemented legislation addressing dredge and fill. The Section 404 permits are particularly important in the biodiversity context because CWA 404 permitting has become the primary federal method for protecting wetlands. Most actions that destroy wetlands deposit some material into the wetlands, and so these actions have generally required a 404 permit. This may change in light of the more restrictive interpretations of the CWA jurisdictional language in a recent Supreme Court decision, discussed below. Under the CWA, the Corps cannot issue a permit "if there is a practicable alternative to the proposed discharge which would have less adverse impact on the aquatic ecosystem" (40 CFR 230.10(a)), the permittee must "minimize the potential adverse effects of the discharge on the aquatic ecosystem" (Id. 230.10(c)), and the permittee must compensate by replacing destroyed wetland habitat (Id. 230.10(d)). Together, this "no net loss" policy has slowed the pace of wetland destruction, although there is still significant functional loss because the replacement wetlands often fail to meet permit requirements or lack the functionality of the original wetlands (Lin 2015).

The 402 and 404 permits are required for discharges into "navigable waters," which has been a very contentious term for much of the life of the act. In the CWA itself, Congress defined the term "navigable waters" to means "waters of the United States" (33 U.S.C. §1362(7)). The EPA and the Corps have issued many regulations defining these terms, and challenges to these rules and other applications of the CWA have produced many Supreme Court decisions addressing the jurisdictional coverage of the act. Essentially, definitions have been inconsistent over time, rendering it difficult still to determine what exactly the act protects. It is clear the act covers waters that are navigable in fact, and that it covers some nonnavigable waters and wetlands that are indistinguishable from the navigable waters (*Sackett v. EPA*, 598 U. S. ___ (2023)). The Supreme Court's recent *Sackett* decision significantly reduced the scope of CWA jurisdiction by eliminating protections for many wetlands and ephemeral streams. More exact definitions will continue to develop from additional judicial decisions and continued agency rulemakings, although it is unlikely that these efforts will produce real clarity in the near term. These definitions are important even beyond the 402 and 404 permits themselves, because the federal permitting requirement often served as a trigger for application of other federal environmental laws like Section 7 of the ESA and the National Environmental Policy Act ("NEPA"), which requires analysis of the environmental impacts of federal actions before the agency decides to proceed with the action.

The second of the two CWA regulatory approaches is a system of state water quality standards (WQSs) that serve as a backstop to the NPDES permit system. The WQS system takes an interesting approach to water quality. To determine the relevant WQS for a given water body or portion of a water body, the state first designates the uses of the water body and then applies "water quality criteria" to ensure that the water body will meet its designated uses (33 USC 1313(c)(2)(A)). For example, the CWA suggests that all waters should be "fishable and swimmable" (33 USC 1251(a)(2)). If a state chooses this use for a given water body, then it would apply the relevant water quality criteria needed to ensure that the water was clean enough for fishing and swimming. States can choose a wide variety of uses, and states may choose uses that protect aquatic biodiversity. For example, California's Water Quality Control Plan for the San Francisco Bay/Sacramento-San Joaquin Delta Estuary (SWRCB 2018) includes use of the Delta for warm freshwater habitat; cold freshwater habitat; migration of aquatic organisms; spawning, reproduction, and/or early development; rare, threatened, or endangered species; and estuarine habitat, among other uses. The water quality criteria for these uses include aspects of water quality related to traditional pollutants like agricultural chemicals and other important aspects like water temperature, volume, and flow timing. The CWA also applies an antidegradation policy to keep states from allowing water quality to drop over time.

When the NPDES permitting system does not offer enough protection for a water body and the water quality does not meet the relevant water quality criteria based on the body's designated uses, the CWA provides a mechanism to tighten the standards for discharge under any relevant NPDES permits. For any water bodies not meeting the relevant criteria, states must prepare a total maximum daily load (TMDL) for the pollutants that push the water body out of compliance. The TMDL establishes the total amount of the pollutant that can enter the water body without the water body exceeding the standards. The TMDL amount is then divided among the natural background sources of the pollutant, the nonpoint sources of the pollutant (like agricultural runoff) and the volume allowed for permitted point sources. This may result in a decrease in the permitted discharge of the TMDL pollutant, via amendment of a discharger's NPDES permit.

For many water bodies, the TMDL and permitting processes will never be sufficient to achieve the WQSs, because nonpoint sources do not require permits and generally cannot be required to be reduced through the TMDL process (Environmental Protection Agency 2023). Indeed, the CWA largely excluded nonpoint pollution, like stormwater, salt from roads, oil from parking lots, agricultural runoff from fields, and other sources of pollution that do not emerge from an identifiable point. The CWA also excludes many sources of agricultural pollution, like agricultural irrigation returns. These exclusions leave the CWA unable to address pollution problems in many water bodies; agricultural and nonpoint sources account for most of the water pollution and most of the impaired waters in the United States. The

CWA does authorize some grant programs to encourage states to address these problems, but they remain a major weakness in U.S. efforts to address water pollution. For example, nutrients from agricultural runoff and other minor sources contaminate the Mississippi River and create a low-oxygen dead zone roughly the size of New Jersey in the Gulf of Mexico; these pollutants are almost entirely beyond the reach of the federal CWA (Szalay 2010), but the dead zone and the upstream pollutants wreak havoc on aquatic biodiversity. Beyond the nonpoint source issue, other CWA weaknesses include insufficient monitoring (only roughly half of US water bodies have been assessed) and increasing water quality challenges related to climate change (GAO 2022).

Despite the CWA's shortcomings, it has been very successful in addressing many water quality problems. Since 1972, the Act has doubled the extent of waters clean enough for fishing and swimming in the United States (Craig 2021). Implementation of the Act has also dramatically reduced the rate of wetland loss in the United States, and levels of pollution in many waterways has significantly declines (Id.). Nevertheless, degraded water quality remains a significant driver of biodiversity loss in the United States, and the CWA's inability to address nonpoint source pollution is a major culprit.

2.3 Federal Power Act

The Federal Power Act provides a regulatory hook to address the ecosystem impacts of some dam projects (16 U.S.C. § 791 et seq.). Under the Federal Power Act, operators of non-federally owned hydropower dams must periodically seek licensing or relicensing from the Federal Energy Regulatory Commission (FERC). Although FERC oversees only roughly 2500 dams out of the 91,000 larger dams in the United States (GAO 2018; FEMA 2023), FERC-licensed dams include many large dams with significant biodiversity impacts. Initial licenses, issued at dam construction, allowed for 50 years of operation; at the expiration of their original licenses, operators can give up operating the facility or apply for relicensing, for a term of another 30 to 50 years (Office of Energy Projects 2017).

Relicensing is a federal action, which triggers other environmental review statutes, like NEPA and Section 7 of the ESA. These laws require consideration of the environmental impacts of relicensing and ensure that relicensing will not drive listed species to extinction. But the relicensing process itself also requires consideration and, often, mitigation of impacts to biodiversity and other natural resources. Under Section 4(e) of the Federal Power Act, in deciding whether to issue the license, FERC "must consider the power and developmental purposes of the project and will give equal consideration to the purposes of energy conservation; the protection, mitigation, and enhancement of fish and wildlife (including related spawning grounds and habitat); the protection of recreational opportunities; and the preservation of other aspects of environmental quality" (Office of Energy Projects 2017). Under Section 10(j), FERC must "include conditions to protect, mitigate damages to, and enhance, fish and wildlife related habitat," provided that they are not inconsistent with other law (Id.). Based on these requirements, new licenses often require significant investments and changes to the project to benefit biodiversity. For example, from 1993 to 2005, FERC "required fish passage improvements or other fish restoration improvements in more than forty-percent of the new licenses" (Kibel 2016, p. 73). In some cases, dam operators have chosen to surrender their licenses and retire dams rather than invest in bringing the projects up to modern environmental standards. For example, the ongoing removal of four dams on the Klamath River in northern California, the largest dam removal project in the world to date, resulted from lengthy relicensing proceedings and Federal Power Act requirements (e.g., volitional passage for fish) for the hydropower dams. The Federal Power Act is a significant legal tool for biodiversity protection in habitats impacted by nonfederal hydropower projects.

2.4 *Wild and Scenic Rivers Act*

The 1968 Wild and Scenic Rivers Act preserves selected rivers or river segments in their free-flowing state (16 U.S.C.A. §§ 1271 to 1287). The Act announces the intent of Congress that "certain selected rivers of the Nation which, with their immediate environments, possess outstandingly remarkable ... values, shall be preserved in free-flowing condition, and that they and their immediate environments shall be protected for the benefit and enjoyment of present and future generations" (16 U.S. C. § 1271 (2000)). Congress can directly designate waterways for protection under Section 5 of the Act, and states can request that the Secretary of the Interior study and approve particular rivers for protection under Section 2 of the Act. Protected rivers are classified as wild, scenic, or recreational, although all classes of rivers are protected from federal resource development like dams, transmission lines, and most other projects. Wild river areas are "rivers or sections of rivers that are free of impoundments and generally inaccessible except by trail, with watersheds or shorelines essentially primitive and waters unpolluted" (16 U.S.C.A. § 1273(b)(1)). Scenic areas "are free of impoundments, with shorelines or watersheds still largely primitive and shorelines largely undeveloped, but accessible in places by roads" (16 U.S.C.A. § 1273(b)(2)). Finally, recreational areas "are readily accessible by road or railroad, ... may have some development along their shorelines, and ... may have undergone some impoundment or diversion in the past" (16 U.S.C.A. § 1273 (b)(3)). The classification level alone does not determine the degree of protection the river or river segment receives under the Act, but rivers are managed to avoid degradation of the "outstandingly remarkable values" the designation of the river is designed to protect, and the classification can inform that management (Blumm and Yoklic 2019). Wild and Scenic designation does not necessarily result in active management of a river and its ecosystem, but the designation does provide significant protection against further degradation of the habitat and loss of aquatic biodiversity.

2.5 *The Pittman-Robertson Wildlife Restoration Act and the Dingell-Johnson Sport Fish Restoration Act*

Overexploitation is one of the top six threats to aquatic biodiversity, as noted above, but hunting and angling groups in the United States have become one of the foremost forces for biodiversity conservation. This has not always been the case; by the late 1800s, market hunting and over exploitation had driven many species of wildlife to near extinction. Wildlife management was seen as a state concern, but the federal government took action to support states and address interstate issues, passing the Lacey Act in 1900 (addressing illegally taken fish, wildlife, and plants moved between states) and the Migratory Bird Treaty Act in 1918. Nevertheless, by the 1930s and 1940s, "wild turkey, whitetail deer, elk, pronghorn antelope, Rocky Mountain sheep, ducks and geese, and a host of other species were at such low numbers that people were predicting that they would soon follow the passenger pigeon to extinction" (Peterson 1998, p. 1). Conservationists, led in part by Aldo Leopold, pushed for professionalization of wildlife management and restoration of habitat to support game species (Id.). Hunters and anglers, led by interest groups, lobbied Congress to tax their equipment purchases to create consistent funding streams for wildlife conservation. Their effort eventually resulted in two bills, the 1937 Federal Aid in Wildlife Restoration Act (16 U.S.C. §§669 et seq., also known as the Pittman-Robertson Wildlife Restoration Act) and the 1950 Sport Fish Restoration Act (16 U.S.C. 777 et seq., also known as the Dingell-Johnson Sport Fish Restoration Act), which together provide much of the funding for wildlife conservation work in the United States. This user-funded model, part of the approach often termed the North American Model of Wildlife Conservation, has been instrumental in restoring habitat essential for aquatic biodiversity (Organ et al. 2012).

The Pittman-Robertson Wildlife Restoration Act is funded by taxes on firearms, ammunition, bows, and arrows. The Dingell-Johnson Sport Fish Restoration Act is funded by taxes on sport fishing equipment, import charges for fishing equipment and pleasure boats, and gas taxes from gas used in small engines and motorboats. These taxes generate significant funds, and the U.S. Fish and Wildlife Service has disbursed over $27 billion from these funds to the states since passage of the acts, matched by state expenditures of $9 billion (FWS 2023). Regulations limit the Pittman-Robertson funds to projects benefitting mammals and birds, but projects often provide ancillary benefits to aquatic biodiversity, through wetland restoration or other habitat enhancement. States and a few territories receive the funding and ultimately determine how the funds are used. Tribal entities are not eligible for the funding, despite their significant land management obligations, and some efforts have been made to amend the acts on this point.

These two acts provide the second most significant source of funding for state fish and wildlife agencies. In 2018, for example, these state agencies had a collective budget of roughly $5.6 billion dollars, with $1.6 billion coming from hunting and fishing license sales and $1.1 billion coming from Pittman-Robertson and Dingell-Johnson funds (Watkins 2019). These expenditures also benefit the fishing and hunting equipment industry, generating a return on investment somewhere between 823% and 1588% (Andrew Loftus Consulting 2011).

This model does pose some problems. For example, it creates incentives that focus management on game species, excludes tribal interests from funding, undervalues nonconsumptive uses of wildlife, and exposes future funding to risks related to the decreasing number of hunters and anglers in the United States (Watkins 2019; Hessami et al. 2021). Efforts by legislators to add additional funding not tied to hunting and angling and available to tribes and other groups are ongoing (Morris 2023), but they have not yet been successful. For the time being, user-financing of wildlife conservation by hunters and anglers seems likely to remain a key piece of habitat and biodiversity protection in the United States.

Tribal Co-Management

Native American nations and people in the United States have a vital role to play in biodiversity management, ranging from sharing traditional ecological knowledge to direct management of biodiversity. For example, the Klamath Tribes have been the primary force behind the political movement that led to the removal of the Klamath Dams beginning in Summer 2023. The indigenous role in biodiversity management has been limited both by tribal resource constraints and by a lack of power to manage nontribal and some tribal lands, despite treaties that often guarantee hunting and fishing rights. Recently, the federal government and some state governments have begun to find ways to restore a measure of indigenous control to public lands, including management of wildlife on those lands. The extent to which these efforts will succeed remains to be seen (Mills and Nie 2021).

2.6 *Presidential Powers: The Biden Administration's 30 × 30 Initiative*

Presidents can issue executive orders to the executive branch of the federal government (consisting primarily of the federal agencies) that direct the agencies to focus on particular priorities, which some presidents have used to protect aquatic biodiversity. The executive orders generally do not make new money available—Congress controls funding allocations—but they can set priorities and direct some funding where agencies have flexibility. For example, on January 27, 2021, within a week of being sworn into office, President Biden issued the "Executive Order on Tackling the Climate Crisis at Home and Abroad" (Exec. Order No. 14008, 2021). Section 216 of the initiative, titled "Conserving Our Nation's Lands and Waters" lays out the administration's goal of "conserving at least 30 percent of [the United States] lands and waters by 2030." This initiative, popularly known as "30 × 30," seeks to "reduce climate pollution; increase resilience to the impacts of climate change; protect public health; conserve our lands, waters, oceans, and biodiversity;

deliver environmental justice; and spur well-paying union jobs and economic growth."

In December 2021, the administration released its first annual report on the 30 × 30 program, which identified several efforts aimed at conserving aquatic biodiversity. These included the National Fish Habitat Partnership program, with "projects in multiple States including Texas, Minnesota, Louisiana, Maryland, and Alaska" (America the Beautiful Interagency Working Group 2021, p. 16); and the EPA Healthy Watersheds Program, which granted funding to "protect an estimated 800,000 acres and 3300 perennial stream miles" (Id.). The report also acknowledges that "freshwater aquatic biodiversity, which includes fish along with a wide diversity of species, is declining at rates roughly double that of marine or terrestrial ecosystems." Executive orders like the 30 × 30 program can be an important part of the United States' biodiversity protection effort, but they are not law and are subject to change based on shifting administration priorities or changes in administration due to elections.

2.7 *Other Federal Law*

The legislation and executive order approaches covered here are the primary federal tools for aquatic biodiversity protection, but many other federal laws play a role in managing and protecting aquatic biodiversity in the United States. For example, the 2022 Inflation Reduction Act and the 2021 Infrastructure Investment and Jobs Act (often called the Bipartisan Infrastructure Bill) both contain significant funding for projects that will address aquatic biodiversity, like coastal resilience projects and wetland conservation and restoration in the Prairie Pothole Region. The National Environmental Policy Act does not contain substantive requirements, but its strict procedural requirements force federal agencies to consider the environmental impacts of their potential actions before they make decisions. Similarly, federal efforts to mitigate or adapt to climate change will likely prove pivotal to the future of aquatic biodiversity in the United States. And federal land laws, particularly in the western United States, control much of the management of aquatic biodiversity on public lands. Further, aquatic biodiversity in marine environments involves additional laws, like the Marine Mammal Protection Act, which fall outside the scope of this chapter. Many indigenous nations have treaty rights to hunt and fish, and these treaties have the force of federal law and can serve as a significant driver of biodiversity protection. For instance, a recent Supreme Court decision required restoration of fish passage through tens of thousands of road barriers across the state of Washington (United States v. Washington, 853 F.3d 946, 952 (9th Cir. 2017), affirmed by an equally divided Supreme Court, Washington v. United States, 138 S. Ct. 1832 (2018)). Other examples include the Reclamation Act, acts authorizing major federal public works like dams and highways, the Coastal Zone Management Act, the National Flood Insurance Act, the Coastal Barrier Resources Act, the Magnuson-Stevens Fishery Conservation and Management Act… the list goes on and on. Practicing in this field requires a learning mindset. The sources listed in the Reference section of this chapter can provide additional background and details on some of these other key laws.

2.8 State Law

Although this chapter focuses on federal laws and policies, much, perhaps most, biodiversity protection in the United States takes place at the state level. This includes direct management of biodiversity though state-level endangered species acts or state statutes requiring analysis of decisions affecting the environment, and indirect management of risks to biodiversity (Revesz 2001). For example, most water law, which determines how much water remains instream and thus available to aquatic ecosystems, is state law. Nearly all land use decision making occurs at the state or local level. State water law doctrines like the public trust doctrine, the reasonable use doctrine, or the state ownership of water doctrine can all provide some protection for the instream flows necessary for aquatic biodiversity to survive. The state laws are beyond the scope of this chapter, but anyone working on aquatic biodiversity conservation should be aware of these additional sources of law that will likely affect their work.

3 Conclusion

The United States has a wealth of aquatic biodiversity, but much of this biodiversity is under threat from habitat loss and degradation, water pollution, overexploitation, flow modification, and interactions with nonnative species. A broad array of federal laws offers approaches to mitigate many of these threats, and state laws offer additional avenues for protection. Conserving this diversity for current and future generations will require both aggressive enforcement of existing laws and successful new approaches to address intransigent problems and emerging threats.

References

Adelman DE, Glicksman RL (2020) Reevaluating environmental citizen suits in theory and practice. Univ Colo Law Rev 91:385. http://lawreview.colorado.edu/wp-content/uploads/2020/02/AdelmanGlicksman_Final.pdf

Alexander K (2010) Warranted but precluded: what that means under the Endangered Species Act (ESA). Congressional Research Service, CRS Report: 7-5700. https://esadocs.defenders-cci.org/ESAdocs/misc/CRS_Warranted_but_precluded.pdf

America the Beautiful Interagency Working Group (2021) Year One Report, America the Beautiful. https://www.whitehouse.gov/wp-content/uploads/2021/12/AtB-Year-One-Report_.pdf

Andrew Loftus Consulting et al. (2011) Financial returns to industry from the federal aid in wildlife restoration program

Biber E, Brosi B (2010) Officious intermeddlers or citizen experts-petitions and public production of information in environmental law. UCLA Law Rev 58:321–400

Blumm M, Yoklic M (2019) The Wild and Scenic Rivers Act at 50: overlooked watershed protection. Mich J Environ Adm Law 9(1):1–75. https://repository.law.umich.edu/cgi/viewcontent.cgi?article=1095&context=mjeal

Bobeldyk AM, Rüegg J, Lamberti GA (2015) Freshwater hotspots of biological invasion are a function of species–pathway interactions. Hydrobiologia 746:363–373. https://doi.org/10.1007/s10750-014-2009-z

Bork K (2019) An evolutionary theory of administrative law. SMU Law Rev 72:81

Bork K (2021) Governing nature: Bambi law in a Wall-E world. Boston Coll Law Rev 62:157

Brewitt PK, Colwyn CLM (2020) Little dams, big problems: the legal and policy issues of nonjurisdictional dams. Wiley Interdiscip Rev: Water 7(1):e1393. https://doi.org/10.1002/wat2.1393

Center for American Progress (2018) The Disappearing West. https://disappearingwest.org/rivers.html

Comte L, Buisson L, Daufresno M, Grenouillet G (2013) Climate-induced changes in the distribution of freshwater fish: observed and predicted trends. Freshw Biol 58(4):625–639. https://doi.org/10.1111/fwb.12081

Craig R (2021) Environmental law in context, cases and materials, 5th edn. West Academic Publishing

Dahl T, Allord G (2023) Technical aspects of wetlands history of wetlands in the conterminous. United States Geological Survey Water Supply Paper 2425. https://water.usgs.gov/nwsum/WSP2425/history.html

Darwell WRT, Freyhof J (2015) Lost fishes: who is counting? The extent of the threat to freshwater fish biodiversity. In: Closs GP, Krkosek M, Olden JD (eds) Conservation of freshwater fishes. Cambridge University Press, Cambridge, England

Dudgeon D (2019) Multiple threats imperil freshwater biodiversity in the Anthropocene. Curr Biol 29(19):R960–R967. https://doi.org/10.1016/j.cub.2019.08.002

Dudgeon D, Arthington AH, Gessner MO, Kawabata I, Knowler DJ, Lévêque C, Naiman RJ, Prieur-Richard H, Soto D, Stiassny MLJ, Sullivan CA (2006) Freshwater biodiversity: importance, threats, status and conservation challenges. Biol Rev 81(2):163–182. https://doi.org/10.1017/S1464793105006950

Environmental Protection Agency (2023) Basic Information about Nonpoint Source (NPS) Pollution. https://www.epa.gov/nps/basic-information-about-nonpoint-source-nps-pollution

Federal Emergency Management Agency (2023) National inventory of dams. https://www.fema.gov/emergency-managers/risk-management/dam-safety/national-inventory-dams

Graf WL (2001) Dam age control: restoring the physical integrity of America's rivers. Ann Assoc Am Geogr 91(1):1–27

Green DM, Weir LA, Casper GS, Lannoo MJ (2014) North American amphibians: distribution and diversity. University of California Press

Greenwald N, Hartl B, Mehrhoff L, Pang J (2016) Shortchanged: funding needed to save America's most endangered species. Center for Biological Diversity, Tucson

Haag WR (2019) Reassessing enigmatic mussel declines in the United States. Freshw Mollusk Biol Conserv 22(2):43–60. https://doi.org/10.31931/fmbc.v22i2.2019.43-60

Haag WR, Williams JD (2014) Biodiversity on the brink: an assessment of conservation strategies for North American freshwater mussels. Hydrobiologia 735:45–60. https://doi.org/10.1007/s10750-013-1524-7

Helfrich LA, Neves RJ (2019) Freshwater Fish Biodiversity and Conservation. Virginia Cooperative Extension. https://www.pubs.ext.vt.edu/content/dam/pubs_ext_vt_edu/420/420-525/CNRE-83.pdf

Hessami M, Bowles E, Popp J, Ford A (2021) Indigenizing the North American model of wildlife conservation. FACETS 6(1):1285–1306. https://doi.org/10.1139/facets-2020-0088

Jelks H, Walsh S, Burkhead N, Contreras-Balderas S, Díaz-Pardo E, Hendrickson D, Lyons J, Mandrak N, McCormick F, Nelson J, Platania S, Porter B, Renaud C, Schmitter-Soto J, Taylor E, Warren M Jr (2008) Conservation status of imperiled North American freshwater and diadromous fishes. Fisheries 33(8):372–407

Jenkins CN, Van Houtan KS, Pimm SL, Sexton JO (2015) US protected lands mismatch biodiversity priorities. Proc Natl Acad Sci 112(16):5081–5086. https://doi.org/10.1073/pnas.1418034112

Johnson PD, Bogan AE, Brown KM, Burkhead NM, Cordeiro JR, Garner JT, Hartfield PD, Lepitzki DAW, Mackie GL, Pip E, Tarpley TA, Tiemann JS, Whelan NV, Strong EE (2013) Conservation status of freshwater gastropods of Canada and the United States. Fisheries 38(6): 247–282. https://doi.org/10.1080/03632415.2013.785396

Katz JV, Jeffres C, Conrad JL, Sommer TR, Martinez J, Brumbaugh S, Corline N, Moyle PB (2016) Floodplain farm fields provide novel rearing habitat for Chinook salmon. PLoS ONE 12(6). https://doi.org/10.1371/journal.pone.0177409

Kibel P (2016) Passage and flow considered anew: wild salmon restoration via hydro relicensing. Public Land Resour Law Rev 37:66–87. https://digitalcommons.law.ggu.edu/cgi/viewcontent.cgi?article=1784&context=pubs

Lin AC (2015) Myths of environmental law. Utah Law Rev 2015(1)., Article 2. https://dc.law.utah.edu/ulr/vol2015/iss1/2

Lomnicky GA, Whittier TR, Hughes RM, Peck DV (2007) Distribution of nonnative aquatic vertebrates in western U.S. streams and rivers. North Am J Fish Manag 27(4):1082–1093. https://doi.org/10.1577/M06-155.1

Male T (2014, March 17) Guest: U.S. is overspending to save salmon. The Seattle Times. https://www.seattletimes.com/opinion/guest-us-is-overspending-to-save-salmon/

Martinuzzi S, Januchowski-Hartley SR, Pracheil BM, McIntyre PB, Plantinga AJ, Lewis DJ, Radeloff VC (2014) Threats and opportunities for freshwater conservation under future land use change scenarios in the United States. Global Change Biol 20(1):113–124. https://doi.org/10.1111/gcb.12383

Mills M, Nie M (2021) Bridges to a new era: a report on the past, present, and potential future of tribal co-management on federal public lands. Public Land Resour Law Rev 44(2):50–184. https://scholarworks.umt.edu/plrlr/vol44/iss1/2

Morris J (2023) Senators Reintroduce Landmark Wildlife Conservation Bill. The Nature Conservancy. https://www.nature.org/en-us/newsroom/rawa-reintroduced-us-senate/

Morrison RR, Simonson K, McManamay RA, Carver D (2023) Degradation of floodplain integrity within the contiguous United States. Commun Earth Environ 4(1):1–10. https://doi.org/10.1038/s43247-023-00877-4

Moyle PB, Leidy RA (2023) Freshwater fishes: threatened species and threatened waters on a global scale. In: MaClean N (ed) The living planet: the present state of the world's wildlife. Cambridge University Press, Cambridge, England

Moyle PB, Mount JF (2007) Homogenous rivers, homogenous faunas. Proc Natl Acad Sci 104(14): 5711–5712. https://doi.org/10.1073/pnas.0701457104

Moyle PB, Kiernan JD, Crain PK, Quiñones RM (2013) Climate change vulnerability of native and alien freshwater fishes of California: a systematic assessment approach. PLOS ONE 8(5): e63883. https://doi.org/10.1371/journal.pone.0063883

National Academies of Sciences, Engineering, and Medicine (2002) Riparian areas: functions and strategies for management. The National Academies Press, Washington, DC. https://doi.org/10.17226/10327

National Caucus of Environmental Legislators (2023) Restoring biodiversity: how U.S. states are protecting life on earth. https://www.ncelenviro.org/articles/how-are-u-s-states-protecting-biodiversity/

Office of Energy Projects (2017) Hydropower primer. https://www.ferc.gov/sites/default/files/2020-04/HydropowerPrimer.pdf.

Organ JF, Geist V, Mahoney SP, Williams S, Krausman PR, Batcheller GR, Decker TA, Carmichael R, Nanjappa P, Regan R, Medellin RA (2012) The North American model of wildlife conservation. Wildl Soc Tech Rev 12(04)

Owen D (2023) The negotiable implementation of environmental law. Stanford Law Rev 75(1): 137–203. https://review.law.stanford.edu/wp-content/uploads/sites/3/2023/01/Owen-75-Stan.-L.-Rev.-137.pdf

Page LM, Burr BM (2011) Peterson field guide to freshwater fishes of North America, North of Mexico. Houghton Mifflin

Panlasigui S, Davis AJ, Mangiante MJ, Darling JA (2018) Assessing threats of non-native species to native freshwater biodiversity: conservation priorities for the United States. Biol Conserv 224:199–208. https://doi.org/10.1016/j.biocon.2018.05.019

Peterson RM (1998) The user fee approach to hunting and fishing finance: the "teaming with wildlife" proposal. Outdoor Recreation: Promise and Peril in the New West (Summer Conference, June 8-10). https://scholar.law.colorado.edu/outdoor-recreation-promise-and-peril-in-new-west/24

Poff NL, Olden JD, Merritt DM, Pepin DM (2007) Homogenization of regional river dynamics by dams and global biodiversity implications. Proc Natl Acad Sci 104(14):5732–5737. https://doi.org/10.1073/pnas.0609812104

Reid AJ, Carlson AK, Creed IF, Eliason EJ, Gell PA, Johnson PTJ, Kidd KA, MacCormack TJ, Olden JD, Ormerod SJ, Smol JP, Taylor WW, Tockner K, Vermaire JC, Dudgeon D, Cooke SJ (2019) Emerging threats and persistent conservation challenges for freshwater biodiversity. Biol Rev 94(3):849–873. https://doi.org/10.1111/brv.12480

Revesz RL (2001) Federalism and environmental regulation: a public choice analysis. Harv Law Rev 115(2):553–641. https://doi.org/10.2307/1342673

Ross ST (1991) Mechanisms structuring stream fish assemblages: are there lessons from introduced species? Environ Biol Fishes 30:359–368. https://link.springer.com/article/10.1007/BF02027979

Ruhl JB (1995) Section 7(a)(1) of the "new" endangered species act: rediscovering and redefining the untapped power of federal agencies' duty to conserve species. Environ Law 25(4): 1107–1163. http://www.jstor.org/stable/43266119

Scott JM, Goble DD, Haines AM, Wiens JA, Neel MC (2010) Conservation-reliant species and the future of conservation. Conserv Lett 3(2):91–97. https://doi.org/10.1111/j.1755-263X.2010.00096.x

State Water Resources Control Board (2018) Water Quality Control Plan for the San Francisco Bay/Sacramento-San Joaquin Delta Estuary. https://www.waterboards.ca.gov/plans_policies/docs/2018wqcp.pdf

Strayer DL, Dudgeon D (2010) Freshwater biodiversity conservation: recent progress and future challenges. J North Am Benthol Soc 29(1):344–358. https://doi.org/40792639

Szalay E (2010) Breathing life into the dead zone: can the federal common law of nuisance be used to control nonpoint source water pollution. Tulane Law Rev 85(1):215–246. https://heinonline.org/HOL/P?h=hein.journals/tulr85&i=217

Taylor CA, Schuster GA, Cooper JE, DiStefano RJ, Eversole AG, Hamr P, Hobbs HH, Robison HW, Skelton CE, Thoma RF (2007) A reassessment of the conservation status of crayfishes of the United States and Canada after 10+ years of increased awareness. Fisheries 32(8):372–389. https://doi.org/10.1577/1548-8446(2007)32[372:AROTCS]2.0.CO;2

Thorp JH, Covich AP, Dimmick WW (2010) Introduction to invertebrates of inland waters. Ecology and Classification of North American Freshwater Invertebrates (Third Edition), pp. 1–23. https://doi.org/10.1016/B978-0-12-374855-3.00001-7

U.S. Fish and Wildlife Service (2023) Over $1.6 billion will support state fish and wildlife conservation and outdoor access. https://www.fws.gov/press-release/2023-03/over-16-billion-will-support-conservation-agencies-and-outdoor-access

U.S. Fish and Wildlife Service & Nat'l Marine Fisheries Serv (1998) Consultation handbook: procedures for conducting consultation and conference activities under Section 7 of the Endangered Species Act
U.S. Government Accountability Office (2017) Information on Endangered Species Act Deadline Suits. https://www.gao.gov/assets/gao-17-304.pdf
U.S. Government Accountability Office (2018) Dam Safety: FERC Should Analyze Portfolio-Wide Risks. https://www.gao.gov/products/gao-19-19
U.S. Government Accountability Office (2022) 50 Years After the Clean Water Act—Gauging Progress. https://www.gao.gov/blog/50-years-after-clean-water-act-gauging-progress
Walsh SJ, Jelks HL, Burkhead NM (2011) The decline of North American freshwater fishes. Am Curr 36(4):10–17
Watkins T (2019) How we pay to play: funding outdoor recreation on public lands in the 21st century. PERC. https://www.perc.org/2019/05/28/how-we-pay-to-play-funding-outdoor-recreation-on-public-lands-in-the-21st-century/
Young K, Bork K (2021) Protecting plants under the existing endangered species act. Harv Environ Law Rev 45:151–194

Stewardship of Tribal Biodiversity in the United States

Serra J. Hoagland and Steven K. Albert

Abstract Indian tribes in the United States manage more land than the National Park Service and have a strong record of effective conservation and wildlife stewardship. Several studies have shown that Indigenous-managed lands have a higher biodiversity than other areas, including conservation lands managed by other entities. Despite these successes, tribes have had to fight hard to maintain the recognition of their inherent sovereignty—a status enshrined in the US Constitution and upheld by numerous Supreme Court cases. In this chapter, we will briefly review the history of tribes' fight for the recognition of sovereignty over land, water, and wildlife; discuss the ramifications of tribal sovereignty and the trust responsibility of the United States as it relates to tribal land and wildlife management; offer suggestions for the proactive coproduction of biodiversity research; and describe how innovative tribal wildlife management projects are reshaping the dialog over land stewardship in North America.

1 Introduction

In the continental United States, tribes have jurisdiction or management influence over more than 140 million acres—a vast and biologically diverse landscape that is larger than that of the National Park Service and 47 of the 50 states. This of course represents a tiny fraction of the land area once stewarded by tribes and First Nations (it is no exaggeration to say that this country was built on stolen land), though the land remaining to tribes in the United States and elsewhere has an unmatched record in the protection of wildlands. Around the world, Indigenous-managed areas have

S. J. Hoagland (✉)
Rocky Mountain Research Station (RMRS) of the USDA Forest Service, Missoula, MT, USA
e-mail: serra.j.hoagland@usda.gov

S. K. Albert
The Institute for Bird Populations, Ramah, NM, USA
e-mail: salbert@birdpop.org

G. Antonelli et al. (eds.), *Biodiversity Laws, Policies and Science in Europe, the United States and China*, https://doi.org/10.1007/978-3-031-56218-1_11

more intact biodiversity than other lands, even those set aside for conservation (Corrigan et al. 2018; Schuster et al. 2018).

Given the accomplishments and strong history of sound stewardship by tribes, it may be surprising to those unfamiliar with the intersection of tribal, state, and federal natural resources law to know that, as late as the 1980s, Native American[1] tribes in the United States lacked the full legal authority to manage their own wildlife and ecosystems. Though tribes have been legally viewed by the US federal government—and the Spanish, Dutch, French, and all other governments before them—as sovereign entities since the first contact between colonizers and Indigenous peoples on this continent, a controlling and paternalistic attitude over tribes tended to prevail, granting tribes sovereign authority only when it was convenient to the US government. It took a deliberate challenge to New Mexico state law regulating elk hunting by the Mescalero Apache Tribe to fully ensure that tribes could be granted the right to harvest the wildlife that they so carefully stewarded (New Mexico v. Mescalero Apache Tribe, 462 U.S. 324, 1983).

2 The Diversity of Tribal Landscapes, Cultures, Attitudes, and Approaches

It is impossible to cover the full range of tribal biodiversity programs, approaches, and projects in a single book chapter. The 574 federally recognized tribes in the United States (and the many involuntarily terminated or unrecognized ones) represent a stunning array of languages, histories, landscapes, and lifestyles, from hunting-based societies to highly complex agricultural megacities (Kraniak 2016). The deep knowledge that tribal peoples have drawn upon to survive and thrive in their milieus is carefully maintained and transmitted across generations and has at times been studied or codified under the rubric of traditional ecological knowledge (TEK) or Indigenous knowledge. The literature on TEK is robust and growing, though somewhat outside the scope of this chapter. Instead, we devote space to describing some of the *current* challenges and approaches faced by tribes, though, as will be shown, the most successful programs and projects maintain traditional values and approaches close at hand, often interwoven with modern approaches, and have produced inspiring results.

These stories have largely not been told. For many reasons, tribal resource professionals tend not to publish in mainstream scientific journals, and they shy away from overt publicity. Humility is a near-ubiquitous core value among Native communities. In our recent book about wildlife stewardship on tribal lands

[1] The usage of terms to describe the first inhabitants of this continent has changed over the years. In this paper, we use Native American, Indigenous peoples, and Indian somewhat interchangeably, though the context of each may be slightly different. Most often, when referring to a specific tribe, we use that tribe's preferred term for themselves.

(Hoagland and Albert 2023), many of the more than 70 tribal authors described their work in writing for the first time.

3 The North American Model and the I-NAM

For most of the past century, the science and practice of biodiversity conservation have centered around the North American Model (NAM)—"the world's most successful system of policies and laws to restore and safeguard fish and wildlife and their habitats through sound science and active management"—as described by the Association of Fish and Wildlife Agencies (AFWA 2023). The seven tenets of the NAM are forthright and seemingly incontrovertible to most wildlife professionals: (1) wildlife resources are conserved and held in trust for all citizens; (2) wildlife may only be killed for a legitimate, nonfrivolous purpose; (3) scientific management is the proper means for wildlife conservation; (4) commerce in dead wildlife is eliminated; (5) wildlife is allocated according to democratic rule of law; (6) wildlife is an international resource; and (7) every person has an equal opportunity under the law to participate in hunting and fishing.

For tribes, the first three of these seven principles are both implicit and explicit parts of their daily life and practice. The next four, while often true for some tribes at some times, may fly in the face of their cultural beliefs, which mandate certain strictures regarding the practice of hunting and other resource use. One element that is missing from the model and most of the dozens of books that have been written to amplify and promote it is any recognition of the people who have been successfully stewarding the continent's biodiversity for the previous several millennia.

The difficulty also arises of how, exactly, the NAM is taught and who, exactly, developed it. In popular nonfiction, in undergraduate and graduate wildlife biology textbooks, and in peer-reviewed articles, John Muir, Theodore Roosevelt, Gifford Pinchot, Aldo Leopold, and Rachel Carson are lauded as the founders of conservation, and their writings and accomplishments form the basis of the modern "conservation ethic." It is undeniable that these individuals were among the first to write from a European perspective about conservation as a distinct discipline, and they promoted and enacted laws and policies that cemented the protection of wildlife as a central American belief leading directly to the formulation of the NAM (granted, after millions of their countrymen drove scores of common species to extinction or its brink). For several thousand years, Native Americans had managed the continent's wildlife quite well—conducting prescribed burns to move and create forage for game, regenerating habitat, and sustainably harvesting wildlife and fish while observing, documenting, and responding to environmental and wildlife population changes—what we now call "adaptive management." As one tribal elder told a colleague of ours, "We have always thought like scientists."

Several of wildlife science's icons were unforgiving (and frankly ignorant) in their views of Native people and traditional forms of land stewardship. In an attempt to convince the American public to suppress all wildfires, Leopold (1920, pp. 12–13) wrote that it was "absurd to think that the Indians had any idea of forest conservation in mind." Leopold called the light-burning practices of tribes a "fallacy" that caused "destructive effects." His writings further insulted Native land management practices and partly led to a century of full fire suppression with disastrous consequences. Pinchot was a proud member of the American Eugenics Society (Wohlforth 2010), and Roosevelt's comments on the Sand Creek Massacre of hundreds of Cheyenne and Arapahoe men, women, and children are frankly disgusting (Schwartz 2020). The Sierra Club has even acknowledged and apologized for Muir's racist views (Melley 2020).

What are Native scholars, practitioners, and students to think of a management system built on the ideas of these people? Recently, many Indigenous and other scholars of environmental and wildlife science have advocated for revising or "indigenizing" the NAM. Eichler and Baumeister (2018) believe that the NAM does not serve tribal interests well, and Hessami et al. (2021) have proposed an intriguing revision known as I-NAM (I for Indigenous). Their model includes the following elements (numbers refer to the elements of the NAM cited above). While there is some similarity to the core tenets of both systems, large and subtle differences point to a fundamentally different view of wildlife, biodiversity, the land, and people's relationship to it:

(1) Rather than wildlife being a public trust, Indigenous wildlife is stewarded through an interwoven set of values and a holistic vision of resource management. Both Indigenous and non-Indigenous governments are held accountable by their respective publics, with the added proviso that the Indigenous public also holds the federal government to account.
(2) Rather than a strict focus on game markets, the I-NAM emphasizes the nonprivate nature of wildlife resources and the importance of multiple user groups.
(3) Rather than a strict reliance on wildlife law, the I-NAM notes the importance of working within multiple governing bodies.
(4) The I-NAM takes issue with the rather vague word "legitimate" as likely culturally biased, instead focusing on conservation and the use of wildlife as the basis for food security, conservation, livelihood, and cultural integrity.
(5) On the point of wildlife being an international resource, there is some agreement, with the I-NAM recognizing the importance of cross-boundary collaboration. Tribes do, of course, understand their own situation to be one in which the integrity of cross-boundary issues between their lands and the rest of the United States is paramount.
(6) Where the NAM emphasizes the role of science, the I-NAM emphasizes the importance of a holistic view of multiple knowledge systems.
(7) Finally, where the NAM codifies democracy as the standard for sharing wildlife, the I-NAM goes further in noting that democracy must include shared decision-making with Indigenous governments.

In general, tribal worldviews on the environment are indistinct from other aspects of Indigenous daily life and spiritual practice, and they implicitly and explicitly informed the conservation ethic claimed by Muir, Roosevelt, Leopold, and others. This misattribution may be partly due to a lack of written records left by the tribal practitioners and the reticence of tribes to speak and write about their ideas and accomplishments, but it is also a result of differing perspectives about what warrants inclusion in the history of science and whose story gets told. Further, there is an uneasiness by some scientists to cross into what is viewed as other disciplines. Traditional or Indigenous conservation practices are often thoughtfully documented in the literature of the anthropological or sociological sciences while remaining unknown to practitioners or students of wildlife conservation. An interdisciplinary approach and including a wider range of voices in discussions about wildlife conservation may change this tendency.

4 Tribal Sovereignty and Trust Responsibility

If there is one theme that underlies almost all of the legal, administrative, and technical challenges faced by tribes in managing their biodiversity in the past century, it is the struggle of tribes to assert their inherent sovereignty. From the earliest contact between foreign nations and the Indigenous people of this continent, the sovereignty of tribes was recognized in law, if not in practice. As US Supreme Court Chief Justice John Marshall noted in 1832, "Indian Nations [have] always been considered as distinct, independent political communities, retaining their original natural rights, as the undisputed possessors of the soil . . . The very term 'Nation' so generally applied to them means 'a people distinct from others'" (*Worcester v. Georgia*, 31 U.S. 515, 559 (1832)).

This ostensibly undisputed right of tribes to manage their own affairs has been challenged, ignored, or actively subverted in countless ways. More than 400 legal treaties signed between the United States and tribes have been unilaterally broken by the United States (Deloria, Jr. 1969). Today, when projects or policies that could affect Indian biodiversity or other resources occur on federal or state land or on tribal land with federal or state funding or support, consultation with affected tribes is legally required by several federal policies and executive orders. Yet tribal interests are often an afterthought or are grouped with those of the general public—one more stakeholder among hundreds, which is a sentiment that is fraught with disrespect and poor regard for the first stewards of the land. As one Hopi elder put it during a recent, highly flawed consultation process: "What does it take for a government agency to involve Hopi at the beginning stages and say, 'Hey, we're planning this project; what do you think?' Try to work with Native communities, instead of [having us be] the last check-off because they have to. What is it going to take for agencies to think that way? Why is the tail wagging the dog? I think some of it is just ignorance. Somebody is responsible for this part of it, somebody's responsible for that part, and there is just lack of communication and overall vision. I think there's a path forward to a better way" (Hopi elder who wished to remain anonymous, Pers. Comm. 2022).

The other core legal concept that greatly affects tribes' ability to manage their own biodiversity and other environmental affairs is the doctrine of trust responsibility: the requirement that the federal government protect and support tribal self-government and provide tribes with the resources they need so their members can have economically and socially prosperous lives. These rights were guaranteed, of course, in exchange for the three billion acres of land that tribes ceded (or had stolen), upon which the entire social and economic life of the United States is built.

The intertwined and counterbalanced concepts of trust responsibility and tribal sovereignty—giving tribes the financial and technical means for their members to carry on their lives on par with the rest of US society while also allowing them the leeway to do so on their own terms—informs nearly every aspect of the federal-tribal relationship, including and especially the protection and management of land and biodiversity. Conflicts over jurisdiction have often played out in the courts as tribes, states, and the federal government spar over who manages what and how. In no arena has this been more contentious than with threatened and endangered species. Tribes rightly believe that they have been good land stewards and should not be punished for poor management in off-tribal areas that have, in some cases, made tribal lands refugia for rare or listed species. The Endangered Species Act does not mention tribes, which under some legal interpretations, including that of tribal sovereignty, leaves them free of its influence. This has not stopped the federal government from declaring critical habitat on tribal lands—in some cases, without any prior consultation with the tribe (Albert and Plumer 2023).

Tribes also face steep challenges in garnering the financial resources necessary to manage their biologically diverse lands. All state wildlife agencies receive funding from the Federal Aid in Fish and Wildlife Restoration program (also known by the sponsors of the original legislation, Pittman-Robertson and Dingell-Johnson), which provides more than $1.5 billion annually to fund fish and wildlife management and conservation. Since the program began, states have received more than $70 billion. Despite having tribal members pay taxes that support these programs, tribes do not receive any of the funding and are forced to run their programs through license sales or by cobbling together federal or private grants, which tend to be short-term and single-project-focused. This type of funding stream often prevents tribes from developing strategic and programmatic level wildlife management, and this may put them into a position where their wildlife is treated as a commodity, which goes directly against most tribal beliefs, and against the stated tenets of NAM.

5 The Unity of All Life

An element of the I-NAM ethic that nearly always comes through in work with tribes is the unity of all life. As one Hopi elder remarked, "Energy is connected throughout the world, through all of us, and these ancient sites. We are all connected . . . There's energy there, and that's how we are connected together . . . [There may be] a forest with a tree on the eastern side of the forest, and another tree way on the west side. It may seem they are far apart, and have no ties together, but actually they do, through the root system. Just like the spider's web, they are all connected together, they are all one. And we are the same way too. We have energy, you have energy, we are all connected together, we're bonded together" (Hopi elder who wished to remain anonymous, Pers. Comm. 2022). This long-held tribal view of the natural world, long dismissed by Western science, has been confirmed with sometimes surprising discoveries. For example, we now know that the aspen trees in a grove constitute a single individual organism, and more recent findings have been borne out of the idea that entire plant ecosystems, including diverse and ostensibly competing species, communicate and share resources through their root networks (Guo et al. 2008; Simard 2018).

While Western science has made impressive strides in understanding discrete elements of the natural world, partly by parsing scientific disciplines into finer and finer areas of specialization, it is important to take stock of what has been lost in the process. For example, the damming, dredging, and channelizing of nearly every major river in the western United States may have enabled the settlement of previously uninhabited areas and the "productive" use of water but at a cost of near extinction of dozens of species and a loss of ecosystem integrity and great beauty. In this sense, perhaps the very term natural "resources"—things to be taken advantage of for utility or profit—is distracting and discordant. Tribes tend to view plants, animals, and humans as equal parts of an integrated system. This perspective generally stands at odds with the nontribal view that the natural world is something apart from people, made for us to profit from or have dominion over. The sentiment was expressed by Fond du Lac Band of Lake Superior Chippewa Vern Northrup: "We feel our place in our soul. . . . For us it is part of our body. It is not that we own it, it is part of who we are. Without it we won't be. We have to take care of it and humble ourselves" (Hoagland and Albert 2023). This nearly universally held tribal view that all species, including humans, are related has moved beyond metaphor to documented scientific fact, with the near-universal acknowledgment of a single origin to all life. Go back far enough in your family tree, and that deer (or mosquito or tree) is your cousin (Weiss et al. 2016).

6 Working Effectively with Tribes to Study, Protect, and Restore Biodiversity

The effective protection and management of biodiversity call for wide and deep collaboration among many entities, including tribes. However, in gaining the trust of Indigenous communities, there is an occasionally ugly history of scientific research gone awry that needs to be overcome. From the earliest years of the "Columbian Exchange," death and disease seemed to follow Europeans in their interactions with Native peoples. Numerous pandemics within little more than a century killed an estimated 90% of the people living in the Americas before contact, wiping out entire cultures (Koch et al. 2019).

Tribal distrust of Western science can be traced back to White attitudes toward Native people as novelties or objects of research. In the early twentieth century, approximately 25% of Native American women were sterilized under the Family Planning Services and Population Research Act of 1970 (Carpio 2004), an effort initiated through researchers and the federal Indian Health Service (Torpy 2000). At the Pueblo of Zuni, the names of Frank Hamilton Cushing and Matilda Coxe Stevenson—to many, obscure nineteenth-century anthropologists—are known by nearly every Zuni tribal member above school age and universally spoken of with contempt more than 130 years after they last set foot on tribal lands (see, for example, LaCapra 2018). Most tribes in the United States have comparable stories of unwelcome scientists poking and prodding them while stealing their physical or intellectual patrimony and sacred objects. For many tribes, the disinterment and theft of human remains and ceremonial items and their removal to study centers thousands of miles away or overseas are part of a living memory, and tribal leaders are still actively fighting to have the bodies of their ancestors returned to their homelands from museums, universities, and warehouses where they are stored (Guilford 1996; Colwell-Chanthaphonh et al. 2010; Kretzler 2015). Former Director of the Hopi Cultural Preservation Office Leigh Kuwanwisiwma estimated that over the course of his career, he took part in the repatriation and reburial of 8000 Hopi ancestors and 16,000 funerary objects (L. Kuwanwisiwma, pers. comm. 2021). The eponym of the Smithsonian Institution's National Museum of the American Indian, George Gustav Heye, was a convicted robber of Native American graves; he once remarked: "It is strange how scientific work sanctions everything."

Tens of thousands of living tribal members retain the emotional scars of the period, which ended only a few decades ago, when children were forcibly removed from their parents, sent to school hundreds or thousands of miles away, forced to cut their hair and adopt non-Indian forms of dress and manners, and beaten for speaking their own language (Adams 1995; Davis 2001; Reyhner 2018). "Kill the Indian to save the child" is a quote attributed to Richard Henry Pratt, who developed the infamous Carlisle Indian School in Pennsylvania. Current revelations surrounding the deaths of nearly 6000 Indigenous children, including 751 in one unmarked mass grave at a boarding school in British Columbia (BBC 2021), attest to the brutality of these places. This loss was exacerbated as tribes as a whole were forced to suppress their practices and adopt European systems of thought and a capitalist view of the world, including the commodification of their biological resources, often entailing management that actively reduced biodiversity. Tribes were encouraged to see their land as a bargaining tool and their resources as currency, a process that deteriorated the landscape, put dozens of tribes on the brink or over the edge of extinction, and left tens of millions of acres permanently degraded (Koch et al. 2019).

If one is tempted to think of these actions as something that happened in the distant past, one need only consider the controversy generated around the Ancient One (generally referred to by non-Natives as Kennewick Man), an ancient Native American male skeleton (Rasmussen et al. 2015) found in Washington state in 1996.

The disposition of his remains created considerable acrimony between tribes, who wanted to rebury their ancestor, and Western researchers, who were keen to glean information (Thomas 2001; Owlsley and Jantz 2014). In the 1990s, Arizona State University was asked to conduct a study on the Havasupai Tribe's diabetes epidemic. However, it was later revealed that one researcher kept blood from tribal members in order to work on new lines of investigation outside of the established agreement—something that only came to light when a Native American undergraduate student observing a lecture asked if the researcher had obtained Havasupai tribal permission. It was eventually revealed that researchers had been using unapproved blood samples on many projects completely unrelated to the original research. Nearly everyone at Havasupai, and tribal communities throughout the region, is well aware of the story (Pacheco et al. 2013).

Subtle forms of intellectual property theft can be found on thousands of Internet sites or by strolling around many cities in the western United States, where Native American themed jewelry and crafts—often made by non-Native people—turn a handsome profit for someone other than the person who created the original design.

Some of the problems with outsiders working on tribal land may stem from differing worldviews. Though widely diverse in their histories and practices, many tribes share a common vision of how to work effectively and a collaborative approach to important decisions. Social scientists recognize that many cultures lie on a continuum of individualistic to collectivist. Individualistic cultures tend to value individual rights, freedom, self-reliance, individual achievement, forthright communication, and individual choice. Australia and the United States are exemplars of this type of approach. In contrast, collectivist cultures tend to value group cohesion, long-term relationships, community objectives, links with historical past, consultation and consensus, and unspoken cues. Japan and most tribal cultures within the United States are representative of this mode of operation.

These issues may seem unimportant or obscure to someone studying the protection of biodiversity. They are not. Distrust of any kind of scientific collaboration with outsiders rightfully runs deep among tribes. However, tribes are now very well positioned to be leaders in protecting, studying, and managing biodiversity in this century. A resurgence in the assertion of tribal sovereignty, and a willingness of federal governments to respect it, means that tribes are now more willing to engage with the federal and state governments and university and private researchers on the tribes' own terms. An elevation of tribal incomes and standard of living (in no small part from casino revenues and oil and gas leases), along with innovative approaches from several forward-thinking academic institutions, have put more tribal members in positions of scientific, administrative, and political leadership.

There are many reasons that non-Indian academics, researchers, and conservation professionals may wish to work with tribes to study biodiversity (adapted from Hickman et al. 2023):

- Tribally held knowledge can provide information about seasonal and annual movements of species, trends in short- and long-term population change, landscape-level habitat shifts, and the impacts of climate change (Polfus et al. 2014; Armstrong and Veteto 2015).

- Indigenous people have a deep connection with natural resources and their homelands (including places where they are no longer active residents) and a deep understanding of local ecology (Blicharska et al. 1981).
- Tribal professionals, elders, hunters, fishers, and other community members offer novel perspectives, methods, ideas, conservation techniques, and ecological knowledge that can inform conservation management in holistic ways.
- Environmental and general research ethics require that all stakeholders have a meaningful voice in projects that may affect their resources (Aggestam 2017).
- Active engagement, collaboration, and coproduction often lead to more successful and sustainable outcomes.
- Many on- and (crucially) *off-reservation* natural resources are considered by tribes as traditional cultural properties, a status conferring federal protection and protocols that may be unfamiliar to those working in the realm of natural resources.
- Many tribal lands are relatively pristine and can serve as reference areas and natural laboratories (Hoagland et al. 2017; Ramírez and Santana 2019).
- Tribal lands share extensive borders and wildlife populations with federal, state, and private lands. The effective conservation of fish, birds, large mammals, and other wildlife species that move across these boundaries requires meaningful collaboration.
- Coproduction with tribes can open new avenues for grants and other financial support.

From a tribe's perspective, work with outside researchers has the potential to make use of the expertise of highly trained professionals to protect habitats and species of cultural and economic importance; strengthen tribal sovereignty by supplying information that tribes can use for more effective and sustainable resource management; amplify tribal voices in land-use planning and in species management and recovery; preserve cultural and ecological information; and provide jobs, income, training, professional development, and technology transfer to tribal staff.

In order to maximize success, and avoid the pitfalls described above, researchers wishing to work with tribes should better understand how conditions might differ from other types of collaborations. Several researchers have developed guidelines for outsiders wishing to work with tribes; these 12 suggestions are adapted from Hickman et al. (2023).

Guidelines for Working with Tribes

1) Make the Tribe an active collaborator from the earliest stages. Meet with tribal officials, administrators, and staff while you are developing your research hypothesis and methods.

(continued)

2) Apply early for all necessary permits. Ask before you go anywhere on tribal lands.
3) Educate yourself about the historical and current contexts of the local community, taking time to learn about the cultural practices, values, and beliefs of the tribe.
4) Visit often and attend community events, especially when invited. When the project is over, return to share your results with the community and the individuals with whom you worked.
5) Try to think at a policy level, dealing with tribes as the sovereign entities they are.
6) Be transparent at all times about everything, including project finances.
7) Make sure your partners have the capacity, willingness, and administrative and financial support they need to carry the project through and that local staff have key (not token) roles. If capacity is lacking, think of ways you can build it so that it is sustained through time. Tribal natural resource departments are often overtaxed and underfunded. Do not make your research a financial or time burden. Find out what the tribe's financial and training needs are and include tribal staff in your budget. Make provisions for capacity building, travel stipends, and compensation or honoraria for local staff, experts, guides, and interview subjects. Consider providing scholarships, internships, or fellowships for local students and young researchers.
8) Be cognizant of different styles of communication. Some tribes and some Native people may not feel comfortable immediately and directly saying no to a proposal. Sometimes "maybe" is a polite way of saying "no." If you feel like you are pushing too hard to make a project happen, you probably are. Be alert for tacit signals: a lack of communication might be an answer, too. In-person communication is always better than phone and video calls. In addition, many tribal elders are more comfortable with their Native language. Expect to use and pay for translation at every step of tribal elders' involvement.
9) Be sure you are working with authorized representatives of the tribe. A single tribal member may not necessarily speak for the tribe, nor do they necessarily understand the sensitivities of cultural information. "Permission shopping" is a common form of researcher abuse. A consensus is developing around the concept of informed community consent, that is, obtaining the consent of an entire community that has had time to be fully informed of any potential research and to carefully consider all the implications (see, for example, Dickert et al. 2021).
10) Be patient. Tribally coproduced projects will usually take much longer than work done with other entities. Many tribes are inherently conservative (in the non-political sense of that word), making decisions

(continued)

deliberatively, by consensus, and approving them only when the benefits are clear. Decision-makers and tribal councils may meet infrequently—plan accordingly.

11) Be sensitive to concerns about intellectual property and academic imperialism (see, e.g., Rakowski 1993). Be explicit about who will own the data, where they will be stored, and who has the right to disseminate and publish the research. If appropriate, develop an intellectual property rights agreement. If some data are sensitive, consider two versions of your final products: a confidential report, which local staff can use as a resource, and a public one, which can be shared more widely or published.
12) Leave something positive behind. Be sensitive to the types of deliverables desired by the tribe. Most academic or professional researchers prefer peer-reviewed publications, but these may not be as important or accessible to tribal staff, who may prefer results they can use immediately and can show to tribal officials and the tribal public. Consider creating reader-friendly reports or summaries in addition to peer-reviewed papers.

Finally, researchers intending to publish their results should reconsider the parameters for authorship. Academic institutions have expanded definitions of authorship-worthy contributions beyond the conventional roles of data analysis and manuscript writing. Harvard University's revised guidelines describe authors as collaborators with "substantial contributions to the conception or design of the work; or the acquisition, analysis, or interpretation of data" (Harvard University 2021). A physics paper in Physical Review Letters (Aad et al. 2015) listed more than 5000 authors—more authors than there were words in the body of the text. For projects with tribes, consider all the members who made the research possible, including translators, facilitators, technicians, and those who might have shaped your conception or design of the research.

Several journals, such as the Canadian Journal of Zoology, have ethical standards for working with Indigenous peoples. Their guidelines state that "submitted manuscripts examining TEK will have to demonstrate that the research was ethically conducted with respect of Indigenous Peoples." The submissions will have to follow these principles:

- The research has received appropriate Indigenous Research Ethics approval.
- True and informed consent was sought before the start of the research.
- Data were returned to the people where they belong for the protection and preservation of their traditional ecological knowledge.

In the past several years, there has been a blossoming of creative, technically proficient, and socially savvy coproduction between tribes and other entities in the service of the protection of both biological and cultural diversity. The entire suite of projects, from Alaska to Florida, is too numerous to catalog, but below we close our chapter and present two briefcase studies that we believe have produced positive and inspirational results.

6.1 Collaborative Management of Protected Areas in the Canadian Arctic

The Canadian Arctic supports many millions of nesting seabirds, waterfowl, and waterbird colonies, including several globally important and management-sensitive species. In recent years, the Canadian government has worked with local First Nations to greatly increase tribal sovereignty in the protection and management of these and other species. For example, Canadian government scientists are working with Nattivak Hunters and Trappers in the community of Qikiqtarjuaq, Nunavut, to census wildlife and document local ecological knowledge to develop two National Wildlife Areas. The parties established a comanagement committee that collaboratively develops management plans and reviews permit applications for take (including the take of many species not normally considered game species for non-Natives in Canada). The committee also codevelops new research initiatives to answer questions of current concern and to adaptively manage the populations of interest, including topics such as the impacts of plastic pollution or environmental contaminants. Mallory et al. (2022), who described their efforts in a recent paper, believe that the key elements of their program success have included:

- Documenting Indigenous knowledge: the importance of listening to tribal elders and others to document their deep understanding of the local environment was a key element in making management and research plans that were accepted by the community.
- Extremely local leadership, priorities, and management: the primary planners and management personnel for these research and management projects are members of the local Indigenous community. Within these programs, the participants hold significant leadership roles and know they have a voice in the way decisions are made, including which topics of research or which management operations will be prioritized.
- Equitable sharing of resources and sampling programs: finally, the comanagement committee has developed an equitable sharing of resources, most importantly including funding.

Restoring the Buffalo

As Berger (2023) writes, for Plains tribes, the buffalo shaped crucial aspects of their economies, cultures, and religions. Buffaloes are widely considered to be a keystone species (Khanina 1998), with their population health being a useful indicator for the functioning of a biologically diverse ecosystem. Efforts by the US government to subdue the tribes were largely centered on a strategy of destroying this means of sustenance. The InterTribal Buffalo Council (ITBC)[2] was founded in 1992 with the goal of restoring buffaloes to tribal ecosystems. The ITBC largely supports both captive and free-ranging buffalo herds on tribal lands throughout the United States. ITBC also works to provide tribes with access to buffaloes and to influence state and federal regulations limiting that access. Today's ITBC includes 69 tribes in 19 states. The organization is governed by a nine-member board of directors, with each tribe voting to elect officers and a representative from their region. ITBC raises and distributes funds to tribal buffalo programs through competitive grants, provides tribes with technical assistance, and secures the distribution of surplus bison from national parks (Berger 2023). Since its inception, the ITBC has worked in a distinctly Indigenous manner, rejecting the treatment of buffaloes as livestock and seeking to restore the buffalo as a wild animal in relationship with Indigenous people and supporting tribal buffalo culture. Tribes now collectively hold four times as many wild buffaloes as the federal government, and results on the biodiversity of tribal landscapes have been dramatic, promoting the spread of native grasses, birds, and terrestrial animals that accompany herds (ITBC 2017).

7 Conclusion

Tribes in the United States have faced a long struggle to gain the full recognition of their constitutionally guaranteed tribal status but have ultimately been successful in protecting the diversity of their lands—in most cases as well or better than private, state, and federal entities. Tribes are eager to partner with other cooperators to study biodiversity but only when they are considered as fully equal partners and their inherent sovereignty is respected. Hundreds of other forward-thinking projects are now regularly springing up on tribal lands across the continent. While conditions differ widely among tribes, the successfully coproduced projects and programs share a common element: the recognition of tribes as sovereign entities and project proponents on all sides who share a common goal of mutual benefits.

References

Aad G et al (2015) Combined measurement of the Higgs Boson mass in pp collisions at $\sqrt{s}=7$ and 8 TeV with the ATLAS and CMS experiments. Phys Rev Lett 114:191803

Adams DW (1995) Education for extinction: American Indians and the boarding school experience, 1875–1928. University Press of Kansas, Lawrence

Aggestam F (2017) Wetland restoration and the involvement of stakeholders: an analysis based on value-perspectives. Landsc Res 39:680–697

[2]The ITBC was originally named the Intertribal Bison Cooperative, but buffalo is the preferred term for this species by most tribes.

Albert S, Plumer R (2023) Tribes and the Endangered Species Act. In: We feel our place in our soul: Wildlife Stewardship on Tribal Lands. Johns Hopkins University Press

American Association of Fish and Wildlife Agencies (AFWA) (2023) North American Model of Wildlife Conservation. https://www.fishwildlife.org/landing/north-american-model-wildlife-conservation. Accessed 22 Aug 2023

Armstrong CG, Veteto JR (2015) Historical ecology and ethnobiology: applied research for environmental conservation and social justice. Ethnobiol Lett 6:5–7

BBC (2021) Canada: 751 unmarked graves found at residential school. https://www.bbc.com/news/world-us-canada-57592243. Accessed 31 July 2021

Berger, BR (2023) The Promise of intertribal wildlife management. In: Hoagland S, Albert S (eds) Wildlife Stewardship on Tribal Lands: We feel our place in our soul. Johns Hopkins University Press, pp 99–119

Blicharska M, Smithers RJ, Kuchler M, Agrawal GK, Gutiérre JM, Hassanali A, Huq S, Koller SH, Marjit S, Mshinda HM, Masjuki HH, Solomons NW, Van Staden J, Brownrigg G (1981) Conserving the natural heritage of Latin America and the Caribbean: the planning and management of protected areas in the Neotropical realm. In: Proceedings of the 18th working session of the International Union for Conservation of Nature's Commission on National Parks and Protected Areas, Lima, Peru, 21–28 June. International Union for Conservation of Nature, Gland, Switzerland

Carpio MV (2004) The lost generation: American Indian women and sterilization abuse. Soc Just 3: 40–53

Colwell-Chanthaphonh C, Maxson R, Powell J (2010) The repatriation of culturally unidentifiable human remains. Mus Manag Curatorsh 26:27–43

Corrigan C, Bingham H, Shia Y, Lewisa E, Chauvenet A, Kingston N (2018) Quantifying the contribution to biodiversity conservation of protected areas governed by Indigenous and local communities. Biol Conserv 227:403–412

Davis J (2001) American Indian boarding school experiences: recent studies from Native perspectives. Organ Am Hist Mag Hist 15(2):20–22

Deloria V Jr (1969) Custer died for your sins: an Indian Manifesto. Macmillan, New York, 296 pp

Dickert NW, Metz K, Fetters MD, Haggins AN, Harney DK, Speight CD, Silbergleit R (2021) Meeting unique requirements: community consultation and public disclosure for research in emergency settings using exception from informed consent. Acad Emerg Med 10:1183–1194

Eichler L, Baumeister D (2018) Hunting for justice: an Indigenous critique of the North American Model of wildlife conservation. Environ Soc: Adv Res 9:75–90

Guilford A (1996) Bones of contention: the repatriation of Native American human remains. Public Hist 18:119–143

Guo D, Mitchell RJ, Withington JM, Fan P-P, Hendricks JJ (2008) Endogenous and exogenous controls of root life span, mortality and nitrogen flux in a longleaf pine forest: root branch order predominates. J Ecol 96:737–745

Harvard University (2021) Faculty of Arts and Sciences guidelines on authorship and acknowledgement. https://research.fas.harvard.edu/links/guidelines-authorship-and-acknowledgement. Accessed 5 July 2021

Hessami MA, Bowles E, Popp JN, Ford AT (2021) Indigenizing the North American Model of wildlife conservation. Facets 6(1):1285–1306

Hickman C, Thorstenson J, Carlisle A, Hoagland S, Albert S (2023) Research with Tribes. In: Our place is in our soul: Wildlife Stewardship on Tribal Lands. Johns Hopkins University Press, pp 229–247

Hoagland S, Albert S (2023) We feel our place in our soul: Wildlife Stewardship on Tribal Lands. Johns Hopkins University Press

Hoagland SJ, Miller R, Waring KM, Carroll O (2017) Tribal lands provide forest management laboratory for mainstream university students. J For 115(5):484–490

InterTribal Buffalo Council [ITBC] (2017) Return of the native: the 25 year history of the InterTribal Buffalo Council. https://itbcbuffalonation.org/return-of-the-native-the-25-year-history-of-the-intertribal-buffalo-council/
Khanina L (1998) Determining keystone species. Conservation Ecology [online] 2:R2
Koch A, Brierley C, Maslin MM, Lewis SL (2019) Earth systems impacts of the European arrival and Great Dying in the Americas after 1492. Quat Sci Rev 207:13–36
Kraniak D (2016) Conserving endangered species in Indian Country: the success and struggles of Joint Secretarial Order 3206 nineteen years on. Col Nat Resour Energy Environ Lit Rev 26:321–349
Kretzler I (2015) Repatriation of "culturally-unidentifiable" human remains: the view from Fort Vancouver. SAA Archaeol Record 2015:21–24
LaCapra D (2018) Understanding others: peoples, animals, pasts. Cornell University Press, Ithaca, New York
Leopold A (1920) "Piute forestry" vs. forest fire prevention. Southwestern Magazine 2 (March):12–13
Mallory ML, Toomasie J, Emond S, Lamarche G, Roberts L, Pirie-Dominix L, Provencher JF (2022) Community-scientist collaboration in the creation, management and research for two national wildlife areas in Arctic Canada. Adv Ecol Res, in press
Melley B (2020) Sierra Club apologizes for founder John Muir's racist views. Washington Post, 22 July
Owlsley DW, Jantz RL (2014) Kennewick Man: the scientific investigation of an ancient American skeleton. Smithsonian Institution Press, Washington, DC
Pacheco CM, Daley SM, Brown T, Filippi M, Greiner KA, Daley CM (2013) Moving forward: breaking the cycle of mistrust between American Indians and researchers. Am J Public Health 103:2152–2159
Polfus JL, Heinemeyer K, Hebblewhite M (2014) Comparing traditional ecological knowledge and Western science woodland caribou habitat models. J Wildl Manag 78:112–121
Rakowski CA (1993) The ugly scholar: neocolonialism and ethical issues in international research. Am Sociol 24:69–86
Ramírez F, Santana J (2019) National parks and biodiversity conservation. In: Ramírez F, Santana J (eds), pp 33–38
Rasmussen M, Sikora M, Albrechtsen A, Korneliussen TS, Moreno-Mayar JV, Poznik GD, Zollikofer CPE, Ponce de León MS, Allentoft ME, Moltke I, Jónsson H, Valdiosera C, Malhi RS, Orlando L, Bustamante CD, Stafford TW Jr, Meltzer DJ, Nielsen R, Willerslev E (2015) The ancestry and affiliations of Kennewick Man. Nature 523:455–458
Reyhner, J (2018) American Indian boarding schools: What went wrong? What is going right? J Am Indian Educ 57:58–78
Schuster R, Germain RR, Bennett JR, Reo NJ, Secord DL, Arcese P (2018) Biodiversity on Indigenous lands equals that in protected areas. BioRxIV 10:1101/321935
Schwartz J (2020) As Teddy Roosevelt's statue falls, let's remember how truly dark his history was. Intercept, 22 June
Simard SW (2018) Mycorrhizal networks facilitate tree communication, learning, and memory. In: Baluska F, Gagliano M, Witzany G (eds) Memory and learning in plants: signaling and communication in plants. Springer Press, New York, pp 191–213
Thomas DH (2001) Skull wars: Kennewick Man, archaeology, and the battle for Native American identity. Basic Books, New York
Torpy SJ (2000) Native American women and coerced sterilization: on the Trail of Tears in the 1970s. Am Indian Cult Res J 24:1–22
Weiss MC, Sousa FL, Mrnjavac N, Neukirchen S, Roettger M, Nelson-Sathi S, Martin WF (2016) The physiology and habitat of the last universal common ancestor. Nat Microbiol 1:16116
Wohlforth C (2010) Conservation and eugenics. Orion Magazine, June

Wildlife, Science, and Law in the United States

Daniel J. Rohlf

Abstract This chapter sets out a framework for how to better integrate science, law, and policy to successfully manage and conserve wildlife and ecosystems. Using various examples, it first discusses standards for managing biodiversity, such as the acceptable risk choices inherent in selecting species for special legal protections. Next, it examines the science process, a term for the choices made in designing scientific determinations as to whether decisions meet applicable standards, as well as for resolving disputes over such determinations. The framework's third element is implementation, including issues such as enforcement and adjusting management regimes to deal with uncertainties and environmental changes. Finally, the chapter explores some of the human elements that affect biodiversity management, including a call for all interested citizens to play a role in making important choices about conserving biodiversity—including scientists. Overall, the chapter strongly advocates better interdisciplinary thinking and communication to improve efforts to manage and conserve biodiversity.

1 Introduction

This chapter considers science related to wildlife in an applied setting. This means focusing primarily on science in a regulatory context—how science plays a role in deciding how we will manage and protect biodiversity and in carrying out those choices. It is not to say that law and policy have no influence on what we often mistakenly think of as "pure" science; for example, law and policy choices often play a crucial role in determining what studies get funded or in determining the point at which a certain researcher has transgressed ethical boundaries. Nevertheless, at a time when we are in the midst of the sixth global extinction event in geological history—this one caused by humans—most of the crucial decisions that will determine the fate of the planet's biological resources involve designing and

D. J. Rohlf (✉)
Lewis and Clark Law School, Portland, OR, USA
e-mail: rohlf@lclark.edus

G. Antonelli et al. (eds.), *Biodiversity Laws, Policies and Science in Europe, the United States and China*, https://doi.org/10.1007/978-3-031-56218-1_12

implementing regulatory mechanisms that govern the most significant threat to biodiversity—us.

Years ago, Professor Oliver Houck wrote an excellent article for the prestigious journal *Science* (Houck 2003) about the intersection of law and science in managing and protecting the environment. In it, he contrasted the amorphous "multiple use" management requirement that applies to vast areas of federal public land with the so-called jeopardy standard of the federal Endangered Species Act, praising the latter as the "most-obeyed" natural resources law.

However, decades of working with the Endangered Species Act (ESA) have taught me a very different lesson, one that holds key lessons demonstrating the importance of understanding the relationship between science and law in managing and protecting biodiversity. At a surface level, it does indeed appear that federal agencies almost always comply with their legal obligation under the ESA to avoid taking or approving an action that would jeopardize the continued existence of threatened or endangered species. To help agencies meet this standard, they must consult with the US Fish and Wildlife Service, which assesses the impacts of proposed actions on protected species. A meta-analysis of nearly 90,000 proposed actions over a nearly 8-year period turned up only *two* cases where the US Fish and Wildlife Service (FWS) found that an agency project would jeopardize listed species (Malcom and Li 2015). While this number suggests an amazing level of compliance with agencies' legal duty to protect threatened and endangered species, a closer look reveals a different explanation. FWS assesses whether a proposed project causes jeopardy to a particular species by considering the site-specific impacts of the action in the context of the species as a whole. In other words, unless a given project will itself imperil the *entire* species, the proposal gets a green light. Since a single agency action almost never has such a severe species-wide impact, FWS finds that virtually all proposed federal actions comply with the ESA. At the same time, this methodology allows for virtually unlimited incremental adverse impacts on listed species and their habitat.

The federal agencies implementing this management system staunchly assert that they protect listed species using the best scientific data available, as the ESA requires. However, the Services' interpretation of the law, which much of the world considers the gold standard for protecting biodiversity, embodies a blueprint for allowing threatened and endangered species to incrementally slide toward extinction.

So how do we untangle what is going on here? To start, this example should raise a number of questions. What exactly does it mean to "jeopardize" a species, and who should make such determinations? What data should we use to assess jeopardy, and what happens if there are disagreements about jeopardy determinations? Does FWS have adequate resources to make reliable jeopardy assessments for the vast number of federal—and federally approved and funded—projects that affect listed species?

To truly understand ESA's role in managing and protecting biodiversity—and indeed the role of any law aimed at these ends—we must reach a systematic understanding of the sorts of questions posed above by identifying the interaction between science, law, and policy choices that together direct how we manage this vital resource. Therefore, this chapter seeks to set out a framework to describe the respective roles of these elements in managing and protecting biodiversity. Its elements include the challenge of creating standards that set the bar for the degree of protection we afford to wildlife and ecosystems—or risks we are willing to take with their future; the science process we employ to assess whether or not we are meeting those standards; and, perhaps most challenging of all, the task of actually implementing what we say we want to do. A framework for thinking about how to integrate science, law, and policy can in turn facilitate better interdisciplinary communication and, ultimately, help scientists, managers, and policymakers cooperate to establish and achieve effective goals for the country's (and planet's) wildlife and ecosystems.

2 Framework Part 1: Standards

Most fundamentally, managing and protecting biodiversity requires us to establish standards. To do so effectively, we must understand what this means, as well as understand the mix of science, law, and policy that goes into setting biodiversity-related standards.

Once again, the US Endangered Species Act provides some good examples of standards. The law does not protect all species that are biologically imperiled; it protects only species placed on two specific lists maintained by FWS and the National Marine Fisheries Service (NMFS). Therefore, the thresholds for designating species as "threatened" and "endangered" constitute important standards for applying the law's protections. At the same time, though perhaps somewhat less obviously, whether a group of organisms qualifies as a "species" also constitutes a key standard. Only species that meet the law's definition of this term—which is not necessarily the same as what some scientists may think of as species—are eligible for listing (Doremus 1997). For example, in 2012, FWS determined that the isolated population of bald eagles that persist in the Sonora desert do not qualify as a "species" and thus are not eligible for protection under the ESA despite concerns about the population's continued viability (FWS 2012).

Aside from the ESA, numerous other standards establish key parameters that are important for managing and protecting wildlife. For example, the federal Migratory Bird Treaty Act protects most wild birds found in the United States, but Congress amended the law in 2004 to exclude protection for birds that are not native to the country (16 U.S.C. 703(b)(1)). Other state and federal laws establish numeric limits on the take of commercially valuable species such as fish stocks and animals hunted or fished; these thresholds play crucial roles in determining the overall level of security for the broader populations of the targeted species. More broadly, other standards play central roles in the future of specific ecosystems. For instance, the Environmental Protection Agency and US Army Corps of Engineers must define which of a wide variety of landforms—streams, ephemeral waterbodies, wetlands, seasonal marshes, wet meadows, etc.—qualify as "wetlands" and thus receive protection under the Clean Water Act. The US Forest Service faces a similar challenge in carrying out its legal direction to manage national forests to "maintain or restore the ecological integrity of terrestrial and aquatic ecosystems and watersheds" (36 C.F.R. §219.8(a)(1)).

While most people are familiar with these sorts of biodiversity-related standards, there is widespread misunderstanding about the nature of these standards and how to establish them. This confusion often undermines effective management and protection of wildlife and habitat. When regulators make important standards decisions, one often hears that they should "let the science decide." Even provisions of the law itself sometimes take this perspective; for example, the ESA requires that FWS and NMFS make decisions about listing and delisting species "solely" on the basis of the best science available (16 U.S.C. §1533(b)1)(A)). At a surface level, this nod to science alone is appealing. Other decision-making scenarios conjure up visions of smoky backroom deals, where shadowy insiders make calls based on expediency rather than data. While it is indeed important to safeguard against such outcomes, the notion that science alone should determine biodiversity standards also raises serious concerns.

A "science as sole decider" perspective suggests that there are right and wrong answers in setting biodiversity standards and that scientists alone can—and should—simply tell us the "correct" answers for decisions such as when species should receive protections, how many individuals in a population we should harvest, and which areas of habitat we should protect. But this view embodies a misunderstanding of science itself. Science describes the world around us and how it works. Experts can use scientific data and an understanding of ecological processes and conservation biology to make probabilistic projections about the future of a given population, species, or ecosystem. However, given the pervasive human influence on biodiversity in the Anthropocene, we constantly have to make decisions that balance species security and ecological function with human needs and desires, as well as economic and political costs. Such decisions, of course, necessarily include value choices.

An insightful biological study provides a good example of nontechnical factors that influence biodiversity standards decisions. Dr. Andrea Easter-Pilcher analyzed decisions by FWS over several years listing species as threatened and endangered under the ESA; she found that mammals listed as threatened had "dramatically" higher number of remaining individuals than birds, reptiles, and fish that were also listed (Easter-Pilcher 1996). These data indicate that agencies implementing the law tend to manage the "cute and cuddly" species that capture more popular attention—most often mammals—to a higher degree of security than other types of organisms. Indeed, FWS itself provided an extreme example of such choices when it refused to list slickspot peppergrass—an imperiled but decidedly uncharismatic species of grass in Idaho—despite finding that the plants had a 64% chance of extinction over the next century (a determination later overturned in court (*Western Watersheds Project v. Foss*, 2005 WL 2002473 (D. Idaho 2005)). Such decisions led Dr. Easter-Pilcher, together with other prominent conservation biologists, to recognize that standards decisions such as determining whether a species is threatened or endangered under the ESA involve significant policy choices.

It should come as no surprise that biodiversity standards decisions involve nonbiological components. After all, no one simply turns over all of her money to an expert and says "invest this for me." Instead, financial planners can provide advice on investing based on factors such as a person's income, years before retirement, market prospects, and similar factors, but the investor herself must still make the key choices of where to put her money based on her own financial goals and tolerance for financial risks. Similarly, in deciding whether a species is threatened or endangered, society must make a number of important value-based choices. What level of security against extinction do we wish to afford other species, recognizing that managing for greater levels of security usually carries greater economic and political costs? Do we wish to provide the same level of security for all species, or should we favor charismatic species or economically or culturally valuable species or keystone species? What distribution of a species do we want? For example, is one population of gray wolves sufficient, or do we want to restore the species throughout its broad former range? Scientists can provide relevant advice on how to answer such questions based on the biological consequences of various options, but they cannot supply "correct" answers.

Interestingly, Congress did not clearly make such standards choices in the Endangered Species Act. For example, the law provides only a vague definition of an endangered species (as a species "in danger of extinction"), which effectively leaves it to FWS and NMFS to decide the point at which species receive (and lose) protections under the law (Rohlf 1991). Yet the Services have set out no generally applicable criteria to define when species are threatened and endangered—in stark contrast to other classification schemes, such as the International Union for the Conservation of Nature's (IUCN) Red List, whose various categories of endangerment are defined by clearly specified biological criteria such as viability over time and percentage of historic range lost (IUCN 2022). This means that FWS and NMFS essentially make ad hoc listing decisions for every listing candidate based on no clear criteria. Even more, stakeholders in listing decisions have limited input into these decisions, and courts are reluctant to overturn the agencies' choices because Congress cast listing decisions as based "solely" on science. Ironically, therefore, pretending that only science can decide which species are threatened and endangered has led to ESA listing decisions that vary widely—often not on the basis of scientific data but depending on factors applied behind the scenes such as what party controls the White House, how charismatic a species happens to be, or the amount of controversy generated by a proposal to protect the species (Kahn 2020).

Therefore, the first step in designing effective standards for managing and protecting biodiversity is to recognize that these standards demand policy choices *informed by* science—letting the science decide is an inaccurate sound bite often employed as a tool by advocates for a particular outcome (Boebert 2022). In reality, we are all on the hook to collectively make what are often tough trade-offs in deciding what elements of biodiversity to protect and how much to protect them.

We should not pretend that someone can simply look at data and give us "correct" answers.

Next, we need to carefully consider who should establish biodiversity standards and how that entity makes its decisions. For example, Congress itself could provide a more specific listing standard for determining when a species is threatened or endangered, and in fact lawmakers have occasionally stepped in to directly make such decisions, such as voting in 2011 to remove ESA protections from the northern Rocky Mountain population of gray wolves. At least in theory, legislators are accountable to the public for their decisions through the ballot box—though as a practical matter, legislatures are unlikely to have the time and attention to make routine conservation decisions on a species-by-species basis, and such an approach is unlikely to produce a coherent overall biodiversity policy. Alternatively, the legislature can empower an administrative entity to make standards decisions, such FWS and NMFS for making listing decisions under the ESA, or state fish and wildlife commissions that in most states establish limits on sport and commercial take of wildlife. It is common for lawmakers to delegate such decisions to "expert" bodies, but these administrative decision-makers should also be accountable to the public by developing means of allowing stakeholders and interested parties to provide input into the value-based aspects of standards decisions.

Entities trusted with establishing biodiversity standards should ultimately formulate actual standards in a manner that allows for both practical application and consistent results. For example, the text of the ESA defines an endangered species by referring to a "significant portion of its range," but the Services have struggled for years to better define the statute's standard for this geographic component of endangerment (Carroll et al. 2010). The lack of a clear threshold for the extent of a species' range loss that should trigger legal protections has led to years of controversy and litigation as FWS has struggled to make listing decisions. In contrast, some states' wolf management plans have set specific population and distribution targets that make their standards for managing the species very clear (with states such as Idaho and Wyoming setting very low standards that reflect their legislatures' antipathy toward wolves). Though biodiversity standards must reflect value judgments, the specific terms used to express those standards should be biologically meaningful and as specific as possible. For example, the ESA defines as threatened species "any species that is likely to become endangered in the foreseeable future...," and neither the statute nor other guidance provides clear definitions of either "endangered" or "foreseeable future" (16 U.S.C. 1532(20)). On the other hand, the "vulnerable" category under the International Union for Conservation of Nature (IUCN) Red List is defined by specific biological criteria for population size, range loss, and the likelihood of extinction over time (IUCN 2022). It is not hard to guess which categorization scheme leads to easier application and produces more consistent results when applied.

3 Framework Part 2: Science Process

Even the best-constructed standards for managing and protecting biodiversity can only be successful at guiding our actions and decisions if we develop means of accurately and reliably assessing whether we are meeting the standards we set. For example, even assuming that a decision-maker establishes a very clear and specific standard for determining when species and their habitat are eligible for special legal protections, we would still need biologists to determine the status and trends of potentially imperiled species and habitat in order to determine which species and/or habitat meet these standards and therefore should receive protection. To ensure trustworthy biological calls on these issues, we also need to ensure the validity of data, assumptions, and models that scientists use in making these judgments, as well as determine how to treat the inevitable uncertainties inherent in all three areas. Finally, biological assessments about of the state of wildlife or ecosystems, and projections of the likely consequences of given impacts to elements of biodiversity, often lead to disagreement and even disputes. Therefore, we must also develop mechanisms to resolve these clashes that stakeholders trust. Taken together, I call the procedures and processes that go into producing trustworthy biological determinations *science process*.

Since making biological determinations requires scientific tools and expertise, it is again tempting to view science process decisions as only the province of science. However, as with setting biodiversity standards, devising sound, workable, and trustworthy science processes also involves making important policy choices.

Here is an instructive illustration. Peer review is of course an important tool of science in helping ensure the reliability of scientific conclusions. However, running a scientific determination through a peer review process often requires substantial time, as well as finding—and perhaps paying—qualified experts who are willing to serve as reviewers. In deciding whether to perform a peer review for a given biological determination, the responsible entity must assess whether the marginal increment of increased scientific reliability that peer review may provide is worth the time, hassle, and perhaps expense necessary to go through the peer review process. Many of the factors that go into making such a decision are thus not scientific, demanding a choice that balances potential scientific benefits against institutional and practical considerations. In an interesting example of this type of science process decision, the Services' peer review policy for ESA listing decisions makes directly opposing choices depending on the listing decision at hand (FWS and NMFS 1994). When it decides to propose a species for listing as threatened or endangered, FWS or NMFS subjects its proposed listing to peer review and considers the results of this review in making its final listing decision. On the other hand, when an agency rejects a petition to list a species, the Service does not seek a peer review of its decision. It is hard to imagine a scientific basis justifying this science process for listing decisions—the Services apparently reached different policy choices about the practical value of peer review in making different types of listing decisions. However, the agencies have never explained to the public *why* they elected to avoid peer review when they reject listing petitions, decisions that often generate considerable controversy.

And perhaps because few people are accustomed to thinking about the science process as a blend of science and policy, no one has ever demanded that the Services provide such an explanation.

More subtly—and more dangerously—science process choices can disguise non-scientific elements as science and then have a determinative effect on the ultimate conclusions of an inquiry. In one of its first assessments of whether plans for operating federal dams on the Columbia and Snake Rivers complied with the ESA, NMFS developed a biological model for assessing whether imperiled salmon populations were likely to improve over time. Noting that its model results showed positive trends, NMFS concluded that the proposed operations complied with the ESA's jeopardy standard. However, when conservation groups challenged this decision in court, the judge noted that NMFS—without explaining why—had chosen to set the model's baseline for comparison as the relatively short time period when salmon populations were at their historic lows. Against this low bar, almost all of the model's projections indicated salmon population growth, and thus NMFS found that the proposed dam operations passed muster under the ESA. The judge threw out the agency's analysis, rebuking it for whitewashing status quo dam operations harmful to listed fish (IDFG case cite). The court found that NMFS had essentially designed its model to provide a predetermined outcome to the scientific question of whether the dam operators' proposal was consistent with the ESA's jeopardy standard. In this case, NMFS had used the science process to covertly *make* a decision rather than to devise an accurate means of assessing whether the consequences of a proposed action complied with the applicable standard.

To be clear, considering nonscientific factors in designing science processes is not inherently problematic. It may be possible to achieve somewhat more accurate results for a given determination by waiting for more complete data, using more sophisticated (and often more expensive) scientific models or scientific instruments, or even seeking out the most qualified or well-known experts. However, absolute accuracy may not be of paramount importance; other important factors relevant to a certain decision may mean that different science process elements are advisable or even necessary. In particular, agencies tasked with managing species and habitats must make decisions within constrained periods of time and with limited resources and personnel. Devising an effective science process thus often involves creating the means of carrying out a scientific assessment that will provide the most accurate answers in light of such constraints. Further, decisions on which assumptions should be built into scientific models can tip the burden of uncertainty in one direction or another. For example, in building a predictive model for a wildlife population, there may be uncertainty as to when individuals in that population become reproductively active. Incorporating into the model an assumption that individuals start to breed as 2-year-olds would mean that the model is more likely to show positive population trends than if the model assumes no breeding until individuals are 3 years old. The first model would thus be more likely to predict that the population could withstand adverse impacts, whereas the second model would effectively give the benefit of the doubt to the species and predict that the species is less able to withstand adverse impacts without decline. Deciding which assumption to employ in the face of scientific uncertainty demands a policy choice of whether it is preferable to err on the side of finding no adverse impact to the species when such impacts actually are taking place or in finding an adverse impact when in reality the species is actually fine.

Therefore, the bottom line is that devising a science process to determine whether a given decision will meet the applicable standard requires an entity to make choices that not only are scientific but also involve policy decisions and judgment calls. Science process choices provide ample opportunity for abuse if the entity creating an assessment process seeks to skew that process toward a given answer. All of this means that stakeholders affected by given scientific assessments—including interested members of the public—should understand the interdisciplinary nature of the science process and examine specific assessments to ensure that they are as objective as possible. Moreover, entities designing a science process to perform a given standards assessment should do so with transparency in order to give stakeholders assurance that the assessment will be as accurate and reliable as possible. Unlike NMFS' actions in designing its peer review process for ESA listing decisions, this means explaining to interested parties the reasons behind important science process choices.

An encouraging trend has emerged that promises to help build a more reliable science process for making standards assessments. The so-called actionable science involves "coproduction," in which managers, policymakers, scientists, and stakeholders identify specific scientific determinations needed in a given situation and jointly define the research questions, methods, and outputs to make these calls (Beier et al. 2017). This sort of transparent and cooperative approach to devising the science process can help guard against potential abuses and avoid conflicts by increasing trust on the part of all parties and stakeholders. If, for example, FWS employed actionable science, instead of its own unilateral analysis, to determine whether proposed dam operations would violate the ESA in light of the likely impacts on protected fish, both stakeholders and the public might have more confidence in the ultimate answer.

In the modern world, disputes that challenge agency decisions affecting biodiversity as inconsistent with appliable standards are inevitable. Such instances implicate another important component of the science process—devising reliable and broadly acceptable methods for resolving disputes over standards determinations.

In the United States, there is a wide variety of means that various entities and jurisdictions employ to resolve disputes about whether a given decision meets applicable biodiversity standards. Federal land management agencies, which oversee hundreds of millions of acres of important habitat, generally have administrative appeal procedures (Congressional Research Service 2013). The federal Data Quality Act allows any party to effectively challenge the integrity of science relied on or disseminated by a federal agency, but the agency itself referees these complaints, and thus successful challenges under this statute have been relatively rare (GAO 2015). The federal Administrative Procedure Act subjects final agency actions and decisions to judicial review—a right uncommon in most countries—so any interested party directly affected by a decision can challenge it in court. However, despite implications to the contrary from endless lawyer shows on TV, such proceedings do *not* entail any sort of trial where both sides present their own evidence and testimony from experts supporting their arguments to a judge or jury. Instead, only a judge considers the administrative record compiled by the agency to support its decision and assesses whether, in light of the information in the record, there was such a disconnect between the facts and the agency's findings so as to render the agency's findings "arbitrary and capricious" (5 U.S.C. 706(2)(a)). This standard of review is very deferential to agencies, effectively putting a thumb on the scale in favor of agency decisions and overturning only those found to involve relatively egregious errors. Though challenges to federal agency decisions are the most common disputes related to wildlife and habitat that end up in a federal court, a smaller number of cases involve citizen suits challenging the actions of landowners or corporations. These cases can involve clashes of opposing experts as part of factual disputes that a judge must resolve.

An analogous but even broader variety of dispute resolution mechanisms for decisions affecting biodiversity exists at the state and local levels in the United States—with a couple of interesting twists. Unlike at the federal level, where disputes related to biodiversity and other environmental issues go to the same courts as all other civil and criminal cases, Vermont and Hawaii have environment courts and Colorado has a specialized court that hears only water disputes. While unusual in the United States, the idea that a dispute resolution mechanism with more experience and expertise in scientific and environmental issues will produce better decisions is quite common in many other countries. In New Zealand, for example, the Environment Court includes scientists as well as lawyers among the members of judicial panels that decide cases, and the court can reach its own independent decisions on a question decided by a regulatory entity rather than simply decide whether or not to uphold the decision of the agency involved. In the state of Washington, the Growth Management Act requires local governments to use the "best available science" in implementing the law's habitat and open space protections. In an effort to provide guidance to both local officials implementing the law and courts that apply it, regulations of the state's Department of Ecology set out a list of "characteristics generally to be expected in a valid science process," which include peer review, quantitative analysis, and "logical conclusions and reasonable inferences" (Washington Administrative Code 365-195-905).

Once again, a better understanding of the role of both science and policy choices in the science process will help improve science processes themselves, as well as facilitate a fairer and more accurate resolution of disputes over decisions and actions that affect biodiversity. Increased interdisciplinary knowledge can help prevent potential abuses hidden in the science process, as well as allow for broader participation in policy-related aspects of science process choices, such as when to apply tools like peer review. Moreover, judges who understand the interaction between science and policy in the science process will be less likely to reflexively defer to agencies' findings merely because they involve scientific determinations, and better recognition of the mix of law and science needed to make standards determinations can potentially even lead to better dispute resolution mechanisms.

4 Framework Part 3: Implementation

Of course, even clear standards and well-thought-out science process designs will not help us meet our goals for protecting and managing wildlife and habitat unless we actually implement these measures. While this may seem obvious, we are clearly slow to learn this lesson; fully implementing laws and policies already on the books remains one of the most significant challenges in managing and protecting biodiversity. And even in this part of the framework, learning to better integrate law, science, and policy can lead to implementation improvements that are especially crucial in an era when conditions influencing wildlife and habitat are changing rapidly.

Not surprisingly, resource availability usually plays a significant role in implementing biodiversity protections and management decisions. Not only adequate funding but also sufficient expertise and personnel are essential ingredients in a successful on-the-ground implementation. For example, Congress in the early 2000s provided funding for state fish and wildlife management agencies to develop Wildlife Action Plans in each state, which include many science-based measures to protect nongame fish and wildlife species and their habitat (Association of State Fish and Wildlife Agencies). However, virtually all state agencies receive the majority of their funding through sources directly linked to hunting and fishing—so the vast majority of state management and protection actions focus on game species that constitute a small percentage of the states' overall biodiversity (Jacobson et al. 2010). Congress also has never allocated meaningful additional funding to the states to help *implement* their Wildlife Action Plans, so these documents have mainly occupied office shelf space rather than made a difference in the real world. This funding situation also affects the expertise available within state fish and wildlife agencies, which tend to hire biologists with backgrounds centered on game species (and even encourage biology programs at colleges and universities to likewise focus on these species) (Jacobson et al. 2010). At the federal level, conservation groups estimate that FWS typically receives from Congress about half of the funding necessary to adequately implement the ESA—a level that sometimes dips even lower when Congress and/or the White House is controlled by elected officials even less favorably disposed to biodiversity protection (Greenwald 2016). These examples demonstrate that even if we develop meaningful standards and effective science processes aimed at protecting ecosystems and other species, we are likely to fall short unless we also allocate sufficient resources to translate words on pages to management actions on the ground.

Enforcement is also a key component of implementation. While everyone touts the ESA as a cornerstone of biodiversity protection in the United States, the plight of listed species on nonfederal land illustrates the central role that enforcement plays in translating law and policy to actual conservation outcomes. The majority of threatened and endangered species have the majority of their habitat on nonfederal land, and the law at least nominally deals with this important biological reality. Section 9 of the ESA bans the "take" of most listed species regardless of where the take occurs, and the broad legal definition of this term encompasses habitat degradation that kills or injures members of a protected species. However, the federal government almost never enforces this prohibition, most likely because of the political sensitivities that come with regulating private property. While citizen enforcement of take restrictions is possible, the resource demands and uncertainties associated with such cases make them uncommon. As a consequence, the difficulty of protecting and restoring imperiled species on private lands remains a major hurdle to stemming the twenty-first century's biodiversity crisis. Similar enforcement challenges in virtually all jurisdictions, the result of both resource and political constraints, also diminish the effectiveness of even well-crafted laws and policies.

The vast and swiftly moving changes to the biosphere brought on by climate change present yet another key implementation challenge. Integrating science, law, and policy into a management strategy for a given species or ecosystem simply starts what is necessarily an ongoing process. Virtually, all such strategies begin with associated biological uncertainties, and chances are that over time, conditions will change in ways that are difficult or impossible to foresee at the outset. To have the best chances of achieving their goals, biodiversity management schemes must include ways to deal with uncertainty and change. While this seems obvious, many barriers to such revisions often prevent implementation success. An agency or decision-maker that finally completed the already fraught process of developing and approving a biodiversity management or restoration plan may be reluctant to revisit difficult trade-offs and reopen finally resolved controversies. Changes may also provoke opposition, and they usually require additional expenditures. Even the law can put hurdles in the way, such as potentially having to update or even redo environmental impact assessments before being able to make management modifications.

Though these potential barriers must be anticipated and dealt with, adaptive management provides a mechanism for coping with uncertainties and changing conditions. The "management as an experiment" and "learning by doing" aspects of adaptive management allow managers to incorporate increased knowledge into management schemes, as well as to revise plans and management schemes themselves over time in response to new circumstances (Center for Progressive Reform 2011). However, adaptive management can also be easily abused as essentially a paper exercise that employs vague assurances of future changes to wave away current shortcomings. Applying best practices such as tailoring adaptive strategies to the problem at hand, developing clear triggers for adaptive changes, and ensuring adequate funding for key elements such as monitoring can help ensure the success of adaptive management (Center for Progressive Reform 2011).

Though implementation challenges can be steep, better cooperation between experts in science, law, and policy can help us translate protections on the books to management actions and protections on the ground. Scientists can help educate both the public and elected officials about the importance of biodiversity; ideally, this education can translate into voter and legislative support for adequate budgets for wildlife agencies as well as prosecutors and judges who appreciate the need to not let wildlife criminals off with a slap on the wrist. Lawmakers and agencies drafting regulations can build into the law's flexibility to change management over time—without onerous and time-consuming procedural requirements—in response to changing conditions. Finally, cooperative interdisciplinary efforts such as those of the Conservation Measures Partnership provide tools for developing adaptive management strategies that can succeed in the face of increasingly dynamic threats to wildlife and ecosystems (Conservation Measures Partnership 2021).

5 Integrative Policies and Human Elements

The framework set out above can hopefully make clearer the interdisciplinary nature of managing and protecting biodiversity and the resulting challenges we face in setting meaningful standards, designing effective science processes, and then actually carrying them out. Even with the framework in place, the question remains: "How can we better integrate science, law, and policy to improve the condition of wildlife and ecosystems in the United States?"

In general, laws and policies in the United States dealing with biodiversity have often done a relatively poor job of transparently considering both the science and value choices inherent in choosing goals for the status and security of wildlife and ecosystems. Instead, legislative bodies often set vague thresholds that effectively empower administrative decision-makers to make ad hoc decisions. Moreover, by erroneously seeing standard setting as involving solely scientific determinations, decision-makers often cut out stakeholders and the public from the standard-setting process. Better understanding the interdisciplinary nature of these decisions would contribute toward developing more transparent and inclusive procedures for deciding biodiversity goals, which in turn could improve the resultant standards themselves.

It is important to note, however, that "better" standards may—or may not—be more protective of all species and ecosystems. Even in light of scientific information on the actual and potential values of biodiversity, it is possible that lawmakers and majorities among the public could nonetheless choose to prioritize values other than robust biodiversity protections. On the other hand, a closer look at existing standards may result in changes to the status quo that would favor strong conservation outcomes. For example, a 2020 study found that 130 recovery plans prepared by FWS for species listed as threatened or endangered under the ESA set goals identifying these species as "recovered" at levels that were below the number of individuals or populations than when the species were first listed, with the agency providing no explanation for these outcomes (Li et al. 2020). If most people recognized that setting these recovery thresholds involves value choices as well as science, it is likely that more interests—and perhaps even the public generally—would raise serious questions about whether FWS' vision of successful restoration outcomes for these species is consistent with the high value that Congress placed on species conservation in the ESA.

Looking forward at the standards challenge through a lens that better integrates science and law, difficult and important decisions loom. For example, ecologists have in recent years learned a great deal about the importance of so-called keystone species, those that play an especially crucial role in a given ecosystem (Ripple et al. 2016); the increase in ecological function in the Yellowstone ecosystem after wolf reintroduction provides a good example of such a species (Ripple et al. 2014). However, most standards in biodiversity management and conservation laws do not give keystone species any increased protection or emphasis. Should they? Additionally, as human alterations to natural systems become increasingly pervasive, direct human intervention in species life cycles is becoming increasingly important for conservation. We transport migrating salmon in barges and trucks, use machines to oxygenate rivers to provide for fish survival, and babysit reintroduced condors in order to recapture them and cleanse their blood when they show signs of all-too-common lead poisoning. Can species that may have to rely on such measures in perpetuity be considered "recovered" and removed from endangered species lists? Finally, given the overwhelming changes wrought by climate change and society's limited resources, should the United States now begin to consider biodiversity triage as some countries are beginning to do, i.e., focus on protecting and restoring the most "save-able" species and ecosystems while letting others slide into oblivion? While such questions are mind-boggling to contemplate, one thing should be clear: science alone cannot provide the answers.

A thoughtful mix of science, law, and policy can also improve the science process. For example, Congress in 2023 amended the National Environmental Policy Act (NEPA), often called the United States's "national charter" for environmental protection, to explicitly require federal agencies to ensure the "scientific integrity of the discussion and analysis in an environmental document" and "make use of reliable data and resources" in carrying out the law (43 U.S.C. 4332). All federal agencies, including those primarily responsible for land management and wildlife protection, must consider how to respond to this legal mandate to ensure a reliable and effective science process. Actions such as developing well-thought-out policies to determine what data are reliable, as well as crafting more standardized scientific tools ranging from population modeling to peer review requirements, could constitute steps in this direction and contribute to the better management and protection of biological resources.

Scientists of course are people, so interdisciplinarity means that we also must not overlook the human element of the science process. Questions involving habitat and species conservation can often have significant economic and political ramifications, so particularly, scientists in public agencies unfortunately often come under pressure to alter their technical findings to suit a particular outcome or face on-the-job retaliation for results that may not fit a desired agency narrative. For example, surveys commonly find that scientists who work for FWS experience political interference in their work or suffer some sort of retaliation due to their technical findings (Center for Science and Democracy 2018). Therefore, an effective science process also involves creating robust internal agency policies to discourage inappropriate pressures on science professionals, as well as adopting and actually implementing meaningful legal provisions to protect whistleblowers. On the other end of the spectrum, sometimes human failings catch up with scientists as well, leading to unethical research practices and professional activities driven by dollars rather than data. Yet despite the prevalence of rhetoric about scientific integrity, the ethical guidelines of many universities and professional societies are vague and unevenly enforced. Better regulation of science itself would thus also improve the science process.

Finally, a fuller implementation of measures to manage and protect biodiversity connects directly to choices made outside the realm of science. Importantly, budgets that support a great deal of biological and ecological research, as well as pay for on-the-ground conservation measures and the personnel who carry them out, are determined by elected executive branch officials and legislators. These same elected leaders also determine government enforcement priorities and appoint judges who will referee disputes about protecting wildlife and habitat. And while the polarized political atmosphere prevailing in Washington D.C. in much of the twenty-first century has generally prevented significant changes in federal law itself, state and even local legislative bodies shape the laws and ordinances that have enormous consequences for the future of biodiversity, particularly on private lands. As a result, the importance we accord to protecting wildlife and habitat is virtually always on the ballot, a fact that many people often overlook.

These undeniable connections between science, management and conservation, and politics raise questions that have enormous implications for efforts to improve the protection and management of biodiversity, which essentially boil down to this: What role should scientists play in politics and advocacy? This issue typically generates strong feelings, with some people arguing that the objectivity idealized by science demands that its practitioners refrain from taking political stands or attempting to influence specific policy decisions (Wilhere 2012). On the other hand, some argue that scientists should not have to put aside their rights as citizens to express their opinions, while others assert that scientists should play a more prominent role in at least *informing* policymakers about scientific issues in order to assist elected officials in making the best choices possible (Carroll et al. 2012).

A better understanding of the roles of science, law, and policy in protecting and managing biodiversity can hopefully help remove some of the vitriol from the debate about scientists' proper roles in policy and politics, as well as remove any stigma from scientists who choose to be active in these areas. For example, the question of whether we should adopt special protections for a species to prevent its extinction involves both scientific and policy elements. Scientists must use their expertise to assess the species' biological risk of extinction. Society then must make a value choice of whether the species' current risk is acceptable—in which case, it does not need special protections—or whether the species faces an unacceptable level of risk and thus should receive such legal benefits. If we have reliable science process procedures in place, there should be no reason that a scientist's policy views about the acceptability of a given risk should affect the reliability of her technical findings about the magnitude of the risk itself, particularly given an understanding of the very different character of these two issues. When the public—as well as the law itself—conflates the distinct science and policy components of standards decisions, it becomes easier to (erroneously) question the integrity of scientists who express views on policies and politics. We therefore need to both improve our level of sophistication in thinking about science and law and invite greater participation by scientists in making challenging and important policy calls—with the understanding that these scientists, like other participants in making policy choices—are expressing a position about values and not some sort of hard-and-fast technical "answer." As such, scientists can contribute to the momentous decisions about the future of biodiversity that the United States and the globe now face.

6 Conclusion

Science has enabled us to do amazing things. We can map the genetic makeup of species and virtually attend conferences with colleagues on the other side of the world. We can even ask artificial intelligence to do everything, from composing sonnets about our friends to building better models to predict wildlife population trends. But we must not forget that there is a lot that science *cannot* do. It cannot provide technical answers to questions such as exactly how much of a species' genetic diversity we should save or whether we should have wolf populations in all of the species' former range; these determinations require us to make value-based choices informed—but not determined—by our technical knowledge. Science also cannot make us connect and communicate with experts in other disciplines despite the many high-tech tools we have at our disposal to do so, and human nature often lulls us into talking just to familiar faces and attending professional conferences where we feel most comfortable.

However, to improve the management and protection of wildlife and ecosystems, the United States—and everywhere else as well—must also better understand the relationships between law, science, and policy and better integrate these disciplines in real-world decision-making. Particularly in a regulatory and management context, the standards/science process/implementation framework can hopefully facilitate such integration. In the end, however, people will a the difference. How much effort we make to work across disciplinary boundaries, develop trustworthy science processes, foster transparency, welcome broad participation in decision-making, and vote for officials who will prioritize support for science and sound stewardship of wildlife and ecosystems will determine the condition of the biosphere that we pass along to future generations.

References

Association of State Fish and Wildlife Agencies, State Wildlife Action Plans: Blueprints for Conserving Our Nation's Fish and Wildlife, available at https://www.fishwildlife.org/afwa-informs/state-wildlife-action-plans

Beier P, Hansen L, Helbrecht L et al (2017) A how-to guide for coproduction of actionable science. Conserv Lett 10:288–296

Boebert L (2022) Rep. Lauren Boebert introduces the Trust the Science Act to delist gray wolves from the Endangered Species Act, available at https://boebert.house.gov/media/press-releases/rep-lauren-boebert-introduces-trust-science-act-remove-gray-wolf-endangered

Carroll C et al (2010) Geography and recovery under the Endangered Species Act. Conserv Biol 24(2):395–403

Carroll C et al (2012) Scientific integrity in recovery planning and risk assessment. Conserv Biol 26(4):743–745

Center for Progressive Reform (2011) Making good use of adaptive management, available at <http://progressivereform.net/articles/Adaptive_Management_1104.pdf>

Center for Science and Democracy (2018) Surveying the U.S. Fish and Wildlife Service, available at <https://www.ucsusa.org/sites/default/files/2019-09/science-under-trump-fws.pdf>

Congressional Research Service (2013) Administrative Appeals in the Bureau of Land Management and the Forest Service, available at https://nationalaglawcenter.org/wp-content/uploads/assets/crs/R40131.pdf

Conservation Measures Partnership (2021) Conservation Measures Partnership Charter Declaration, available at <https://drive.google.com/file/d/1Gs4e8aCVWertz7GSuik_C-3Y7xqB6DG_/view>

Doremus H (1997) Listing decisions under the Endangered Species Act: why better science isn't always better policy. Wash Univ Law Q 75:1029–1153

Easter-Pilcher A (1996) Implementing the Endangered Species Act. BioScience 46:355–363

Fish and Wildlife Service (2012) 12 Month Finding on a Petition to List the Sonoran Desert Area Bald Eagle as Threatened or Endangered 77 Fed. Reg. 25792

Fish and Wildlife Service and National Marine Fisheries Service (1994) Notice of Interagency Cooperative Policy for Peer Review in Endangered Species Act Activities 59 Fed. Reg. 34270

Government Accountability Office (2015) Information Quality Act: Actions Needed to improve Transparency and Reporting of Correction Requests, GAO-16-110 (available at www.gao.gov/assets/gao-16-110.pdf)

Greenwald N (2016) Shortchanged: Funding Needed to Save America's Most Endangered Species, Center for Biological Diversity report available at www.biologicaldiversity.org/programs/biodiversity/pdfs/Shortchanged.pdf

Houck O (2003) Tales from a troubled marriage: science and law in environmental policy. Science 302(5652):1926–1929

IUCN (2022) Guidelines for Using the IUCN Redlist Categories and Criteria, available at http://cmsdocs.s3.amazonaws.com/RedListGuidelines.pdf

Jacobson C et al (2010) A conservation institution for the 21st century: implications for state wildlife agencies. Wildl Manag 74(2):203–209

Kahn B (2020) Trump has listed the fewest endangered species of any president ever, Gizmodo, available at https://gizmodo.com/trump-has-listed-the-fewest-endangered-species-of-any-p-1845854952

Li Y, Malcom J, Che-Castaldo J et al (2020) Recovery plans need better science to support decisions that allow species to decline in abundance but be recovered, available at <https://www.biorxiv.org/content/10.1101/2020.02.27.966101v1.full>

Malcom J, Li Y (2015) Data contradict common perceptions about a controversial provision of the Endangered Species Act, available at https://www.pnas.org/doi/10.1073/pnas.1516938112

Ripple WJ, Estes JA, Beschta RL et al (2014) Status and ecological effects of the world's largest carnivores. Science (1979) 343. https://doi.org/10.1126/science.1241484

Ripple WJ, Estes JA, Schmitz OJ et al (2016) What is a trophic cascade? Trends Ecol Evol 31:842–849. https://doi.org/10.1016/j.tree.2016.08.010
Rohlf D (1991) Six reasons the endangered species act doesn't work – and what to do about it. Conserv Biol 5:273–282
Wilhere GF (2012) Inadvertent advocacy. Conserv Biol 26:39–46

Biosafety Regulation in China: Progress and Challenges

Ancui Liu

Abstract The Convention on Biological Diversity (CBD) and its protocols require their parties to ensure the safe transfer, handling, and use of genetically modified organisms (GMOs) that may have an adverse effect on the conservation and sustainable use of biodiversity. Partially due to the determination to fulfil its international obligations, China has adopted several laws, regulations, and administrative measures to regulate the safe use of GMOs. This chapter will analyse to what extent the Biosecurity Law, which went into effect in April 2021, will affect the legal framework on GMOs and the institutional arrangements and concrete measures. Furthermore, this chapter will discuss challenges facing China in relation to the application of the precautionary principle and public involvement, capacity building, risk management, and liability and redress rules. The chapter will end with a brief discussion on how the current biosafety regulation in China will be harmonised with the Biosecurity Law on the one hand and be improved to be fully consistent with the CBD and its protocol on the other hand.

1 Introduction

As stated by a spokesperson for the Legislative Affairs Commission of the Standing Committee of the National People's Congress (NPC) in October 2022, China has established a comprehensive legal framework for environmental protection (Xi 2022). This legal framework consists of the Environmental Protection Law (EPL), a central and fundamental piece of environmental legislation, and several specialised laws covering various environmental protection sectors, such as pollution prevention, nature conservation, and the management of geographical areas (Xi 2022; Lyu 2023a, b). While the Chinese environmental legal framework grows broader, an immediate question is how to ensure its coherence and coordination. Practical solutions include developing new legislation for environmental issues not

A. Liu (✉)
Nankai University, Tianjin, China
e-mail: liuancui@nankai.edu.cn

G. Antonelli et al. (eds.), *Biodiversity Laws, Policies and Science in Europe, the United States and China*, https://doi.org/10.1007/978-3-031-56218-1_13

yet covered by the legal framework, amending already existing pieces of environmental legislation, and even enacting an environmental code (Lyu 2023). Biodiversity law is an integral part of the above-mentioned legal framework and, to be specific, the nature conservation law. Current laws and regulations on biodiversity are scattered and, in some cases, inconsistent. Following the idea of systematically regulating biodiversity, Qin recommends enacting a biodiversity law that provides for overarching objectives, principles, and measures for the conservation and sustainable use of biodiversity and further supplements this biodiversity law with laws and regulations that address specific biodiversity-related topics (Qin 2022; similar discussions see Yu and Hu 2022). Among the specific laws and regulations on biodiversity is the biosecurity/biosafety law.

The Biosecurity Law (BL) is a recent addition to the biosecurity/biosafety legal system. It was adopted in 2020 and became effective on 15 April 2021. The systematic lawmaking approach regarding environmental protection and biodiversity discussed above may provide some insight into the analysis of the BL. The BL could be positioned and examined under different legal frameworks, such as an environmental law framework, a biodiversity legal system, or a national security law framework. For instance, viewed from the biodiversity law perspective, the BL regulates the development and use of biotechnology (including genetically modified organisms (GMOs)), the invasion of alien species, and genetic resources (Yu and Hu 2022), and thus, an effective implementation of the BL would contribute to the perfection of the biodiversity law. An often-discussed question is how to coordinate the rules in the BL with a more systematic legal system on biodiversity.

The research, development, and commercialisation of GMOs are accompanied by concerns that they may have adverse effects on the environment and human health (Grumet et al. 2011; Liu 2022). International law has been implemented to address biosafety concerns on GMOs. China is parties to the Convention on Biological Diversity (CBD), the Cartagena Protocol on Biosafety (CPB), and the Nagoya-Kuala Lumpur Supplementary Protocol on Liability and Redress to the Cartagena Protocol on Biosafety (the Supplementary Protocol) and thus bears international obligations to ensure the conservation and sustainable use of biodiversity and human health. As GMOs were developed and commercialised, many nations adopted rules to, on the one hand, control risks thereof and, on the other hand, promote technological development. The Chinese government also adopted some regulations and measures to specifically address biosafety issues, with the Regulation on the Administration of the Safety of Agricultural Genetically Modified Organisms (the 2001 Regulation) being the central one. China has enacted laws and regulations applicable to GMOs since the 1990s. The 2001 Regulation was adopted by the State Council in 2001 and later revised in 2011 and 2017. The recently adopted BL, on the one hand, is a new vehicle for China to implement the international law requirements and, on the other hand, provides an opportunity for legislators to systematically update GMO-related laws and regulations. It is perhaps too early to evaluate the effects of the BL as a whole. However, it is meaningful to discuss how the BL would contribute to the better regulation of GMOs in China. It is also urgent and meaningful to discuss this issue against the backdrop of the demand to implement effectively the Kunming-Montreal Global Biodiversity Framework (GBF).

This chapter is structured as follows. Section 2 explains three interrelated terms, i.e. biosafety, biosecurity, and biodiversity. Their links will be clarified by exploring the history of GMO regulation in China and their connections among different types of legal frameworks. Section 3 introduces the key requirements under the CBD and its protocols and then discusses the challenges that China's GMO regulation needs to respond to. Following the discussion on international obligations and domestic regulation on GMOs in Sect. 3, Sect. 4 first explains the key aspects of the BL and then analyses changes caused by the BL to the GMO regulation in China. This section also explores the remaining challenges even after the BL has been enacted regarding the GMO regulation. Section 5 concludes.

2 Biosafety, Biosecurity, and Biodiversity

The Chinese term "shegnwu anquan" can be translated as both "biosafety" and "biosecurity". The piece of legislation adopted by the Standing Committee of the NPC in 2020 is officially translated as "the Biosecurity Law" while being translated as "the Biosafety Law" in some publications (Han 2021). Clarification of the two terms is crucial in understanding the BL adopted in 2020 (Cao 2021). A brief description of how they are understood in the literature might help elaborate on their distinctions. Traditionally, environmental law literature discusses biosafety issues in view of adverse effects that may be caused by modern biotechnology; a typical example is GMOs (Redick 2003; Abdollahi et al. 2011; Yu and Wang 2012; Segger et al. 2013; Espinosa 2014; Perron-Welch 2017). This actually follows the understanding of the CBD, which defines the rules on biotechnology as measures that lead to biosafety (Mackenzie et al. 2003). A literature review on biosafety/biosecurity law carried out by Mo shows that before the BL was enacted in 2020, a great deal of literature specifically discussed GMO regulation (Mo 2020).

The literature occasionally defines a broader biosafety law as addressing not only the adverse effects related to GMOs but also those related to "biological technology, alien species invasion, extinction of species and the health of humans and animals, etc." (Nie 2005). Similar ways to differentiate between biosafety in a narrow sense and a broad sense are also found in other publications (Yu 2020; Cao 2021; Wei 2022). Besides drawing the distinction between different sizes of "biosafety", Cao deems that they altogether refer to the protection of humans, animals, plants, and the environment from biological hazards or potential risks (Cao 2021). Zhou and Song do not specifically differentiate biosafety (in a narrow sense or in a broad sense) and biosecurity. Instead, they describe biosafety/biosecurity as "a nation's ability to respond effectively to biological threats and related factors" (Zhou et al. 2019). The biological threats discussed in this sense include the "prevention and control of major emerging infectious diseases, defensive action against biological weapon attacks, the prevention of bioterrorism attacks, the prevention of biotechnology abuse, the protection of laboratory biosafety, the protection of special biological resources, and the prevention of invasion by alien organisms" (Zhou et al. 2019). The BL regulates biosafety in a broad sense, and the term biosecurity is hence used. As shown by article 2 of the BL, biosecurity is defined as a status where "the state effectively prevents and responds to the threat of dangerous biological agents and related factors, biotechnology can develop steadily and healthily, neither the lives and health of the people nor the ecosystem is relatively in danger or under threat, and there is capability in the biological field to maintain national security and sustainable development".

Cao further explains the differences between "biosafety" and "biosecurity" by examining sources of risks: biosafety relates to "protection from the risks and hazards caused inadvertently by working with microorganisms and toxins"; biosecurity relates to "protection from the hazards that may arise in connection with deliberate theft, misuse, or diversion of biotechnology" (Cao 2021). Qin also makes this distinction and further emphasises that the scope of biosafety/biosecurity is dynamic as new types of biological risks may emerge in the future (Qin 2020a, b). The way biosecurity issues are categorised in the BL is consistent with the observation that the scope of biosafety/biosecurity is dynamic. Article 2 of the BL covers seven types of biosecurity issues (i.e., preventing and controlling a major new or sudden outbreak of an infectious disease or an epidemic in animals or plants; researching, developing, and applying biotechnology; biosecurity management of pathogenic microbe laboratories; biosecurity management of human genetic resources and biological resources; preventing the invasion of alien species and protecting biodiversity; responding to antimicrobial resistance; and preventing biological terrorist attacks and defending against biological weapon threats) plus one miscellaneous provision (other biosecurity-related activities). The miscellaneous provision leaves room for interpreting more biosecurity risks to be covered by the BL (Wei 2022).

For the convenience of discussion, despite different definitions of biosafety and biosecurity in the literature, this chapter uses "biosafety" to refer to the status of protection from risks caused by GMOs and "biosecurity" in relation to biological risks covered by the BL. Furthermore, either biosecurity law or biosafety law has close connections with biodiversity law. The BL's link to biodiversity law can be observed from the environmental law system, its objectives, and key measures. First, the BL is often mentioned in the environmental law system in China as a key piece of legislation that deals with nature conservation and biodiversity protection (Wang and You 2021; Lyu 2022; Yue 2022; Lyu 2023). Measures on alien species and biotechnology directly contribute to the protection of biodiversity and the environment (Qiu and Hu 2021). Second, article 1 of the BL defines the protection of the environment as one of its objectives. Moreover, article 34 and article 60 of the same law define the preservation of biodiversity as objectives of controlling modern biotechnology and alien species, respectively. Third, chapter 2 of the BL has a series of risk assessment and risk management measures, and one of the considerations is to examine whether certain activities will cause adverse effects on the environment and biodiversity.

The biosafety law relates closely to biodiversity law, partially due to the incorporation of biosafety issues into the agenda of the CBD (Segger et al. 2013). The literature often suggests that biodiversity protection be considered when designing and implementing national biosafety laws (Yan and Yan 2012). It is observed that biosafety is one of the well-explored research areas among biodiversity topics but still demands research that delves deeply into it (Morgera 2017). Meanwhile, it deserves noting that in addition to international biodiversity law, international laws on food safety, trade, and plant protection are also relevant (Mampuys and Brom 2015).

3 Implementation of International Biosafety Law in China: Requirements and Barriers

The GBF, as adopted in December 2022, has new targets and requirements regarding biosafety issues and hence further highlights the necessity to continue studying the ways to achieve biosafety goals in China. It is thus necessary to review how China has fulfilled its obligations regarding GMO regulation or, in other words, how China will contribute to the effective implementation of the goals and targets set by the GBF in relation to biosafety. The first step is to summarise what international biosafety law requirements are. This section will then continue describing Chinese laws and regulations on GMOs and analysing to what extent China has implemented international obligations. Lastly, this section will explain current challenges in China to properly regulate GMOs. All these will provide a basis for discussing the questions in Sect. 4 of the chapter.

3.1 Biosafety Requirements in CBD and Its Protocols

Under the umbrella treaty, the CBD, two of the three protocols address biosafety issues. Article 19.3 of the CBD requires its parties to consider making a protocol setting out appropriate measures "in the field of the safe transfer, handling and use of any living modified organism resulting from biotechnology that may have adverse effect on the conservation and sustainable use of biological diversity". This task was done in 2000 when the CPB was adopted. As its name shows, the CPB addresses exclusively biosafety issues. Later in 2010, another protocol, the Supplementary Protocol, was adopted to elaborate on liability rules in relation to biosafety. In addition, article 8(g) and article 19 of the CBD provide for biosafety measures in a general and abstract way.

The CPB aims to ensure to following:

> an adequate level of protection in the field of the safe transfer, handling and use of living modified organisms resulting from modern biotechnology that may have adverse effects on

> the conservation and sustainable use of biological diversity, taking also into account risks to human health, and specifically focusing on transboundary movements. (Article 1 CPB)

The CPB follows a precautionary approach and introduces several biosafety measures. The precautionary approach in the CPB has its root in principle 15 of the Rio Declaration, which requires that the lack of scientific certainty regarding the adverse effects of GMOs shall not prevent the parties of the CPB from taking measures to prevent or avoid the potential adverse effects (article 10.6 and article 11.8 of the CPB). Key biosafety measures as designed by the CPB include the advance informed agreement procedure, labelling and documentation requirements, and public involvement measures (Perron-Welch 2017; Liu 2022). Supporting measures include information sharing, establishing biosafety clearing houses, capacity building, monitoring and reporting, and financial mechanisms. Liability rules in the CPB were not detailed until the Supplementary Protocol was adopted in 2010.

The GBF is an integral part of the CBD and was adopted in Decision 15/4 of the CBD COP 15. It highlights the importance of effectively implementing the CBD and its protocols. Long-term and mid-term targets both cover biosafety aspects. Among 23 action-oriented global targets for urgent action over the decade to 2030 is target 17:

> Establish, strengthen capacity for, and implement in all countries in biosafety measures as set out in Article 8(g) of the Convention on Biological Diversity and measures for the handling of biotechnology and distribution of its benefits as set out in Article 19 of the Convention.

An effective implementation of the CBD and its protocols largely relies on national implementation. The GBF, the Implementation Plan, and the Capacity-Building Action Plan further elaborated on the relevant goals and criteria. The Implementation Plan for the Cartagena Protocol on Biosafety (CP-10/3, Implementation Plan) and the Capacity-building Action Plan for the Cartagena Protocol on Biosafety and the Nagoya-Kuala Lumpur Supplementary Protocol on Liability and Redress (CP-10/4, Capacity-Building Action Plan) were adopted in COP-MOP 10 in 2022. The Implementation Plan breaks down the requirements in the CPB into 14 goals. For instance, the first goal is that parties of the CPB have in place functional national biosafety frameworks. For each of the goals, the Implementation Plan offers detailed objectives, indicators, and outcomes so that the implementation of parties can be quantified and evaluated. The Capacity-Building Action Plan takes a similar approach to the Implementation Plan to facilitate the improvement of the capacities of the parties to the CPB to implement the CPB and to achieve goals and targets set out in the GBF.

3.2 *China's Implementation of International Obligations*

China has actively participated in the implementation of the CBD and its protocols (Liu 2022). China participated in capacity-building projects on the promotion of national regulatory frameworks and submitted four national reports on the implementation of the CPB. According to the latest report, the 2019 Chinese national report, national measures on the implementation of the CPB have been fully in place; moreover, China has integrated biosafety into China's biodiversity strategy by adopting the China National Biodiversity Conservation Strategy and Action Plan (2011–2030) (China Biodiversity Strategy). The Chinese Biodiversity Strategy describes the *status quo* and challenges regarding biodiversity in China and elaborates on the objectives, priorities, targets, and supporting measures in relation to biodiversity conservation in China. One of the priorities focuses on GMO biosafety, which consists of improving risk assessments of GMOs, detection and monitoring of risks that may be caused by GMOs, and participating in negotiations on international biosafety rules.

Again, according to the 2019 national report, the National Biosafety Administration Office in the Ministry of Ecology and Environment (MEE) coordinates environmental management in relation to biotechnology; MEE's Department of International Cooperation works as the focal point of the CPB in China and is responsible for international cooperation and exchanges in the field of biosafety; the Office of Agricultural GMO Safety Management within the Ministry of Agriculture and Rural Affairs (MARA) is designated as the key agency in supervising and managing the safety of agricultural GMOs according to the 2001 Regulation; the Biosafety Management Office established by the National Forestry and Grassland Administration is responsible for managing the safety of forest GMOs; and the General Administration of Customs (GAC) is responsible for the inspection and quarantine management of genetically modified products entering and exiting the territory.

The enactment of the BL is a very recent complement to the implementing activities of China. Besides the BL and the 2001 Regulation, the legal framework on GMOs in China consists of several relevant pieces of legislation and administrative measures (for a summary of GMO laws and regulations, see Wang 2020). For instance, the EPL regulates biosafety issues by stipulating in its article 30.2 that "in the introduction of alien species and the research, development, and utilisation of biotechnologies, measures shall be adopted to prevent any damage to biodiversity". Principal measures applicable to GMOs include risk assessment, risk management, public involvement, labelling, and liability rules. Special rules are made to fulfil requirements in the CPB regarding the import and export of GMOs.

A hidden linkage between biosafety law and biosecurity law in China can be found by reviewing the history of the enactment of the BL. Since the enactment of the 2001 Regulation, the literature has frequently made recommendations to improve Chinese GMO laws and regulations. A key question is how to develop proper laws and regulations on GMOs so that risks and damages caused by GMOs can be well addressed. Typical recommendations include adopting laws at the NPC level and designing better risk assessment and risk management rules (Yu and Wang 2012; Monien and Cai 2018). The EPL, in its article 30.2, is specifically about biotechnology regulation, and its aim is to prevent adverse effects on biodiversity. It is general and focuses only on biodiversity aspects. These two limitations hinder the EPL from being a leading NPC-level law for GMO regulation.

Some authors specifically suggest that NPC or its standing committee enact a biosecurity law (Yu 2009; Xiang 2012; Hu 2014; Liu 2016; Chang 2020; Mo 2020). Some authors suggest making specific laws on GMOs (Xu et al. 2007; Yan and Yan 2012; Wang 2016). Legislators had, to some extent, responded to the academic recommendations mentioned above by proposing a draft biosafety law. The State Environmental Protection Administration (now the MEE) started considering adopting a GMO biosafety law in 2005 (Bian and Yu 2006; Xiang 2012; Cao 2021). However, the attempt was not a success (Chen 2015) until the BL was adopted in 2020 (Liu and Zhou 2022). Some of the key drivers for China adopting the BL are a gene-editing scandal conducted by Jiankui He and the outbreak of COVID-19 (Song and Joly 2021; Wang et al. 2021; Liu 2023). The enactment of the BL, to some extent, ended the stagnation regarding the enactment of the biosafety law and, thus, is a step forward for improving biosafety regulation in China.

3.3 Challenges in Implementing the CBD and Its Protocols

The literature has constantly focused on the better implementation of the CPB and, in a broader sense, on how to improve biosecurity regulation in China. In addition to calling for comprehensive and systematic laws on biosafety or biosecurity, there are other concerns. These concerns are still felt and emphasised even after the BL has been enacted (Shi and Zhao 2023).

First, laws and regulations are not systematic. Although these laws and regulations have been revised several times, there are still problems in this system. For instance, the 2001 Regulation was revised in 2011 and 2017; the Administrative Measures on the Safety Assessment of Agricultural GMOs adopted by MARA was revised in 2004, 2016, 2017, and 2022. Procedures regarding risk assessment kept being improved. However, critics remain. After the enactment of the BL, the 2001 Regulation still plays a leading role in GMO regulation in China. However, how to make them consistent is challenging. Moreover, the 2001 Regulation is exclusively about the safety management of agricultural GMOs; this means other types of GMOs and environmental aspects of agricultural GMOs are not fully examined. Another challenge hence is how to construct a wholesome GMO legal system on the basis of the BL (Shi and Zhao 2023). On the one hand, some measures, such as labelling and safety assessment, are abstract and general (Shi and Zhao 2023), and liability rules are not effective and systematic (Liu 2016; Shi and Zhao 2023). On the other hand, some key measures and mechanisms, for instance post-authorisation measures, are not in place, and emergency responding measures are still lacking (Shi and Zhao 2023).

Second, the problem of coordination of administrative authorities still exists. If seen from the perspective of the implementation of the CPB, the MEE bears the major responsibilities in implementing the CPB. Therefore, some authors suggest that the MEE be the proper one to coordinate biosafety management in relation to GMOs (Wang 2006; Lu and Xiao 2009; Zhang and Liu 2014). As explained in Sect.

3.2 of this chapter, other governing agencies, such as MARA and GAC, are also involved in biosafety management. It can be anticipated that different governing agencies have their own aims and priorities, and thus there might be conflicting views. To solve this problem, article 5 of the 2001 Regulation sets an inter-ministerial joint conference to coordinate different views. However, some research has shown that the coordination effects are not good (Liu 2016). One reason might be that the position of the 2001 Regulation in the hierarchy of GMO-related legislation is not high enough to persuade all ministries to consider fully the biosafety issues.

Third, the CPB's requirements are not clearly shown in the Chinese legal framework on GMOs. For instance, the precautionary principle and environmental concerns are not fully addressed. Although article 3.2 of the 2001 Regulation reflected the idea of the precautionary principle, the precautionary principle is not clearly stated. Moreover, risk assessment and management measures should be updated to reflect the precautionary measures as required by the CPB (Liu 2016). Article 30.2 of the EPL provides an environmental law basis for preventing or avoiding biosafety risks. However, as the provision states, it is merely about biodiversity protection, ignoring wider concerns about environmental protection (Wang 2016). Another example is socio-economic considerations as required by the CPB. According to the 2019 Chinese national report on the implementation of the CPB, there are no specific approaches or requirements that facilitate how socio-economic considerations should be taken into account in GMO-related decision-making.

Fourth, the CPB has requirements regarding public involvement by explicitly stating them in article 23 and also by implicitly providing for requirements on precautionary measures, labelling, and socio-economic considerations (Zhao 2021). Although public involvement principles and measures under the EPL can be applied, the fact that there are no specific public involvement requirements in GMO-related laws and regulations affects the public's access to information and participation in decision-making regarding GMOs (Wang 2020). Suggestions to ensure public access to GMO-related information, participating in the public's rights in GMO decision-making, and ensuring judicial remedies have been made (Zhao 2021), and enhancing public involvement in risk assessment and risk management is also recommended (Liu 2016).

4 Biosecurity Law and GMO Regulation: Contribution and Remaining Challenges

Since there are still challenges faced by China in regulating GMOs and the BL adds some rules to the legal framework on GMOs, it is necessary to analyse how the BL has contributed to solving these problems; furthermore, the remaining challenges after the BL is considered. Before analysing these two aspects, this section will first describe the key measures that are applicable to GMOs in the BL.

4.1 Structure and Key Measures of the Biosecurity Law

The BL has ten chapters with 88 provisions. Chapter 1 and chapter 2 are respectively about general provisions and biosecurity risk prevention and control systems. Chapters 3–7 contain rules on concrete biosecurity risks; chapter 4 is about research, development, and the application of biotechnology, which is relevant to GMO biosafety issues. As for GMO biosafety issues, the BL conspicuously does not give detailed and specific rules, perhaps to avoid conflicts with currently existing laws and regulations on GMOs (Cao 2021). Chapter 8 and chapter 9 are about capacity building and liability rules, respectively. Chapter 10 has supplemental provisions. When focusing specifically on GMO regulation, special attention should be paid to chapters 1, 2, 8, and 9.

Article 1 of the BL provides for the objectives:

> This Law is enacted for the purposes of maintaining national security, preventing and responding to biosecurity risks, safeguarding the lives and health of the people, protecting biological resources and the ecology and environment, promoting the sound development of biotechnology, boosting the construction of a community with a shared future for mankind, and achieving the harmonious coexistence of man and nature.

It should be noted that the BL has more holistic and macro aims than merely focusing on biodiversity protection: maintaining national security, balancing risk prevention and biotechnological development, and achieving the harmonious coexistence of man and nature (Chen and Yang 2022; Wu 2022; Xiao 2022). The National Security Law as enacted in 2015 is a core piece of legislation that governs traditional and non-traditional security issues. Specifically, biosecurity risks belong to non-traditional security issues (Wei 2022). The BL is adopted under the "holistic view of national security" (You 2020; Cao 2021; Qiu and Hu 2021) and is designed as a fundamental national biosecurity law and a policy-oriented law (Qin 2020; Han 2021; Ma and Tian 2022; Lyu 2023). Within the national security law system, it is a specialised law on biosecurity risks, one of the non-traditional security risks, while if positioned in the biosecurity law system, the BL is the very fundamental one under which are laws and regulations that govern concrete types of biosecurity risks (Qin 2020).

The BL has established the monitoring and early warning system (article 14), risk investigation and assessment system (article 15), review system (article 20), and emergency response measures (article 21). These form a whole process and life-cycle system (Wei 2022). Other supporting measures include information sharing and release system (articles 16–17), category and list system (article 18), standards system (article 19), and capacity-building measures (articles 66–71). A whole and comprehensive liability mechanism is also established (Wei 2022).

4.2 Contribution and Remaining Challenges

The BL stresses the harmonious relationship between human activities and nature (Wei 2022). This point is consistent with the aims of the CPB and environmental protection objectives. Enacting the BL is also an example of mainstreaming biodiversity into national laws and policies (Liu 2021). Meanwhile, by being incorporated into the BL, the GMO biosafety regulation becomes a part of biosecurity regulation and an even broader national security system (Shi and Zhao 2023). In this vein, the guiding principles for biosecurity governance, the principles for balancing security and development, and the general provisions of chapter 2 of the BL must apply to GMO regulation. Consequently, future adjustments to the legal framework on GMOs and coordination between GMO laws with other relevant laws, such as the EPL, food safety law, and agriculture law, all need to take the above-mentioned factors into account.

The precautionary principle is deemed to be essential for formulating an effective GMO regulation. It is also required by the CPB. However, Chinese laws and regulations on GMOs did not explicitly stipulate it until it was formulated as one of the guiding principles of the BL (article 3, the BL). This principle is further concretised by measures such as the monitoring and early-warning system on biosecurity risks (Lan and Qin 2021; Qin 2021). The incorporation of the precautionary principle in the BL is part of China's efforts to implement the precautionary approach as required by the CPB.

The institutional arrangements in the BL are made to coordinate multiple administrative authorities. A central leading group on national security is responsible for major decision-making, drafting and implementing biosecurity strategies and policies, planning and coordinating major biosecurity matters and work, and establishing the Coordination Mechanism for National Biosecurity (article 10, the BL). The Coordination Mechanism is established to recognise and analyse biosecurity risks and coordinate and supervise national biosecurity-related work (article 11, the BL). Biosecurity risks related to GMOs will also be supervised and coordinated under the central leading group and the Coordination Mechanism.

The BL's risk surveillance, management, and communication systems are applicable to all types of biosecurity risks, including biosafety risks caused by GMOs. In this vein, if the risk control measures in current laws and regulations on GMOs are not consistent with the former ones, they need to be revised. Recent revisions to GMO regulations are such examples. The Administrative Measures on the Safety Assessment of Agricultural GMOs was revised in January 2022, making the authorisation procedure simpler (Xiao and Kerr 2022). The enactment of the BL ensures that gene editing regarding animals and plants is regulated to prevent potential risks (Jiang 2023). Gene editing regarding plants is now managed by the Guide for Biosafety Measurement of Gene Edited Crops, which was adopted by MARA in April 2023 (Xiao and Kerr 2022).

Fulfilling international obligations regarding biosafety and biosecurity is one of the drivers for China to enact the BL (Cao 2021; Han 2021; Qiu and Hu 2021). The

BL in turn facilitates China's implementation of relevant international treaties (Cao 2021; Han 2021). Article 6 of the BL sets out the general requirements for international cooperation, which are also applicable to GMO regulation. To be specific, the BL stipulates that China is to fulfil the international obligations it has concluded or participates in, to support participation in exchanges and cooperation on biological science and technology and in international aid for biosecurity incidents, to participate in the research and drafting of international biosecurity rules, and to promote global biosecurity governance. Furthermore, the BL specifically promotes capacity building regarding biosecurity in China in its chapter 9 (Cao 2021; Qiu and Hu 2021). If fully implemented, international cooperation activities and capacity-building initiatives will also contribute to the effective implementation of the CBD and its protocols and the GBF.

4.3 Remaining Challenges

The provisions of the BL, as analysed in Sect. 4.2 above, have been integral components of the legal framework on GMOs. The enactment of the BL, to a certain extent, responded to the need for biosafety regulation by adding NPC-level laws to the legal framework on GMOs. They provide guidance for addressing biosafety risks from the perspectives of objectives, principles, risk management, and international cooperation. In view of responding to challenges regarding GMO regulation in China, as discussed in Sect. 3.3 of this chapter, this section will continue analysing what still needs to be done to improve the current Chinese laws and regulations on GMOs.

Since the BL aims to achieve multiple objectives other than merely biodiversity protection and environmental protection and is a policy-oriented law, the next step is to enrich the laws and regulations under the umbrella of the BL and to ensure that each of these laws and regulations coordinates with each other (Qin 2020; Ma and Tian 2022; Wei 2022; Yue 2022). Of equal importance is the effective implementation of the BL (Ma 2022). Since the BL mainly provides for abstract and general rules, more elaborated rules are needed (Cao 2021; Ma and Tian 2022). First, the BL mainly consists of seven types of biosecurity issues and is framework legislation for biosecurity; hence, it needs to be supplemented by laws and regulations that specifically address each of the biosecurity risks in the future (Wang and You 2021). Second, the BL needs to be coordinated with other national security laws and regulations (Han 2021; Qiu and Hu 2021) and other more general laws, such as the Wildlife Protection Law (Qiu and Hu 2021). This point is to ensure that the objective of maintaining biosecurity is balanced with other sustainable development goals.

Considering the close connection between laws and regulations on GMOs in China and the BL/biodiversity law, the following question must be addressed: Is it still necessary to adopt a GMO biosafety law? As discussed above, making a GMO biosafety law has been frequently recommended in the literature (Wang 2006; Xu et al. 2007). How to deal with the relationship between laws and regulations on GMOs and the biosecurity law has been carefully considered during the draft of the BL (Mo 2020; Qin 2020). It is observed that such a biosafety law is still needed even after the BL is effective (Shi and Zhao 2023). Once legislators decide to adopt a GMO biosafety law, it should be considered how to coordinate with institutional settings and the key risk management measures as provided for in the BL. Coordination with biodiversity law should also be taken into account (Mo 2020; Tan 2022; Yu and Hu 2022). The GMO biosafety law, especially the 2001 Regulation, should be revised if the rules do not confirm with the principles and measures of the BL (Qin 2020).

The enactment of the BL is an important step towards implementing international biosafety as it provides a legal basis for China to participate in international cooperation regarding biosafety. To implement the CPB more effectively, China needs to seek ways to incorporate international law requirements into the legal framework on GMOs in an explicit way. Detailed rules on public involvement in socio-economic considerations and liability need to be incorporated into the GMO legal system. Moreover, other international treaties than the CBD and its protocols should also be considered so that China can participate in and lead the international biosafety governance.

5 Conclusion

The enactment of the BL is not the end of disputes on GMO regulation but a new start. It partially responds to challenges regarding GMO regulation, and some challenges remain. From an international biosafety perspective, enacting and implementing the BL is also a practice of mainstreaming the requirements of biodiversity protection into national laws (Qin and Liu 2022). Subsequent tasks should include ensuring the effective implementation of the BL, revising current laws and regulations on GMOs to make them consistent with the BL, and constantly participating in international cooperation activities on biosafety and biosecurity governance.

References

Abdollahi M, Ghavamabadi MHR, Shafee MS (2011) A critical introduction to Iran biosafety law. US-China Law Rev 8:401

Bian Y, Yu G (2006) The evolution of Chinese laws on gene modified organisms. China Law (4): 106–108

Cao C (2021) China's evolving biosafety/biosecurity legislations. J Law Biosci 8(1):lsab020–lsab020

Chang J (2020) National biosecurity legal system should be accelerated (in Chinese). Study Times: 001

Chen J (2015) Legal attitudes towards issues about GMOs: how should lawyers think about scientific problems (in Chinese). Leg Res (9):118–128

Chen L, Yang P (2022) Ecological security in the national security system and its legal improvement (in Chinese). J Southwest Univ Polit Sci Law 24(05):98–112

Espinosa J-FE (2014) The international biosafety regime and the world trade system after ten years of the Cartagena Protocol. Eur Energy Environ Law Rev 23(4):127–142

Grumet R, Hancock JF, Maredia KM, Weebadde C (eds) (2011) Environmental safety of genetically engineered crops. Michigan State University Press, East Lansing

Han W (2021) Introduction on biosafety law of the People's Republic of China and linkage thereof with international and domestic regulations. Biotechnol Law Rep 40(2):95–103

Hu T (2014) Principles of making legislation for regulating genetically modified crops and food (in Chinese). J Sci Technol Law (1):114–127

Jiang L (2023) Dilemma and solution of the legal regulation of genome editing in plant (in Chinese). Law Sci (05):125–138

Lan Y, Qin T (2021) Applying the precautionary principle to emerging zoonotic disease: lessons from China's response in environmental law. J Environ Law 34(2):331–342

Liu Q (2016) The international experience of the legislation on agricultural genetically modified organisms biosafety and its lessons to China (in Chinese). World Agric 7:114–120

Liu Z (2021) Situation and implications of the negotiations on the convention on biological diversity (in Chinese). Int Econ Rev (03):155–176+158

Liu A (2022) Regulating genetically modified crops in view of environmental risks: China's implementation of international obligations. Springer

Liu Z (2023) Classification and legal regulation of ethical issues of genome editing (in Chinese). J CUPL (03):126–139

Liu C, Zhou S (2022) Problems and countermeasures in legalization of life and health governance in China (in Chinese). J Sichuan Police College 34(04):1–9

Lu Q, Xiao X (2009) Selection of security policy pattern of Chinese agricultural genetically modified organisms (in Chinese). J Nanjing Forestry Univ (Human Soc Sci Edn) (02):68–78

Lyu Z (2022) On attribute of administrative field legislation of environmental code (in Chinese). Law Rev 40(04):1–14

Lyu Z (2023a) A new journey to Chinese construction of environmental rule of law (in Chinese). Local Legis J 8(01):1–13

Lyu Z (2023b) Ten-year review of the construction of environmental rule of law and prospect of codification of environmental law (in Chinese). J Beijing Univ Aeronaut Astronaut (Soc Sci Edn) 36(01):18–31

Ma F (2022) Building a national security implementation system by rule of law systematically (in Chinese). Theor Explor (01):12–22

Ma F, Tian B (2022) Research on the path of improving the legal system of national security (in Chinese). J Southwest Univ Polit Sci Law 24(04):54–66

Mackenzie R, Burhenne-Guilmin F, Viña AGML, Werksman JD, Ascencio A, Kinderlerer J, Kummer K, Tapper R (2003) An explanatory guide to the Cartagena Protocol on Biosafety. IUCN, Cambridge

Mampuys R, Brom FWA (2015) Ethics of dissent: a plea for restraint in the scientific debate about the safety of GM crops. J Agric Environ Ethics 28(5):903–924

Mo J (2020) Some reflections on speeding up the construction of national biosafety legal system (in Chinese). J Xinjiang Normal Univ (Edn Philos Soc Sci) 41(4):78–93

Monien J, Cai Y (2018) Genetically modified organisms law. In: Hartel I (ed) Handbook of agri-food law in China, Germany, European Union. Springer, pp 517–549

Morgera E (2017) Introduction to volume III: The research challenges of international biodiversity law. In: Razzaque J, Morgera E (eds) Biodiversity and nature protection law, vol 3. Edward Elgar, Cheltenham, pp 1–9

Nie X (2005) International conventions, policies, law and management: a comparative study on the biosafety. China Oceans Law Rev 2005(1):525–551

Perron-Welch F (2017) Biosafety law. In: Razzaque J, Morgera E (eds) Biodiversity and nature protection law, vol 3. Edward Elgar, Cheltenham, pp 226–236
Qin T (2020a) The design and discussions on the biosecurity law (in Chinese). Soc Sci J (3): 134–147
Qin T (2020b) Perfection of legal regulation to laboratory biosafety (in Chinese). J Gansu Univ Polit Sci Law (03):1–11
Qin T (2021) On the development of risk prevention principle in environmental law: a combination with the investigation of “Biosecurity Law” (in Chinese). China Law Rev (02):65–79
Qin T (2022) On the systematic legal regulation of biodiversity conservation (in Chinese). Leg Forum 37(1):119–128
Qin T, Liu S (2022) A re-examination of China’s legal system for biodiversity convention in the context of the CBD negotiations (in Chinese). Yuejiang Acad J (6):95–104
Qiu S, Hu M (2021) Legislative moves on biosecurity in China. Biotechnol Law Rep 40(1):27–34
Redick TP (2003) Biopharming, biosafety, and billion dollar debacles: preventing liability for biotech crops. Drake J Agric Law 8:115
Segger M-CC, Perron-Welch F, Frison C (eds) (2013) Legal aspects of implementing the Cartagena Protocol on Biosafety. Treaty implementation for sustainable development. Cambridge University Press, New York
Shi X, Zhao T (2023) Environmental risk regulation of genetic resources utilization from the perspective of ecological security (in Chinese). North Forum (03):57–65
Song L, Joly Y (2021) After He Jianku: China’s biotechnology regulation reforms. Med Law Int 21(2):174–192
Tan B (2022) Optimization of wildlife protection enforcement in the post-epidemic era—based on the interpretation of the decision of the Standing Committee of the National People’s Congress (in Chinese). J CUPL (01):50–64
Wang X (2006) Biosafety and biosafety law in China (in Chinese). J Ningbo Univ Liberal Arts Edn 19(4):118–124
Wang K (2016) Legal discussions on the prevention of environmental risks that may be caused by GMOs (in Chinese). Law Soc Dev 132(6):132–147
Wang K (2020) An outline of the construction of national biosecurity rule of law system with Chinese characteristics (in Chinese). Stud Foreign Soc Sci (12):4–19+94
Wang H, You M (2021) Annual review of Chinese environmental law developments: 2020 comments. Environ Law Rep 51(6):10478–10484
Wang L, Wang F, Zhang W (2021) Bioethics in China’s biosecurity law: forms, effects, and unsettled issues. J Law Biosci 8(1):lsab019–lsab019
Wei J (2022) The constitutional logic of the biosafety law (in Chinese). J Shanghai Univ Polit Sci Law 37(03):63–75
Wu K (2022) Classification and system attribution of environmental legal norms under the background of codification (in Chinese). Law Sci (06):158–174
Xi Y (2022) China’s legal system for ecological, environmental protection takes shape, 25 October 2022. https://www.globaltimes.cn/page/202210/1277968.shtml
Xiang W (2012) International liability and redress for genetically modified organisms and challenge for China’s biosafety regulation. In: Sancin V (ed) International environmental law: contemporary concerns and challenges. GV Založba, Ljubljana, pp 581–600
Xiao J (2022) On the systematic construction of national security legal system (in Chinese). J Southwest Univ Polit Sci Law 24(04):43–53
Xiao Z, Kerr WA (2022) Biotechnology in China – regulation, investment, and delayed commercialization. GM Crops Food 13(1):86–96
Xu J, Li J, Zhang W, Li J (2007) Biosafety in China: questions, current regulations, and recommendations (in Chinese). Environ Prot (13):25–30
Yan H, Yan X (2012) Prevention and control of GMO biosafety risk--legislation on GMO biosafety law from the perspective of biodiversity (in Chinese). Environ Prot (12):45–47

You M (2020) Changes of China's regulatory regime on commercial artificial breeding of terrestrial wildlife in time of COVID-19 outbreak and impacts on the future. Biol Conserv 250:108756
Yu W (2009) On biosafety legislation (in Chinese). Tsinghua University Press
Yu W (2020) The legal principles and approaches for biosecurity (in Chinese). Explor Free Views (04):160–166+290
Yu W, Hu Z (2022) Systematization of biodiversity legal institution from the perspective of ecological civilization (in Chinese). J Henan Normal Univ (Philos Soc Sci) 49(05):37–45
Yu W, Wang C (2012) Agro-GMO biosafety legislation in China: current situation, challenges, and solutions. Vermont J Environ Law 13(4):865–883
Yue X (2022) Systematic path of regional ecological protection legislation under the background of environmental code compilation (in Chinese). Hebei Law Sci 40(11):119–138
Zhang Z, Liu X (2014) Study on legal approaches towards the prevention of ecological risks regarding biotechnology (in Chinese). Environ Rule Law 2:1–24
Zhao J (2021) A study on the system of public participation in the regulation of genetically modified organisms: taking the EU experience as an example (in Chinese). J Northeast Normal Univ (Philos Soc Sci) (5):101–107
Zhou D, Song H, Wang J, Li Z, Xu S, Ji X, Hou X, Xu J (2019) Biosafety and biosecurity. J Biosaf Biosecur 1(1):15–18

Legal Practice of In Situ Biodiversity Conservation in China: From the Perspective of Nature Reserves

Weiwei Duan

Abstract In situ conservation is an important measure for the coordinated conservation of species resources, genetic resources, and ecosystems in China's biodiversity conservation, which not only has the function of conserving wildlife species and regional natural ecosystems but also pays attention to the protection of the rights and interests of different stakeholders, and the establishment of a nature reserve system with national parks as the main body has become an important part of the on-site conservation of biodiversity in China in the new era. Under the background of the new era, this chapter takes the nature reserve system as the perspective to systematically analyze the legal practice of biodiversity conservation in place in China. This chapter will systematically discuss the legal system of nature reserves, including national parks, the administrative supervision and management system of nature reserves, and the judicial protection of nature reserves. At the end of this chapter, a brief discussion will be made on the challenges and future development direction of the rule of law in China's biodiversity conservation in situ.

1 Introduction

China is rich in biodiversity resources. According to the 2022 China Ecological Environment Bulletin issued by the Ministry of Ecology and Environment on May 29, 2023, China's natural ecosystems currently include forests, grasslands, deserts, wetlands, islands, bays, mangroves, coral reefs, seagrass beds, estuaries, and upflows, and there are artificial and semi-artificial ecosystems such as farmland and cities. It has a rich natural ecosystem. Most of these rich biodiversity resources are systematically and scientifically protected by means of in situ biodiversity conservation represented by nature reserve systems. In situ conservation of biodiversity refers to the goal of protecting and restoring species populations and their habitats, as well as safeguarding and improving ecosystem services, through the establishment and management of nature reserve systems and in combination with

W. Duan (✉)
Zhengzhou University of Aeronautics, Zhengzhou, China

G. Antonelli et al. (eds.), *Biodiversity Laws, Policies and Science in Europe, the United States and China*, https://doi.org/10.1007/978-3-031-56218-1_14

other effective area-based conservation measures (OECMs) outside nature reserves.[1] For a long time, China has been striving to achieve the overall and systematic protection of biodiversity resources through the establishment of a nature reserve system, which is an in situ protection method. At present, China has established more than 10,000 nature reserves at all levels and of all kinds, of which the area of the red line of land ecological protection accounts for more than 30% of the land area.

Under the scientific leadership of the Chinese government and the joint efforts of all sectors of society, remarkable results have been achieved in the in situ conservation of biodiversity in China, and in this process, the important supporting value of the rule of law system for China's construction of a nature reserve system cannot be ignored. In practice, the establishment of a nature reserve system with national parks as the main body requires not only a scientific layout in light of the characteristics of the natural ecosystem but also a clear scope of the powers and responsibilities of the relevant government departments for the construction of nature reserves and a reasonable regulation of various acts of using biodiversity resources to ensure the effective protection of biodiversity resources by the nature reserve system. Against this background, the rule of law system with legislation, law enforcement, and justice as the main contents is an important guarantee to ensure the on-site protection of biodiversity. The rule of law system not only provides the institutional basis for the development and construction of the nature reserve system but also restricts the destruction of biodiversity resources through strict punitive measures.

This part mainly discusses the practice of the rule of law in the construction of China's nature reserve system and analyzes how the Chinese style can ensure the smooth development of biodiversity conservation in situ through three main ways of the rule of law, namely, the construction of a legal system, supervision and management, and judicial protection.

2 Policy and Legal System for the In Situ Conservation of Biodiversity in China

2.1 Relationship Between Policy and Law

The List of Biological Species in China 2023 consists of 148,674 species and subspecies, particularly 135,061 species and 13,613 subspecies, including the animal kingdom, the plant kingdom, the bacteria kingdom, the pigment kingdom, the fungus kingdom, the Protozoa kingdom, viruses, etc. When protecting these rich resources, China mainly protects species diversity, genetic resource diversity, and ecosystem diversity among biodiversity by establishing a nature reserve system dominated by national parks. The legal practice of on-site biodiversity conservation

[1] Zhou and Jin (2021), pp. 1583–1590.

in China mainly clarifies the scope of functions, basic principles, and important systems of the construction and management of natural reserves through the establishment of a scientific and systematic legal system, as well as the legal resources that damage biodiversity resources. However, when discussing the legal practice of in situ conservation of biodiversity in China, the first step should be to clarify the guiding role of national policies in legal practice. The national policies of nature reserves determine the direction and content of the legal system construction, and the content of the legal system also reflects the current Chinese government's philosophy and goals for the construction of nature reserves.

Compared to the law, although policies can be more flexible and in line with social reality in terms of formulation procedures and timeliness, there are shortcomings in terms of stability, execution, and authority. Therefore, the legalization of policies remains an important aspect of achieving good law and governance. Policies that have been proven mature and stable through practical testing, and have been adjusted to regulate social relations over a long period of time, are elevated to national law by state organs with legislative power in accordance with legal authorities and procedures, ensuring that these policies have legal validity and national coercive power. Against the backdrop of China's clear recognition of the importance of biodiversity conservation, building a systematic legal system for biodiversity conservation and providing specific normative behavioral norms for various entities can achieve the specific implementation of policy guidance from the perspective of legal regulation.[2]

2.2 *Policy Orientation for Biodiversity Conservation and Nature Reserves in China*

In 2021, China issued the "Opinions on Further Strengthening Biodiversity Protection," proposing to "ensure the comprehensive protection of important ecosystems, biological species, and genetic resources, and integrate the concept of biodiversity protection into the entire process of ecological civilization construction," emphasizing "accelerating the improvement of biodiversity protection policies and regulations."[3] This provides a policy basis and requirements for the current legislative work on biodiversity conservation, including the construction of natural reserve systems. In 2019, China issued the "Guiding Opinions on Establishing a Nature Reserve System with National Parks as the Main Body," emphasizing "accelerating the construction of relevant laws, regulations, and systems for nature reserves, and increasing the efforts to reform, abolish, and release laws and regulations," which further strengthened the construction of a nature reserve legal system with national

[2] Chen (2001), pp. 64–66.

[3] Chinese Government Website (2021).

park protection as the main content.[4] In addition to providing policy guidance for the construction of the legal system of the nature reserve system, China's national policy on nature reserves has, to some extent, filled the gap in the legislation of nature reserves. In addition to the Guiding Opinions on Establishing a Nature Reserve System with National Parks as the Main Body, national policies such as the Wetland Protection and Restoration System Plan, the Overall Plan for Establishing a National Park System Plan, and the National Park Spatial Layout Plan all provide a direct work basis for the construction of the nature reserve system in the context of relevant legislative deficiencies.

2.3 Legal System for the In Situ Conservation of Biodiversity in China

China has currently formed a preliminary legal system for nature reserves, providing a reliable and complete institutional basis for the on-site protection of biodiversity. This section mainly introduces the legal systems of three main nature reserves, namely, national parks, nature reserves, and natural parks, based on the Chinese government's classification of the nature reserve system.

In terms of national park legislation, China launched the legislative work of the National Park Law in 2018. Currently, the draft of the National Park Law has been included in the annual legislative work plan of the State Council for 2023 and is ready to be submitted to the Standing Committee of the National People's Congress for review. At present, the main content of the draft National Park Law includes planning and establishment, protection and management, public services, financial security, law enforcement supervision, legal responsibility, and other content on national parks. The promulgation and implementation of this legislation will provide a specific basis for establishing a natural reserve system with national parks as the main body. At the same time, the China Forestry and Grassland Administration issued the "Interim Measures for the Management of National Parks" in 2022, which is a legal system that focuses on clarifying the scope of authority of national park managers and provides a legal basis for relevant government departments to carry out national park construction and management work.[5]

As nature reserves are an important part of China's biodiversity in situ conservation work and one of the earliest types of nature reserves to carry out legislative practice, China has now formed a relatively complete legislative system for nature reserves. In terms of national laws, there are the Environmental Protection Law, the Forest Law, and the Grassland Law. In terms of administrative regulations, there are the Regulations on Nature Reserves. In terms of departmental regulations, they include the Management Measures for Forest and Wildlife Nature Reserves, the

---

[4] Chinese Government Website (2019).

[5] Du (2023), pp. 32–47.

Management Office of Marine Nature Reserves, and the Land Management Measures for Nature Reserves. At present, the legislation on nature reserves in China is mainly based on the "Regulations on Nature Reserves" issued by the State Council, which uniformly regulates the construction and management of different types of nature reserves at the national level. On the other hand, China's natural resource regulatory authorities have stipulated the specific types and work matters of nature reserves through departmental regulations, achieving an effective connection between macro and specific legislation on nature reserves in China.

China has currently introduced legal systems such as the Regulations on Scenic Spots, the Management Measures for Forest Parks, the Management Measures for National Forest Parks, the Wetland Protection Law, and the Management Measures for Geological Heritage Protection, forming a relatively complete legislative system for natural parks. At the same time, due to the fact that natural parks include various types such as forest parks, geological parks, ocean parks, and wetland parks, there are significant differences in the legislative basis for different types of natural parks. For example, in terms of wetland parks, the Wetland Protection Law provides a national legal basis for the construction and management of wetland parks. Although the number of forest park legislation is large and the system is relatively complete, the main legislative body is the Ministries of the People's Republic of China of the State Council of China, and the legislative rank is relatively low. In terms of geopark legislation, China has not yet formed a specialized legal system for addressing parks.

In addition to the legislative system for specific types of nature reserves such as national parks, nature reserves, and nature parks, national-level legislation, such as the Constitution, Environmental Protection Law, Water Law, Yangtze River Protection Law, and Yellow River Protection Law, also provides legislative support for the construction and management of nature reserves in China. At the same time, local governments in China have also introduced a series of local-level legal systems for nature reserves based on the practical background of local nature reserve management work, such as the Yunnan Provincial Regulations on the Management of National Parks, the Hainan Provincial Regulations on Nature Reserves, and the Interim Measures for the Supervision of the Ecological Environment of Nature Reserves in Gansu Province. These local legislation and national legislation together form the legislative system for nature reserves in China in the new era.

2.4 Development Direction of China's Legal System for Biodiversity Conservation In Situ

In addition to integrating systems based on the integrity and diversity of legal regulatory objects, clarifying the boundaries of power and responsibility between administrative and social entities is also an important part of building China's systematic legal system for biodiversity protection. In this section, the institutional configuration of the legal system should pay more attention to the integrity of the government's exercise of functions. By weakening and eliminating conflicts of interest between government departments, we can overcome the phenomenon of administrative isolation and fragmentation among some government departments and clarify the functional positioning of the central government's unity, authority, and local and government departments' auxiliary and cooperative nature so as to truly achieve unity and coordination in the government's administrative function of biodiversity protection. With the development of biodiversity work in China, the establishment of a natural reserve system with national parks as the main body has become an important way to protect biodiversity in situ, and the legislative system of natural reserves with national parks as the main body is also constantly improving. As a country rich in biodiversity resources, China has long attached great importance to protecting natural resources through legal systems and has formed different types of legal systems for nature reserves. On this basis, as the Chinese government proposes to establish a nature reserve system with national parks as the main body, national policies pay more attention to the integrity of the natural ecosystem, and China's nature reserve legislative system will also develop toward unity and systematicity based on the existing legislative system.

3 Regulatory System for Nature Reserves in China

In the practice of biodiversity conservation, in addition to establishing a relatively complete legal system for nature reserves, China has also formed a systematic and effective regulatory system for nature reserves, providing reliable guarantees for the legislative implementation and construction management of nature reserves. In this process, the development of China's national park system represents the direction of the development of China's nature reserve regulatory system in the new era.

3.1 The Important Role of the Chinese Government in the Construction and Management of Nature Reserves

The public environmental interests in biodiversity protection are mainly based on the sustainable use of biodiversity resources and the sustainable development of biodiversity Systema Naturae.[6] The government, on behalf of the country, performs the function of safeguarding public interests because it has a wide range of interest subjects and a unified interest orientation. The public environmental benefits of biodiversity conservation are first reflected in achieving sustainable development of the natural ecological environment system, that is, conserving and protecting biological species resources, genetic resources, and related ecosystems and

[6] Yu and Hu (2022), pp. 71–78.

achieving harmonious development between humans and nature. In this process, on the one hand, the government, as the administrative subject with administrative supervision functions, actively exercises the power to maintain public environmental interests based on its own legal functions. On the other hand, the government is also entrusted by a wide range of public interests, representing the state in managing and protecting the ownership of natural resource assets for public environmental interests. When such rights and interests are infringed upon externally, the relevant infringers are compensated through the ecological environment damage compensation litigation mechanism. Therefore, the public environmental interests in biodiversity conservation often have the meaning of the government acting as a representative of public interests to protect and achieve. This is reflected not only in the government's legal function as an administrative entity to maintain public interests but also in the exercise of the national ownership of natural resource assets entrusted by the public based on the government's advantage in safeguarding public environmental interests.

3.2 *Structure of the Regulatory System for Nature Reserves in China*

In 2013, China's national policy explicitly proposed the establishment of a national park system for the first time, and in 2015, the "Pilot Plan for Establishing a National Park System" was released, proposing the establishment of a national park system with Chinese characteristics. In 2018, China set up the National Forestry and Grassland Administration for the first time when it was carrying out the reform of national institutions, which is responsible for the supervision and management of various nature reserves and biodiversity conservation. At the same time, in order to unify the management functions of national parks, the Chinese government has also set up the National Park Administration Bureau in the National Forestry and Grassland Administration, which is responsible for the construction and management of national parks. This institutional reform has clarified the management structure of China's natural reserve system, with national parks as the main body, and promoted the unity and synergy of the Chinese government's on-site biodiversity conservation work. On the basis of the current national park management system, China has also proposed the implementation of a natural reserve management system with national parks as the main body, natural reserves as the foundation, and various natural parks as supplements, achieving coordinated development between the natural reserve management system and the legal system.

In addition to the National Forestry and Grassland Administration and the National Park Administration, which are specifically responsible for the construction and management of China's national parks, other departments of the Chinese government are also currently responsible for the construction and management of the nature reserve system. As the administrative department in charge of national natural resources protection and development, the Ministry of Natural Resources of China will exercise the function of unified management of China's natural reserve system. The National Forestry and Grassland Administration and the National Park Administration under the Ministry of Natural Resources will assume the function of building and managing national parks. In addition, the Ministry of Ecology and Environment is mainly responsible for the supervision and management of the ecological environment quality of nature reserves, while the Ministry of Agriculture and Rural Affairs is mainly responsible for rural areas and agricultural matters related to nature reserves. Government departments such as the Ministry of Water Resources, the Ministry of Finance, and the Ministry of Public Security are also responsible for managing the construction of nature reserves within their respective powers. Against the backdrop of the Chinese government's proposal to establish a unified nature reserve system, a unified management system with national parks as the main body, nature reserves as the foundation, and natural parks as supplements will be the development goal and direction of China's future nature reserve supervision system. In this context, the Ministry of Natural Resources and its affiliated National Forestry and Grassland Administration and National Park Administration will uniformly exercise the functions of building and managing China's natural reserves, and other government departments will also work with the above departments within their own responsibilities to form a regulatory system for China's natural reserves in the new era.

In addition to forming a regulatory system led by the natural resource management department at the national level, other relevant departments collaborate to establish a regulatory system for the on-site conservation of biodiversity in China. Due to the large number and types of nature reserves in China, as well as the significant differences in their distribution areas, the construction and management of nature reserves in China also have certain regional characteristics. In this context, the Chūgoku region's local governments have also formed a management model of local nature reserves with regional characteristics according to the actual needs of the construction and management of nature reserves in the region. For example, the first batch of national parks set up in China includes five national parks: Sanjiangyuan National Park, Giant Panda National Park, Northeast Tiger and Leopard National Park, Hainan Tropical Rainforest National Park, and Mount Wuyi National Park. These five national parks are distributed in different regions of China, and there are significant differences in the biodiversity resources and natural environment within the national parks, making it particularly necessary to establish a natural reserve management system that is in line with local natural and cultural factors. For example, in the management practice of Sanjiangyuan National Park, although the ownership of natural resources in the national park is directly exercised by the Chinese government, in the current management practice, the management authority is exercised by the Qinghai Provincial Government. The Sanjiangyuan National Park Administration, as the agency of the People's Government of Qinghai Province, is responsible for the management of various state-owned natural resource asset owners within the pilot area of Sanjiangyuan National Park and Sanjiangyuan National Nature Reserve in Qinghai Province. At present, the Sanjiangyuan National

Park Management Bureau, Management Committee, and Conservation Management Station are responsible for the construction and management of relevant natural reserves in the national park, forming a natural reserve management system with distinct local characteristics.

3.3 Cooperation Between the Government and Social Organizations in the Management of Nature Reserves

Although the Chinese legal system has given the National Forestry and Grassland Administration, the National Park Administration, and other government departments the power to manage nature reserves, in practice, non-governmental organizations, especially environmental protection groups, and the public also play an important role in the management of nature reserves in China. Taking Sanjiangyuan National Park as an example, since 2016, the World Wide Fund for Nature (WWF) and GAC Trumpchi have jointly promoted activities related to ecological protection of Sanjiangyuan National Park. In 2018, representatives of the three parties officially signed a strategic cooperation framework agreement (MOU), with the goal of "establishing and improving the institutional mechanism for social participation in the construction and management of national parks," and jointly committed to carrying out and implementing ecological protection and environmental education related to national parks.[7] In the practice of natural reserve management in China, social organizations often actively participate in natural reserve management practices through publicity and education, species resource survey and monitoring, local community cooperation, ecological services, and product development, becoming an indispensable and important part of China's biodiversity in situ conservation work. Government and other administrative authorities are also more willing to accept their professional opinion, and even on some issues, they would like to provide advice as a basis for decision-making.[8] At the same time, due to the current lack of specialized legislation on the participation of social organizations in natural reserve management, it is difficult for experienced social organizations to participate in policy formulation and decision-making consultation activities related to natural reserve management. In addition, in the absence of a clear legal basis, cooperation between government departments responsible for managing nature reserves and social organizations is often in the exploratory stage, which affects the normalization and diversification of cooperation between government departments and social organizations. In the context of the clear proposal of "improving social participation mechanisms" in the "Overall Plan for Establishing a National Park System," social entities, including environmental protection organizations, experts and scholars,

[7] People's Daily Online (2016).

[8] Wang (2006), p. 175.

enterprises, the public, and other government departments, will also form a new era of China's nature reserve supervision system.

4 Judicial Protection System for Nature Reserves in China

4.1 Professional Trial Mechanism for Cases in Nature Reserves

In 2022, the Supreme People's Court of China issued a report on the judicial protection of biodiversity in China. The report shows that since 2013, Chinese courts at all levels have concluded a total of 182,000 first-instance cases involving biodiversity protection, covering different types of wildlife and their living environments, fisheries and forestry resources, animal and plant inspection and quarantine, and new plant varieties, effectively protecting biodiversity resources. The Chinese judicial system has provided solid guarantees for the construction and management of natural reserves in China through specialized case trials, the issuance of judicial interpretations and policy documents, the issuance of guiding cases, and the strengthening of international cooperation and exchange.

According to the report "Judicial Protection of Biodiversity in China," there are a total of 2426 environmental resource trial-specialized agencies or organizations established by courts nationwide.[9] These trial-specialized agencies often use natural ecosystems and ecological functional zones as jurisdictional standards when trying cases involving biodiversity protection and comprehensively protect these cross-administrative ecological functional zones. At the same time, to ensure that these innovative judicial institutions can smoothly carry out case trials, the Supreme People's Court of China has also issued 15 judicial policy documents, 21 judicial interpretations, and 26 environmental resource-specific guidance cases, providing solid legal guarantee for biodiversity protection.

4.2 Cooperation Between Judicial Organs and Social Organizations

Due to the wide range of regions, complex geographical environment, and ecological elements involved in nature reserves, it is often difficult for the trial mechanism that defines the jurisdiction based on administrative regions to effectively hear cross-regional cases. In this context, Chinese judicial organs have clearly defined the scope of jurisdiction based on natural elements and ecosystems, achieving the connection between judicial trials and the demand for on-site biodiversity protection. The

[9]The Supreme People's Court of the PRC (2022).

Supreme People's Court has guided local courts to fully consider the integrity of ecosystem types and explore cross-administrative division centralized jurisdiction based on the ecosystem, national parks, nature reserves, and other ecological functional areas according to the needs of ecological environment governance and the characteristics of environmental resource cases. Under the guidance of this concept, the Chūgoku region's local people's courts at all levels have carried out a series of effective judicial practice exploration activities. For example, the Jiangsu court implemented the "9+1" centralized jurisdiction mechanism with the Nanjing Environment and Resources Tribunal as the core and the nine ecological function area courts as the support. The Jiangxi court established the centralized jurisdiction courts for the Yangtze River, Poyang Lake, and other provinces in the "one river, one lake and five rivers" basin, effectively promoting systematic protection and overall governance.

Biodiversity protection involves not only adjusting the relationship between human behavior in the development and utilization of natural resources and the sustainable development of the ecological environment but also balancing interests between individual interests and public interests, social and administrative rights, natural resource development, and national security. Building a systematic legal system for biodiversity conservation involves balancing diverse conflicts of interest in the field through legal regulatory means, while clarifying the overall objectives of biodiversity conservation, in order to ensure the coordination between legal regulatory effectiveness and practical social needs. The protection of interests in the field of biodiversity conservation not only focuses on the overall protection of ecosystems, biological species, and genetic resources but also emphasizes the reasonable regulation of the behavior of each subject in order to maximize the interests of each subject in this field. On the one hand, the government representing the country in carrying out biodiversity conservation work not only needs to fulfill its duties in accordance with the law but also should avoid administrative isolation caused by departmental conflicts of interest within the government. On the other hand, social entities such as the public, experts and scholars, and social organizations should also be given the right to participate and work together with administrative entities to seek the maximization of common interests in the field of biodiversity protection. In this context, a systematic legal system for biodiversity protection can provide a reliable institutional basis for balancing the conflicts of interests between different subjects, achieving the integrity of government administration, and ensuring the interaction and cooperation between social and administrative subjects.

In carrying out the work of protecting nature reserves, Chinese people's courts at all levels not only try cases involving biodiversity protection in accordance with the law but also pay attention to cultivating public awareness of the rule of law. Through various means, they play the guiding and educational role of ecological environment justice in society and advocate for the active participation of the whole society in biodiversity protection work. With the progress in the construction and management of nature reserves in China in recent years, the number of nature reserves in China has been continuously increasing. While effectively protecting biodiversity resources, it has also had a certain impact on the production and life of indigenous residents within the scope of nature reserves. Chinese judicial organs, on the other hand, strengthen communication with these indigenous residents and make local residents aware of the importance of protecting biodiversity by publicly hearing cases, inviting them to participate in judicial practice activities, and conducting legal lectures. At the same time, Chinese judicial organs are actively collaborating with the administrative departments of nature reserves to work together to build a nature reserve system with national parks as the main body.

4.3 Improving the Judicial Guarantee System for Global Nature Reserves

In addition to giving full play to the positive value of judicial functions in protecting domestic nature reserves, China's judicial organs have also made positive contributions to improving the rule of law for global biodiversity conservation. The Supreme People's Court of China and the United Nations Environment Programme held the World Conference on Environmental Justice and promoted the adoption of the Kunming Declaration of the World Conference on Environmental Justice. The Kunming Declaration of the World Conference on Environmental Justice pointed out that the current judicial systems of various countries should systematically respond to the three major global ecological and environmental crises, including biodiversity loss, climate change, and environmental pollution, and adhere to the principles of fairness, common but differentiated responsibilities and respective capabilities, protection and sustainable use of natural resources, and liability for damage. These all provide feasible solutions for global environmental governance, including biodiversity conservation. At the same time, the Supreme People's Court of China has guided courts at all levels to perform their obligations under international environmental treaties concluded or acceded to by China, such as the Convention on Biological Diversity; in judicial cases emphasized the judicial position of attaching importance to the rules of international law; and implemented the solemn commitment to biodiversity protection, which has played a positive role in improving the judicial security system of global nature reserves.

5 Public Participation Mechanism in Nature Reserves in China

5.1 Information Disclosure of Government Nature Reserves

China's Environmental Protection Law for the first time expresses public participation as a basic principle and specifies the contents of public participation, indicating that public participation in environmental governance has been recognized and guaranteed by the Environmental Protection Law. The Measures for the Implementation of Government Information Disclosure by the Ministry of Ecology and Environment and the Measures for Environmental Information Disclosure by Enterprises and Institutions promulgated by China have also promoted the development process of public participation in environmental governance in China from the perspective of information disclosure. The Measures for Public Participation in Environmental Protection promulgated in September 2015 comprehensively and specifically stipulate the ways, procedures, and guarantees for public participation in environmental governance and clarify the responsibility of the government for assistance and guidance in it, indicating that China's environmental law construction has developed from focusing on the protection of the rights and interests of public environmental entities to giving consideration to the protection of environmental procedural rights and interests. Therefore, with the continuous improvement of China's environmental legal system, information disclosure has become an important part of public participation in China's environmental protection, including the construction of nature reserves.

Relevant environmental laws and regulations of China, including administrative regulations or guarantees based on the public's right to know or the performance of the duties of administrative organs, all recognize and guarantee that the subject of the right to environmental information disclosure is a citizen. But in the group of citizens, according to the environmental information available, laws and regulations divide it into all citizens and specific citizens. Among specific citizens, the Regulations on the Disclosure of Government Information stipulates that "the public may apply to the departments of the State Council, local people's governments at all levels and local people's government departments at or above the county level for relevant government information according to their special needs in production, life and scientific research." However, in the process of the construction of nature reserves, many stakeholders are often involved, and the division of such subjects of environmental information disclosure rights is conducive to defining and guaranteeing citizens' right to know the environment, realizing public participation in the environmental field according to the environmental information obtained, and promoting the development of environmental protection undertakings. On the other hand, the confirmation of the subject of environmental information disclosure will also help strengthen the obligation of governments and administrative departments to disclose environmental information.

In China's legal system for the in situ protection of biodiversity, nature reserves have not yet been fully and uniformly named as such, but it has established different terms for different protected objects and formulated relevant legal documents. In the field of nature reserves, especially in the normative legal documents on nature reserves for different protected objects, there are provisions requiring the disclosure of information on the establishment and protection of relevant protected areas. In addition to the provisions of Articles 11, 19, and 20 of the Measures for the Disclosure of Environmental Information (for Trial Implementation), some laws and regulations on the management of special nature reserves also stipulate the scope of environmental information disclosure. According to the summary of these special legal documents on the management of nature reserves, the disclosure of environmental information in the field of nature reserves also includes the scope and boundaries of nature reserves, the construction and management of nature reserves, the environmental information of nature reserves, and relevant registration items of the ownership of nature reserves. For example, Article 11 of the Measures for the Administration of Nature Reserves in Sichuan Province provides: "Nature reserves are divided into core areas, buffer areas and experimental areas in accordance with the provisions of the State, and peripheral protection zones can also be delimited when necessary. After approval, the scope and boundaries of nature reserves shall be announced by the local people's governments." On the other hand, Article 12 of the Measures for the Administration of Nature Reserves in Fujian Province states: "The administrative departments of environmental protection at or above the county level and the administrative departments of relevant nature reserves shall strengthen the information statistics of the construction and management of nature reserves within their jurisdiction and publish them in the annual environmental status bulletin." Meanwhile, paragraph 1 of Article 14 of the Regulations of Guizhou Province on the Administration of Forest Land stipulates: "The registration authority shall examine the application materials submitted by the applicant for the registration of forest land ownership. Those that conform to the provisions of relevant laws, regulations, and these Regulations shall be accepted, and the relevant materials shall be announced in the place where the forest land is located within 10 working days from the date of acceptance, and the announcement period shall be 30 days." These provisions apply to the disclosure of local environmental information, but because they specify the requirements of the relevant parties, they are more conducive to the disclosure of environmental information in nature reserves.

5.2 *Public Participation in the Daily Management of Nature Reserves*

China's environmental laws have systematic provisions on the right of the public to participate in environmental governance. The Environmental Protection Law of the People's Republic of China clarifies the right of the public to participate in environmental governance through public consultation, supervision and reporting of illegal activities, and filing public interest lawsuits in Articles 56, 57, and 58. Local legal documents also stipulate that the public has the right to report and accuse acts that damage nature reserves. For example, Article 4 of the Regulations of Yunnan Province on the Administration of Nature Reserves states that "All units and individuals have the obligation to protect the natural environment and natural resources in nature reserves, and have the right to report and accuse units and individuals who destroy or occupy nature reserves"; Article 5 of the Regulations of Yunnan Province on the Administration of the Dabaoshan Black Necked Crane National Nature Reserve in Zhaotong provides that "Any unit or individual has the obligation to protect the reserve, and has the right to stop, report and accuse acts that damage the ecological environment of the reserve, damage black necked cranes and other wildlife"; Article 15, paragraph 3, of the Regulations of Henan Province on the Protection and Administration of Forest Land stipulates: "It is forbidden for any unit or individual to endanger or destroy forest land. All units and individuals have the right to report and accuse acts that endanger or destroy forest land"; and Article 7 of the Regulations of Sichuan Province on the Protection and Administration of Drinking Water Sources provides: "All units and individuals have the obligation to protect the safety of drinking water sources, and have the right to stop and report acts that pollute and damage drinking water sources. Local people's governments at all levels and relevant departments shall protect informants and commend units and individuals who have made outstanding contributions to the protection of drinking water sources."

Nature reserve management activities are a general term for the construction, development, utilization, and protection of nature reserves in daily life, especially in the process of daily protection. The actual management effect of nature reserves has a direct bearing on the actual operation, protection, and development of corresponding nature reserves. Therefore, strengthening the management of nature reserves is one of the important contents related to the sustainable development of nature reserves. At present, the management of nature reserves in China mainly relies on the special nature reserve management agencies set up for each nature reserve. These management responsibilities are an important part of the management activities of the relevant nature reserves and an important means to promote the development of nature reserves. As some management agencies are short of personnel and management responsibilities, it is particularly necessary for the public to assist the management agencies in participating in the management of nature reserves. The public may supervise and administer the management activities of nature reserves in accordance with the Regulations on Nature Reserves, the Environmental Protection Law, and other relevant legal documents. The Regulations on Nature Reserves stipulate that "all units and individuals have the obligation to protect the natural environment and natural resources in nature reserves, and have the right to report and accuse units and individuals who destroy or occupy nature reserves." In addition, the Environmental Protection Law and the Civil Procedure Law establish the environmental public interest litigation system, which provides legal relief channels for citizens to participate in the supervision and management of nature reserve management activities.

In the legal documents related to local nature reserves, the ways for the public to participate in the management of nature reserves are generally not directly defined or are generally explained in terms of "properly handling the relationship with local economic construction and residents' production and life." For example, the Regulations of Yunnan Province on the Administration of Nature Reserves stipulates that "the protection, construction and management of nature reserves shall adhere to the principle of 'comprehensive planning, active protection, scientific management and sustainable utilization', and properly handle the relationship with local economic construction and the production and life of residents." This article makes general provisions on public interests but does not make clear provisions on specific public participation.

5.3 Public Participation in the Formulation of Policies and Laws on Nature Reserves

The construction and management of nature reserves in China cannot be separated from the participation of social organizations, experts, scholars, scientific research institutions, and other social subjects, and public participation is an important part of the in situ conservation of biodiversity in China. In the process of compiling the National Park Spatial Layout Plan in China, strict procedures such as multiple rounds of expert demonstration, soliciting opinions from relevant departments, and third-party evaluation have been followed.[10] At the same time, the opinions of experts and scholars in different fields, such as scientific research institutions and universities, non-governmental organizations, deputies to the National People's Congress, and members of the Chinese People's Political Consultative Conference (CPPCC), have been solicited as well as revised and improved in light of the results of mass online voting. We can say that the whole compilation process fully reflects public participation in the construction and management of nature reserves in China. The policies, laws, regulations, and other normative legal documents related to nature reserves are important bases for guiding and promoting the development of nature reserves in China, and at the same time, they also put forward legal requirements for us to strengthen the construction of nature reserves, requiring us to actively assume corresponding legal responsibilities so as to realize the sustainable development of nature reserves.

China's Legislation Law stipulates that "legislation should adhere to and develop people's democracy throughout the process, respect and safeguard human rights, and safeguard and promote social fairness and justice. Legislation should embody the will of the people, carry forward socialist democracy, adhere to the openness of legislation, and ensure that the people participate in legislative activities through various means." In the process of formulating relevant laws, regulations, and other normative legal documents on nature reserves, the public may put forward their own opinions on the relevant draft legal documents and reflect them to the relevant legislature through certain channels so as to participate in the formulation of relevant laws, regulations, and other normative legal documents by influencing the activities of the relevant legislature. When publishing relevant draft legal documents, relevant legislative bodies will also choose to make them public in various ways and accept the public's legislative proposals through letters, networks, and other means. At the same time, in the legislative process, the Chinese legislature will also invite experts and scholars, professional institutions, social organizations, and other

[10] Xinhua News Agency (2022).

representatives of all sectors of society to participate in the drafting of relevant legislative documents, and these forms of public participation in legislation are also reflected in the legislative activities of nature reserves in China.

6 Conclusion

With China's successful hosting of the 15th Conference of the Parties to the Convention on Biological Diversity (COP15), China's unremitting efforts in the field of biodiversity conservation have not only made great achievements but have also been recognized by the international community. With the proposal of China's national policy to build a natural reserve system with national parks as the main body, the construction and management of the natural reserve system to achieve on-site biodiversity conservation will be an important part of China's biodiversity conservation work.[11] In this process, China's legal system will also provide strong guarantees for the construction of a natural reserve system with national parks as the main body, natural reserves as the foundation, and natural parks as supplements in multiple aspects.[12]

Driven by national policy guidance and the demand for the rule of law in biodiversity conservation, the current legislation in the field of biodiversity conservation in China has shown characteristics of multi-point dissemination and mutual response. The national level biodiversity protection laws, represented by the Biosafety Law, Wildlife Protection Law, and Forest Law, not only regulate specific areas of biodiversity protection, such as biological species resources, genetic resources, and natural ecosystems, but also reflect the close connection between biodiversity protection legislation and the overall system protection of biodiversity. Therefore, although national legislation on biodiversity protection has not yet been introduced, there are many specific areas of biodiversity protection that involve legislation on species resources, genetic resources, and natural ecosystems. With the gradual deepening of the overall system protection concept of biodiversity protection, in the future, China's biodiversity protection field will also form a legal and regulatory system with complete external forms and internal normative connections. In terms of administrative supervision, in addition to the National Forestry and Grassland Administration performing the function of biodiversity protection supervision at the national level, the Ministry of Ecological Environment, the State Oceanic Administration, the Ministry of Natural Resources, and other departments also assume the function of biodiversity protection supervision in different fields according to law. At the same time, the administrative supervision mechanism for local biodiversity protection also presents a collaborative feature of multiple departments based on the requirements of overall biodiversity protection. In terms of

[11] Qin and Liu (2022), pp. 95–104.

[12] Xinhua News Agency (2019).

judicial protection, with the advancement of environmental judicial specialization in China, biodiversity protection has formed not only a professional judicial protection mechanism in terms of trial institutions, trial basis, typical cases, etc., but also social entities such as experts and scholars, professional appraisal opinions from third-party institutions, etc. have begun to provide reliable support for the judicial protection mechanism of biodiversity protection.

References

Chen T (2001) On the coordination and connection of policies and laws. Theor Explor 1:64–66

Chinese Government Website (2019) Guiding opinions on establishing a nature reserve system with national parks as the main body. https://www.gov.cn/gongbao/content/2019/content_5407657.htm?ivk_sa=1024320u. Accessed 8 June 2023

Chinese Government Website (2021) Opinions on further strengthening biodiversity protection. https://www.gov.cn/zhengce/2021-10/19/content_5643674.htm. Accessed 8 June 2023

Du Q (2023) Review and prospect of the construction of the rule of law for China's nature reserves. J Beijing Univ Aeronaut Astronaut (Soc Sci Edn) 1:32–47

People's Daily Online (2016) GAC Trumpchi joins China's first national park construction plan. http://www.people.com.cn/big5/n1/2016/1107/c347407-28841297.html. Accessed 8 June 2023

Qin T, Liu S (2022) A re-examination of China's legal system for biodiversity conservation in the context of the CBD negotiation. Yuejiang Acad J (6):95–104

The Supreme People's Court of the PRC (2022) Exploring the path of judicial protection of biodiversity with Chinese characteristics. https://www.court.gov.cn/zixun-xiangqing-381891.html. Accessed 18 June 2023

Wang J (2006) Comparative study on environmental impact assessment system – the legal procedure for the environment and development decision-making. Peking University Press, p 175

Xinhua News Agency (2019) The General Office of the Central Committee of the Communist Party of China and the General Office of the State Council opinions on establishing a nature reserve system with national parks as the main body. https://www.gov.cn/zhengce/2019-06/26/content_5403497.htm. Accessed 8 June 2023

Xinhua News Agency (2022) Promoting the construction of national parks in a high-quality manner-interpretation of the plan for the spatial distribution of national parks. http://www.forestry.gov.cn/search/28864. Accessed 10 June 2023

Yu W, Hu Z (2022) Improvement of biodiversity rule of law in the context of ecological civilization. J Beijing Inst Technol (Soc Sci Edn) (2):71–78

Zhou Z, Jin X (2021) Policy, legal system analysis and suggestions for the protection and management of wild plants in China. Biodiversity Prot 12:1583–1590

The Governance of Traditional Knowledge in China: Past, Current, and Future

Yiding Li

Abstract Traditional knowledge, especially traditional Chinese medical knowledge, is a typically symbolic figure of ancient Chinese civilization and is still a heated topic in the governance of both biodiversity and cultural diversity. The governance of traditional knowledge includes and is no limited to ideal, goal, subject and stakeholder, object, model, tool and measure, etc. According to literature review, no theoretical research on a similar topic has been conducted in China so far. Through comprehensively checking and examining the history of the governance of traditional knowledge in China from three different development stages, China has chosen the kinds of rules, such as policies and legislation at different levels, to use as governance tools; built up governance relationships; and formatted a governance model of heteronomy. Looking forward to the future, China should persist on a legislation process, select other governance tools, and create more governance models in the field of governance in traditional knowledge.

1 Introduction

China is a country with the longest history, richest biological resource, and most splendid culture in the world. Different kinds and categories of traditional knowledge form the basis or component of the biodiversity and cultural diversity of this country. Even after ratifying the *Convention on Biodiversity* and signing the *Nagoya Protocol*, China is still faced with urgent, real, and clear pressure on the fulfillment of international law and the implementation of national law.

Recently, it can be found that there are a large number of studies from the perspective of environmental science, ecology, or ethnobotany, but only a few have discussed the topic related to this chapter in English, such as Changhua and Man (2011), Chenguo (2018), Hua (2022), Dilixiati and Xiaoting (2023), Nan (2023), etc.

Y. Li (✉)
Guizhou University, School of Law, Guiyang, Guizhou Province, China

G. Antonelli et al. (eds.), *Biodiversity Laws, Policies and Science in Europe, the United States and China*, https://doi.org/10.1007/978-3-031-56218-1_15

This chapter, titled "The Governance of Traditional Knowledge in China: Past, Current and Future," tries to discuss the protection of traditional knowledge from a distinct perspective. This chapter consists of five parts. The first part is a brief literature review of studies conducted by Chinese scholars, which aims to show what have happened or emerged in China in terms of theoretical research. The second part makes a concise introduction to "governance" from a Chinese theoretical or practical perspective. In the third part, it begins to describe process of governance of traditional knowledge in China from a historical point of view, dividing it into "the past stage," "the current stage," and "the future stage" only based on time quantum. The fourth part is the most essential part of this chapter, which attempts to show the whole picture of the governance of traditional knowledge in China currently. The last part presents comments and identifies problems and solutions for the future in this field.

2 A Brief Literature Review

This part firstly traces back to the theoretical results relates to traditional knowledge in the context of China, hoping to draw the outline of Chinese research on this issue. A search on the journal *China National Knowledge Infrastructure* (CNKI) shows that nearly 600 chapters containing "traditional knowledge" in their titles were published from 1989 to 2023. But in Chinese, "traditional knowledge" can have different meanings under different backgrounds or contexts, and studies that relate to the topic of this chapter may be fewer. This phenomenon suggests that traditional knowledge may still not be a popular issue in theory, not only in the discipline of law.

The earliest chapter related to traditional knowledge was published in (2004), which was written by Prof. Dr. Zhu Xuezhong, a famous intellectual property (IP) expert in China. Then Prof. Dr. Qin Tianbao published his doctoral thesis titled *The Research on Legal Issue on Access and Benefit-Sharing to Genetic Resource* in (2005), which was the first study made from the perspective of environmental law and which filled the gap in theoretical research in this field. Prof. Dr. Yan Yonghe also published his doctoral thesis titled *The Intellectual Property Protection to Traditional Knowledge* in the same year (2006), which was the first study made from the perspective of intellectual property law. Prof. Dr. Song Xiaoting published his first monograph on this, titled *The Legal Protection on Traditional Chinese Medicine Knowledge*, in 2009.

In 2010, Prof. Dr. Xue Dayuan and Prof. Dr. Guo Luo released newly researched results with their study titled *On Concept and Protection of Traditional Knowledge* (Dayuan and Luo 2019). In this paper, from the field survey, Xue and Guo divided traditional knowledge into five categories, respectively knowledge to traditional utilize to agriculture biological genetic resource, knowledge of traditional utilization of medical and biological resources, traditional technical innovation or life style related to biologic resource utilization, traditional culture or custom law related to the conservation and utilization of biological resources, and traditional geographical label production.

When it comes to the definition of "traditional knowledge," Chinese scholars always follow the meeting process of *WIPO-IGC* and other legislation in advanced countries, such as India, Brazil, South Africa, Peru, etc. Understanding the concept is not unusual. In this context, a lot of researchers focused on the relationship between traditional knowledge and intellectual property, mention challenge, intellectualization and suitability, specifically from international law or domestic law. Discussions in this field have nearly failed, for they failed to draw self-consistent conclusion by themselves and problems aroused from the regime of intellectual property itself. They have argued that strong IP rights either harm the developing world, as when they raise the costs of medicines, or disproportionately benefit advanced industrial democracies, whose citizens and firms hold most patents, trademark and copyrights (Munzer and Raustiala 2009). A few studies, such as *Traditional Knowledge Digital Library of India* by Prof. Dr. Li Yiding (Yiding 2020), mentioned country samples. Only one scholar, Prof. Dr. Zhang Chenguo, mentioned traditional knowledge as *sui generis* (Chenguo 2015).

But in the context of traditional Chinese medicine knowledge (TCMK), there is another scene. Due to the special position and demonstration to Chinese culture, TCMK still needs to be paid attention to. Comparative to the research on traditional knowledge, theoretical prospect may be deeper and in detail. For example, Prof. Dr. Ma Zhiguo and Prof. Dr. Zhou Fang mentioned some values of TCMK legislation (Zhiguo and Fang 2008). Prof. Dr. Liang Yan proposed non sui generis model to traditional knowledge in *Law on Traditional Chinese Medicine* (Yan 2017). Dr. Song Jian discussed the categories of subjects of right in the field of TCMK (Jian 2019). Prof. Dr. Chen Qing stipulated limited rules on the rights of stakeholders in the field of TCMK (Qing 2022). Dr. Wang Hua and Dr. Hu Qin showed the benefit sharing right to TCMK (Hua and Qin 2017). Dr. Zhang Jiwang etc. talked about the basic principles of TCMK legislation (Jiwang et al. 2013).

But what is traditional knowledge? Maybe introducing self-experience samples is more specific than making a definition. Early summer every year, Yunnan Province, which is located in the western part of China and which is the richest in biodiversity and cultural diversity, enters the "season of mushrooms." In this period, you will see that the daily life of local people in that place is to have a mushroom hotpot. Due to a large number of mushroom unnamed or unrecognized, there are always poisoned people sent to the hospital. The disease control and prevention center of local governments even released folk songs to warn citizens not to misunderstand and eat toxic mushroom. The traditional knowledge included in this anecdote is permutation and combination of mushrooms and chicken boiled together. First, when you go to any restaurant, you will see that the categories, kinds, or numbers of mushrooms are different. Second, boiling mushrooms with chicken, instead of pork or beef, is the best choice and has a delicious taste. The author asked about the reason of this combination, but the waiter did not give an answer but replied that it was the custom. And in the process of boiling, the waiter always warn that we should not stir with the chopsticks to so as to prevent toxics, and mushrooms with chicken usually need to be boiled for 12 minutes. After that, without putting any seasoning, you should drink a soup first and enjoy it. This case is a typical case of traditional knowledge, fit for nearly all characteristics of the concept in theory. From the case, you will take a glance of traditional knowledge. "[W]hat is called traditional, it only means model of access or utilize to knowledge belongs to the part of cultural tradition in specific folk or local community" (Zuxue 2006). In this way, we present some typical definitions made by Chinese scholars, and you will see that they are close to the mainstream understanding in the world. "Traditional knowledge is the intellectual innovative achievement that appeared and inherited by generation after generation in a specific region, which features remarkable unique value, and a close connection with specific culture and population" (Xiaoting 2006).

3 Governance

The word "governance" is an exotic word that is not original from China. The concept defined by *The Commission on Global Governance* is more representative and authoritative. In *Our Global Neighborhood*, "governance" means the sum of the many ways individuals and institutions, public and private, manage their common affairs (*The Commission on Global Governance* 1995). It is a continuous process through which conflicting or diverse interests may be accommodated and cooperative action may be taken. Now the world is entering an era of comprehensive and deep governance. For the scholars in the field of politics or management in China, it is a new theoretical issue or topic compared with government and regulation. Prof. Dr. Yu Keping, a famous scholar, said: "From the perspective of politics, governance means the process of politic management. It includes rule basement of politic authority, model of politic affairs track with and the management of common resources" (Keping 1999). This issue has upgraded to become a national strategy officially, as shown in *Several Major Issues on Persisting and Improving the System of Socialism with Chinese Characteristics, Promoting the National Governance System and Modernizing National Capacity for Governance* decided by the Central Committee of the Communist Party of China in 2019.

The ideal of governance demonstrate the differences in terms of subject, goal, mode, tool, etc. For example, the subject of governance may not only be the government at different levels but also include the citizens, non-government organizations, communities, enterprises, etc. The goal of governance should stratify the interest at best and sustain the public interest. The models of governance may include self-governance, mutual governance, governance in common, etc. The tool of governance should not be limited but should include moral, ethic, law, intelligence, standard, etc. In view of this, the following section reviews and provides comments on the development process of traditional knowledge conservation in China from the perspective of governance.

Unlike in the context of the Western world, "governance" in China embodies Chinese features. From the *Guide Opinion on Establishing a Modern Environmental*

Governance System by the General Office of the Communist Party of China and the State Council in 2020, China wanted to build a governance system "led by the Committee of the Communist Party of China, dominated by the government, with enterprises as the priority, and participated by social organizations and citizens." In the system, government is the key subject in the governance of environment. This judgment also applies in the field of governance of traditional knowledge in China.

4 The Past Stage

Officials in China has begun to focus on related issues since 1990s. The *Decisions on Enhancing Environment Protection* by the State Council required local governments to lay emphasis on the protection of species resources. The *China Biodiversity Conservation Action Plan* (2002) was the first action plan promulgated by the Bureau of Environmental Protection in 1994. The *Notices on Enhancing Biological Species Resource Conservation and Management* by the General Office of the State Council in 2004 aimed to solve the problem of disappeared or lost species in China. Then some other guidelines were also stipulated and implemented, such as the *National Guidelines on Conservation and Utilization of Biological Species (2006–2020)* (2007), *China Biodiversity Conservation Strategy and Action Plan (2008–2020*; "*Strategy and Action Plan" as follows)*. But it is a pity that a lot of policies mentioned above did not contain the issue of traditional knowledge from the beginning, except the *Strategy and Action Plan*. The main reason may be the consciousness of officials.

The *Strategy and Action Plan* mentioned above may be the first appearance of traditional knowledge in official documents. It was updated once in 2011. This content was mainly drafted by the *Ministry of Environmental Protection* (whose name was changed to the Ministry of Ecological and Environment in 2018), with the participation of other 28 ministries, national administrations, etc. During the whole process, traditional knowledge is affiliated with genetic resources emerged in policies, goals, etc. In the 2011 version of the *Strategy and Action Plan*, the situation was changed dramatically for it had to suit the *Nagoya Protocol*, which was passed at that time. "Traditional knowledge" or "traditional knowledge associated with genetic resource" appeared in the parts of principles, missions, prior areas and actions. The essence of all these clauses was an attempt to establish the regime of access and benefit sharing and realize rescuing conversations. To achieve this goal, one task is the survey and documentation of traditional knowledge.

At this stage, China completed the third revision of *Law on Patent*. At this time, the legislation first involved the validation on patent related to biodiversity. Clause 2 article 5 said that "if access to or utilization of genetic resources violate laws or regulations, the related patent must be invalid." The *Enforcement Regulation on Law on Patent* further supplemented it. Progress in the field of patent achieved the goal of protection of biodiversity, but it seems that it is has no relation to the governance of traditional knowledge in China for it only suits genetic resources and cannot be explained in a broad sense. China adapted a very different pathway to disclosure, not belongs to voluntary, mandatory or proof of legal acquisition (Fuguo and Jisong 2008).

5 The Current Stage

This stage has seen two types of legislation. One is the *Law on Intangible Cultural Heritage* (ICH), and the other is the *Law on Traditional Chinese Medicine*.

Due to the impact of the *Convention on the Conservation of Intangible Cultural Heritage*, China passed the *Law on Intangible Cultural Heritage* in 2011, although there was previously a *Law on National Folk and Culture (Draft)*. In this law, China transferred international experience into its national practice, examples being representative programs of ICH inheritors at different levels. Based on this legislation, China had stipulated a comprehensively, overly and systematically legal regime in this field. In Article 2 of this legislation, traditional technology, medicine, and calendar fall in the category of ICH in China. Traditional Medicine, the traditional knowledge relates to this issue should be conserved by *Law on ICH*. But it aroused the doubt of why this legislation did not embrace "knowledge and practice related to nature and atmosphere" in the definition of ICH, that emerged in the convention mentioned above. The possible reason may be the expression of the convention is not clear enough to understand for China, but this category of ICH is truly the traditional knowledge in literal. Now, China had 43 categories of heritages selected into the *Intangible Culture Heritage List of UNESCO*. Till 2020, there are 1557 national intangible culture heritages, and 3063 inheritors of national intangible culture heritages (China Artistic Institute 2023).

Local places in China have a lot of legislations and practice in this field. This process changed the tendency of legislation status quo in China, which the central legislation never mentioned before, and it also reflects the ideal of access and benefit sharing. Local legislation on ICH from Tianjin, Sichuan Province, Jiangxi Province, Yunnan Province, Zhejiang Province, Gansu Province, etc. regulate that the interview, entity object assembling, photograph, and record should be with a prior informed consent. Local legislation on ICH from Jiangxi Province, Gansu Province, Liaoning Province, Anhui Province, Henan Province, Shanxi Province, Chongqing, Guizhou Province, etc. also require that the application of ICH programs be with prior informed consent. Article 44 of the *Regulation on Conservation on ICH* of Jiangsu Province, Article 20 of the *Regulation on Conservation on ICH* of Yichang, Hubei Province mention that the natural right or legal right related to ICH, traditional knowledge, genetic resources and folk culture technology should be protected.

The *Law on Traditional Chinese Medicine* was the first time in which the right to TCMK was discussed. The reason of drafting this legislation is to inherit TCMK, and to safeguard and promote the development of traditional Chinese medicine. In clause 1 of Article 43, it was stated that "the state establishes the regime of database, conservation list, etc." In clause 2, it opined "stakeholders of TCMK" have the right to inherit and utilize TCMK held by them, and that they also have the right to prior informed consent and benefit sharing. From the wording of the article, this kind of right is not intellectual property right obviously. At least, innovation of legal regime like this dispel a part of scholar's doubt. A *sui generis* intellectual property model to protect traditional knowledge will not eliminate the need to enforce and protect existing intellectual property rights (J. Janewa Oseitutu 2011). It is very meaningful to the situation or status of governance of traditional knowledge in China. Firstly, it created a new governance relationship between stakeholders and other subjects, which has enriched the governance model in this field. We will see that not only in the first stage, but in the preliminary phase of the second stage, the relationship was still that between the governments at different levels and other subjects which appeared popular. In spite that local legislations of ICH have mentioned some elements, they had always been not clearly or directly enough. For example, when it comes to what is natural right or legal right to ICH, traditional knowledge, genetic resource and folk culture technology, we might not find a solution in local legislations. Secondly, it offered an innovative right relief tool to cope with possible right prejudice, although it may only implement in board. An example is the phenomenon of "biopiracy," especially in the field of TCMK, China is still coveted by neighboring countries. Along with the staff or work of investigation or documentation of TCMK, the identification, status, etc. may be delimited gradually, the judicial needs require legislation preparation. "To offer subject *sui generis* to traditional knowledge, stimulating inner impetus on conservation or inherit to the maximum extent, traditional knowledge should be conserved, inherited, utilize in effective and development" (Fang 2011). Thirdly, it pushed legislative process extremely in this field for China. Contemporary to *Law on Traditional Chinese Medicine*, the *Regulation on Administration on Access and Benefit-Sharing to Genetic Resource (Draft)* initiated by the Ministry of Environmental Protection (now called the Ministry of Ecological and Environment).[1] This attempt perhaps was the option of comprehensive one. The advantage of this option is that it can address all issues related to GR and its related TK in a single legal instrument (Tianbao 2009). But it is regretful that there is no coincidence to the authority of administrative authorities, this regulation still needs to be promoted further. After *Law on Traditional Chinese Medicine* was passed, it has not filled the gap of legislation, but it primarily established a legal system in this field.

But some terms should be explained theoretically. For example, who are the "stakeholders" of TCMK? Does it refer only to owners? What are the categories? The first notion is that the understanding of "stakeholder" needs to be wide. The range of stakeholders should not be limited to owners but should rather be extended to possessors, managers, and other subjects. ". . .[S]takeholders include providers of biological resources, investors related to the research and development of Chinese

[1] In the regulation, some articles mentioned traditional knowledge associated with genetic resource, such as article 2(definition), article 5(conservation of traditional knowledge), article 6(documentation of traditional knowledge), article 7(collective management of traditional knowledge), article 35 (redistribute to benefit-sharing based on collective management organization), article 43(legal responsibility of collective management organization), ect.

Traditional Medicine and innovators related to the production of Chinese Traditional Medical Knowledge" (Yanhui and Xiaoting 2013). In terms of published chapters, the ownership *status quo* of TCMK in China shows very different patterns (Yiding 2013). Many kinds of TCMK are posited in public domain, only a little has specific right declaration, and some kinds are possessed by common communities, collectives, etc. Traditional knowledge may be known within one particular indigenous or local group or only by specific members of a particular group (e.g., healers) or, more commonly and complicatedly, by a discrete number of neighboring groups within a geographical area (Varadaranjan 2011). But in the real world, who are the representatives of possessors or managers? Some scholars mentioned that "communities" should be the stakeholders (Changjian and Haiping 2007; Bingbin 2007); however, "community" is not an accepted term in China's legal system but only an expression used within the sociology or anthropology discipline. But in communities, we will organize or combine subjects that fit for the legal identification, rural collective economic organization is the prior option from *Civil Code.* And collective management organization in the *Regulation on Administration on Access and Benefit-Sharing to Genetic Resource (Draft)* is a new expression, perhaps after it becomes effective, it will be another suitable option. "Considering these conditions, for convenience to manage TCMK and safeguard the benefit of stakeholders, it is necessary for the state to establish united collective management organizations, so that subjects of right can trusted the management of intellectual properties to collective manage organizations" (Xiaoyu and Wushuang 2009).

After the *Law on Traditional Chinese Medicine* entered into effect, National Administration of Traditional Chinese Medicine launched the program on draft on *Regulation on Conservation on Traditional Chinese Medical Knowledge*, serving as the matching rules to the articles related to *Law on Traditional Chinese Medicine.* This program become the critical issue of the national intellectual property strategy. *The Plan on Implementing National Intellectual Property Strategy Deeply, and Enhancing the Establishment of an Intellectual Property Powerhouse* (2018) required to push the staff of database on TCMK, conservation list on TCMK, and to enhance the intellectual property protection on ancient classical prescription. In *The Plan on Implementing the National Intellectual Property Strategy Deeply, and Enhancing the Establishment of an Intellectual Property Powerhouse (2019)*, it first mentioned to promote the legislative process of *Regulation on the Conservation of Traditional Chinese Medical Knowledge.* And this viewpoint was also referred to in *The Opinion on the Inheritance and the Innovative Development of Traditional Chinese Medicine* by the Central Committee of the Communist Party of China and the State Council.

National Administration of Traditional Chinese Medicine of China had stipulated *Regulation on the Conservation of Traditional Chinese Medical Knowledge (Draft)* in 2021 for public consultation. Till now, this legislation remains in process and is much expected. As the matching rules to *Law on Chinese Traditional Medicine* mentioned above, this legislation attempts to draw the outline of bundle of rights on TCMK, but it aroused the paradox that this legal practice may disobey the principle of law reservation on *Law on Legislation* in China. And other confusion is about what kinds of obligation correspond with the bundle of rights on TCMK. Now neither the *Law on Chinese Traditional Medicine* nor the *Regulation on the Conservation of Traditional Chinese Medical Knowledge (Draft)* has been clearly demonstrated. As we know, the subject of obligation may stem from state, government, individual, etc. According to the context, obligations suitable for the bundles of rights on TCMK is almost at the state level, a kind of positive obligation that advices the government (which is the representative of the state) to fulfill its duty of conservation, registration, documentation, etc. Some of the obligations are perhaps at the individual level, involving enterprises, communities, or other subjects. When encountering the situation of access to traditional knowledge, individuals should obey the rules in due diligence, as to safeguard or implement the right to prior informed consent or mutual agreed terms from the stakeholders of TCMK.

Law on Traditional Chinese Medicine has driven the perfection of local legislations. The issue of TCMK related to local legislations has been divided up into four fields. First is to set obligations for governments above the county level. These obligations include collection, disposal, exploration, and utilization. Shanxi Province, Guangdong Province, Guangxi Zhuang Autonomous Region, Gansu Province, etc. have complied with this article. The second one refers to the requirement on benefit sharing. Article 49 of *Regulation on Traditional Chinese Medicine of Guizhou Province (2021)* allows classic prescription, secret prescription, proved recipe, diagnosis and treatment technology, process drug technology and research achievement related to this to be transferred or to be an intelligence to contribution of capital, and should cooperate to benefit sharing during the process. The third one is to establish the obligation on disclosure. Clause 4 Article 45 of *Regulation on Traditional Chinese Medicine of Jiangxi Province* stipulated that without the consent of the right holder, anyone cannot disclosure, utilize or permit others to utilize classic prescriptions, secret prescriptions, proved recipes, diagnosis and treatment technology, process drug technology. The fourth one is to create a database or conservation list on TCMK at local levels. Qinghai Province, Beijing, Zhejiang Province, Jiangsu Province, Hubei Province, etc. had fulfilled this article. We have also seen news stating that a lot of provinces in China have begun such documentation as well as registration of TCMK. One facet is the performance to abide by local legislation in this field, another facet is the implementation of *Law on Traditional Chinese Medicine* into real practice.

During the first stage of CBD COP-15 convened in Kunming, it is a very rare opportunity to promote public consciousness, complete propaganda and deploy work related to biodiversity. The *Opinion on Further Enhancing the Conservation of Biodiversity* was issued by the General Office of the Central Committee of the Communist Party of China and the State Council. This policy pushed China directly into a new era of biodiversity governance. This shows the requirement, principle, goal, mission, and priority in the near future.

This document proposed "...to research and draft the *Regulation on the Conservation of Traditional Knowledge Related to Biodiversity*." It also designed "...to implement the investigation or documentation of biological genetic resources and those associated with traditional knowledge." The latter one is not a novel expression, but the first point reminds that the legislative situation in China may turn into "a third trail model." The legal system in this field is combined with ICH, TCMK and traditional knowledge related to biodiversity.

What is the meaning of traditional knowledge related to biodiversity? In essence, this definition is the same as the expression "biological genetic resources associated with traditional knowledge." one explanation is that two different expressions should not appear in one policy such as this one, other argument is comparative study between advisory standard and regulation drafted from the Ministry of Environmental Protection (now called the Ministry of Ecological and Environment). From the *Technological Rules on Taxonomy, Investigation and Category Related to Traditional Knowledge Related to Biodiversity (for Trial Implementation)* (2014) and *The Regulation on Administration on Access and Benefit-sharing to Genetic Resources (Draft)*, although they have chosen different words, but the implication is the same, pointing out "the knowledge, innovation and method that benefited for biodiversity conservation and sustainable utilization, which is invented, inherited and developed by people of all nationalities and local communities."

Why has the "a third trail model" emerged? The critical reason may be the departmental legislation orientation. In China, legislation and legislative iteration are advocated by administrative authorities, whether at the central or local level. Legislation or legislative iteration from administrative authorities is generally based on their needs for administrative regulation, even if mutual consultation between administrative authorities during the legislation process, it always leads to potential application conflicts. It is undeniable that before the *Law on Chinese Traditional Medicine*, a part of traditional knowledge, especially TCMK, were conserved by means of the *Law on ICH*. We also see that inheritors, especially those in the field of traditional medical medicine, have been included in the "stakeholders of TCMK" in the process of related legislation.

The main points of establishing the *Regulation on the Conservation of Traditional Knowledge Related to Biodiversity* are as follows: (1) significance – why should China enact this legislation? There may be two reasons. One is to perfect the legal system for biodiversity conservation in China, and the other is to create duties such as those of the Ministry of Ecological and Environment. (2) Location – it means the position of this legislation in the biodiversity legal system in China. Compared with the *Regulation on the Conservation of Traditional Chinese Medical Knowledge (Draft)*, the relationship between these two drafts is special and general, which implies that even though they are different in subject and object, they should coordinate with each other in practice. If China restarts the process of *Regulation on Administration on Access and Benefit-Sharing to Genetic Resources (Draft)*, the object should include traditional knowledge related to biodiversity (synonyms as biological genetic resources associated with traditional knowledge), for reason that the *Regulation on the Conservation of Traditional Knowledge Related to Biodiversity* is a specific one which can be substitute for article in the former. (3) Source of law – one direct source is the *Law on Environmental Protection*. Article 30 thereof was the first time in which the term "biodiversity conservation" was introduced. Another indirect source is *Law on ICH*, which may support or assist the legal regime of traditional knowledge related to biodiversity in operation. (4) Goals – the legislation should accept the idea of pluralism when it comes to its goals. Conservation should be the priority, but it should also promote sustainable utilization and the protection of the right or benefit of the local people and communities. (5) Principles – these should include the principle of conservation as a priority: the principle of regulating categories; the principle of cooperation and benefit sharing; the principle of public participation; the principle of conservation as a priority, matching the goal of the legislation; the principle of regulating categories, considering the *status quo* of traditional knowledge in China; the principle of cooperation and benefit sharing according to the spirit of the *Convention on Biodiversity* and the *Nagoya Protocol*; typical principles under the *Law on Environmental Protection*. As the source of this legislation, the principle of this law should be referred to. (6) Ideal – undoubtedly, the ideal of this legislation is governance. Compared with the general regulation of ecological environment affairs, governance focuses more on the transfer of subjects, tools, models and effects, etc. Governance of traditional knowledge related to biodiversity should follow the value of equity, fairness, mutual benefit sharing and cooperate. The subjects include governments, enterprises, non-government organizations and citizens, etc. Besides laws or policies, governance should concentrate on other tools of function or effects, such as ethic, standards, intelligence, etc. The model should not only emphasize self-governance but must also highlight mutual governance and common governance. (7) Regimes – these should include the regime of investigation and registration, of prior informed consent, and of mutual agreed terms. Nowadays, China has no plans of initiating this draft legislation program; maybe we still need time and energy to prepare for it.

6 The Future Stage

This section is divided into three parts. After finishing our discussion on the history development on the issue of governance of traditional knowledge in China, we should make comments. Then it is necessary to propose problems and find solutions, so as to construct the governance in the future.

6.1 Comments

In nearly 20 years of practice, the governance of traditional knowledge in China has had the following characteristics: first, government orientation. This phenomenon is manifested by lots of policies and legislations promulgated, although "governance" advocated. The categories of policies include strategies, opinions, notices, etc. On the other hand, the categories of legislation include central legislation, such as law and regulation, and local legislation. especially in the field of local legislation in ICH, it changed the status of "top-down" legislation to a certain degree. This is also reflected in the fact that legislative authorities or governments in China are gradually paying more attention to this topic, and we hope that the situation will get better in the future. Second is multiple relationships. Accompanied by the process of policies and legislation, China has formatted various kinds of governance relationships. One is the general regulate relationship between the government and administrative stakeholders. The circumstance existed during the governance of ICH and TCMK. Following the narration above, *Law on ICH* kept the ideal or pattern from the *Convention on the Conservation of Intangible Culture Heritages*. As typical legislation innovation, *Law on Chinese Traditional Medicine* proposed rights of stakeholders to TCMK, although there is no sample till now, it depicted potential concerns between stakeholders and others. Basically, it is an equally and mutually beneficial relationship. Third singularity tool. Currently, the governance of traditional knowledge in China mainly uses rules (in a broad sense) as governance tools. Despite emerged model agreement, guidance in the aspect of microbiological resources does not include TCMK. It still only a thought to bring ethic into scientific research or local communities where the obstacles are consciousness and capability. Fourth, simpleness mode. Based on policies and legislation, governance of traditional knowledge in China focusing on heteronomy, self-governance or mutual governance has not yet been established.

6.2 Problems

In the context of "a three-trail model," the primary problem is the coordination or linkage between pieces of legislation at different levels. The *Opinion on Enhancing the Conservation of Intangible Culture Heritages* by the General Office of the Communist Party of China and the State Council in 2022 said that ". . .to establish regime of access and benefit to intangible culture heritages. . .," which implied that intangible cultural heritages had become the object of the regime of access and benefit sharing. If one kind of traditional knowledge belongs at the same time to intangible cultural heritage and TCMK, how should be the regime of access and benefit sharing operate? What are the key points during the whole progress?

Firstly, inheritors should be considered in the operation of access and benefit sharing. China had stipulated the regime system of inheritors, who are the providers or users of access and benefit sharing. Inheritors are only an identity certificated by administrative authorities, and they are accessors of intangible cultural heritages from local communities or other stakeholders. Indeed, access and benefit sharing happened between inheritors and other stakeholders, such as customers, producers, etc. Secondly, regime designers should reject the "secondary benefit-sharing" in one object. If a kind of traditional knowledge completed the progress according to one legislation, the administrative authority should fulfill the obligation of announcement, other administrative authorities should confirm this practice and should not repeat the process again for the equality and fairness. As customers or producers access to intangible culture heritages from inheritors directly, it should not initiate benefit sharing with local communities or other stakeholders because they are not offering resources.

Another problem is the possibility of introducing new governance tools. One side of the coin is that the object or sphere of rules, no matter legislation or policies, should be limited. The spirit of governance also advocated multiple tools to be chosen and adapted, ethic, standards, intelligence may be the prioritized ones. Ethic may be substitution for legislation when it does not take into effect on condition. Standards may offer technological assistance or support, intelligence may be a typical decision instrument for resource security.

6.3 Solutions

One solution should face the "a three-tail mode" legislation in this field. The different administrative authorities, such as the Ministry of Culture and Tourism, the Ministry of Ecological and Environment, and the National Administration of Chinese Traditional Medicine, should communicate or coordinate with one another in a timely manner. The key point is to leave vacancy for other legislation draft or implement which is administrative authority oriented. And in general, it should give the deliberative coordination bodies play their role in this issue. For effectiveness and efficiency of administrative regulations, China (2016, 2022) has established lots of temporary organizations, such as the inter-ministerial joint meeting on intangible cultural heritages and Chinese Traditional Medicine. Access and benefit sharing should be taken into account during the process.

Then it should place great hopes on the *Regulation on the Conservation on Traditional Chinese Medical Knowledge*. After the stagnation of the *Regulation on Administration on Access and Benefit-Sharing to Genetic Resources (Draft)*, the *Regulation on the Conservation of Traditional Chinese Medical Knowledge* becomes the sole legislation in this field currently in China. The ideal of "…establishing regime of access and benefit to intangible cultural heritages…" and "…researching and drafting *Regulation on the Conservation of Traditional Knowledge Related to Biodiversity*…" is still in the phase of official will. China still lacks clear and practical rules in the aspect of access to and benefit sharing of biological genetic resources and those associated with traditional knowledge, such as prior informed consent and mutually agreed terms; this legislation has perhaps yet to fill the gaps. Whereas the pressure increases after adopting the *Nagoya Protocol*, entering into *Regional Comprehensive Economic Partnership* and preparing to join *Comprehensive and Progressive Agreement for Trans-Pacific Partnership*. All these international economic laws include articles relates traditional knowledge, which should be carefully considered or closely concerned. In the context of international laws mentioned above, this legislation also face with new circumstances or environments, and it may become a huge challenge to legislators or administrative authorities. From this perspective, the legislation taking a relatively long time scale will be justifiable.

Except legislations mentioned above, China should also extend the object of *Law on Patent* to traditional knowledge. Even though there are defective rules, traditional knowledge is not included in the fourth revision on *Law on Patent(2020)* which could be deemed as a pity. China National Intellectual Property Administration have not explained why they made such a choice, but this practice may aggregate "biopiracy" potentially by the reason that patent application related to traditional knowledge has the same position as biological genetic resources. The function of object extension is to further build the legal regime structure of traditional knowledge in China such as disclosure, so as to enrich governance models. Voluntary disclosure is not suitable for the governance status or situation in China, mandatory disclosure would break the balance between appliers (accessors) and the public (providers as the representative), mode of proof of acquisition should be the optimum choice in the field of traditional knowledge patent application.

China should also encourage spontaneous and non-mandatory rules in the process of governance. It reckoned that China should bring ethics into the research community and local communities. Ethic values would be revealed by guidelines. Ethic itself represent self-governance or heteronomy model, which is implied through ethic, and behaviors would be influenced or changed. If ethic is applied to specific groups, members or stakeholders should be "controlled" but not in the same way as the operation of law, but mainly through consciousness. Just like Germany, which adopted research guidelines related to the access and benefit sharing to biological genetic resources (DFG DFG 2021). Nowadays, China attaches importance to the issue of scientific and technological ethics. A lot of research institutes and universities have established committees on research ethic for ethical review and regulation. But the priority area is the kinds of assessment on impact of experiment, biotechnology development to human, animals or environment. Access and benefit sharing also influence human, resources and the environment, which we have merely noticed. We passionately expect that committees on research ethic would lay emphasis on research related to biological genetic resources, traditional knowledge and even biodiversity, it is so clear that relevant ethic should be contemporary. Traditional knowledge in China emerged or existed in local communities, which have always been "heavy afflicted areas" with a lack of rules. As we know, legislation, no matter at what level, usually plays no role in it; people here pay more attention to their own rules, such as custom law. Like Alaska in the United States, this country had enacted Guidelines for Respecting Cultural Knowledge (Alaska Native Traditional Network 2000). Governments, especially those at local levels, would invite citizens or villagers from local communities to formulate guidelines and model agreements related to biodiversity conservation and access to and benefit sharing of biological genetic resources and associated traditional knowledge. And we also expect relevant industries, enterprises, and companies to introduce the ideal of access and benefit sharing into their business.

All tasks cited above can be accomplished through capacity building. This issue should be the priority after finishing rulemaking and the legislation process. Also from the field experience, when the pilot program related to access and benefit to biological genetic resource and associated with traditional knowledge supported by

Global Environment Facility came to China during the years from 2017 to 2021, we found that lots of subjects, especially in local places, were not had basic cognition on this issue. The answer to the question "what capacity development does" is "implementation (to conserve and sustainably manage biodiversity for present and future generations), impact (to cope with environment degradation), synergies (to enhance cooperation and collaboration and foster partnership for action) and value for money (to ensure returns on investments mode) (IUCN 2018). Maybe capacity building is the most difficult step in the governance of traditional knowledge, but still it is a delight to see more and more non-governmental organizations devote their time to this field.

7 Conclusion

For nearly 20 years, China has gone through two stages in the field of governance of traditional knowledge, and now it is about to enter the next stage. Although there still some gaps to achieve status or situation of governance in the true sense, it is without any doubt that progress, achievement of governance in traditional knowledge in China have been greatly realized, such as the ideal, element, and performance. Governance of traditional knowledge is a new topic for China, and governments, citizens, enterprises, local communities, researchers, etc. must not only have awareness but also take actions.

References

Alaska Native Traditional Network (2000) Guidelines for Respecting Cultural Knowledge. Available at http://ankn.uaf.edu/publications/Knowledge.pdf

Bingbin L (2007) Community as the right holder of traditional knowledge basic: theoretical issues. Presently Law Sci 8(2):64–68

Central Government of the People's Republic of China (1990) Decisions on Enhancing Environmental Protection. Available at https://www.gov.cn/zhengce/content/2010-12/17/content_5263.htm

Central Government of the People's Republic of China (2004) Notices on Enhancing Biological Species Resource Conservation and Management. Available at https://www.gov.cn/govweb/gongbao/content/2004/content_62739.htm

Central Government of the People's Republic of China (2016) Approval on Inter-Ministerial Joint Meeting on Traditional Chinese Medicine, by the State Council. Available at https://www.gov.cn/zhengce/content/2016-08/25/content_5102220.htm

Central Government of the People's Republic of China (2018) The Plan on Implementing National Intellectual Property Strategy Deeply, and Enhancing the Establishment of an Intellectual Property Powerhouse (2018) Available at https://www.gov.cn/xinwen/2018-11/09/content_5338779.htm

Central Government of the People's Republic of China (2020) Guide on Opinion on Establishing a Modern Environmental Governance System, Available at https://www.gov.cn/gongbao/content/2020/content_5492489.htm

Central Government of the People's Republic of China (2022) Letter on Adjusting and Perfecting the Inter-Ministerial Joint Meeting on Intangible Cultural Heritages by the General Office of the State Council. Available at https://www.gov.cn/zhengce/content/2022-02/17/content_5674176.htm
Changhua L, Man G (2011) Protecting traditional knowledge of Chinese: concepts and proposals. Front Med 5(2):212–218
Changjian L, Haiping X (2007) Justification of protecting traditional knowledge by intellectual property law taking communities as the new subject of right simultaneously. Presently Law Sci 5(3):11–17
Chenguo Z (2015) On the establishment of sui generis of traditional knowledge in China-combined with definite of subject of right of traditional knowledge materialized. Polit Law 1:79–92
Chenguo Z (2018) How is the owner of 'Traditional Knowledge Right'? A perspective of international law and the case of China. J Legal Ethical Regul Issues 21(2):1–14
China Artistic Institute (2023) China Intangible Culture Heritage Website Available at https://www.ihchina.cn/#page9
Dayuan X, Luo G (2019) On concept and protection of traditional knowledge. Biodiv Sci 17(2): 135–142
Dilixiati D, Xiaoting S (2023) Benefit-sharing model of traditional knowledge based on substantive fairness in China. Queen Mary J Intell Prop 13(1):75–96
Fang Z (2011) Defining the rights of traditional knowledge from legal perspective. J Xi'an Jiaotong Univ (Soc Sci) 31(5):91–98
Fuguo D, Jisong Y (2008) A study on creation a mechanism of the origin disclosure of traditional knowledge. Hebei Law Sci 26(12):100–103
Hua W (2022) Protecting traditional Chinese medicine's traditional knowledge: on application of research of benefit-sharing right. Forest Chem Rev 4:2425–2433
Hua W, Qin H (2017) A study on the benefit-sharing right of traditional Chinese medicine knowledge. J NanJing Univ Tradit Chinese Med (Soc Sci) 18(3):165–170
IUCN (2018) Capacity Building and Synergies across the Biodiversity-related Conventions: Contributing to the Design and Subsequent Implementation of a Long-term Strategic Framework for Capacity Building beyond 2020, p. 8
Janewa Oseitutu J (2011) A Sui Generis regime for traditional knowledge: the cultural divide in intellectual property law. Marquette Intellect Prop Law Rev 15:171
Jian S (2019) Discussion on the types of subject of right of traditional Chinese medicine knowledge: on the improvement of legislation in China. J Guizhou Normal Univ (Soc Sci) 5:152–160
Jiwang Z, Meihong W, Ye R (2013) The basic principles of legislation on traditional Chinese medicine knowledge protection. China Health Law 21(4):9–12
Keping Y (1999) The introduction to governance and good governance. Marxism Reality 5:39
Ministry of Ecological and Environment of the People's Republic of China (2002) China Biodiversity Conservation Action Plan. Available at https://www.mee.gov.cn/ywgz/zrstbh/swdyxbh/200607/t20060725_91260.shtml
Ministry of Ecological and Environment of the People's Republic of China (2007) Guidelines on National Biological Species Conversation and Utilization (2006-2020), Available at https://www.mee.gov.cn/gkml/zj/wj/200910/t20091022_172479.htm
Ministry of Ecological and Environment of the People's Republic of China (2014) Announcement on Technological Rules on Taxonomy, Investigation and Category Related to Traditional Knowledge Related to Biodiversity (for Trial Implementation), Available at https://www.mee.gov.cn/gkml/hbb/bgg/201406/t20140606_276593.htm
Munzer SR, Raustiala K (2009) The uneasy case for intellectual property rights in traditional knowledge. Cardozo Art Entertain Law J 27:51
Nan X (2023) Intellectual property protection for traditional medical knowledge in China's context: a round pig in a square hole? Med Law Rev 00:1–33
National Administration of Traditional Chinese Medicine (2021) Notice on Seeking Public Opinions on the Regulation on the Conservation of Traditional Chinese Medical Knowledge (Draft

for Public Consultation), Available at http://www.natcm.gov.cn/fajiansi/gongzuodongtai/2021-10-25/22994.html
Qing C (2022) On the construction of restriction rules for the rights of holders of traditional knowledge-with the law on traditional Chinese medicine as an opportunity. Hebei Law Sci 40(2):148–161
Senate Commission on Fundamental Issues of Biological Diversity of the German Research Foundation (DFG) (2021) Guidelines for Research and/or Development Projects involving Access to Genetic Resources and/or to Traditional Knowledge Associated with Genetic Resources
The Commission on Global Governance (1995) Our Global Neighborhood
Tianbao Q (2005) The research on legal issue on access and benefit-sharing to genetic resources. Wuhan University Press, Wuhan
Tianbao Q (2009) The process of legislation on access and benefit sharing in China-a new long March. In: Kamau EC, Winter G (eds) Genetic resource, traditional knowledge and the law. Earthscan, pp 225–241
Varadaranjan D (2011) A trade secret approach to protecting traditional knowledge. Yale J Int Law 36:399
Xiaoting S (2006) On law on sui generis to traditional Chinese medical knowledge and framework design. Intellect Prop Right Law Res 2:57–80
Xiaoting S (2009) Legal protection on traditional knowledge medical knowledge. Law Press, Beijing
Xiaoyu Z, Wushuang H (2009) On the establishment of a new legal regime on the conservation of benefit of traditional medical knowledge. J Chongqing Inst Technol (Soc Sci) 5:53
Xuezhong Z (2004) A study on legal protection of traditional knowledge. J Central China Normal Univ (Human Soc Sci) 43(3):31–40
Yan L (2017) On the no sui generis model to traditional knowledge-the opportunity brought about by the law on traditional Chinese medicine. Gansu Soc Sci 6:148
Yanhui W, Xiaoting S (2013) The construction of the benefit-sharing in traditional knowledge of Chinese medicine. Hebei Law Sci 31(9):121
Yiding L (2013) The legal empirical analysis of access and benefit-sharing of traditional knowledge of common pools in China. Sci Technol Law 1:7–12
Yiding L (2020) The development trend and enlightenment of governance system of traditional knowledge database of India. Intellect Prop 3:86–96
Yonghe Y (2006) The intellectual property protection to traditional knowledge. Law Press, Beijing
Zhiguo M, Fang Z (2008) Protection of traditional Chinese medicine knowledge-a study on the legislation value. J Xi'an Jiaotong Univ (Soc Sci) 28(1):44–49
Zuxue G (2006) On the ability of traditional knowledge to obtain intellectual property. J Xiamen Univ (Soc Sci) 2:13

Current Situation and Future of Legislation on Precaution of Alien Species Invasion in China

Wang Luquan

Abstract China has focused on the issue of invasive alien species as early as 1982 in the Regulations on Import and Export Animal and Plant Quarantine, which were followed by the Entry-Exit Animal and Plant Quarantine Law, Marine Environmental Protection Law, Grassland Law and Seed Law. The Biosecurity Law (2020) and the Management Measures for Alien Invasive Species (2022) further refine the institutional context of the prevention and control of invasive alien species. However, there are still deficiencies in existing legislation and systems. It is necessary for China to establish higher-level laws on the prevention and control of invasive alien species at the national level; strengthen the early warning system and process tracking system, etc.; and establish cross-departmental and cross-regional coordination mechanisms at the national and local levels. China needs to enhance the awareness and capabilities of various stakeholders while fulfilling the requirements of the global biodiversity framework and continue to play the role of active participants and emerging leaders.

1 Introduction

Article 8 of the 1992 Convention on Biological Diversity (CBD) requires member countries to prevent the introduction, control or eradication of alien species that threaten ecosystems, habitats or species. As a party to the CBD, China's awareness of invasive alien species has largely kept pace with the rest of the world. As early as 1982, China promulgated the Regulations on Import and Export Animal and Plant Quarantine, which provided for the prevention of the import of diseases, insects, weeds and other pests that harm plants and animals from abroad and within the country. Subsequent enactments such as the Law on Entry-Exit Animal and Plant Quarantine, the Law on Marine Environmental Protection, the Law on Grassland, the Law on Seeds and the Law on Animal Husbandry have all made provisions for the prevention of invasive alien species.

W. Luquan (✉)
Jiaxing University, Jiaxing City, China

G. Antonelli et al. (eds.), *Biodiversity Laws, Policies and Science in Europe, the United States and China*, https://doi.org/10.1007/978-3-031-56218-1_16

The Biosecurity Law adopted in 2020 makes more comprehensive provisions for the prevention of invasive alien species, requiring all relevant departments to clarify the division of responsibilities, improve the list of invasive alien species and develop management measures. In particular, in 2020, a paragraph was added to the Criminal Law Amendment (XI) after Article 344 to provide for the offence of illegally introducing, releasing and discarding invasive alien species. In May 2022, China's Ministry of Agriculture and Rural Affairs, Ministry of Natural Resources, Ministry of Ecology and Environment and General Administration of Customs jointly issued the Management Measures for Alien Invasive Species (MMAIS). The purpose of the legislation is to prevent and respond to the hazards of invasive alien species; to ensure the sustainable development of agriculture, forestry, animal husbandry and fisheries; and to protect biodiversity, and this legal document ended the lack of specific legislation in the field of prevention and control of invasive alien species in China.

However, the relevant provisions of the Biosecurity Law are relatively principled and simple. The management responsibilities of relevant regulatory departments in MMAIS are not detailed enough, and the design of relevant systems has not yet covered the entire chain and process of managing invasive alien species. Therefore, it is necessary to analyze the problems and shortcomings of the current legal system by sorting out the process of legislation on the prevention and control of invasive alien species in China so as to provide a reference for the formulation of special legislation or comprehensive biodiversity protection laws of a higher rank in the future. At the same time, attention should also be paid to the interface between China's administrative law on invasive alien species and the relevant provisions of criminal law in the future.

2 Historical Review: Changes in Legislation on Precaution of Alien Species Invasion

2.1 National-Level Legislative Process

China's attention to the issue of invasive alien species has largely kept pace with that of other countries around the world. Even before the formation of the Convention on Biological Diversity, the Chinese State Council promulgated the Regulations on the Quarantine of Imported and Exported Animals and Plants (1982), which began to focus on the quarantine of foreign animals and plants entering the country. The Law on the Quarantine of Imported and Exported Animals and Plants, adopted by the Standing Committee of the National People's Congress in 1991, stipulates that if there is a special need to introduce state-prohibited items for scientific research or other reasons, an application must be made in advance and approved by the state animal and plant quarantine authorities' approval. The main purpose of this law is to prevent the invasion of dangerous species such as pests, diseases and weeds into the country, and due to differences in understanding and inadequacies, the control of alien species has not yet been carried out from the perspective of ecological security.

In 11th June 1992, China signed the Convention on Biological Diversity (CBD), which requires member countries to prevent the introduction, control or eradication of alien species that threaten ecosystems, habitats or species. Based on this, the relevant Chinese authorities began to pay attention to the control of alien species from the perspective of ecological security and to take action for compliance. Subsequently, in 1997, Yu Kongjian of Peking University and other scholars first introduced the concept of Invasive Alien Species in a Chinese journal (Kongjian and Dihua 1997). At that stage, however, there was no uniform definition of Alien Species or Invasive Alien Species in Chinese legislative documents.

In 1999, the Standing Committee of the National People's Congress amended the Marine Environmental Protection Law, stipulating for the first time in the form of a national law that "the introduction of marine animal and plant species shall be subject to scientific proof to avoid causing harm to the marine ecosystem"; in 2002, the amended Grassland Law stipulated that the introduction of grass seeds from outside the country must be approved in accordance with the law; in the same year, the amended Agriculture Law also stipulated that the import and export of biological species from outside the country must be registered or approved in accordance with the law and that corresponding safety control measures must be taken. The Agriculture Law, amended in the same year, also stipulates that the introduction of biological species resources from abroad shall be registered or approved in accordance with the law, and corresponding safety control measures shall be taken.

The Fisheries Law, amended in 2004, stipulates that the import and export of aquatic seeds shall be subject to quarantine to prevent the introduction of diseases into and out of the country. The Seed Law, amended in the same year, also stipulates that those who introduce germplasm resources from abroad shall go through the procedures of examination and approval and application in accordance with the law. According to the Animal Husbandry Law of 2005, those who import livestock and poultry genetic resources from overseas should apply for approval. If the genetic resources of livestock and poultry imported from abroad are found to be harmful or potentially harmful to the genetic resources and ecological environment of domestic livestock and poultry, the relevant administrative department of the State Council shall, in consultation with the relevant competent department, take corresponding safety control measures.

At that stage, relevant provisions on the prevention and control of invasive alien species began to be added to the relevant animal and plant epidemic prevention legislation and biological resources legislation. At the same time, there were also some governmental normative documents with relevant provisions. The National Ecological Environmental Protection Programme (2000) prepared by the State Environmental Protection Administration (now the Ministry of Ecology and Environment) first proposed to strengthen biosecurity management and that "risk assessment must be conducted on the introduction of exotic species, and import quarantine work must be strengthened to prevent foreign harmful species from entering the country".

In 2003, the State Environmental Protection Administration (SEPA) and the Chinese Academy of Sciences (CAS) formulated and released the First List of Invasive Alien Species in China after a study; at the same time, SEPA also issued the Circular on Strengthening Prevention and Control of Invasive Alien Species. From 2003 to 2005, multiple provinces and cities in China carried out detoxification and pest control actions against key invasive species such as ragweed, *Bauhinia grandiflora*, and water peanut, achieving certain results.

It is worth noting that from the very beginning, China has regarded invasive alien species as potentially damaging to the sustainable development of agriculture, forestry, animal husbandry and fisheries and to the conservation of biodiversity, and therefore the relevant management work is mainly the responsibility of the competent agricultural departments. The General Office of the State Council issued the Regulations on the Main Responsibilities and Staffing of the Ministry of Agriculture in 2008, which specifies that the leading management of invasive species is one of the main responsibilities of the Ministry of Agriculture, which has an Office of Invasive Species Management within the Ministry of Agriculture to undertake work related to invasive species management.

In addition to the aforementioned legislation on animal and plant disease prevention and biological resources, some legislation on environmental protection and ecological protection also contains elements of the prevention and control of invasive alien species. For example, Article 30 of the Environmental Protection Law stipulates that "measures shall be taken to prevent damage to biodiversity in the introduction of foreign species and in the research, development and use of biotechnology". Article 12 of the Wildlife Protection Law states that "the introduction of exotic species, the creation of monoculture forests and the excessive application of pesticides in nature reserves are prohibited or restricted, and other acts that interfere with and threaten the habitat and reproduction of wildlife are also prohibited". Article 30 of the Wetland Protection Law provides that "the introduction and release of exotic species into wetlands is prohibited; if such introduction is necessary, a scientific assessment shall be conducted and approval shall be obtained in accordance with the law". Article 42 of the Yangtze River Protection Law stipulates that "it is prohibited to breed or release exotic species or other non-native species of germplasm in the open waters of the Yangtze River basin". Article 42 of the Law on the Protection of the Yellow River provides that "It is prohibited to breed or release exotic species and other non-native species germplasm resources in the open waters of the Yellow River basin."

The Biosecurity Law adopted in 2020 includes the prevention of invasive alien species and the protection of biodiversity as important regulatory elements of the law; Articles 60 and 81 of the law stipulate the main national systems for preventing and responding to invasive alien species and the related penalties. It can be seen that at this stage, China has already considered the risk of invasive alien species as an important part of national biosecurity and has thus built a relevant system of Prevention at Source – Monitoring and Early Warning – Treatment and Restoration.

In addition, on 22 April 2022, the Ministry of Agriculture and Rural Affairs adopted the Management Measures for Alien Invasive Species (MMAIS).

At the same time, the Criminal Law Amendment (XI) Act of 2020 added a new offence: the offence of illegally introducing, releasing or discarding invasive alien species. The provision reads as follows: "Anyone who illegally introduces, releases or discards an invasive alien species in violation of state regulations, and the circumstances are serious, shall be sentenced to fixed-term imprisonment of not more than three years or detention, and shall be fined or fined alone."

2.2 Introduction to Relevant Local Legislation

In addition to laws and regulations at the national level, some Chinese provinces and cities have gone a step ahead by adopting special legislation to regulate the prevention, control and management of invasive alien species in their regions due to the relatively serious phenomenon of invasive alien species. For example, in 2011, the Regulations on the Management of Invasive Species in Hunan Province (amended in 2020) was enacted by the Standing Committee of the Hunan Provincial People's Congress and is the first local regulation specifically regulating invasive species in China, with the legislative aim of protecting ecological security and maintaining biodiversity in Hunan Province. The Regulations on the Management of Exotic Species in Hunan Province have relatively scientific and reasonable legislative objectives, and the legal system for the prevention and control of invasive alien species is reasonably designed, innovative and operable. In 2019, Guigang City, Guangxi Autonomous Region, issued the Measures for the Management of Invasive Alien Species in Guigang City, with the main objective of preventing and controlling the hazards of alien species, protecting biodiversity, maintaining biosecurity and ecological safety and safeguarding human health.

In addition to special local legislation, some provincial and municipal local regulations and normative documents on environmental resources and border management also have content on the prevention and control of invasive alien species. The typical ones are the Measures for the Protection of Wild Plants in Zhejiang Province and the Emergency Plan for Major Harmful Organisms and Alien Biological Invasion of Fisheries of Zhejiang Provincial Bureau of Ocean and Fisheries; Shaanxi Qinling Ecological Environment Protection Regulations and Shaanxi Provincial Water Conservancy Scenic Area Management Measures; Yantai Marine Ecological Environment Protection Regulations, Xuzhou Luoma Lake Water Environment Protection Regulations, Yuxi Xinping Ailaoshan County Level Nature Reserve Regulations, and Shijiazhuang Hutuo River Protection Regulations; and the Xinjiang Uygur Autonomous Region Border Management Regulations, Gansu Province Border Management Regulations, etc.

In particular, the Shaanxi Provincial Regulations on Ecological Environmental Protection of the Qinling Mountains (revised in 2019), which were enacted in 2007, aim to protect the ecological security of the Qinling Mountains in Shaanxi Province, with Chapter 5 of the regulations being Biodiversity Protection. Article 41 of the Regulations specifies that "within the Qinling Mountains, the illegal introduction and release of exotic species and the free release of wild animals are prohibited", and Article 30 stipulates that "the provincial administrative departments of agriculture and rural areas and forestry shall, in accordance with their respective responsibilities, formulate risk plans for the impact of invasive exotic species on the ecological environment of the Qinling Mountains". This is to protect the biodiversity of the Qinling Mountains in Shaanxi and to prevent the invasion of alien species. Later, in 2022, the Shaanxi Provincial Forestry Bureau issued the Emergency Response Plan for Invasion of Exotic Species (Animals and Plants) in Qinling Forestry in Shaanxi Province. The 2016 Gansu Province Border Management Regulations (revised in 2022), Article 10, stipulates that "the people's governments at all levels where the border is located shall take measures to prevent the introduction of infectious diseases, animal and plant epidemics, invasive alien species, as well as floods and fires, from the land border or their spread or spread at the border".

As can be seen from the above, the existing local regulations for the prevention and control of invasive alien species in China are relatively few and insufficient to prevent and control invasive alien species in the entire region of China. The laws, regulations and policies related to the management of invasive alien species are scattered at different levels, with different effects and different sectoral laws, and the relevant provisions are highly homogeneous, with the content and institutional design of the provisions lagging behind, and some of the provisions may even be inconsistent with the higher laws.

3 Latest Developments: Relevant Provisions of the Biosecurity Law and the Management Measures for Alien Invasive Species

3.1 Relevant Provisions of the Biosafety Act

China's Biosecurity Law was promulgated in 2020, and the law was primarily designed to address the various risks and management pressures on biological resources and ecological environmental protection arising from the rapid development of human biotechnology. The biosafety risks in modern society are both in terms of biological resources and ecological environmental protection and in terms of promoting the healthy development of biotechnology, as well as in terms of the prevention and control of major new and unexpected infectious diseases and animal and plant epidemics. Biosecurity is directly related to people's safety and security, scientific and technological progress and social and economic development and reflects the capacity and level of national governance.

Prevention and response to invasive alien species is an important part of the regulation of biological resources security. Articles 60 and 81 of the Biosecurity Law provide as follows:

Article 60

The State strengthens the prevention of and response to invasive alien species and protects biodiversity. The competent department of agriculture and rural areas under the State Council, in conjunction with other relevant departments of the State Council, has formulated a list of invasive alien species and management measures.

The relevant departments of the State Council shall, in accordance with the division of responsibilities, strengthen the investigation, monitoring, early warning, control, assessment, removal and ecological restoration of invasive alien species.

No unit or individual may introduce, release or discard invasive species without approval.

Article 81

Where, in violation of the provisions of this Law, an alien species is introduced without approval, the relevant department of the people's government at or above the county level shall, in accordance with the division of responsibilities, confiscate the introduced alien species and impose a fine of not less than 50,000 yuan but not more than 250,000 yuan.

Where an alien species is released or discarded without approval in violation of the provisions of this Law, the relevant department of the people's government at or above the county level shall, in accordance with the division of responsibilities, order the capture and retrieval of the released or discarded alien species within a specified period of time and impose a fine of not less than RMB 10,000 yuan but not more than RMB 50,000 yuan.

In fact, prior to the introduction of the Biosecurity Law, the Regulations on the Safe Management of Agricultural Genetically Modified Organisms (2001) had already focused on the safety of the introduction of agricultural genetically modified organisms (GMOs) from outside China and established a corresponding system of application, approval, inspection and quarantine, and penalties.

According to Article 30 of this regulation, if agricultural genetically modified organisms are introduced from outside China for research and testing, the introducing unit shall apply to the agricultural administrative department of the State Council. Only those who meet the following conditions can be approved by the agricultural administrative department of the State Council: (1) They have the application qualifications stipulated by the agricultural administrative department of the State Council. (2) The introduced agricultural genetically modified organisms have undergone corresponding research and experiments, both domestically and internationally. (3) Corresponding safety management and prevention measures are in place.

By comparing and observing the relevant contents of the Biosecurity Law and the Regulations on the Safety Management of Agricultural Genetically Modified

Organisms, it can be seen that the Biosecurity Law stipulates the approval system for the introduction and release of alien species (Article 60, Paragraph 3), but does not establish systematic institutional norms for the introduction, approval, investigation, monitoring, clearance, etc. of alien species, and only stipulates in principle that the state strengthens prevention and response and authorizes competent departments such as agriculture to be responsible for developing a list of invasive alien species and management measures. In contrast, the Regulations on the Safety Management of Agricultural Genetically Modified Organisms (GMOs) have earlier taken note of the safety risks of foreign GMOs and have provided for the competent authorities for the approval of the introduction of GMOs, inspection and quarantine, and customs clearance procedures, which have a strong practical guidance role (Zhao Tengyu 2022).

However, it must be clear that the previous laws and regulations, including the Biosecurity Law, have failed to pay attention to the tracking, monitoring and control of invasive alien species introduced into China by "natural means", such as water flow and air currents, and none of them has established a system of approval, survey and monitoring of the introduction of all types of biological species. This calls for special legislation on invasive alien species in China after the Biosecurity Law to focus on the establishment of a system with a comprehensive process and coverage, integrate the relevant provisions of the aforementioned laws and regulations and fill the regulatory gaps of the past principled and fragmented legislation.

3.2 The Main System Constructed by the Management Measures for Alien Invasive Species

On 1 August 2022, the Management Measures for Alien Invasive Species (MMAIS), jointly issued by China's Ministry of Agriculture and Rural Affairs, Ministry of Natural Resources, Ministry of Ecology and Environment and General Administration of Customs, came into force. This is another important piece of legislation in the field of maintaining national biosecurity and protecting biodiversity in China, following the Biosecurity Law. MMAIS clarifies that the introduction of an invasive species can be by natural or man-made means, including all parts of the species that may survive and reproduce. At the same time, Invasive Alien Species is defined as alien species that have been introduced to colonize and pose a threat or hazard to ecosystems, habitats and species, affecting China's ecological environment and undermining the sustainable development of agriculture, forestry, animal husbandry and fisheries, and biodiversity.

MMAIS makes it clear that the management of invasive alien species adheres to the principles of risk prevention, control at source, comprehensive management, coordinated cooperation and public participation. Under the national inter-ministerial coordination mechanism for the prevention and control of invasive alien species, a list of invasive alien species will be drawn up, a database of invasive alien species will be established and technical specifications for risk assessment, monitoring and early warning, prevention, and control and management of invasive alien species will be improved. The core legislative contribution of MMAIS is that it clarifies and refines the management system for invasive alien species in China and establishes a full chain of prevention and control systems for prevention at source, monitoring and early warning, and treatment and restoration. Specifically, these include:

- Responsibilities of relevant authorities, including the Ministry of Agriculture and Rural Affairs, the Ministry of Natural Resources, the Ministry of Ecology and Environment, the National Forestry and Grassland Administration and the Customs Department (Articles 4–9)
- Institutional provisions to strengthen prevention at source (Articles 10–14)
- Strengthening mechanisms for the monitoring and early warning of invasive alien species (Articles 15–19); and
- Measures to promote the management and ecological restoration of invasive alien species (Articles 20–24).

Regarding the responsibilities of the relevant authorities, the Ministry of Agriculture and Rural Affairs, as one of the most important authorities for the management of invasive alien species, is responsible for establishing an inter-ministerial coordination mechanism for the prevention and control of invasive alien species in conjunction with the relevant departments of the State Council, studying and deploying national work on the prevention and control of invasive alien species and coordinating and resolving major issues. Customs needs to improve the early warning and emergency-handling mechanism for risks outside the country and strengthen quarantine supervision at ports of entry for invasive alien species in channels, such as inbound cargo, means of transport, consignments, passenger luggage, cross-border e-commerce and border markets. Agricultural and rural authorities are responsible for the supervision and management of invasive alien species in farmland ecosystems, fisheries waters and other areas. The department in charge of forestry and grassland is responsible for the supervision and management of invasive alien species in forests, grassland, wetland ecosystems and nature reserves. The department in charge of natural resources (marine) is responsible for the supervision and management of invasive alien species in near-shore waters, islands and other areas. The department in charge of ecology and the environment is responsible for the supervision and management of the impact of invasive alien species on biodiversity. The supervision and management of invasive alien species in areas such as along highways, urban green belts and flower and seedling trading markets is the responsibility of other relevant authorities of local people's governments at or above the county level.

Regarding prevention at source, MMAIS strengthens the system of prevention at source in three main aspects. First, it regulates the management of the introduction of seeds. The introduction of crop and forestry seedlings, aquatic seedlings and other exotic species from abroad for special needs, such as breeding of varieties, shall be subject to import approval and quarantine approval in accordance with the approval authority. If it is the first time to introduce, the introduction unit should conduct a risk analysis and submit a risk assessment report to the approval department. Second, it strengthens port prevention and control. Customs shall strengthen prevention and control at ports; crack down on the illegal introduction, carrying, sending and smuggling of exotic species; and dispose of the invasive species found in accordance with the law. Third, it strengthens quarantine within the territory. Agricultural and rural, forestry and grassland authorities at or above the county level should strengthen the quarantine supervision of the transfer of crops and forestry seeds and seedlings, plant products and aquatic seedlings across the territory to prevent the spread of invasive alien species.

With regard to strengthening monitoring and early warning and keeping abreast of the status of invasive alien species, MMAIS has mainly made three main provisions. The first is to carry out surveys and monitoring. A census and monitoring system for invasive alien species will be established, a national census will be organized once every 10 years, a national monitoring network for invasive alien species will be built and regular monitoring will be carried out. The second is to issue early warning forecasts. The competent departments of agriculture and rural areas, forestry and grassland at or above the provincial level and customs shall strengthen the sharing of monitoring information, analyze and judge the occurrence and proliferation trends of invasive alien species, issue early warning forecasts in a timely manner and guide prevention and control. Third, standardize the release of information. The overall situation of invasive alien species in the country shall be unified and released by the Ministry of Agriculture and Rural Development in consultation with relevant departments. The occurrence of invasive alien species in relevant areas shall be released by the relevant departments of the State Council in accordance with their responsibilities. The provincial agricultural and rural authorities, in consultation with the relevant departments, will unify the release of information on invasive alien species in their administrative areas.

Regarding the promotion of the management and ecological restoration of invasive alien species, MMAIS stipulates that the Ministry of Agriculture and Rural Affairs, the Ministry of Natural Resources, the Ministry of Ecology and Environment and the State Forestry and Grassland Administration shall, in accordance with the division of responsibilities, study and formulate strategic measures for the prevention and control of invasive alien species, and localities shall formulate prevention and control management plans and implement prevention and control measures in accordance with the actual situation. For the management of invasive alien plants, measures such as manual uprooting, mechanical eradication, spraying of green chemicals and the release of biological natural enemies can be taken during critical growth periods such as the seedling, flowering or fruiting stages, according to the actual situation. For the management of invasive pests and diseases, measures such as the selection of pest-resistant varieties, seedling pre-treatment, physical removal, chemical eradication and biological control should be taken to effectively stop the spread of pests and diseases. For the management of invasive aquatic animals, measures such as targeted fishing should be taken to prevent their further spread and harm. In addition, MMAIS specifies the adoption of measures such as planting native plants and releasing native species in accordance with local conditions to restore the ecosystem in areas where invasive alien species occur.

4 Ideal State: Shortcomings and Improvement Direction of Existing Legislation

4.1 Inadequacies of Existing Legislation and Room for Improvement

Faced with the increasing problem of invasive alien species in China, relying solely on the Biosafety Law, departmental regulations and several local legislation is still insufficient. Although existing legislation has made breakthroughs in administrative management systems and criminal sanctions, the shortcomings are also very obvious.

Firstly, a system for the whole process has not yet been established. Due to the invasion of new ecological environments by alien species and the emergence of the dominant species, it is a complex chain process. It can be roughly divided into four steps: introduction, colonization, naturalization and spread (Jin et al. 2009). The concept of whole process control is therefore particularly important in legislation on the management of invasive alien species. The whole-process control concept or principle refers to the need to strengthen the safety management of introduced invasive species and to monitor the whole process, from research and testing to trading and management to domestication and release, as well as other aspects that may have environmental impacts and ecological risks. The principle of full control is based on the scientific uncertainty of the impact of alien species on the environment and the limited knowledge of human beings about the survival of the species, so full control should be implemented to prevent management loopholes. The implementation of the precautionary principle of environmental law in the field of invasive alien species prevention and control is particularly inadequate in China's existing laws and regulations. In particular, the lack of an early warning system has resulted in some alien species that could have been controlled becoming more dangerous invasive species. In fact, the probability of an alien species eventually evolving into an invasive species is only 10% (Bo and Jiakuan 2002), which makes it very interesting for humans to consider how to predict, warn and manage in advance. The lack of prevention efforts not only reflects the lack of a legal system but also indicates that the current level of biosecurity prevention and control techniques needs to be improved.

Secondly, the existing legislation on legal liability (including civil liability, administrative liability, etc.) is relatively simple. This is demonstrated by the fact that MMAIS only stipulates that if the perpetrator introduces, releases or discards an alien species without approval, Article 81 of the Biosecurity Law is invoked to impose penalties, while MMAIS itself does not have a clear punishment system. In fact, the legal relationships arising from invasive alien species are complex and can not only damage civil rights and interests but also cause damage to the ecological environment. The damage caused by invasive alien species to the ecological environment is often difficult to quantify and determine, especially as some of the damage is not apparent at the time and only gradually becomes apparent over time (Chuanqiu 2016). In terms of civil liability determination, the current application of only the relevant provisions of the Civil Code on tort liability is a difficult solution to the problem of potential ecological damage and economic loss. In terms of administrative penalties, the relevant laws only provide penalties for the intentional introduction of invasive alien species but not for the unintentional introduction. In general, the existing provisions on administrative liability are fragmented and lack a strong accountability mechanism; civil liability only focuses on short-term economic and environmental losses and does not take sufficient care of long-term and potential ecological damage. In turn, this is not conducive to the effective regulation of invasive alien species and may even encourage uncontrolled and unintentional introductions.

Thirdly, post-event response strategies and cross-regional cooperation mechanisms are lacking. Exotic species that have been introduced into the country need to be subject to long-term detection and assessment, while those that have shown destructive power after successful invasion need to be controlled and removed. Although existing legislation provides for the obligation of relevant authorities and local people's governments at or above the county level to formulate prevention and control management programmes for invasive alien species in their own areas and regions, the relevant provisions are very general and principled, which is not conducive to the implementation of post-event response work. Generally speaking, for alien species that have been introduced, the relevant authorities should conduct risk assessments on a case-by-case basis whenever possible and take reasonable preventive or control measures in a timely manner. If an alien species is found to have caused or is likely to cause the extinction of local species or has endangered or is likely to endanger human health or public property or has damaged the local ecological balance, the relevant competent authorities should immediately activate the emergency plan and take reasonable and effective measures to control and remove the alien species.

In addition, the legal possessor of an alien species also has the obligation to control and remove the alien species in situations where it is at risk. Cross-regional cooperation mechanisms are designed to prevent the spread of invasive alien species across provincial and municipal boundaries, a problem that has received less attention in existing legislation. As China is a vast country and the administrative boundaries between provinces and municipalities are not the natural boundaries of ecological units, the migration of invasive alien species inevitably raises the issue of coordinated prevention, monitoring and management across regions.

It can be seen that there is still much room for improvement in China's legislation and institutional system on the prevention and control of invasive alien species. On the one hand, there is a need to update the legislative concept, focus on the value of ecological and resource security and implement the concept of whole-process control and the principle of prevention. On the other hand, it is also necessary to fill in the gaps in the system, focusing on establishing a closed-loop system of risk prevention, process control, accountability, and ecological restoration and related coordination mechanisms.

4.2 *Suggestions on Improving the Prevention and Control Legislation of Alien Invasive Species*

With regard to the proposal to improve the legal system for the prevention and control of invasive alien species in China, this section focuses on the legislative hierarchy, legislative concepts and principles, key institutions, coordination mechanisms and public participation.

In terms of the hierarchy of legislative documents, the existing special legislation is at a low level and fails to properly address issues such as the responsibilities of the authorities in charge of invasive alien species, cross-departmental coordination mechanism and legal responsibility. Therefore, it is recommended that a comprehensive, high-ranking law or administrative regulation dedicated to the prevention of invasive alien species be introduced in the future to harmonize the provisions of existing laws and regulations with the different competencies of various departments and to supplement the many institutional gaps in the prevention and control of invasive alien species. Future amendments to existing legislation or the enactment of new legislation should focus on updating the legislative philosophy and principles and suggest that legislation on the prevention and control of invasive alien species adhere to the principles of risk prevention, control at source, comprehensive management, synergistic cooperation and public participation. More importantly, holistic systems thinking and the theory of biological symbiosis need to be introduced into the invasive alien species management and legal system (Liu Tongtong 2021).

Regarding the core system, it is recommended that future legislation should focus on building and improving the whole chain of control systems, such as the early warning system, the approval and filing system, the tagging system, the process tracking system and the post-event treatment and repair system. Among them, the early warning, marking system and process tracking system are relatively lacking in existing legislative documents and institutional systems.

At the same time, the operation of the core system also requires dynamic cross-departmental and cross-regional (including cross-city and cross-province) coordination mechanisms to ensure it. At the national level, it is recommended to establish a cross-departmental National Committee on Invasive Species, responsible for leading and coordinating the prevention and control of invasive species nationwide. The members of the National Committee on Invasive Species shall be responsible persons from the competent departments of the State Council, including ecological environment, agriculture, forestry and grassland, urban and rural construction, transportation, health, marine, inspection and quarantine, customs, etc. The people's governments of each province and city should set up provincial and municipal committees for the prevention and control of invasive alien species and establish a regular and coordinated cross-regional mechanism for the prevention and control of invasive alien species with relevant provinces and cities.

Public participation, as a basic principle of China's Environmental Protection Law, should permeate the entire field and process of environmental and resource protection and utilization. Therefore, the law should encourage individual citizens and social groups to participate in the prevention and control of invasive alien species. Invasive alien species committees at all levels should establish invasive alien species databases to provide various information related to invasive alien species and ensure that the public can easily access this information in order to participate in relevant prevention and control or decision-making activities. Relevant regulatory departments at all levels can promote and popularize knowledge about invasive alien species to the public through channels such as the Internet, television, movies, radio and newspapers. At the national level, attention should also be paid to exchanges and cooperation with foreign and international government and non-governmental organizations in the field of alien species invasion prevention and control in order to jointly resist this global problem.

It should be noted that the 15th Conference of the Parties to CBD formally adopted the Kunming-Montreal Global Biodiversity Framework. The Framework reaffirms invasive alien species as one of the five direct drivers of natural change with the greatest global impact. The target six emphasizes: By identifying and managing the pathways for introducing alien species, preventing the introduction and settlement of important invasive alien species, eliminating, minimizing, and mitigating the impact of invasive alien species on biodiversity and ecosystem services, reducing the introduction and settlement rate of other known or potential invasive alien species by at least 50% by 2030, and eliminating or controlling invasive alien species, especially in priority sites such as islands. Therefore, it is necessary for China to leverage the requirements of the global biodiversity framework in the future to ensure that decision-makers, practitioners and the public have access to the best available data, information and knowledge through domestic legislation, policies, etc., in order to guide the effective management of invasive alien species and the participatory management of biodiversity.

In addition, considering that the international community has paid close attention to the issue of digital sequence information (DSI) of genetic resources in recent years, many countries, including China, can use cutting-edge technologies such as synthetic biology to help early warning, in-process tracking and identification of alien invasive species, as well as post-treatment and ecological restoration. Of course, as a latecomer country, China still needs to carefully learn and understand the experience of other countries in the prevention and control of invasive species, as well as legislation, especially how to integrate the prevention and control of invasive species with biodiversity conservation and biosafety management, as well as advanced management systems and cross-departmental linkage mechanisms abroad.

5 Conclusion and Future Work

China has developed rapidly in the field of invasive alien species management and the rule of law in recent years, and the relevant provisions of the Biosecurity Law, the Measures for the Management of Invasive Alien Species and the Amendment to the Criminal Law (XI) have constructed the basic institutional framework for the prevention and control of invasive alien species in China, which has basically reached a level where there are laws to follow and clear systems. However, it should also be noted that there are shortcomings in the existing legislation; for example, the whole process of the institutional system has not yet been established, the existing legislation is relatively simple in terms of legal liability and there is a lack of an ex post response strategies and cross-regional cooperation mechanisms.

In this regard, it is necessary for China to consider enacting a higher-ranking law on the prevention and control of invasive alien species at the national level, to focus on building and strengthening the early warning system and the process tracking system in the core system, to consider establishing cross-departmental and cross-regional coordination mechanisms at both national and local levels and to improve the knowledge and capacity of national policymakers, practitioners and the public in accordance with the requirements of the post-2020 global biodiversity framework. The government should learn from the experiences of other countries and use cutting-edge technologies such as synthetic biology to help prevent and control invasive alien species.

Admittedly, due to the limitations of space and research methods, this paper has paid less attention to the contingent model and institutional content of China's future legislation on invasive alien species management and has not sufficiently analyzed the ideal invasive alien species management system and the boundaries of powers and responsibilities of the relevant authorities. Therefore, further exploration is needed in future research on how to effectively improve the prevention and control system for invasive alien species, enhance the legislative level and attract more managers, social organizations and the public to participate within the existing legal framework of biosafety in China. In the future, China will continue to play a role as an active participant and emerging leader in the global affairs of biodiversity conservation and will certainly play a more important role in the field of invasive alien species prevention and control by building a better legal and institutional system.

References

Bo L, Jiakuan C (2002) Ecology of biological invasions: achievements and challenges. World Sci Technol Res Dev 2:26–36

Chuanqiu X (2016) Legal control of invasive alien species in China. J Harbin Coll 37(07):51–55

Jin W, Shekun W, Houfu Y (2009) Resisting invasive Alien species: comparison and choice of legal regulation models. Beijing University Press, Beijing, p 10

Kongjian Y, Dihua L (1997) Landscape ecology model of urban-rural and regional planning. Foreign Urban Plan 03:27–31

Tengyu Z (2022) Building a rule of law system for biodiversity in the context of ecological civilization. New Econ 552(04):10–14

Tongtong L (2021) A holistic system view: the logic of biodiversity legislation protection in China. Theor Mon 478(10):130–141

China Promotes the Practice of Participatory Biodiversity Conservation

Jing Wu

Abstract The Convention on Biological Diversity (hereinafter referred to as "The Convention") and Aichi Biodiversity Targets acknowledge the importance of involving efforts. This approach fully utilizes their resources and advantages, and provides a normatice framework for participatory conservation. It also guides the legitimacy, legatity, inclusiveness of global biodiversity protection efforts, while exploring the functional value of paticipatory conservation. In order to fulfill and efficiently fulfill this international obligation, China acknowleges the importance of participatory norms to biodiversity legal mechanisms. We are enhancing the design and institutional innovation of paticipation mechanisms in legislation, law enforcement and justice. We are also regulating and guiding the operation of mechanisms for non-state actors to participate in biodiversity conservation. This chapter is based on the practical experience of NGOs in China engaging in in biodiversity conservation, while also highlighting existing issues and inadequacies. From a legal perspective, this chapter provides recommendations and perspectives on the legal syetem, engagement capabilities, and collaboratice potential. Finally, this chapter will explain how China's current participatory biodiversity conservation practices are coordinated, consistent and synchronized with the Convention and Aichi goals.

1 Introduction

The Convention on Biological Diversity affirms the status of participatory conservation in the global biodiversity regulatory mechanism, It operates through key node implementation mechanisms such as the Biodiversity Strategic Plan 2011–2020, Aichi Biodiversity Targets, and the Kunming-Montreal Global Biodiversity Framework. To effectively implemet, the Chinese government issued the biodiversity conservation action plan and the China biodiversity conservation strategy and action plan (2011–2030), the "citizen participation protection" in strategic important

J. Wu (✉)
Hebei University of Economics and Business, Shijiazhuang, China

G. Antonelli et al. (eds.), *Biodiversity Laws, Policies and Science in Europe, the United States and China*, https://doi.org/10.1007/978-3-031-56218-1_17

position, and specific legal norms[1] constitute the Chinese biodiversity participatory protection legal system. The participatory mechanism is the expansion energy that adjusts to the natural biological interests of the overall structure. China stimulates participatory multiple values, explores the functional space of traditional knowledge and skills, innovates the normative mechanism path of biodiversity conservation, and gradually corrects, adapts to and improves the overall harmony in the biodiversity ecosystem in China.

2 Functional Value of the Participatory Biodiversity Conservation

2.1 The Legal Status of the Participatory Biodiversity Conservation

First, let us define the conception of biodiversity conservation: paticipation is rooted in the principles of democratic theory. In 1970 Pateman published the "Theory of Participation and Democracy," which officially opened the criticism of contemporary democracy theory. The contemporary democratic theory reflects civic participation through a representative system model, which essentially expresses the interests and will of the national level and political elites but deliberately ignores "the cultivation of individual citizens' democratic participation ability with corresponding conditions" at the micro level.[2] From Rousseau to John Stuart Mill, Carole Pateman deepened her understanding of participation in democracy, believing that "participation has a broader function and is key to the establishment and maintenance of a democracy. Democracy is not only as a "national representative system" but also a "participatory society."[3] Participation in democracy is enhance the public's expression in the public sphere, including political norms and public life, and optimizes the legitimacy of representative democratic entities and procedures. Rousseau proposed three major functions for participating in democracy: educational function, decision-making participation function and integrated function. Law is an effective way for the public to realize these functions, especially for the latter two functions belong to the key link of democratic politics. Participatory

[1] Participatory normative documents mainly include: the environmental protection law, the environmental impact assessment law, the environmental protection public participation, the environmental impact assessment of public participation, on strengthening the development and standardize social organizations of environmental management guidance, "about the reform of social organization management system to promote the healthy and orderly development of social organization opinions", "about encourage and support social capital to participate in ecological restoration," opinions on further strengthening the protection of biodiversity conservation".

[2] [Us] Carol (2006), p. 7.

[3] [America] Carol Pettman, The Theory of Participation and Democracy. By Chen Yao, Shanghai Century Publishing Group, 2006 edition. Jianlin and Tianpeng (2012), p. 88.

regulation is to give the coercive force of participation democracy in the law, so that the public participation has normative value, and the Participatory biodiversity conservation is the concrete embodiment of this coercive force in the legal mechanism of biodiversity. Public participation is an integral part of the biodiversity standard protection mechanism. It can participate in the whole legal operation of legislation, law enforcement, justice, law-abiding and legal supervision, and integrate the interests of a wide range of subjects and the naturalization of biological resources and environment into the mainstream of environmental rule of law.

Secondly, the legal status of the rules on biodiversity of utmost inportance. Biodiversity is a holistic, systematic and independent natural ecosystem. Various actors interact with resource factors based on their behavioral capacity to meet the needs and development of production and life, and have a dominant position in ecological resources within a certain range. The legal path of biodiversity protection is a compulsory constraint based on the principle of national sovereignty of natural resources, and integrates all kinds of behaviors to form a unified, dynamic and integrated legal behavior system. International law and domestic law are the leading parties guiding all kinds of behaviors, and participatory protection is in an auxiliary and secondary position. Through the existing interactive ability of ecological resources, nonstate actors optimize the effect of legal norm mechanism, realize the transformation of decentralized and diversified behavior modes to a unified and systematic normative mechanism, and complete the legal positioning of participatory protection.

First of all, an analysis of the norms level: international environmental law is the composition of international law. The ledge recognition of international law forms the basis for the entitlement of non-state actors to partake in the governance of global biodiversity regulation. is the legal recognition of international law. The consultative status of non-governmental organizations (NGOs) and the status of international treaties are confimed by the United Nations Economis and Social Council. Additionally, the Aarhus Convention defines the public's right to know in environmental governance, participation in decision-making and recourse to law. Consequently, this convention lays the international groundwork for non-state actors to participate in the global biodiversity regulation mechanism.

Although the Convention does not have clear participatory protection provisions, the Cartagena Biosafety Protocol, the Nagoya Protocol, the Strategic Plan, the Aichi Goals, and the Kunming-Montreal Global Biodiversity Framework all confirm the legal status and mechanism operation of participatory protection to varying degrees. From international law to the international norms of biodiversity, confirming the auxiliary orientation of participatory protection to the operation of international law.

Secondly, China has established a systematic framework for biodiversity conservation through a scientific approach, despite the absence of a dedicated law specifically for this purpose. The inclusion of "ecological civilization" in the Constitution has elevated the legal status of environmental protection, laying the foundation for standardizing the preservation of biodiversity. Mediated by *The National Biodiversity Strategy and Action Plan*, *Environmental Protection Law*, *Guiding Opinions on Construction of a Modern Environmental Governance System*, *Opinions on*

Enhancing Biodiversity Conservation, and *Guiding Opinions on Establishment of a Nature Reserve System with National Parks as the Mainstay*, along with other regulatory documents and regional ecological development strategies, form the normative foundation for participatory conservation to become an integral part of the overall standardization mechanism of biodiversity. Additionally, the *Measures for Public Participation in Environmental Conservation*, *Measures for Public Participation in Environmental Impact Assessments*, *Guidelines for Strengthening the Guidance and Standardized Management of Environmental Conservation Social Organizations*, *Opinions on Reforms to the Management System of Social Organizations to Promote the Healthy and Orderly Development of Social Organizations*, *Opinions on Encouragement and Support for the Participation of Social Capital in Ecological Conservation and Restoration*, and other regulatory documents provide a legal scope for the broadening and deepening of their systematic operation, solidifying the position of participatory support mechanisms.

China's participatory normative practice gradually moves from passive assistance to active evolution. In terms of legislation the normative path of legislative proposals and international conference side meetings provides a formal platform for the interest demands of non-state subjects; In law enforcement, the specialization and sustainability of NGOs protection practices, the supply chain effect of green management responsibility of enterprise entities, and the flowering of green and low-carbon innovation methods of the broader public enrich the normative mechanism content of participatory protection. In the judiciary, the system improvement of the democratic mechanism of the whole process of environmental justice has become the normative realization of the participatory protection value, The trial function of expert technology and the judicial connection of multiple dispute resolution will implement the value of participation into the whole judicial process.

Therefore, in China, biodiversity and participatory protection, while adhering to the auxiliary position, experience an improvement in the participation ability from macro to concrete, from passive to active, and construct the biodiversity participatory protection modern rule of law with Chinese characteristics.

2.2 The Functional Value of the Participatory and Normative Protection of Biodiversity Conservation

Firstly, it is necessary to balance the biodiversity normative value of biodiversity. Biodiversity value and biodiversity normative value are two sistinct concepts. Biodiversity value is derived from the biodiversity ontology, and encompasses the external value of providing useful resources for human survival and development from economic, scientific, aesthetic, and comfort perspectives. The intrinsic naturality of biodiversity from extrinsic value sources is a factual evaluation based on the objective characteristics of biological resources. The fact is the existence of objectivity or mandatory force, the value is the guarantee of effectiveness.

The effective integration of the two can be achieved through legal norms.[4] The normative value of biodiversity is the beneficial standard formed by the convergence of the expectation of harmonious coexistence between man and nature around the universally recognized behavior pattern.[5] The legitimacy of law carries the value rationality, and the legal system has the dynamic function of maintaining the value stability, and is the interest consensus path for the realization of biodiversity value. But the law belongs to the purposeful behavior, the legislative power main body in pursuit of their own interests maximization will tend to choose to serve the specification of its own value design. Elite groups become accomplices and beautify their legitimacy through legal form, not only covering the expression of objective laws but also distorting the human value of biodiversity, leading to a lack of legitimacy. The participatory regulation of biodiversity protects the power structure of equitable sovereign subjects. Through the natural association between non-state actors and biodiversity, the dynamic framework is based on ecological value, and explores the adaptation of external value and the normative value of biodiversity.

Second, the scientific nature of biodiversity norms: the scientific nature of norms is an external that requires human activities to be based on the objective laws of the ecosystem.[6] This involves respecting the objective laws of the ecosystem, balancing the relationship between protection and development, and maintaining the bottom line of the ecosystem tolerance.

With the Convention as the boundary, the previous standard system was mostly aimed at a separate species, an ecological problem and a certain type of pollution, which was targeted for restoration and behavioral restrictions, and then transformed into sustainable development based on protection. The transformation of the value pattern promotes the transformation of legal norms and mechanisms, and integrates the respect for the ecological environment into the standardized operation of the utilization. Participatory protection norms are precisely the dynamic drivers of this shift. Nonstate actors will bring the traditional wisdom of adapting to the survival of biodiversity into the normative and normative mechanism of biodiversity protection, fill in the lack of scientificity, fairness and legitimacy in legislative decision-making, implementation and judicial disputes, and enhance the interest harmony ability of all links of the biodiversity legal operation.

Thirdly, the mainstream of biodiversity conservation: mainstreaming of biodiversity conservation is the fundamental outlet to address biodiversity loss. The close interdependence between biology and ecosystems and human beings proves the responsibility of everyone towards environmental protection. The public sector plays a leadership role in establishing and implementing standard systems, while the private sector serves as the executor of the standards. Participatory protection is the social subject's tolerance to the biodiversity specification system, especially the non-governmental organizations, private groups, indigenous groups, civil society

[4] Xiaoqing (2019a), p. 38.

[5] Xiaoqing (2019b), p. 42.

[6] Minzhong (2010), p. 115.

and biological resource stakeholders and interest-linked actors. Through their diverse abilities and resources, they contribute to the sustainable inplementation of biodiversity conservation at the specification level. Even at the international and national levels, non-state actors implement supervisory rights to ensure that the overall value of biodiversity norms is upheld. Therefore, participatory conservation not only promotes the construction and implementation of biodiversity conservation in the global system, but also determines the core position of sustainable utilization, and enhances the status of ecological value in the normative mechanism, which is the dual mainstream promotion of the content and form of biodiversity conservation.

3 The Practical Status of Participatory Normative Conservation of Biodiversity in China

The participatory normative regulatory protection mechanism is a governance based operation that relies on the three powers of legislation, law enforce and judiciary. It aim to enhance innvation of informal normative system through a legal framework, with a priamry focuses on nongovernmental organizations, enterprises, community citizens, and other non-state actors.

3.1 Standardizing the Practice of NGOs Participating in Biodiversity Conservation

According to the *Guidelines on Strengthening the Guidance of the Development and Standardized Management of Environmental Social Organizations*, environmental NGOs in China are mainly divided into three types: environmental social organizations, environmental protection foundations, and environmental social service organizations. By the end of 2021, there were a total of 902,000 social organizations, including 371,110 social organizations, 8,877 foundations, and 521,883 private non-enterprise units.[7] With a focus on the ecological space of protected natural areas, these non-governmental organizations aimed to protect precious, endangered, fragile, and key biological species and habitat resources. They constantly strive to enrich and expand the standard path of participating in protection, optimize and fill in the absence of protection, and deepen the multiple participation mechanism.

Firstly, in order to participate in legislative decision-making, it is important to formulate a text that sounds native and fluent. The strictness of the legislative main body of the state is always sacred and unbreakable. The authority of NGOs to participate in international biodiversity norms does not belong to the scope of national implementation and transformation. As the biodiversity regulation

[7] The Statistical Bulletin on the Development of Civil Affairs in 2021.

mechanism deepens, the Chinese government is constantly opening up the decision-making path of legislation, enforcement and justice, and is actively seeking the participation and influence of NGOs' beneficial knowledge and technology.

First of all, it is recommended that the proposal be subject to legislative participation. Since 2016, the China Green Development Council has set up a platform for the "Two Sessions/Proposal and Suggestions Conference" for several years, which collects suggestions and opinions from all over the country, and discusses the research with NPC deputies and members of the CPPCC National Committee. This platform optimizes the path for NGOs to participate in environmental legislation. This is similar to the way NGOs participate in the negotiations and decision-making of international environmental conventions and enter into formal dialogues. Additionally, with the increase of China's influence in the international environment and governance mechanism, China's environmental NGOs have also become a key force in safeguarding the global ecological interests. In 2022, China hosted a new round of contracting conferences of the International Convention on The Wetlands and the Convention on Biological Diversity. Environmental NGOs, together with other social organizations, academic organizations, think tanks, talent organizations, will promote negotiations on the Convention and fully express the interests and suggestions of nonstate subjects.

Secondly, participate in the refinement of protection execution: biodiversity execution is the main battlefield of biodiversity conservation practices. The Environmental Impact Assessment Law will solicit regulations from relevant units, experts and the public for special planning and construction projects, so as to realize the standardized status of the participation mechanism. The Measures on Public Participation in Environmental Impact Assessment and the Regulations on Environmental Impact Assessment in Planning specify the scope and procedures of public participation, as well as the procedural guarantee for the adoption of suggestions and deep doubts, so as to build a participation mechanism for micro-ecological utilization. At the same time, the standard mechanism of nature reserves with national parks as the main body adheres to the management mechanism of government supervision, local government and administrative support, nonstate and main participation and cooperation, so as to build an implementation paradigm of weakening conflicts of interests and converging values. Environmental protection NGOs are able to attack actively, innovate paths, and supplement the effective scope of protected natural areas. The Sustainable Global Enviroment Research Institute (GEI) use as the combination of bottom-up and top-down community participation in protection mode, in Inner Mongolia, Ningxia cloud mountain nature reserve GaZha village, Sichuan baoxing county, Qinghai region and Burma (Thanbayarkhon, TBK) village promotion, to expand different cooperation modes of community agreement protection mechanism, help yunwu mountain reserve administration and surrounding communities a model household to reach an agreement. In addition, various public welfare conservation areas explore the types of cooperation among multiple stakeholders, and become a social force connecting the complete system of biodiversity conservation.

Once more, the ecology of the judicial trial is a topic discussion. The qualification of litigation subject of NGOs has opened up a new idea of environmental public interest litigation. The friends of nature enviroment research institute in Beijing' chaoyang district filed the first national wildlife protection preventive public interest litigation, known as the "green peacock case". This case was named one of the top ten typical cases for world environmental judicial protection at the 2021 World Encironmental Justice Conference by the United Nations environment program. Additionally, it was named one of the "Top Ten Cases to Promote the Rule of Law Process in the New Era 2021" by the Supreme People's Court and the central radio and television reception desk. Judicial trials play a crucial role in establishing a consensus on the value of biodiversity and legitimizing its protection. named "new era to the rule of law process 2021 top ten cases." Judicial trial assumes the legal function of biodiversity value consensus and legitimacy output. On the basis of the existing public participation system, To enhance the existing public paticipation of the increase the scientific proportion of trial opinions and enhance the substantive participation of the people's jury system. Futhermore, a multiple dispute resolution mechanism based on the connection between people's mediation and trial functions should be constructed to resolve the interest disputes of biological resources with people's feelings and common sense.

Second, the implementation methods of biodiversity conservation norms: leaning upon initiatives pertaining to protected areas, environmental conservation nongovernmental organizations have actively expanded the three traditional practice paths of charity, volunteer service and education and publicity, transforming from pure blood transfusion assistance to growth aid of "input + output" (Table 1).[8]

As can be seen from this table, environmental conservation nongovernmental organizations break through the idea of pure fund transfusion for people in need, and turn to the concept of the relationship between man and nature through multiple paths of capital, technology, ideology and culture, so as to realize the purpose of saving resources, improving the environment, reversing the loss of biodiversity and sustainable development. This is the most basic, the most ordinary, but the most indispensable practice field in biodiversity conservation, and is the key and difficulty to achieve the goal of biodiversity mainstream.

3.2 *Enterprises Shall Participate in the Standardized Operation of Biodiversity Protection*

China's Biodiversity Conservation Strategy and Action Plan 2011–2030 explicitly establishes the partnership among stakeholders in biodiversity conversation and actively fulfill the obligations of "Global Partnership between Enterprises and Biodiversity" (Global Partnership on Business and Biodiversity (GPBB)). Chinese

[8] Jing (2021), p. 44.

Table 1 Traditional practices of environmental protection and social organizations

Type	Classify	Brief introduction	Example illustration	Legislative authority	Remarks
Charity	Charitable fund	Philanthropic foundation	Mangrove Foundation, Alxa Ecological Foundation, Peach Blossom Source foundation	The Charity Law and the Regulations on the Administration of Foundation Registration	–
	Social donations	Social donations are made based on the project terrace.	Shanshui Nature Protection Center: monthly donations, public welfare outlets		–
	Financial support	We will support environmental welfare entrepreneurship projects.	The SEE Foundation supports the Green Home Project.		Target with entrepreneurial projects
Volunteer service	Volunteer service	Organize volunteer services with projects as the platform	The China Conservation and Green Development Foundation of Biodiversity (hereinafter referred to as the Green Development Association) The "Power Generation and Cooperation Center" has 11,000 environmental volunteers and established 45 service stations, covering 12 provinces and nearly 70 counties (cities and districts).	Regulation of Voluntary Service (Dec.2017), On the support and development of voluntary service organizations Opinion (July 11, 2016)	–
	Professional consulting services	Law, international affairs, and technology	"Environmental public interest litigation", China Environmental Federation provides consulting services for enterprises to participate in international environmental protection exchanges, and Alxa SEE Foundation organizes "Jinpeer" Technology to support		–

(continued)

Table 1 (continued)

Type	Classify	Brief introduction	Example illustration	Legislative authority	Remarks
			public welfare institutions move		
	Knowledge training	Enhance public protection skills	China Wildlife Conservation Association: National wildlife rescue Nursing technology research and experience exchange training		–
	Learning through practice	Organize field landscape learning.	Taohuayuan Ecological Protection Foundation organizes the super volunteer program.		–
Education oriented	Institutional education	School education model	Gea Nature School and Mangrove Foundation, established by Friends of Nature in 2016, focus on Shenzhen Bay Wetland and cooperate with multiple units. Operating three nature education centers/nature schools	–	–
	Publicity activity education	University education model on promoting biodiversity knowledge, enhance conversation capacity and protection through media and specialized platforms.	–	–	–

enterprises quickly adapt to the demand for corporate social responsibility towards sustainable development, pledging their Commitment of the Corporate Biodiversity commitment. They dedicated to transparetly reporting enterprise information and contructing a participatory soft law arrangement, which includes the internal management system for green production and operation and supply chain external operation mechanism. The green production and operation management system constitutes a built-in biosphere conservation and sustainable utilization mechanism for enterprises, serving as the pivotal core within the operational and production newworks. The elevated blueprint for High-level green development, strict resource selection standards, advanced low-carbon operation technology, and precise monitoring and implementation execution have emerged as the authoritative source of the external operation mechanism within the industrial chain. They enhance the sustainability of resource utilization, and constitute a self-recycling system of harmonious coexistence between enterprises and biological resources.

Yili has became the first Chinese company to sign the Enterprise and Biodiversity Commitment Letter (2016). To ensure sustainable and healthy management of Yili, the company has implemented the "Community-Based Sustainable Development (CSD) System". This system requires the external packaging operation chain adhere to the FSC forest certification standards, while the raw material procurement chain adhere to RSPO certification standards. In addition, the company has committed to sustainability in the selection of development sites, production process, manufacturing cycles, transportation and logistics. These efforts collectively form a soft legal mechanism for biodiversity conservation. Procter & Gamble China, State Grid Jibei Electric Power Co., LTD., Longji Green Energy Technology Co., LTD., Sky Battery Group and so on are all excellent examples of China's green supply chain mechanism construction.

China's green finance development is undergoing a shift and upgrade in line with the goal of achieving carbon neutrality. Since 2017, the State Council has implemented a pilot program for local green finance reform, resulting in the establishment of 238 green finance business divisions or specialized institutions in each pilot area by the end of 2020. The focus is on establish a diversified financial product system that includes green credit, green fund, green insurance, green trust and green PPP, with a high focus on the financing needs of the carbon-brown industry, such as steel, building materials, fossils, paper making, chemical fiber and textile. The six large commercial banks have outstanding green loans reached 6.27 trillion yuan, and Bank of China, China Construction Bank, Industrial and Commercial Bank of China, Agricultural Bank of China, and Bank of Communications have all invested in the National Green Development Fund Co., Ltd., to promote the transformation and upgrading of green industries. The focus is on biological resources, including environmental protection, pollution prevention and control, ecological restoration, and territorial space greening. Green finance is now geared toward biodiversity conservation.

3.3 Civic Participation in Biodiversity Conservation

The maintenance of biodiversity in natural resources is of great importance in China, with high spatial distribution in northeast and southwest and low distribution in northwest.[9] Biodiversity is diversitied in remote and poor ethnic areas. China is a multicultural country with 56 ethnic groups. The natural dependence between local residents and biological resources determines that it is an important subject of biodiversity conservation, and national cultural customs provide spiritual support. The year-round use of slash-and-burn in the Yi nationality is an ecological operation adapted to the mountain forest environment. Due to extensive tillage, the soil forms a protective layer and the vegetation provides a cultivation period, which constitutes a protective film for the local biodiversity.[10] Wild vegetables in the food culture of wa residents; sugar gum tree and gentian in medical culture; kapok tree in brocade dress culture, dragon bamboo and water wax gourd tree in traditional architectural culture all reflect the relationship between biodiversity and cultural diversity. The worship culture of biological resources is the inheritance and upgrading of this dependence relationship. The people of Baise area have preserved a large number of ancient trees through the culture of "sacred tree" and "geomantic tree" culture; the belief of turning off evil spirits and praying conveyed through the culture of "life tree" and "land god" makes the diverse biological resources concerned and protected.[11] Folk culture keeps biodiversity conservation stable in local minds.

Culture is an endogenous force for development. With the promotion of sustainable development theory and the adoption of green and low-carbon paths, the folk culture of biodiversity has evolved from a unipolar self-closure to a more adaptable and diverse approach. Through the implemention of supportive policies, technologies and experiences at all levels, we can explore the development path of a green ecological economy and realize the diversified values of ecological products.[12] For instance, we can establish women's handicraft teams to develop sustainable livelihoods through the production of yak down felt products. In Chaoyang Village as an "enclave" between the Evergreen Reserve and Fuping Reserve, the local community has established an informal "nature protection team" to engage beekeeping, palm leaf picking and tea picking economy, and establish rural economic revitalization industry, etc.[13] By combining the ecological elements, cultural inheritance, and labor skills of village communities are combined with scientific and adaptive general

[9]Yingdi and Jijun (2022), p. 23.

[10]Rongkun (2016).

[11]Jiaoli et al. (2014), p. 41.

[12]Landscape Nature Conservation Center, Jiatang Protected Area: Exploring the Road to Ecological Protection and Community Development, https://mp.weixin.qq.com/s/UEsdu-VQinmQkX7h8ykcZA.

[13]Peach Blossom Foundation, From Mountain to Ecological Consciousness, a Village and Her Green Destiny.

utilitarian guidelines, we can promote innovation and improve the mainstream mechanism of biodiversity protection.

Citizens' awareness of participating in biodiversity conservation has gradually increased, and volunteers, forest rangers and rangers have become symbols of biodiversity conservation in the new era. Their perseverance provides the information basis for biodiversity to adapt to social development, and gradually establishes a mainstream-oriented society for biodiversity protection in China through points and lines.

4 Successful Experience of Participatory and Normative Conservation of Biodiversity in China

4.1 Building an Inclusive Legal Mechanism for Biodiversity

The naturalness of biodiversity determines the integrity and systematization of the legal mechanism, while the timeliness of biodiversity determines the adaptability and development of normative guidance. Therefore, it is particularly important to establish an inclusive mechanism of general coercion and specific positioning. Specifically, China will establish a biodiversity legal operation mechanism that includes the structure of yuan, namely, species, heritage resources and ecological legal system and the protection of biodiversity security, space layout, protection area, technology, capital ratio, intellectual property, and cost-benefit development policy synthesis. This mechanism will, adhere to the legal logic of multiple values, multiple factors, and multiple space and moderately adapt to the specification operation. It is mainly reflected in two aspects: on the one hand, the appropriate adaptation between the internal elements of biodiversity and China's economic structure, political culture, legal level, scientific and technological level, international status and development goals; on the other hand, the appropriate adaptation between the state and non-state subjects in the distribution and management of biodiversity ownership.

Participatory protection is a comprehensive legal mechanism that involves both state subjects and non-state actors subjects. It mobilizes the energy and wisdom of non-state actors in legislation, enforcement and justice, and improving the soft regulations for biodiversity conservation, Green sustainability standards should connect the behaviors of various actors in cities, towns, villages and regions. For instance, the All China environmental Protection Federation has formulated the "Technical Specification for Rare Earth Industrial Waste Water Treatment Engineering" and "Technical Specification for Petroleum Refining Industrial Waste water Treatment Engineering". The sustainable utilization path and scope of biological resources should be developed and supplemented to expand the consensus mechanism of multiple co-governance based on nature. Environmental should be supervised, and the specialized mechanism of integrating into environmental justice should be improved. A green cultural force for environmental justice should be built to promote the modernization of China's biodiversity legal regulation mechanism as a whole.

4.2 Adjust and Adapt to the Operation Logic of Biodiversity Conservation and Management

The implementation of national biodiversity conservation is a comprehensive legal project that which requires the coordination between top-down regulatory guidance and bottom-up dynamic innovation. The original operational logic of public power involves fine compulsory guidance under the provisions, and the local norms and social rules must strictly adhere to laws and policies. The integrity and diversity of biological resources determine the inclusiveness and adaptability of the operation of state power operations. Relevant laws and policies should be positioned under the macro guidance of strategic, principled and directional principles. Local and non-state entities can adopt different power operation tracks based on the characteristics of biological resources, operational resources and cost budget. This can be summersized as follows:

To begin with,it is crucial to establish a strict power structure from the grassroots level and enhance operational efficiency through subject cooperation. Biodiversity conservation necessitates strict legal coordination, which aligns with China's system of state ownership of natural resources. As the power subjects responsible for legal operations,governments at all levels and environmental protection agencies must carry out specialized and multilevel standardization and expansion operations, with the assistance of multiple stakeholders. Non-state entities should establish informal protection mechanisms in various forms and content, and enrich the scope of normative mechanisms through cooperative efforts.This rigorous power structure represents a strategic adjustment for the country to adapt to the internal laws of biodiversity and adjust the logic of power operations.

Secondly, there should be multilevel cooperation to explore the innovation and breakthrough of the local standard mechanism. The natural protected area mechanism, with the national park as the main body, should be the basis of the natural protected plan under the regional environmental development mechanism. This will help to break the administrative power of environmental resources and establish new biodiversity legal norms mechanism through the collaboration of all levels of government, administrative departments, social organizations, research experts, and the interests of folk customs, and behavior standards, as well as public-private cooperation to establish new biodiversity legal norms mechanism.

4.3 Exploring Scientific and Innovative Protection Methods

The rich biodiversity gives rise to a diverse array of non-state actors who participate in conservation efforts, ranging from unconscious and decentralized protection to conscious and scientifically-informed protection. As such, non-states actors are increaingly recognizing the importance of scientific rationality in conservation.

Firstly, a path towards good governance for ecological security and economic optimization should be established: This solution should be based on meeting human development needs while respecting the ecological value and minimizing ecological impact. It is to balance the good governance within nature and between humans and nature, and to become an innovative force that ensure the bottom line of ecological security and breaks through the path of economic optimization. For instance, sustainable global environmental research is widely applied to community protected areas through the "protocol protection mode," aiming to create regional characteristics of biodiversity conservation.

Secondly, prevention, classification strategies, and flexible responses are key to addressing the normative governance of biodiversity. The unique interplay between biological resources and multiple environments determines the boundaries and scope of the governance mechanism. Non-state actors can adapt to the specificities, respect the ecological boundaries, and flexibly explore the intervention range. For instance, in response to the threat of flora to wetlands and tidal flats, relevant stakeholders should classify and treat the land based on characteristics, such as replacing miflora with mangroves in suitable area and building breeding areas for shellfish in beach areas. Respecting the particularity of nature is the foundation of scientific respect. China's biodiversity conservation standard mechanism has provided a relaxed and innovative environment and practical space for non-state actors to participate, and promoting the continuous emergence of scientific and innovative protection methods.

5 Problems Existing in the Practice of Participatory Normative Biodiversity Conservation in China

Participatory conservation is the practice of biodiversity governance practice that is driven by globalization. The Convention on Biological Diversity establishes a connection between formal and informal norms, resulting in a consistent participatory norms system. For a country, the principle of natural resources and the theory of public trust give it absolute authority over biological resources. This is also true for China, where the dominant ownership of natural resources and the invisible ownership of the whole population place the legal system and subject capacity of biodiversity conservation will be at a disadvantage.

5.1 The Participatory Standard System of Biodiversity Needs to Be Improved

Firstly, the content of biodiversity needs to be deepened.

Since the implementation of the ecological civilization strategy, China has accelerated the development of policies and legal system for biodiversity protection, progressing from initial optimization to the fine-tuning. Participatory mechanism and composition are essential for optimizing ecosystem functionality and enhancing governance effectiveness. To achieve this, normative logic must evolve to maxmize effectiveness. The Environmental Protection Law of the People's Republic of China (2014) and China's Biodiversity Conservation Strategy and Action Plan (2022–2030) (hereinafter referred to as the Strategic Plan) establish the participatory status in the biodiversity regulation system. The Environmental Protection Law includes a chapter on "Information Disclosure and Public Participation" to determine the specific content of citizens' right to participate in three aspects: obtaining environmental information, participating in and supervising environmental protection. The Strategic Plan elevates "public participation" to a basic principle and places "participation" at the top of the macro level. Currently only the environmental impact assessment law and related rules involve procedures and species, genetic resources, ecosystem legislation lack clear participatory mechanisms. For instance, the grassland law of the People's Republic of China has no relevant content, the agricultural law, "forest law," "seed," the Yangtze river protection law simplify the specific content of citizen participation, essentially copying the environmental protection law. The revised the wildlife protection law aims to enhance citizen awareness and paticipation in wildlife protection through various means such as reporting, accusation, and participation in publicity and education activities. The principle of citizen participation is specified, and the channels for paticipation are encoruaged by the state for citizens, legal persons and other organizations to paticipate in wildlife protection activities through donation, funding, and volunteer service. Howerve, the multifaceted power function of public participation in environmental elements has not been fully explored. The paticipatory standard is principled and strong, but the biodiversity standard system is not yet formed, and the supporting operation mechanism is insufficient. The construction of the legal mechanism also needs improvement. The mechanism system construction of obtaining information, participating in decision-making and appealing to litigation is not systematic, which does not fully stimulate the initiative and creativity of civil society.

Secondly, the legal guarantees for participatory subjects need to be improved.

The effectiveness of participation lies in the value of the existence of its public participation mechanism, and the key to improving efficiency is the adaptation and improvement of the relevant legal rules governing paticipation. The mechanism of public participation in biodiversity can be distinguished from two perspectives: collective and decentralized. Collective paticipation mainly involves environmental NGOs, market enterprises, think tanks, communities and other rules that collaborate through public-private cooperation and private cooperation to establish rules for the use of biological resources. Examples of collective paticipation include natural protected areas, public protection, environmental protection projects, education, normal education, ecological industry development, and collective voluntary service and charity action. Decentralized participation involves individuals or small groups with special ability who help protect biodiversity, focusing on voluntary service, charitable donations, photography and other behaviors. Currently only the revised "charity law" (2016), the volunteer service regulations, the public welfare donation, but there is no corresponding system to support public paticipation in biodiversity protection. As a result, there is no the legal protection for public welfare, participate in species monitoring and patrol protection personnel rights and interests protection, local financial support, ecological products proprietary market management and tax incentives. At the same time, in addition, if the public's rights and interests are damaged during participation, they can only seek relief through traditional civil infringement norms. Environmental infringement relief, ecological environment damage compensation litigation and environmental public interest litigation are only format relief after the citizens' environmental interests are violated, and other interest protection has not been paid attention to.

5.2 The Participation Ability of the Participatory Normative Protection Subject Needs to be Strengthened Urgently

At present, currently the primary participants in biodiversity conservation are non-governmental organizations, enterprises, and citizens. Based on the economic and technological characteristics of enterprises participating in biodiversity conservation, their ability to improve mainly stems from the internal concept and rule positioning. From the perspective of the operation process, the participation ability of non-governmental organizations can be categorized into organizational management ability, practical experience ability, capital operation ability, professional training ability, strategic planning ability and the ability to maintain relevant stakeholders networks. Generally, national and provincial NGOs should participate in legislative proposals, formulate behavioral standards, file environmental public interest lawsuits, and organize projects for protected areas. Local NGOs should mainly carry out education on environmental protection and volunteer services. The degree and scope of participation determine the capacity-building needs of NGOs. At present, except for several national leaders, other levels will face the problems of insufficient professional personnel, insufficient personnel quality, insufficient source of funds and insufficient continuity of professional promotion. The development of the low-level organization is threatened: on the one hand, the limited foundation; on the other hand, there is less support and insufficient cooperation resources, which limits the organizational expansion of nongovernmental organizations. A few excellent NGOs alone cannot cover the whole country in the promotion of biodiversity conservation. The fragmentation of urban biodiversity, the restoration of nonendangered species, the connectivity of dispersed habitats, and the diversified and sustainable green development of agricultural products all need extensive public support at the grassroots level. This is the only to achieve mainstream construction of biodiversity, and it is also the next stage task of biodiversity conservation in China. It is a closed-loop junction related to the effectiveness of biodiversity conservation and sustainable development strategy. Therefore, improving the overall capacity of NGOs, and the improvement of the hierarchical guarantee system and mechanism support should be put on the agenda.

Individual citizens participate in conservation actions mainly through national regulatory agencies and non-governmental organization biodiversity conservation projects. On the one hand, local residents participate in the daily management of protected areas and protection projects, and continuously enhance the effectiveness of protection and monitoring capacity through ability training and new technology external; on the other hand, they integrate protection and development to innovate the production and life track of farmers. In December 2019, the farmers seed network in the United Nations development program global environment fund small grant program (UNDP-GEF-SGP), with the support of "promote three niang bay in Guangxi fishery community protection and sustainable development pilot project" in three niang bay, aims to improve the villagers to community natural resources protection consciousness and reengineering ability, alleviate the pressure of the Marine ecological environment at the same time, the development of fishery community sustainable livelihood. These two points reflect that citizens lack of active awareness to participate in the improvement of biodiversity protection ability and the orientation. The most important reason is that the overall social protection atmosphere is weak and the mainstream of education has not yet been established. The natural ecology deep in the forest needs to be brought to the city, and the hot tropical rain forest needs to be known by the Greater Hinggan Mountains. Teaching education, perception education and experiential education should be consistent with biodiversity conservation, and form a conservation ideology that is compatible with local and migration, and consciousness and action.

5.3 *The Level of Participation Needs to Be Deepened*

The term "participatory" has moved beyond mere accepted by the biodiversity regulation mechanism and has entered the level of substantive integration. In both formal and informal normative mechanisms, non-state actors can paticipate in decision-making and implementation. However, there is still a certain gap between participation and effectiveness.

The essence of the global active implementation of participation is the innovation of the value of ecological resources system, and the application of the knowledge accumulated in civil society to fit ecological resources and national concepts to the various links of biodiversity decision-making and implementation. This requires not only the implementation of legislation, but also the corresponding implementation and docking. However, the actual situation in China is different: the principle of "public participation" in the biodiversity law is thin; the scope of "public" in environmental impact assessment is unclear, and there are the limited opporrunities for participation in decision-making. The lack of guaranteed participation and loopholes in the legislative mechanism have resulted in fragmentation of the non-state participation in biodiversity operation mechanism, which limits the depth of participation level and hinders the effectiveness of participatory protection.

6 Suggestions and Prospects on Promoting the Conservation of Participatory Biodiversity

6.1 *Improve the System and Dynamic System of Improving the Laws and Norms of Biodiversity*

Firstly, optimize the participation section of biodiversity legal norms.

The close relationship between biodiversity and human beings determines the important position of the participatory status in the legal norm system. The dynamic change between the two also highlights the importance of a solid participatory legal status for the long-term legal function of biodiversity. At present, the participatory legal status has been established, and the optimization needs to start from two aspects: one is the solid public participation as the foundation of the biodiversity legal standard system, provide the optimization direction for individual elements that have not been clearly positioned; the second is the content and mechanism construction of public participation standards should include three rights: the right to obtain information, the right to participate in policy suggestions and the right to file litigation. The content and scope of public participation should be expangded on the basis of respecting the bottom line of power patterns. The connectivity mechanism with public participation in operation should be improved to enhance the effectiveness of the participatory mechanism.

Simultaneously, participatory legal guarantees must evolve with the times. Capacity and funding are the two primary obstacles that limit public participation. Firstly, the protection projects, which include the public's involvement in forest protection and monitoring, should focus on labor rights and interests, such as the post, wages, insurance, the protection of data resources, and the construction of forest rangers, monitors, data analyst, and a improved the protection system for public participation behavior; secondly, the supervision and management system for public participation should quantify the public participation behavior indicators, standardize the daily management institutionalization, and integrate it into the biodiversity co-governance system.

Second, the dynamics and systematization of the legal system for biodiversity: The legal normative system for biodiversity is a systematic mechanism that adheres to the holistic theory, usually adhering to the horizontal and vertical perspectives. The vertical perspective inclues the Constitution, the basic law of environmental protection, and policy normative documents, while the horizontal perspective involves legislation on species, ecosystems and genetic resources. Together, these two pathways constitute a static system of the normative system of biodiversity method, However, the dynamic coordination between the two still requires two breakthroughs in the legal relationship between the ownership of natural resources and the distribution of power among subjects. On the one hand, in the face of differences in interests at the natural resource level, it is necessary to optimize the hierarchy of the value orientation, legal orientation and mechanism path of biological resources, pursuing the embodiment of a hierarchical mechanism on the basis of holism. On the other hand, it is important to adhere to the vertical and horizontal distribution of power, To coordinate the transboundary protection mechanism of the regions and river basins, promote protection and achieve coordination through interest goals, create and optimize the collaborative coordination mechanisms, and form a multisubject mechanism model based on the relationship between human and nature.

6.2 Construct the Capacity Development Mechanism of Participatory Protection

In generally, legal qualifications and funding are the main constraints on public participation in biodiversity conservation. The conclusion is drawn from the limitation of public participation in the normative operation of biodiversity, and the asymmetry in the legal status confirmation of legislation, enforcement and justice and the lack of effective mechanisms. To solve this problem, policy guidance and path innovation approaches are needed to encourage, non-governmental organizations, market entities, and citizens to accumulate effective management, professional skills, system practice effective and to get more policy support and social recognition. This will enhance the legitimacy of the state's behavior, develop innvation participatory mechanism, and absorb the financial support and funding, ultimately improving the soft power of public participation in biodiversity conservation. Additionally, given the loose organizational struture, limited mangement rules, and professional and technical levels non-governmental organizations, marketnetities, and citizens, to participate in the operation of loose organization structure, systematic management rules, professional and technical level, limited real state, by it is neccessary to strengthen the interaction between high and low levels, exchange funds management experience exchange reverse local NGOs, and enhance the organization management ability of local NGOs and small and medium-sized enterprises. By seizing the key to participatory mechanism and improving internal hardware strength, the public's participation in biodiversity conservation can bi effectively inproved.

6.3 Strengthen the Integration and Construction of Local Regulatory Mechanisms for Biodiversity Conservation, and Deepen Public-Private Cooperation

Citizens' participation in biodiversity conservation is promarily focused on the protected natural area system centered on national parks. It is important to integrate citizen values into the existing standard system and the concentration of public power, in order to achieve the comprehensive goals of biodiversity conservation such as natural resource protection, national security guarantee and economic development promotion.[14] However, the centralized advantage of natural protected areas only standardizes the goal of high-quality biodiversity, and cannot achieve the whole of mainstream. At present, the sustainable and standardized governance of the ecosystem in the watershed and regional blocks is a systematic exploration of the transboundary environment overall and systematic. The fragmentation and coherence of grassroots ecology have become a challenging area for the improvement of the legal system and legal transformation of biodiversity protection in China. The key to standardizing the rule of law is to realize the synergistic balance between biological resources and local industrial structure adjustment and economic development transformation. This mainly needs to rely on the transformation of the survival path of market entities and civil society, so that the weight of public participation is actually enhanced. Specifically, the construction of a local biodiversity conservation framework, which includes macro regulations and policies based on biological resources and ecosystem protection, as well as micro-participation of non-state subjects at all levels, can deepen the public-private cooperation and promote the standardization of local biodiversity conservation as a whole. This presents an opportunity and challenge for the participatory deep regulation of biodiversity conservation, and a new stage of breaking through the harmonious coexistence between man and nature.

7 Conclusion

A consensus has been reached on the global governance system for biodiversity, and it has entered a stage of precise commissioning of a multitier mechanism. The biological l origin promotes the participation space of non-state subjects, balancing adherence between following the legal logic and breaking through the compulsory orders. This is not a traditional rule of law review based on legal qualifications, normative attributes, legitimacy evaluation and other criteria, but rather an adaptive rule of law based on the inherent material dynamics of biodiversity. Participation will become the driving force of normative cognition. In line with the development

[14] Tianbao (2022), p. 119.

law of a community with a shared future for mankind, China has transformed from a learner to a leader in the exploration of global biodiversity norms, Non-state entities in China have evolved from followers to innovators, which has constructive significance for strengthening the rational rule of law for biodiversity in China, and is an important source for enhancing the compatibility between human and modern values in the future, and contributing to the global ecological good governance.

References

Carol P (2006) The theory of participation and democracy (trans: Chen Y). Shanghai Century Publishing Group, p 7

Jianlin S, Tianpeng J (2012) From generation to Participation—Carol Petman's pursuit of participatory democracy. Guang Xi Univ (Philos Soc Sci Edn) 6:88

Jiaoli H, Ke H, Jianmin T (2014) Ethnic and folk plant worship culture and biodiversity conservation in Baise region. Guangxi Plants 11:41

Jing W (2021) Difficult inspection and path optimization of environmental social organizations' participation in biodiversity conservation in accordance with the law. China Environ Manage 4: 44

Minzhong H (2010) On the science and value of norms. Ningxia Soc Sci 6:115

Rongkun L (2016) Symbiosis of forest people: a study on forest culture and changes of Yi nationality. Doctoral thesis of Yunnan University, May

Tianbao Q (2022) On the systematic legal regulation of biodiversity conservation. Legal Forum 1: 119

Xiaoqing C (2019a) On facts, values and legal regulations. Soc Sci Forum 5:38

Xiaoqing C (2019b) On facts, values and legal regulations. Soc Sci Forum 5:42

Yingdi W, Jijun M (2022) Evaluation and analysis of the importance of ecological Services of China's natural resources in space pattern. Nat Resour 37(1):23

GPSR Compliance

The European Union's (EU) General Product Safety Regulation (GPSR) is a set of rules that requires consumer products to be safe and our obligations to ensure this.

If you have any concerns about our products, you can contact us on ProductSafety@springernature.com

In case Publisher is established outside the EU, the EU authorized representative is:

Springer Nature Customer Service Center GmbH
Europaplatz 3
69115 Heidelberg, Germany

Batch number: 10726133

Printed by Printforce, the Netherlands